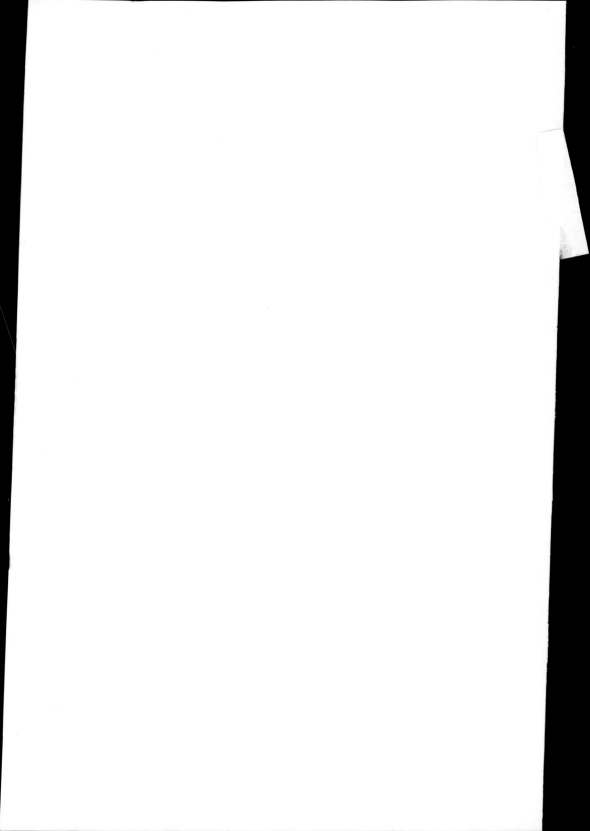

The Design
of Relational
Databases

The Design of Relational Databases

Heikki Mannila

University of Helsinki

Kari-Jouko Räihä

University of Tampere

ADDISON-WESLEY
PUBLISHING
COMPANY

Wokingham, England · Reading, Massachusetts · Menlo Park, California · New York
Don Mills, Ontario · Amsterdam · Bonn · Sydney · Singapore
Tokyo · Madrid · San Juan · Milan · Paris · Mexico City · Seoul · Taipei

Cover designed by Chris Eley incorporating photograph © ANT/Paddy Ryan/NHPA which shows termite mounds commonly seen across northern Australia and printed by The Riverside Printing Co. (Reading) Ltd.
Typeset by the authors, using LaTEX
Printed in Great Britain at the University Press, Cambridge

First printed 1992.

British Library Cataloguing in Publication Data
A catalogue record for this book is available from the British Library

Library of Congress Cataloging in Publication Data
Mannila, Heikki
    The design of relational databases/Heikki Mannila, Kari-Jouko Räihä.
        p.   cm.
    "December 1991."
    Includes bibliographical references and index.
    ISBN 0–201–56523–4
    1. Data base design. 2. Relational data bases. I. Räihä, Kari
    -Jouko. II. Title.
QA76.9.D26M37   1992
005.75′6—dc20   92–4567
                                                              CIP

Preface

This is a graduate-level textbook and reference on the design of relational databases. It is based on the use of the entity-relationship model on the conceptual level of database design, and combines this with a rigorous treatment of the design of relational schemas. The book presents practically applicable design theory and methods in a unified way.

We emphasize iterative two-level design, where relational schemas and ER-schemas can be used simultaneously, and changes in one are mapped to the other. Some issues in design are easier to solve on the ER-level, some on the relational level, and hence a two-level methodology is useful.

Simple and intuitive integrity constraints, namely functional and inclusion dependencies, are used to develop relational design theory. These constraints correspond to the notions of keys and referential integrity, and they are easy to understand and occur in all practical design tasks. They are also sufficiently powerful to model complicated situations.

The book also presents algorithms and methods for the use of example databases in database design. Automatically generated example databases can give the designer important feedback about the design decisions. We also show how existing database instances can be analyzed and how the integrity constraints holding in them can be inferred. This makes it possible to produce conceptual schemas for existing databases.

The design method described in the book is supported by a design tool, called Design-By-Example, currently under development. The tool has been developed for several years in a project supported by the Academy of Finland and by the Technology Development Center of Finland. It should be ready for release in 1993.

Structure of the book

This book consists of four parts. The first part (Chapters 1 through 6) introduces our approach to database design, presents basic definitions of data models, and discusses the properties a good database design should have. After the introductory Chapter 1, Chapter 2 discusses the database design process, the properties a design methodology should have, and the Design-By-Example design tool. Chapter 3 presents the ER-model, while Chapter 4 covers the basic concepts of the relational data model and its query languages. Chapter 5 discusses object-oriented data models, which seem to be the next important step in data models. The desired properties of database schemas are presented in an informal way in Chapter 6.

The second part, Chapters 7 through 10, concentrates on the relational model. Chapter 7 discusses different types of integrity constraints, their role in database design, and their use in database management systems. Chapter 8 gives formal definitions and examples of the desired properties of relational database schemas. Chapter 9 studies the properties of integrity constraints and gives the axiomatizations for the important classes of functional and inclusion dependencies. Chapter 10 covers basic algorithms for the manipulation of database schemas and database instances under functional and inclusion dependencies.

The third part (Chapters 11 and 12) gives algorithms for mapping an ER-diagram into a relational schema and vice versa. The latter mapping is possible only for schemas in appropriate normal form; corresponding schema transformation algorithms are presented in Chapter 12.

In the fourth part, Chapters 13 through 15 deal with questions that arise from the unique features of Design-By-Example. Chapter 13 defines concepts that can be used in producing fast algorithms for traditional design problems and also for generating example databases. Chapter 14 investigates the use of example databases and gives methods for producing such databases. Finally, Chapter 15 investigates the problem of inferring the dependencies that hold in a database.

Prerequisites

The book presupposes no knowledge about database systems or design, although some experience in database systems is useful. If the book is used as a textbook in a graduate course, the students should have access to a database management system so that practical experiments can be made. The reader should be familiar with the basic notions and notations of set theory and algorithms. In certain chapters some knowledge about graphs and logic are useful.

Some exercises are exceptionally hard or require knowledge of a field that is not covered in the book. These are marked with the symbol **.

Acknowledgements

Various versions of the material that evolved into this book have been used by the authors in database courses that they have taught in the following universities: Cornell University, University of Helsinki, University of Oregon, University of Tampere, and University of Turku. The feedback from students on these courses has been most useful.

Several people have read the manuscript and made numerous suggestions for improvements. The comments by Jyrki Nummenmaa and Peter Thanisch are gratefully acknowledged. We also thank our editor, Nicky Jaeger, for useful comments and suggestions.

Finally, we owe a debt of gratitude to the implementors of the Design-By-Example tool: Martti Kantola, Harri Siirtola, and Jyrki Tuomi. Their hard work has made it possible to try out the ideas, and insight obtained from practical experience has often guided the development of the design method.

Heikki Mannila[1]
University of Helsinki

Kari-Jouko Räihä[2]
University of Tampere

June 1992

[1]University of Helsinki, Department of Computer Science, Teollisuuskatu 23, SF-00510 Helsinki, Finland. E-mail: mannila@cs.Helsinki.fi.

[2]University of Tampere, Department of Computer Science, P.O. Box 607, SF-33101 Tampere, Finland. E-mail: kjr@cs.uta.fi.

Contents

Chapter 1

Introduction

The purpose of this chapter is to introduce some terminology and to clarify our perspective on the subject matter of the book.

1.1 Why database management systems?

Programming has changed profoundly from the early days of computing. The essential and difficult part of programming used to be the specification of the computation, not the interfaces of programs and users. As a case in point, the definition of input and output statements was completely missing from the definition of the ALGOL 60 programming language.

In today's programs, the code for the actual computation may form a small fragment of the entire program. More and more effort goes into the specification and implementation of various interfaces. Increasingly often, a networked computer does not even carry out the entire processing itself; instead, it may rely on services provided by various other components, such as a window server (that makes it possible to use the capabilities of bitmapped workstations), a communications server (that allows a program to communicate with the outside world), and a database server (that provides access to large, shared storages of data).

Such a modularization of the various facets of a program has several advantages. *Maintainability* is the most apparent benefit provided by this style of programming. A clear separation of different functions makes it easier to modify a part of a program without affecting the other parts.

1

Thus, for instance, the user interface of a well-structured program can be changed without altering the computation carried out by the program.

Similarly, it should be possible to access the data used by a program without concern about how that data is actually stored. Before the era of databases, large masses of data were stored in file systems. Perhaps the main goal of switching to the use of more complex database management systems has been *data independence*: if, for some reason, it becomes necessary to restructure the input file of a program, this should require little, if any, changes in the program. This goal was not obtainable when the input and output operations of a program were directly dependent on the file structures.

A *database management system* (dbms) is a program intended for storing and accessing data. Though even a file system would satisfy this definition, a true database management system typically provides many services not offered by conventional file systems, such as:

- Consistency: the system ensures that the updates to the data do not violate a specified set of constraints.

- Concurrency: several users can read and update the data simultaneously.

- Access control: users can have various access rights, and the system prevents unauthorized access to the data.

- Reliability and recovery: very little data is lost in case of, say, a program error that abnormally halts the execution of the program. Even in the case of more extensive crashes, backups and logs that are automatically maintained by the system allow restoration of much of the lost data.

A *database* is a collection of data stored using a database management system. A *database system* is the part of an information system that deals with data access; it consists of the actual database, the database management system, and the information system's interface with the database management system.

Database management systems are no panacea for data management problems. They are well suited for large masses of data, in applications where the logical organization of the data and concurrent use of the database are important. For small scale data management problems there are other solutions that may do the job better. For personal use, various file management programs often offer a modern interface and more advanced report generation features. The UNIX^{TM} environment contains several filter programs that are extremely convenient for expressing associative queries and for manipulating textual data.

1.2   Data models and database design

Databases are intended for a variety of users, often running different applications. This sets high requirements on the organization of the data in the database. Quite different queries must be handled efficiently. Efficiency aside, it must be possible to *formulate* such queries. The database must be organized in a manner that allows the users to store, update and query the data they desire, without posing restrictions other than those necessary for maintaining the consistency of the data. The task of database design is to achieve this goal.

On the other hand, a database should also form a coherent collection of data. Users with exceptional requirements may have to resort to other databases or manage the additional data personally. The focus in this book is on the logical organization of data within one database, but the proper division of labor among several databases should not be forgotten in application design.

The *relational data model* was proposed in the early 1970s by E. F. Codd as a logically sound basis for describing both the structure of the data and data manipulation operations. Early implementations of the relational model were very inefficient compared to systems based on more operationally-oriented data models. However, the relational model has been steadily gaining in popularity, and today most new database management systems and database applications use the relational model.

There are several reasons for the success of the relational model. It has very few basic concepts, and they are simple: one can think of the data as being stored in tables, a familiar concept from everyday life. This makes the model easy to learn. It has a firm theoretical basis. It allows arbitrary queries based on comparing values in different columns in the tables – a sharp contrast with competing data models (such as the hierarchical data model and the network data model), where the user can move from one part of a database to another only if a pre-programmed link exists for that purpose in the database.

In the framework of the relational model, the main task of database design is to find suitable tables for storing the data. If a table has too many fields, storing and updating the data becomes difficult: in order to store a fact that a user is interested in, he or she may have to provide additional information, not relevant for that particular fact. On the other hand, using tables that are too small may make it impossible to combine the data in different tables to create interesting derived facts using the connections between the data in different tables.

Keeping track of all the information necessary for designing large databases is hard. It is customary to divide the design process into successive phases to make the process more manageable. Some higher-level data model is typically used to describe the conceptual structure of the data before laying out the table structure within the framework of the relational model. The most widely used of such conceptual data models is the *entity-relationship model* or ER-model, for short. Though similar modelling constructs had appeared in earlier data models, the work of Peter P.-S. Chen is generally considered to be the starting point of the development of the ER-model. As with the relational model, the ER-model has only a few simple concepts and is easily learned, contributing to its popularity.

In this book, we shall use the relational model and the entity-relationship model to express our methods and algorithms for database design.

The theory of relational databases is mature: it has been intensively studied for two decades. Many characteristic properties of good databases are known, and algorithms for designing such databases have been developed. In spite of the richness of this theory, it has limitations when applied to real-world design problems. Databases can be huge, containing hundreds or thousands of different tables and fields. To be useful in designing such large databases, a design methodology or algorithm must have several properties.

- Most research on relational database design has been done solely within the relational model. Practical algorithms must support *multi-level database design*, providing transformations between data models with different levels of abstraction.

- The first attempt to design a large database probably produces a design with shortcomings, forcing the designer to return to a previous phase in the design process to make appropriate modifications. The design algorithm must support *iterative* design, so that in a multi-level design process a restart from the beginning is not necessary each time a problem is found.

- Suppose that it is indeed possible to return to a previous design phase to make a change in the design data. The changed design should correct some problem in subsequent phases, but the change should leave the other parts of the design intact. The design algorithm must in other words be *incremental*.

- Often during a design process there may be many ways to proceed. Typical design algorithms make an arbitrary choice between alternatives that, theoretically, are equally good. In real database design the designer would certainly like to be informed of such choices, and to have the possibility to override the choices made by the algorithm. The algorithm must be based on *interaction* with the designer.

- Databases typically live for a long time. The conditions that prevailed when they were first designed – such as the database management system used, or the typical applications using the database – may change. Often many applications rely so heavily on an existing database that it is impossible to have a fresh start with a completely new database system. Therefore it should be possible to redesign a database according to changing needs. The term *reverse engineering* refers to the process where an existing design is analyzed and used to construct another description (usually on a higher level of abstraction). A good design algorithm should support schema evolution using reverse engineering techniques.

Traditional algorithms for designing relational databases do not have these properties – at least not all of them. The main goal of this book is to develop the theory of interactive, iterative, and incremental database design.

A design method with the above characteristics is most useful when it is supported by computerized tools. Such tools are increasingly common. This is understandable: proper comprehension of the design theory requires mathematical maturity from the designer. When databases are more and more designed by persons familiar with the application but not necessarily with database management systems, it is not realistic to assume that the designer knows the state-of-the-art methods for database design. A good design tool should hide the theory from the designer and provide an intuitive, easy-to-use interface for manipulating the various descriptions of the database.

Another reason for the increasing use of computerized design tools is that not only database design, but the design of the entire information system is being supported by CASE (Computer Aided Software Engineering) tools. Such tools typically contain as one component a program that supports database design.

Our approach to database design forms the basis of an existing design tool called Design-By-Example. The name Design-By-Example comes from the special emphasis given to example relations in the tool. Such examples are generated automatically by Design-By-Example to illustrate the properties of a candidate database design; they can also be used to test queries on the database.

In Design-By-Example, the example databases are formed using attribute values given by the designer. The examples have the property that they satisfy exactly the conditions given by the designer, and hence they are helpful in spotting omissions and mistakes in the design. In fact, one of the main problems that has been noted with the use of automated design tools is getting all the necessary design information from the designer into the tool; the examples are intended to alleviate that problem.

They allow the designer to approach schema validation systematically.

The Design-By-Example tool itself is not discussed any further in this book, but most of the design methods and algorithms that are presented have been implemented within Design-By-Example.

Exercises

Exercise 1.1 Discuss how well a database management system is suited for the following applications. What other types of software might be used?

(a) The handling of course evaluation questionnaires. A reply form could contain both free-form comments and suggestions, as well as opinions on various issues (such as course organization, lecture presentation, pace of course etc.) on a fixed scale from poor to excellent.

(b) Managing a collection of n bibliographic references, where $n = 50, 300$, or 3000.

(c) Guiding an assembly robot. The instructions of the guiding program are of the form 'move the assembly arm to position x'. The operations have to be carefully monitored because they are not necessarily carried out as intended: the arm may move imprecisely, there may be sudden obstacles on the way, and so on. The robot has several sensors feeding information about the location and speed of the assembly arm and the forces acting upon it. This sensor data is used to guide the execution of individual instructions. Also, when the same sequence of instructions is repeated, the history information about what happened in the previous round is used to modify the way the instructions are executed.

Bibliographic notes

The various aspects of database management systems are explained in many books, including those by Date [Dat90a], Korth and Silberschatz [KS86], Ullman [Ull88, Ull89], Elmasri and Navathe [EN89], and Vossen [Vos90]. The AWK programming language [AKW88] is a good tool for the manipulation of textual data in the UNIX^{TM} environment.

References for the ER-model and the relational model are given in Chapters 3 and 4, respectively. General expositions of data models can be found in the books by Tsichritzis and Lochovsky [TL82] and Teorey and Fry [TF82a].

Two of the most advanced database design tools are DATAID and DDEW (Database Design and Evaluation Workbench). DATAID has been developed in Italy. It consists of a set of cooperating tools; they are described in a series of papers by Atzeni, Batini and others [Cer83, ABLV83, AC83, BDD84, DD85b, DD85a]. DDEW was originally developed at the Computer Corporation of America. Its main architects are Reiner and Rosenthal [RBB+84, RBF+86, RR89].

Several other research prototypes for computer-aided database design exist [CL80, SKK83, BDRZ84, BH84, Wed84, MBGW84, BGM85, Fer85, WP87, HPBC88, CMNK88, Kan88, BC89, SC89, NO89, NN90, CFT91]. Commercial products have also mushroomed, either strictly for database design [ERD, ERV, Mas] or within CASE tools [IEF, IEW, Exc, Des, DEF]. CASE tools and their use in database design have been treated in several books, including those by McClure [McC89] and Fisher [Fis88].

The present version of Design-By-Example is documented in [KMR+91].

Chapter 2

An Overview of Database Design

In this chapter we review the database design process to illustrate how the methods developed later in the book fit into the whole. We pay special attention to one design principle, the use of feedback in all design phases, and discuss the effects this principle has on the design method. We also present an example that is used extensively throughout the book.

2.1 Phases of database design

Information systems design is usually based on either the *data-driven* or the *function-driven* approach. In the data-driven approach the emphasis is in finding out what data has to be stored and manipulated in the system. The function-driven approach puts emphasis on the applications that the system has to support. In this book we concentrate on the data-driven approach.

It has become fairly standard to divide the database design process into four phases: requirements analysis, conceptual design, logical design, and physical design.

The first phase, *requirements analysis*, produces an operationally-oriented description of the database. Its purpose is to ensure that the database contains the data necessary for the functions and applications where the database is used.

The prevailing view used to be that requirements analysis should be done mainly by experts in database design who interview the users to find out their needs. Then requirements analysis becomes a *knowledge acquisition* problem: the knowledge has to be transferred from the users to the designers, who describe it using appropriate means. A more modern approach is *participatory design*, where the users and designers together construct a description of the database and its usage. This approach has been made possible by the development of more intuitive modelling techniques and tools that support their use. A consequence of this trend is that the borderline between requirements analysis and conceptual design is getting fuzzier; it is nowadays considered wise to merge the two steps and have the users participate also in conceptual design.

There exists no commonly accepted notion of how requirements analysis should be done and how its results should be represented. While some formal models have been developed, they have not gained popularity. A formal representation is of little use unless it helps in the next design phase, conceptual design. We shall be satisfied either with a list of actions (queries and updates) to which the database should be able to react, or with a more general description of the purpose of the database and the tasks where it will be used. The descriptions will be given in natural language.

While requirements analysis produces information about the actions and operations where the data in the database is used, all the subsequent phases yield descriptions of the structure of the data in the database. The descriptions produced during conceptual and logical design are given in terms of some data model. The models used in these phases differ in their degree of abstraction.

In the function-driven approach to information systems design, an important task is *functional analysis*, which aims at finding the functions demanded from the information system. As a tool, functional design methods usually use dataflow diagrams. From our point of view functional analysis can be considered to be a part of requirements analysis.

Conceptual design produces a description of the database using some *conceptual data model*. The intent is to describe the structure of the data in high-level terms. The concepts should be natural for the *target of the database*, a term that refers to those notions (objects and abstractions) whose data is stored in the database. The term *universe of discourse* is often used with the same meaning in database jargon. The resulting description of the database is called a *database schema*. In contrast, the term *database instance* may be used to refer to the data stored in the database.

The conceptual data models typically offer a rich collection of modelling concepts that do not necessarily have an obvious implementation using file structures. In fact, some conceptual data models ignore the database instance altogether, and concentrate solely on the logical relationships among the data.

The main task of conceptual design is to find the essential concepts from the operational description that was produced by requirements analysis. This is a nontrivial task. Users may refer to the same concept using different terms, or use the same term for several concepts; such contradictions must be sorted out. It is not necessarily wise to store in the database instances of all the concepts mentioned, since some of them might be computable from other concepts. An essential goal of database design is to store each fact only once in order to trim off redundant information and thereby decrease the possibility of having inconsistent data in the database.

We use the entity-relationship model as the conceptual data model. It distinguishes between two kinds of concepts: entities and relationships. Both give rise to data items that must be stored in the database. Making the distinction allows the designer to understand the contents of the database better and also helps in finding the proper representations in subsequent design phases.

Deciding whether a concept should be an entity or a relationship is not always obvious. In fact, the database may have more than one 'correct' conceptual description; one man's entity may be another man's relationship.

Logical design is the third phase of the database design process. The name stems from the desire to separate this design phase from the final phase, physical design. The result of logical design is a description of the structures used for storing the database. Questions about file organization are postponed to the last phase.

The data models used in logical design are typically based on concepts that are abstractions of physical database structures, not abstractions of the universe of discourse. We use the relational model, where data is stored in tables, natural abstractions of files.

In relational database theory, logical design has often been identified with a process called *normalization*: construction of table structures that avoid redundant storing of data and are free from various update anomalies. In our multi-level approach to database design, normalization need not be visible to the designer at all, if automated tools are used. The normalization process is embedded in the transformation from entity-relationship structures into relational structures.

Still, it is the task of the database designer to examine the result of the transformation and to check that it is natural. Finding the right tables for storing the data is extremely important, since the queries of the application will be formulated and executed in terms of the tables. One cannot rely solely on a mechanical transformation from the entity-relationship model; it does not necessarily produce optimal structures.

The designer may also wish to rearrange some of the tables, for instance by grouping together data that is needed for computing answers to the most frequent queries. This process, in which some desirable properties of the database schema are consciously sacrificed for the sake of efficiency, is called *denormalization*. It occurs regularly in practice, indicating that real-world database design is not for purists: it requires the ability and willingness to find compromises between conflicting goals.

The designer also has to decide what the type (string, numeric, and so on) of each data item is, how many bytes of storage it needs, and what are the allowed values. This can be done in the conceptual or the logical design phase, or even postponed to physical design. It often serves as a good testing point of whether the attributes and entities really are suitably defined.

Finally, *physical design* produces the file structures needed for storing the database structures created by logical design. It is natural (though not necessary) to represent each table as a separate file. Then the main question becomes that of deciding what indices to maintain, and how to organize the indices.

Proper physical design needs information not only of typical queries, but also of their expected execution frequency. A good file structure is found by trying to optimize the overall performance of the system, so that most frequently executed queries can be handled fast. Such performance data may be difficult to get right before the actual use of the system. Therefore physical design may well continue during the use of the database system. Because of the data independence provided by the higher level data models, changing the file structures should not have an effect on the correctness of application programs.

The focus of this book is on the logical design phase. We shall also study in detail the entity-relationship model used in conceptual design and the mappings between conceptual and logical schemas.

2.2   Using feedback in database design

The phase structure of database design described in the preceding section does not support the validation of the results of intermediate design phases. One has to go through every design step and actually form the database to check whether it functions as desired. Errors made in the early stages can remain unnoticed for a long time.

A good design methodology and tools based on it should provide feedback on every possible level. The designer should be able to see the consequences of the design decisions immediately. Instead of four consecutive phases, we would like to structure the design process as in Figure 2.1.

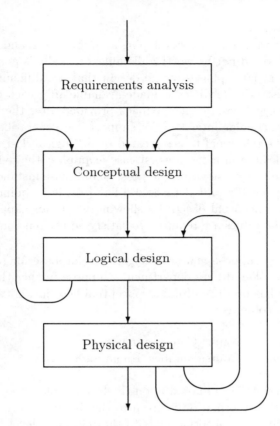

Figure 2.1   Iterative database design.

The iterative structure depicted in Figure 2.1 puts additional requirements on the design methodology. For instance, suppose that a conceptual
description of the database is transformed into one based on the relational
model, and that some errors or omissions are later noted in the relations.
Then it is quite natural to correct the problems on the relational level.
However, this may be dangerous, since it causes inconsistencies between
the two levels of database description (ER and relational). This inconsistency can surface later, if the conceptual description is modified for some
other reason and the transformation is applied anew. Then the old error
is again present. Thus it seems necessary either to make all corrections on
the conceptual level or to map the changes made on the relational level
back to the conceptual level.

The first alternative is not good, since it prevents fixing an error directly and forces the designer to look for the ER-construct that would
give the desired relational schema. Therefore we shall develop algorithms
that support the mapping of changes from lower to upper levels in the

design process.

The extra work put into developing an incremental and reversible design method would not be worthwhile unless it really is possible to make observations in later phases of the design that are difficult earlier, that is, unless illustrative feedback is made available after each phase. As our focus is on logical design, the feedback provided after the logical design phase is of particular interest. We support the generation of examples for each of the relational tables created in the logical design phase. The example tables are in a sense worst-case examples: they violate all constraints (conditions restricting the possible database instances) that have not been explicitly required to hold. The goal is to point out possible omissions in conceptual design by showing what can happen unless the contents of the tables are required to satisfy additional conditions.

Example 2.1 Suppose you are designing a database for recording data about courses offered by a department. Suppose further that the logical design phase has produced from a conceptual description two tables with the following columns:

Courses: Name, Course number
Class times: Course number, Room number, Time

No constraints are imposed upon the latter table.

Suppose this information is given to the designer as the result of the mapping from the conceptual level to the relational level. What should the designer do? All that is known about the database has already been specified. The designer is not likely to spot any problems in the result of the transformation.

However, the design probably does not reflect the real world accurately. For instance, nothing prohibits many courses from meeting in the same room at the same time, nor one course from meeting in two rooms at any given time. Such details can easily be overlooked in conceptual design.

The worst-case example (the so-called Armstrong relation) that can be automatically generated would have the following form.

Course number	Room number	Time
CIS 551	PAC 30	M 9:30
CIS 510	PAC 30	M 9:30
CIS 510	DES 200	M 9:30
CIS 510	DES 200	W 13:30

In this example the problems discussed above are evident.   □

The fact that a constraint is not required to hold is very easy to spot from an example table: one only needs to compare two rows. Noticing that a constraint does hold is more difficult, since one has to inspect the whole table. Therefore the designer should be able to view two complementary representations of the constraint set: the list of constraints and the example table.

When two representations for the set of constraints are used, the designer should be able to work with either one of them. Thus the designer can update a set of dependencies, and the tool should generate a corresponding example relation. If the example relation does not satisfy the user, it can be edited, and a new set of constraints should be inferred from the relation. Algorithms for generating examples and for inferring dependencies belong to the repertoire developed in this book.

2.3   An example

In this section we present an example database application that will be used throughout the book. Here we look at a small part of the application and discuss how the design could have proceeded in this case.

Example 2.2 Consider a small database that might be used by the organizers of a scientific conference, such as the annual *ACM SIGACT-SIGMOD-SIGART Symposium on Principles of Database Systems*. The complete example is described in Chapter 3, but we start here with some tidbits.

The papers presented in a scientific conference are selected by a program committee, whose members are either selected in the previous conference or invited by the program committee chairperson. The program committee composes a call for papers, and interested authors submit their papers for consideration.

The program committee then evaluates the papers. Here the practice varies: either all members of the program committee read all the papers – a formidable task – or the papers are distributed among program committee members so that each member gets only a subset of the papers. The evaluations are usually both verbal and quantitative: the members may be asked either to grade the entire paper, or to evaluate its originality, significance for the theme of the conference, and so on.

After all the evaluations are obtained, the program committee meets and decides which papers are accepted for presentation at the conference. The accepted papers are grouped to form coherent sessions, and usually the session chairpersons are chosen among the members of the program committee.

Databases are intended for several users. They are therefore *integrated* storages of data, containing more information than any single user might need. This is also true for our conference database, which is intended to serve program committee members, organizers, and perhaps even participants alike.

Suppose that in the requirements analysis phase the chairperson of the program committee, a member of the program committee, and a researcher are interviewed. Here are some queries that they might wish the database system to be able to handle:

Program committee chairperson

(1) 'List the papers in decreasing order according to their average score.'

(2) 'List the papers in their order of arrival.'

Program committee member

(3) 'List the papers in decreasing order according to the grades given by me.'

(4) 'List those papers where my grade differs from the average significantly.'

Researcher

(5) 'Did my paper get accepted?'

(6) 'What was the rejection percentage?'

In addition, some requirements are so obvious that they probably do not even come up in the interviews. For instance, each session should be assigned a time and room; the names and addresses of program committee members should be stored because of the correspondence involved in the selection process; and so on. Such general requirements could best be called common knowledge about the target of the database and should be treated just as the knowledge acquired from individual users.

Here we shall focus on conceptual design on the basis of the queries found during requirements analysis; common knowledge is incorporated into the full example in Chapter 3. To begin, 'submitted paper' is clearly one of the entities that must be stored in the database; are there any others? The third query gives a clue: it talks about 'grades given by [a program committee member]'. Indeed, it is natural to consider the program committee members as entities. The query indicates that submitted papers and program committee members are related, and that the grade given for a paper by a program committee member is a property of that relationship.

What else can we learn from the example queries? The first query seems to indicate that 'average score' could be an appropriate property of submitted papers. But certainly that value can be computed from the individual scores – after realizing that the committee chairperson has used 'score' in the same meaning where 'grade' was used by the committee member. Therefore it is not wise to keep the average score as a part of the database; rather, it should be recomputed each time the first query is executed.

The second query indicates that it must be possible to sort the papers by their order of arrival. This could be achieved by making arrival date a property of submitted papers. An even simpler solution that we adopt here is to number the papers consecutively when they arrive. In a realistic database, recording also the date of arrival is certainly a good idea.

The answer to the fourth query can be computed from the data we have already decided to store.

The fifth query indicates that it must be possible to determine which papers have been accepted. Our first reaction might be to make this a property of submitted papers. However, that is usually unwise: such a property is known much later than the other properties of submitted papers. Therefore we would temporarily have to use some kind of a null or blank value for that particular property, until its true value can be determined after the program committee meeting. The entity-relationship model does not deal with such blank values. An entity or relationship is supposed to have valid values for all its properties.

But the entity-relationship model does provide a concept that is ideally suited for our case: sets of entities can be partitioned into subsets. We therefore represent accepted papers as a subset of all submitted papers. Chapter 3 explains the details of how this can be done.

The fifth query also shows that authors are an interesting property of papers. Even storing the names of authors is not as straightforward as one might imagine. Every author knows how important it is that the names of all the authors appear in the same order everywhere – in the header of the paper, in the conference program, and so on. This indicates that the list of authors should be a single, undivided data item associated with a submitted paper.

But then answering queries like the fifth query becomes difficult: the application program must retrieve information about *every* accepted paper and use a string matching algorithm to decide whether the interested researcher is among the authors of the paper. If we consider this an important question and wish to get help from the database management system in answering it, then we must also treat individual authors as entities in the database. Then authorship becomes a relationship between authors and papers.

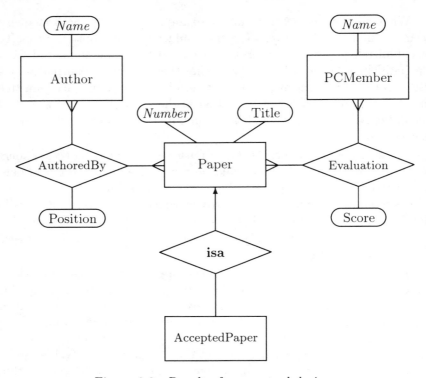

Figure 2.2   Result of conceptual design.

We adopt the latter solution. However, we must still be able to list the authors of a paper in the correct order. Therefore we add a property, say 'position', to the relationship that connects authors and papers. The position of the first author will be 1, the position of the second author will be 2, and so on. In a sense, this is information that does not exist in the target of the database (at least not in this form). It is not unusual that such artificial data has to be stored in a database so that it is possible both to organize the data in a logical manner and to answer all the necessary queries. An ideal solution for queries of this type would be to have string manipulation features combined with the query facilities of conventional database management systems.

Finally, the answer to the sixth query can again be computed on the basis of the stored information.

It is convenient to represent the result of conceptual design in graphical form. Figure 2.2 shows the entity-relationship diagram that summarizes the preceding discussion. The components of the diagram are explained in Chapter 3, but it should be understandable even without explanations.

Let us go on with the design. For storing the concepts depicted in Figure 2.2, the automatic transformation would suggest six tables: one for program committee members, one for papers, one for evaluations, one for accepted papers, one for authors, and one for associating authors with papers. The columns in the tables would be:

PC members:	Name
Papers:	Number, Title
Evaluations:	Name (of reviewer), Number, Score
Accepted papers:	Number
Authors:	Name
Authors of papers:	Number, Name (of author), Position

In addition, the transformation yields information about the keys (identifying columns) of the tables; for instance, a reviewer can give at most one score for each paper, implying that Name (of reviewer) and Number are together a key of Evaluations. This information must be provided during conceptual design. Additionally, the transformation also produces constraints that the database must satisfy. For instance, one such constraint could state that the table for evaluations can have an entry for a paper only if the number of the paper appears in the table created for papers; another could state that all paper numbers found in the table for accepted papers must also appear in the table for submitted papers.

In this small example, the result could be acceptable as such, and no manual changes are necessarily needed in the logical design phase.

In physical design we have to decide the index structure of the files (assuming that we create a separate file for each table). For this phase we really do not have enough information. Maintaining the indices is both a time and space consuming task for the computer system, at least if the database is updated frequently. One cannot therefore have an index for every possible data item that might be used for searching a table. In our example, indices based on paper numbers seem crucial; the others depend on the importance of the corresponding queries.

In physical design we might also decide to store several tables in one file. For instance, it would make sense to combine the tables for submitted papers and accepted papers, and to use simply one field to record the acceptance information (yes / no / not yet known). Although the conceptual data model does not allow unknown values, they can be used on a level that is hidden from the database user.

The *view* is a common mechanism that can be used to achieve such hiding of implementation specific decisions. The user of the database could access it through the view that corresponds to the original table structure. The tables stored in the database could still be the optimized ones. It would be a task of the database management system to map queries expressed using the view into queries that operate on the tables that are actually stored.   □

Exercises

Exercise 2.1 Design a small database for a target that is familiar to you. For instance, your target could be course and grade data, library data, or bibliographic data. The database need not be large, but you should carry out all four phases of database design in an informal manner. Evaluate the result of your design.

Exercise 2.2 Example 2.2 is obviously incomplete. List some entity types and attributes that a real application would need.

Bibliographic notes

The four-phase structure of database design has been discussed extensively by Teorey and Fry [TF82a].

An interesting modern treatment of functional design and its relationship to conceptual modelling with the entity-relationship model, resulting in a methodology combining data-driven and function-driven approaches, is given in [BCN92].

Silva and Melkanoff [SM81] were the first to suggest the use of example relations for providing feedback to the database designer. The idea has been developed further in a series of papers by Mannila and Räihä [MR86a, Man87, MR87, MR88]. A similar approach has also been suggested by Tseng, Mannino, and Choobineh [TM89, CMT92].

Chapter 3

The Entity-Relationship Model

In Chapter 2 we saw that data models are used for describing databases. What exactly is a data model? Its primary purpose is to describe in a formal and exact way the *logical organization of data*. In addition, a data model often provides means for expressing *integrity constraints* and *database queries*. Integrity constraints provide additional information about the target of the database. They express conditions that the database instance must satisfy. Database queries are used for updating and querying the database instance[1].

A distinction is often made between so-called *semantic data models* and *syntactic data models*. The semantic data models are used for conceptual design, that is, for describing the structure of data in high-level terms that are natural for the universe of discourse. Some semantic data models do not explicitly consider the database instance at all, in the sense that they do not specify how the instances are represented. Then, of course, questions such as how to query the database become mute.

As explained in Chapter 2, the conceptual schema is transformed into a representation based on a syntactic data model before the database can be used. Syntactic data models are based on concepts that are abstractions of physical database structures, not abstractions of the target of the database. The possibilities offered by direct manipulation interfaces may, however, make the transformation unnecessary in the future. Tools for

---

[1]In database jargon, the term 'query' indeed refers not only to read operations, but also to operations that may change the data in the database.

accessing the database instance through a visual, conceptual level schema already exist in laboratories, and they may eventually make their way into commercial database systems.

The entity-relationship model is the semantic data model used in this book. In this chapter we describe the semantics of the entity-relationship model: the meaning of each modelling concept and the conditions that an entity-relationship schema must always satisfy. Chapters 6 and 8 provide more advice on how the modelling concepts *should* be used to obtain a database schema that can be used without problems. Expressing integrity constraints in the entity-relationship model is treated in Chapter 7. No query language is associated with the entity-relationship model.

3.1   Entities and relationships

The entity-relationship model views the target of the database as consisting of *entities* and *relationships*. Roughly, entities are 'things' that exist independently of other entities, whereas relationships are connections between entities. We hasten to point out that this is an oversimplification: actually there are two kinds of entities, *strong entities* and *weak entities*. The existence of a weak entity depends on the existence of some strong entity.

Relationships connect two or more entities. The entities are said to be the *participants* in the relationship. Entities and relationships are jointly called *objects*. Objects have *attributes* that describe the properties of the objects. Each attribute is associated with a *domain*, the set of possible values that the attribute can assume.

Deciding how to model a particular concept is not always easy. Each alternative (using an entity, a relationship, or an attribute of some object) may have some merit. Experience is probably the best help in making good decisions. Often a single 'correct' solution does not even exist.

Example 3.1 Consider the conference database of Example 2.2. Assume the database is used for the *Eighth ACM SIGACT-SIGMOD-SIGART Symposium on Principles of Database Systems (PODS'89)*. The strong entities are submitted papers (such as the paper on constant-time-maintainability of databases [Wan89]), authors (such as Ke Wang), and program committee members (Catriel Beeri, Ashok K. Chandra, and others). The evaluations are relationships between program committee members and submitted papers. Finally, accepted papers are weak entities, since they are dependent on the existence of a corresponding submitted paper.
□

Entities and relationships are objects that are stored in the database. A database contains many objects with the same structure (that is, with the same set of attributes). On the schema level we therefore talk about *entity types* and *relationship types* or, collectively, *object types*. The database contains an *object set* for each object type in the database schema. All the objects in an object set have the structure described by the corresponding object type[2]. The word 'attribute' is used on both the schema level and the instance level: an object type has an attribute exactly when every object in the corresponding object set has the attribute.

Each object type has a unique name in the entity-relationship schema. Attribute names, on the other hand, need not be unique. Several object types can have attributes that are identically named.

A relationship has always at least two participants, but they need not necessarily belong to different entity sets. For instance, a Descendant relationship could have two participants, both of which belong to entity set Person. In the database schema, therefore, relationship type Descendant would have two participants, both of which are of type Person. To avoid confusion, *role names* must be associated with the different participants. For the Descendant relationship type the roles of its participants could be Parent and Child. We require that role names be unique and distinct from the names of object types.

An entity-relationship schema is usually represented in a graphical form, called an *entity-relationship diagram* or ER-diagram, for short. Competing visual representations have been proposed for ER-diagrams. Ours is a hybrid that borrows features from different proposals.

Figure 2.2 shows a small ER-diagram. Entity types are represented using rectangles, relationship types using diamonds, and attributes using ovals. Attributes are connected to their object types using lines, and the entity types participating in a relationship type are connected to the relationship type using lines with some additional adornments – their meaning is explained soon. An ER-diagram may not show all the information in the entity-relationship schema, for instance role names may be omitted to avoid clutter.

An entity type is an abstraction of the entities that share the same structure. The name of an entity type could equally well be in plural or singular form, depending on whether the focus is on the set of entities or on the individual entities belonging to the same set. Experience has shown that using the plural form makes finding natural names for relationship types sometimes more difficult. We shall therefore consistently name all entity types using a singular form, such as 'PCMember' and 'Paper'.

---

[2]The terms are sometimes used with a different meaning in the literature. Object sets are here defined to constitute the database instance, but some authors use object sets in the same meaning where we have used object types: as a description of the database schema.

In a formal setting we use calligraphic letters such as $\mathcal{A}$, $\mathcal{E}$ or $\mathcal{R}$ to denote the concepts in an entity-relationship schema.

For each entity type $\mathcal{E}$, a subset of its attributes forms the set of *identifying attributes* of $\mathcal{E}$. This set of attributes is called the *key* of $\mathcal{E}$. The entity set that corresponds to $\mathcal{E}$ cannot contain two entities whose key attributes have the same values. Another property required from keys is that they must be minimal. Thus for any subset of a key, an entity set can contain several entities that have identical values for the attributes in the subset.

Note that a key identifies an entity only within one entity set. The database may well contain several entities that have the same attributes and the same values for all the attributes, as long as the entities belong to different entity sets. To fully identify an entity in a database, one has to know both its type and the values of its key attributes.

An entity type can have several alternative keys. One of the keys is designated as the *primary key*. It is denoted in the ER-diagram by italicizing the names of the attributes that belong to the primary key.

The members of a relationship set are identified by the key values of the participating entities.

Relationships are of varying *cardinality*. Consider first a binary relationship type $\mathcal{R}$ having participants $\mathcal{E}_1$ and $\mathcal{E}_2$. We say that $\mathcal{R}$ is

- *one-to-many* from $\mathcal{E}_1$ to $\mathcal{E}_2$, if any entity in the entity set that corresponds to $\mathcal{E}_2$ can participate in at most one relationship that belongs to the relationship set that corresponds to $\mathcal{R}$;

- *many-to-one* from $\mathcal{E}_1$ to $\mathcal{E}_2$, if any entity in the entity set that corresponds to $\mathcal{E}_1$ can participate in at most one relationship that belongs to the relationship set that corresponds to $\mathcal{R}$;

- *one-to-one* between $\mathcal{E}_1$ and $\mathcal{E}_2$, if it is one-to-many and many-to-one; and

- *many-to-many* between $\mathcal{E}_1$ and $\mathcal{E}_2$, if it is neither one-to-many nor many-to-one.

If the cardinality of a relationship type is many-to-one from $\mathcal{E}_1$ to $\mathcal{E}_2$ (or one-to-one between $\mathcal{E}_1$ and $\mathcal{E}_2$), we say that the relationship type is *functional* with respect to $\mathcal{E}_2$.

Example 3.2 Consider two entity types: Course and Teacher, and a relationship type TaughtBy between the two entity types. The relationship type is

- many-to-one from Course to Teacher, if each course has only one teacher, but each teacher can teach several courses; and

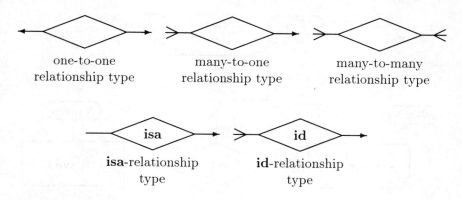

one-to-one
relationship type

many-to-one
relationship type

many-to-many
relationship type

isa-relationship
type

id-relationship
type

Figure 3.1   The relationship symbols used in an ER-diagram.

- one-to-many from Course to Teacher, if each course can have several teachers, but each teacher can teach at most one course.   □

In an ER-diagram, the line that connects the $\mathcal{R}$ diamond to the $\mathcal{E}$ rectangle is drawn with an arrowhead, if $\mathcal{R}$ is functional with respect to $\mathcal{E}$. If $\mathcal{R}$ is not functional with respect to $\mathcal{E}$, the connection of the line and the $\mathcal{E}$ rectangle gets a delta-like tail. Thus the ER-diagram shows explicitly the cardinality of each relationship type: 'many' corresponds to a delta-like tail, and 'one' corresponds to an arrowhead. See Figure 3.1 for the relationship symbols used in ER-diagrams.

The notion of functionality generalizes to relationship types with more than two participants: if an entity in a participating entity set $\mathcal{E}$ can be related to at most one collection of entities of the other participating entity sets, the relationship type is functional with respect to $\mathcal{E}$. Functional participants are indicated by arrows (from a relationship type to the entity type) in ER-diagrams.

Example 3.3 Consider again the classroom assignment problem discussed in Example 2.1. A possible entity-relationship diagram for modelling the situation is shown in Figure 3.2.

Given a course in the entity set that corresponds to Course and given a particular Time, the entity set for Room can contain at most one room such that the three would be connected by a relationship in MeetsIn. Therefore the line that connects MeetsIn and Room ends with arrow. A similar argument explains the second arrowhead in Figure 3.2. On the other hand, a course can meet in the same room several times a week – thus a delta-like tail for the connection between MeetsIn and Time.

The functionalities should not be misinterpreted. An arrowhead in an ER-diagram means that if we know *all other* participants of the relationship, then the remaining component (the one with the entering arrow)

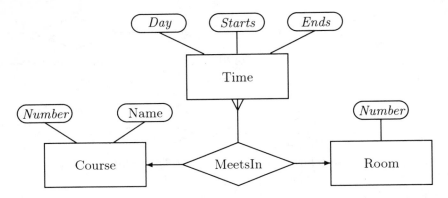

Figure 3.2   An entity-relationship diagram for class schedules.

is uniquely determined. Thus, knowing Time and Room uniquely determines the course that meets in that room at the given time. Figure 3.2 does, of course, *not* indicate that given a particular Time, we would know the unique Course and Room associated with that time. To put it differently, the lines connected to a relationship type with more than two components should be interpreted as running 'from head to a set of tails', not 'from tail to a set of heads'.   □

Note that the definition of cardinalities uses the phrase 'at most one'. What would change if the phrase was replaced by 'exactly one'? Then the relationship would turn into an *existence constraint*. Adding an entity to an entity set whose type participates in such a relationship type would be impossible, unless a corresponding relationship was simultaneously added to the relationship set. We shall not deal with existence constraints except in the special case of weak entities, the topic of the next section.

3.2   Weak entities

So far we have encountered only entities whose existence does not depend on the existence of other entities. Such strong entities can, for example, be added to or deleted from the database instance, no matter what other entities exist in the database.

When hierarchical structures are modelled, the entities on the lower levels of the hierarchy typically *inherit* various properties from the entities on higher levels in the hierarchy. As an example, consider the accepted papers and submitted papers in Example 2.2. An accepted paper has, of course, all the properties that any submitted paper has, but it also has additional properties – in this case simply the information that the paper has indeed been accepted. We could define accepted papers as a strong entity type and let that entity type have the same attributes as the entity type for all papers. Such a solution would, however, be dangerous: then the set of accepted papers could easily contain papers that have not even been submitted, papers with the same number could have different titles in the two entity sets, and so on.

We would like the ER-diagram to express the fact that accepted papers are a subset of submitted papers. This is exactly what the **isa**-*relationship* type used in Figure 2.2 (page 18) does: it is an existence constraint stating that an entity can only exist in the entity set for accepted papers if an entity with the same value for the attribute Number exists in the set for all submitted papers.

In addition to expressing existence constraints, weak entities allow the sharing of information among various entities, so that all the data does not have to be repeated for accepted papers. Instead, accepted papers inherit the key attribute (number of the paper) from the strong entity type, and this allows access to the information that is stored for all submitted papers.

An **isa**-relationship type is not named, and no attributes are associated with it. Therefore in the database instance no relationship set is created for **isa**-relationship types.

The weak entity that depends on the existence of another entity is called the *child* of the relationship, and the other entity is called the *parent*. The child entity may have some attributes of its own (an example can be found in Figure 3.6). In addition, by virtue of being the child in the **isa**-relationship type, it also has as its attributes the attributes that constitute the primary key of the parent. These inherited attributes form the key of the child entity type.

In an ER-diagram, **isa**-relationship types are denoted by drawing the symbol **isa** inside the corresponding diamond. The line that connects the diamond to the parent entity type ends with an arrowhead. Since at most one child entity of a given type may be associated with any parent entity, the tail of the line from the child entity type to the diamond does *not* get the usual delta-like adornment.

The inherited attributes of a weak entity type are not shown in the ER-diagram.

We also use the brief textual notation $\mathcal{E}$ **isa** $\mathcal{F}$ to indicate that $\mathcal{E}$ and $\mathcal{F}$ are connected by an **isa**-relationship type, and that $\mathcal{E}$ is a child of $\mathcal{F}$.

An **isa**-relationship is used for modelling the partitioning of a set into subsets. As we just saw, both the child and the parent have the same key. Another common situation arises when the parent entity is in some sense a generalization of the child entity. In this case some attributes of the child (in addition to the inherited key attributes) are needed for identifying the weak entity. The **id**-*relationships* are used for this situation.

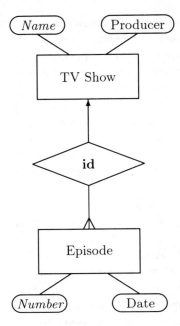

Figure 3.3   An entity-relationship diagram for TV-shows and their episodes.

An **id**-relationship (whose name comes from 'identification dependency') is used to model specialization into subclasses. The only formal difference between **isa**-relationships and **id**-relationships is their effect on the keys of the weak entity type. With **isa**-relationships, the child and the parent have the same key, whereas in the case of **id**-relationships, the key of the child is a superset of the key of the parent.

In an ER-diagram, an **id**-relationship type is denoted by drawing the symbol **id** inside the corresponding diamond. Since several children may inherit the properties of the same parent, this time the delta-like tail *is* used for connecting the child type to the **id**-diamond. The textual notation $\mathcal{E}$ **id** $\mathcal{F}$ is used to denote **id**-relationship types.

Example 3.4 Figure 3.3 shows an example of the use of **id**-relationship sets.

Individual episodes are here considered as instances of a series of TV-shows. To identify a particular episode, one needs to know the name of the show (the inherited component of the key) and the number of the episode.   □

For brevity, we shall refer to **isa**-relationship types and **id**-relationship types jointly as *existential relationship types*. The other relationship types are called *standard relationship types*.

Some restrictions apply to the use of **isa**-relationship types and **id**-relationship types. Though several relationship types in general can have the same participating entity types, at most one **isa**-relationship type or **id**-relationship type is allowed between two entity types. This is a natural requirement for several reasons. For example, these special relationship types are not named, and their multiple occurrences could not be distinguished from each other.

Another restriction is that no cyclic dependencies are allowed. To make this condition more exact, we define the *reference graph* for an ER-diagram $\mathcal{D}$ as a directed multigraph $ref(\mathcal{D}) = (V, S)$. The node set V consists of the entity types and the standard relationship types in the ER-diagram. The edge set S is formed as follows. Each connecting line between a relationship type $\mathcal{R}$ and an entity type $\mathcal{E}$ gives rise to a directed arc from $\mathcal{R}$ to $\mathcal{E}$. Since an entity set may participate in multiple roles in a relationship type, $ref(\mathcal{D})$ may have several arcs from a relationship set into an entity set – hence $ref(\mathcal{D})$ is really a multigraph, not a simple directed graph. Moreover, if $\mathcal{E}_c$ **isa** $\mathcal{E}_p$ or $\mathcal{E}_c$ **id** $\mathcal{E}_p$, the multigraph has a directed arc from $\mathcal{E}_c$ to $\mathcal{E}_p$. We say that the ER-diagram contains no directed cycles if the reference graph contains no directed cycles.

Such directed cycles could only be caused by existential relationship types. (Actually, any path in the reference graph consists of possibly one arc from a relationship type to an entity type and then arcs between entity types.) A situation where $\mathcal{E}$ **isa** $\mathcal{E}'$ and $\mathcal{E}'$ **isa** $\mathcal{E}$ for two entity sets $\mathcal{E}$ and $\mathcal{E}'$ is unnatural. The same holds for longer cycles and for **id**-relationship sets as well. Therefore we shall require the ER-diagram to be acyclic.

We shall also need the undirected version of the reference graph. It is called the *connection graph* and denoted by $conn(\mathcal{D})$. Cycles are allowed in the connection graph.

Example 3.5 The ER-diagram shown in Figure 3.4 has a cyclic connection graph but an acyclic reference graph. □

Our third and final rule restricts the simultaneous use of existential relationship types. The restriction says that if a weak entity type inherits several keys through different paths, then all the keys must satisfy the condition of minimality: no inherited key may be a subset of another.

Example 3.6 Consider the ER-diagram in Figure 3.5. In this diagram, entity type $\mathcal{X}$ inherits key A through the **isa**-relationship type that connects $\mathcal{X}$ to $\mathcal{Z}$. However, also another path connects $\mathcal{X}$ to $\mathcal{Z}$. The key of $\mathcal{Y}$ consists of attributes A and B, and the key is inherited by $\mathcal{X}$ because of the **isa**-relationship type between $\mathcal{X}$ and $\mathcal{Y}$. This creates a contradiction: both A and the catenation of A and B cannot simultaneously act as keys of $\mathcal{X}$. □

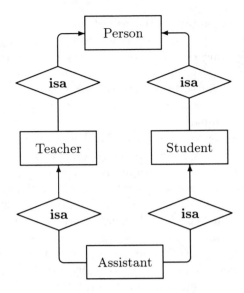

Figure 3.4   An entity-relationship diagram for assistants, faculty members, students, and persons.

We shall present more principles for the use of existential relationship types in conceptual modelling in Section 6.6.

3.3   An example: The conference database

The full ER-diagram for our example of a conference database is shown in Figure 3.6.

We have added several attributes to the fragment in Figure 2.2 (page 18): Address (of PCMember), Comments (of Evaluation), and Title

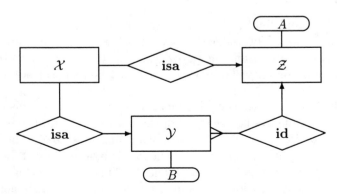

Figure 3.5   A forbidden entity-relationship diagram.

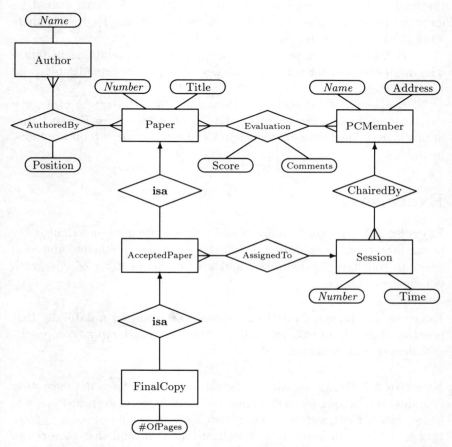

Figure 3.6   An entity-relationship diagram for a conference database.

(of Paper). A new strong entity type, Session, has also been added; it participates in relationship types ChairedBy and AssignedTo.

Finally, a new weak entity type, FinalCopy, has been added to keep track of whether the final copy of an accepted paper has already been received or not. If this was our only interest, then we could simply add a Boolean attribute, say Received, to AcceptedPaper. But we assume that the editor of the proceedings wants to know the number of pages in the final copy, so we need an attribute like #OfPages. This cannot be an attribute of AcceptedPaper: it has a valid value only for those papers whose final copy has indeed been received.

Note how keys can be inherited along a chain of relationship types. The attribute Number serves as the key of Paper, AcceptedPaper, and FinalCopy.

This example is, of course, fairly small: the ER-diagram of a large database application can contain hundreds of entity types. For such diagrams more refined drawing techniques and computerized tools are indispensable.

Exercises

Exercise 3.1 The words 'scheme' and 'schema' are used interchangeably in the literature. Look up the definitions of 'scheme', 'schema' and 'diagram' in your favorite dictionary and see whether or not you agree with our choice of words.

Exercise 3.2 Design an entity-relationship schema for a database that contains data about concert halls, orchestras, conductors, composers, symphonies, and concerts.

Exercise 3.3 Design an entity-relationship schema for a database that contains data about football teams (such as name of franchise, owner, home town), their rosters, game schedules, and results of games. Note that franchises can move from one city to another, and that players can be sold. Thus your database should somehow indicate when a data item has been valid.

Exercise 3.4 Draw an ER-diagram for a database to be used in a departmental library for storing data about books, borrowers, and loans. Estimate how many object types a real library database would have, and also estimate how many megabytes of space some local library would need for the storage of its data.

Bibliographic notes

Data modelling has been treated extensively in several books, of which those by Tsichritzis and Lochovsky [TL82] and Teorey and Fry [TF82a] are among the most widely cited. Some choices in data modelling (for instance, how to decide whether an object is an entity or a relationship) are discussed by Kent [Ken82]. A survey of semantic data models is given by Hull and King [HK87].

The seminal article on the entity-relationship model was published in 1976 by Chen [Che76]. Teorey [Teo90] gives an overview of the many proposed additions to the model. The proceedings of the annual *Conference on the ER-Approach* is a good source for recent developments on the ER-model. An unofficial effort to standardize the concepts and terminology is currently under way [STH91].

The three best-known suggestions for representing ER-diagrams are due to Bachman [Bac69], Chen [Che76], and Martin [Mar87]. Goldstein and Storey [GS89] study the intuitiveness of ER-diagrams.

Graphical interfaces to systems based on the entity-relationship model are described in [ZM83, RC88] (see also [HK87, Ioa92]).

Chapter 4
The Relational Model

This chapter defines the basic concepts of the relational model and also two query languages that can be used for accessing a relational database. Integrity constraints are treated in Chapter 7.

4.1 Schemas and relations

In the relational data model, data is stored in tables. The columns in the tables are named, and the names are called *attributes*. We use capital letters from the beginning of the alphabet (like A, B and C) to denote attributes when they occur in formal definitions and proofs.

Attribute sets are denoted by capital letters from the end of the alphabet, such as X, Y and Z. A set consisting of a single attribute is denoted by the attribute itself, and concatenation is used to denote set union. Thus ABC denotes the set $\{A, B, C\}$, and XY stands for $X \cup Y$.

An *attribute sequence* is an ordered set of attributes. Attribute sequences are written by enclosing the attributes in angle brackets, as in $\langle A_1, \ldots, A_n \rangle$. The same symbols are used to denote both attribute sets and attribute sequences. Thus, X, Y, and Z can denote sequences, and ABC can denote the sequence $\langle ABC \rangle$. Attribute sequences can be used as arguments in set operations; then the ordering of the elements is simply ignored. Similarly, sets can be used as sequences by ordering the elements in some way.

Each attribute A has an associated *domain*, denoted $Dom(A)$. If a table has an A-column, all values appearing in the column must belong to $Dom(A)$. For a set of attributes X, we define

$$Dom(X) = \bigcup_{A \in X} Dom(A).$$

The rows in a table consist of values for all attributes labelling the columns of the table. The rows are called *tuples*, and the set of all tuples in the table is called a *relation*. These terms come from set theory: if the attributes of a table are $A_1, \ldots, A_n$, the table is a subset of $Dom(A_1) \times \cdots \times Dom(A_n)$, that is, a relation in the set theoretical sense. Small letters are used to denote tuples (for example t, u, v and w) and relations (for example r and s). We allow both domains and relations to be infinite sets. For some properties this is essential; in such cases it will be explicitly mentioned.

Let r be a relation whose attributes are $A_1, \ldots, A_n$. The attributes define the structure of the data that is stored in the table. In relational terms, we say that r is a relation *over* $\{A_1, \ldots, A_n\}$, and that $\{A_1, \ldots, A_n\}$ is the *relation schema* of r. It is useful to give names to relation schemas; capital letters are used for this purpose. Thus, if $R = \{A_1, \ldots, A_n\}$, relation r is over R. We also say that r is an *instance* of R. Sometimes it is useful to indicate which attributes belong to a relation or a relation schema. Then we can also write $r(A_1, \ldots, A_n)$ and $R(A_1, \ldots, A_n)$ instead of r and R, respectively.

Let r be a relation over R. Formally, each tuple $t \in r$ is a mapping $t : R \to Dom(R)$ such that $t(A) \in Dom(A)$ for each $A \in R$. This is in contrast with mathematical relations, where the order of the components in a tuple is important. Here, a tuple is an unordered set of components, but the components are named. When a relation is displayed in tabular form, the columns can therefore be freely permuted without changing the relation. (The same holds for rows as well, since the relation is an unordered set of tuples.)

Either alternative (defining a relation as a set theoretical relation or as a set of mappings) could be used to develop the relational model, and each has its virtues. Our choice, defining a relation as a set of mappings, makes many proofs and constructions slightly more pleasant, since the relation schema is part of the definition of the mappings. In a mathematical relation the column names do not belong to the relation instance; they are extraneous information that would somehow have to be incorporated into the notation to make the definitions unambiguous. In some cases, however, the definition of a relation as a set of mappings causes some notational problems. Therefore we sometimes interpret a relation as a set of sequences.

Finally, a relational database is composed of several tables. A *database* is a set of relations, and a *database schema* is a set of relation schemas. In fact, this is a simplification that will later be changed. Besides the structure of the database (the set of relation schemas), the integrity constraints are also an essential part of the database schema. After the integrity constraints have been introduced in Chapter 7, we shall adopt a notation where the set of relation schemas is just one of the three components that together form a database schema, the other two components being sets of integrity constraints. But for now, a database schema is simply a set of relation schemas.

Bold letters are used for database objects: small letters (such as **r** and **s**) for databases, capital letters (such as **R** and **S**) for database schemas. Even though a database is a set, it is usual to use parentheses instead of braces when listing the component relations of the database. Thus we write **r** $= (r, s, q)$, not **r** $= \{r, s, q\}$. The same convention is used for database schemas, too. The set of attributes appearing in the relation schemas that form a database schema is usually denoted by U (for the *universal* set of attributes).

A *relational schema* is a term used of schemas expressed within the relational model. Be careful to notice the difference between a relation schema and a relational schema.

The most important form of integrity constraints are *keys* of relation schemas. They correspond exactly to the keys in the ER-model: a key of a relation schema is a set of attributes whose values are sufficient for identifying the tuples in the relation instance. Keys will be defined formally in Chapter 7, but in the examples we already indicate the key attributes of a schema by italicizing the names of the attributes.

An ER-diagram can be transformed to a relational schema basically by producing a relation schema from each entity set and a relation schema from each relationship set. Parts of the transformation are complicated: in particular, some attributes may have to be renamed. We discuss the algorithm in detail in Chapter 11. The reverse transformation, a mapping from relational schemas into ER-diagrams, is also presented there.

Example 4.1 For implementing the conference database of Figure 3.6 (page 31) we could use the following relation schemas:

> AcceptedPaper (*Paper_Number*),
> AssignedTo (*Paper_Number*, Session_Number),
> Author (*Author_Name*),
> AuthoredBy (*Author_Name*, *Paper_Number*, Position),
> ChairedBy (*Session_Number*, Chairperson_Name),
> Evaluation (*Paper_Number*, *Reviewer_Name*, Score, Comments),
> FinalCopy (*Paper_Number*, #OfPages),
> Paper (*Paper_Number*, Title),
> PCMember (*PCMember_Name*, Address), and
> Session (*Session_Number*, Time).

Fragments of two relations are shown below.

Paper_Number	Title
47	Updating Databases in the Weak Instance Model
16	Attribute Agreement
86	Can Constant-time-maintainability be More Practical?
33	Bottom-up Beats Top-down for Datalog
28	On the Power of Alexander Templates
75	Safety of Datalog Queries over Infinite Databases
77	Proof-tree Transformation Theorems and Their Applications

Author_Name	Paper_Number	Position
Paolo Atzeni	47	1
Riccardo Torlone	47	2
Y. C. Tay	16	1
Ke Wang	86	1
Jeffrey D. Ullman	33	1
Hirohisa Seki	28	1
Yehoshua Sagiv	75	1
Moshe Y. Vardi	75	2
Raghu Ramakrishnan	77	1
Yehoshua Sagiv	77	2
Jeffrey D. Ullman	77	3
Moshe Y. Vardi	77	4

□

4.2   Relational algebra

The relational model has two equally expressive formalisms, *relational algebra* and *relational calculus*, for writing queries. Of the two, relational algebra is more compact and therefore extensively used in database research. It is sufficient for our purposes, too, and we shall therefore not deal with relational calculus at all.

Relational algebra contains a set of basic operations for manipulating data given in tabular form. In addition, several derived operations (operations that can be expressed as a sequence of basic operations) are also used. In a formal query language, the set of basic operations should be nonredundant: none of the operations should be expressible using the other basic operations. This core of the relational algebra can be chosen in different ways. In the following we present one possibility.

Set operations

Formally we have defined relations to be sets. Therefore all operations in relational algebra are set-oriented: they take sets as arguments and produce a set as their result. Conventional set operations are useful for manipulating relations. We shall include *union, intersection* and *difference* (denoted by $r \cup s$, $r \cap s$ and $r \setminus s$, respectively) as the basic operations in relational algebra. The operations have their standard meaning:

$$r \cup s = \{t \mid t \in r \text{ or } t \in s\},$$
$$r \cap s = \{t \mid t \in r \text{ and } t \in s\}, \text{ and}$$
$$r \setminus s = \{t \mid t \in r \text{ and } t \notin s\}.$$

Care must be taken to ensure that the resulting set is a relation, in the sense that it has a schema. Therefore $r \cup s$, $r \cap s$ and $r \setminus s$ are defined only if r and s are relations over the same schema.

More interesting are the operations that are specifically designed for database relations. There are three such operations: *projection* for stripping columns from tables, *selection* for choosing rows from tables, and *join* for combining data from several tables. A fourth operation, *renaming*, is also useful for the handling of attribute names.

Projection

The purpose of the projection operation is to trim a table so that only the data in the interesting columns remains.

Formally, let r be a relation over R, and $X \subseteq R$. For a tuple $t \in r$ we define the *projection* of t on X, denoted $t[X]$, as the mapping $t' : X \to Dom(X)$ such that $t'(A) = t(A)$ for each $A \in X$. Intuitively, $t[X]$ is simply shorter than t: it is defined only for the attributes in X, but for those attributes it has the same values as t.

The projection of relation r on X is now defined as

$$r[X] = \{t[X] \mid t \in r\}.$$

Sometimes the notations $\pi_X(t)$ and $\pi_X(r)$ are used with the same meaning as $t[X]$ and $r[X]$, respectively.

A side effect of projecting a relation is that the number of tuples may decrease. If the argument relation over R is projected on a set of attributes X, and if relation r over R contains two tuples that agree on the X attributes but differ on some attribute in $R \setminus X$, the projected tuples would be identical. Such identical tuples are commonly called *duplicates*. Since relations are sets, they cannot contain duplicates, and only one representative of each duplicate is retained. Because this feature is implicit in the concept of a set, it does not show up in the definition of the projection operation.

This point, incidentally, is one where commercial database systems often differ from the pure relational model. In real implementations, relations are stored as files. Files, of course, *can* contain several identical records. Checking the uniqueness of records could take a lot of time. It is therefore customary that relations in commercial database management systems can contain duplicates.

Example 4.2 Consider relation schema $R(A, B, C)$. The following figure shows a relation r over R and the results of operations $r[AB]$ and $r[AC]$.

A	B	C
5	7	3
8	6	4
5	7	4
5	9	2

r

A	B
5	7
8	6
5	9

$r[AB]$

A	C
5	3
8	4
5	4
5	2

$r[AC]$ □

If $t \in r$ and $A \in R$, then $t[A]$ is in principle a mapping from the singleton set $\{A\}$ to $Dom(A)$. We identify $t[A]$ with the value of this mapping on A (which formally is $t[A](A) = t(A)$) and use the notation $t[A]$ also for the value of t on attribute A.

Sometimes it is notationally advantageous to consider projection as an operation that returns a set of sequences, rather than a set of mappings. For example, if we want to say that tuple t has as its X-columns the same sequence of values as tuple u on its Y-columns, we write $t[X] = u[Y]$ and consider both sides of the equation as sequences. Whenever we write an expression relating two projections with different attribute sets we consider the values of projections to be sequences or sets of sequences. In addition to the above, examples of this usage are the expressions $r[X] = s[Y]$ (equality of sets of sequences), $t[X] \in r[Y]$ (membership of a sequence in a set of sequences), and $r[X] \subseteq s[Y]$ (subset relation between two sets of sequences).

Selection

While projection is used to trim a relation horizontally, *selection* can be used to trim it vertically by selecting a subset of the tuples in a relation. Another name often used for this operation is *restriction*.

An essential part of a selection operation is the condition that specifies which tuples should be selected. We omit a detailed definition of how conditions are formed, and simply say that a condition is a formula that is composed of constants, attribute names, comparison operators, and the logical operators $\vee$ (or), $\wedge$ (and), and $\neg$ (not). Then the selection operation based on condition ψ is defined as

$$\sigma_\psi(r) = \{t \in r \mid t \text{ satisfies } \psi\}.$$

Here satisfaction is defined in the obvious way; for instance, if ψ is "$A = 5 \wedge B < 3$", tuple t satisfies ψ if $t[A] = 5$ and $t[B] < 3$.

Example 4.3 Consider again relation schema $R(A, B, C)$. The following figure shows the result of two selection queries.

A	B	C
5	7	3
8	6	4
5	7	4
5	9	2

r

A	B	C
5	7	3
8	6	4
5	9	2

$\sigma_{A>5 \vee C \leq 3}(r)$

A	B	C
5	7	3
5	7	4
5	9	2

$\sigma_{A<B}(r)$ $\square$

Join

Both projection and selection are used for cutting off data from a relation. The next operation, *join*, is used for connecting data that is stored in two different relations. In the relational model, all connections between data items are implicit, in the sense that no 'links' are stored in the database. Two tuples are connected if the attributes that are common to both tuples have the same values.

The join operation combines connected tuples from the argument relations. Thus the join of r and s contains the rows that can be formed by pasting together a row of r and a row of s so that the values for the common attributes are the same.

Formally, let r and s be relations over R and S, respectively. The join of r and s, denoted $r \bowtie s$, is a relation over $R \cup S$. It is defined by

$$r \bowtie s = \{t \mid \text{there exist tuples } u \in r \text{ and } v \in s \text{ such that } t[R] = u \text{ and } t[S] = v\}.$$

Example 4.4 Consider relation schemas $R(A, B, C)$ and $S(A, B, D)$. The following figure shows the result of a join operation when applied to two relations over these schemas.

A	B	C
5	7	3
8	6	4
5	7	4
5	9	2

A	B	D
5	7	3
5	2	4
5	7	8
8	6	2
4	4	2
5	9	6
5	9	4

A	B	C	D
5	7	3	3
5	7	3	8
8	6	4	2
5	7	4	3
5	7	4	8
5	9	2	6
5	9	2	4

r s $r \bowtie s$ □

The join operation can be defined in several equivalent ways. We present an alternative definition after introducing our final basic operation of the relational algebra.

Renaming

All previous operations have produced new relations from their argument relations. The final operation, *renaming*, does not change any data values; instead, it modifies the *schema* of the argument relation. The renaming operation is typically used to carry out a transformation that allows a relation to be used as an argument of one of the other operations, such as union or intersection (which require the schemas of the argument relations to be identical) or join (where the common attributes of the schemas influence the result).

Let again r be a relation over R, and let $A \in R$ and $B \notin R$. Then r with A renamed to B, denoted $\rho_{A \to B}(r)$, is a relation over the attribute set $(R \setminus \{A\}) \cup \{B\}$. It is defined by

$$\rho_{A \to B}(r) = \{t \mid \text{there exists a tuple } u \in r \text{ such that}$$
$$t[B] = u[A] \text{ and } t[C] = u[C] \text{ if } C \neq B\}.$$

Example 4.5 The effect of renaming one of the columns is shown below.

A	B	C
5	7	3
8	6	4
5	7	4
5	9	2

A	D	C
5	7	3
8	6	4
5	7	4
5	9	2

r $\rho_{B \to D}(r)$ □

This completes the description of the basic operations in relational algebra. Before looking at some derived operations, let us see how relational algebra can be used in querying the conference database.

Example 4.6 Consider the relation schemas of Example 4.1. Here are some example queries expressed in relational algebra:

(1) 'Give the titles of the papers that are longer than ten pages.'

$$\pi_{\text{Title}}(\text{Paper} \bowtie \sigma_{\#\text{OfPages}>10}(\text{FinalCopy}))$$

(2) 'Give a list of the first authors of the papers whose final copy is still missing.'

$$\pi_{\text{Author\_Name}}(\sigma_{\text{Position}=1}(\text{AuthoredBy} \bowtie ($$
$$\text{AcceptedPaper} \setminus \pi_{\text{Paper\_Number}}(\text{FinalCopy}))))$$

(3) 'Which program committee members did not evaluate any papers?'

$$\pi_{\text{PCMember\_Name}}(\text{PCMember}) \setminus \pi_{\text{PCMember\_Name}}($$
$$\rho_{\text{Reviewer\_Name} \rightarrow \text{PCMember\_Name}}(\text{Evaluation}))$$

☐

We now turn to some derived operations. An operation closely related to the join operation is the Cartesian product. The Cartesian product of two relations, r over R and s over S, is a relation with $|R| + |S|$ columns and $|r| \cdot |s|$ rows containing all the rows obtainable by placing a row of s at the end of a row in r. This relation has two occurrences of all attributes that appear both in R and in S.

For a more formal definition, assume first that R and S have no common attributes. For tuples $t \in r$ and $u \in s$ the *concatenation* w of t and u is a tuple over the relation schema $R \cup S$ such that for each attribute $A \in R$ we have $w[A] = t[A]$ and for each attribute $B \in S$ we have $w[B] = u[B]$. The concatenation is denoted by tu.

The *Cartesian product* $r \times s$ of relations r and s is a relation over $R \cup S$ consisting of all concatenations of tuples from r and tuples from s, that is,

$$r \times s = \{tu \mid t \in r \wedge u \in s\}.$$

If schemas R and S contain attributes with the same name, the Cartesian product is defined by first renaming an attribute B in $R \cap S$ as $R.B$ in R and as $S.B$ in S. That is, we consider the Cartesian product to be a relation over the schema

$$T = (R \setminus S) \cup (S \setminus R) \cup \{R.B, S.B \mid B \in R \cap S\}.$$

Example 4.7 Consider the schemas $R(AB)$ and $S(BC)$, and assume the relations r over R and s over S are as follows.

A	B
0	1
3	2

B	C
1	4
2	6
2	5

r 　　　　　　　　 s

The relation $r \times s$ over $T = \{A, R.B, S.B, C\}$ is shown below.

A	R.B	S.B	C
0	1	1	4
0	1	2	6
0	1	2	5
3	2	1	4
3	2	2	6
3	2	2	5

□

The Cartesian product and the join operation are closely related. A simple observation is that if two relations have no attributes in common, then their join and Cartesian product are identical. But the correspondence goes much further. In fact, the Cartesian product could replace the join operation as one of the basic operations in relational algebra: then join could be defined using the basic operations. Intuitively, the join of r and s can be obtained from the Cartesian product of r and s by first selecting all tuples with the same values for the attributes occurring in both R and S. Then the duplicate occurrences of attributes are dropped using projection.

Formally, let

$$r \bowtie' s = \sigma_\phi(r \times s),$$

where

$$\phi = \bigwedge_{B \in R \cap S} (R.B = S.B)$$

is the *join condition*, defining which tuples from the Cartesian product belong to the join. The second step is that for each attribute $B \in R \cap S$, attribute $S.B$ must be removed and attribute $R.B$ renamed back to B. Thus

$$r \bowtie s = \rho_{R.B \to B | B \in R \cap S}(\pi_X(r \bowtie' s)),$$

where $X = T \setminus \{S.B \mid B \in R \cap S\}$.

Example 4.8 Continuing Example 4.7, the relations $r \bowtie' s$ and $r \bowtie s$ are shown below.

A	$R.B$	$S.B$	C
0	1	1	4
3	2	2	6
3	2	2	5

$r \bowtie' s$

A	B	C
0	1	4
3	2	6
3	2	5

$r \bowtie s$

□

The joins we have been considering so far are so-called *natural joins*: the join condition is an equality over common attributes. One can define other types of joins by letting condition ϕ be an arbitrary Boolean expression among the attributes in the schema of the Cartesian product.

The following theorem states a fundamental property of the join operation: the join of two projections of a relation r contains all the tuples in r (and usually some more), provided that all attributes appearing in r appear in at least one of the projections.

Theorem 4.1 Let r be a relation over R. Assume that $X \subseteq R$ and $Y \subseteq R$ are attribute sets such that $X \cup Y = R$. Then

$$r \subseteq r[X] \bowtie r[Y].$$

Proof. Since $XY = R$, the relation $r[X] \bowtie r[Y]$ is also a relation over R. Given a tuple $t \in r$, we have to show that it belongs to the join. Since $t \in r$, we have $t[X] \in r[X]$ and $t[Y] \in r[Y]$. Thus by the definition of join we have $t \in r[X] \bowtie r[Y]$.   □

The inclusion in Theorem 4.1 may be proper. An example can be found in Example 4.2, where $r[AB] \bowtie r[AC]$ contains the tuple $(5, 7, 2)$, although it does not belong to r.

Some additional properties of the operations in relational algebra are dealt with in the exercises.

Although relational algebra provides a powerful set of operations for expressing a wide variety of queries, there exist some fairly natural queries that cannot be formulated using relational algebra. The lack of recursion is the most notable omission. Properties of recursive queries and even more general queries expressed using first-order logic are subjects of intensive research. This research, however, has not yet had an effect on database design.

4.3   The SQL query language

Relational algebra is a good and compact notation for developing the design theory of relational databases. For database management systems we need another language with, for instance, an alphabet without any special symbols such as π, σ and $\bowtie$. *SQL* (for Structured Query Language) is the standard adopted by most vendors. Here we shall only introduce the basic structure of SQL programs to be able to use it in examples and exercises.

In SQL, a relation schema is defined by giving the name of the schema, and by listing the attributes together with their domains. The set of possible domains is predefined. It includes some common data types, such as several kinds of numbers and character strings.

Example 4.9 The schema Evaluation of the conference example can be defined by the following SQL statement.

> **create table** Evaluation (
>   Paper_Number **decimal**(3),
>   Reviewer_Name **char**(20),
>   Score **decimal**(2),
>   Comments **char**(255)
>)

We shall see in Chapter 7 how this definition can be augmented with conditions that help in ensuring the correctness of the data stored using this schema.   □

In SQL, indices are defined by a **create index** command, by listing the attributes that the index is based on.

Example 4.10 Continuing Example 4.9, we could define an index on table Evaluation as follows.

> **create index** EvaluationIndex on
>   Paper_Number   □

All the operations of relational algebra can be expressed using SQL, but the correspondence between the operations and the statements of SQL is by no means one-to-one. SQL has one fundamental statement structure, called the *select statement*, that can be used to express all but the standard set operations of relational algebra. The select statement has the following form:

> **select** $A_1, A_2, \ldots, A_n$
> **into** $B_1, B_2, \ldots, B_n$
> **from** $r_1, r_2, \ldots, r_k$
> **where**   list of conditions

The third line, the *from clause*, specifies the relations to which the SQL statement is applied. The fourth line, the *where clause*, specifies the conditions that the tuples in those relations must satisfy to be accepted into the result of the statement. The first line, the *select clause*, then specifies which attributes of the participating relations should appear in the result. It corresponds to the projection operation of relational algebra (*not* the selection operation). Finally, the second line, the *into clause*, can be used for renaming the attributes in the result relation, typically for specifying the schema of the result.

The where clause is used for representing both the selection and the join operations of relational algebra. For a selection operation, the selection conditions are simply listed in the list of conditions of the where clause, separated by the keywords **and**, **or**, and **not**. The join operation is represented in a manner that resembles the alternative definition of join, based on the Cartesian product. The join conditions are listed in the where clause of the select statement. In SQL, arbitrary joins and natural joins can thus be expressed with equal ease.

If some relations in the from clause have common attributes, the attribute names must be prefixed by a dot and the name of the relation when they appear in the select clause or where clause. If all attributes of participating relations should appear in the result, the list of attributes in the select clause can be replaced by a star.

The into and where clauses may sometimes be omitted, but the select and from clauses are mandatory.

Example 4.11 Let r and s be relations over ABC and ABD, respectively. The following four SQL statements illustrate how the operations of relational algebra can expressed in SQL.

$\pi_{AB}(r)$:
    select A, B
    from r

$\sigma_{A<5 \wedge C \geq 10}(r)$:   **select**   *
    from r
    where $A < 5$ **and** $C >= 10$

$r \bowtie s$:   **select** $r.A, r.B, C, D$
    from r, s
    where $r.A = s.A$ **and** $r.B = s.B$

$\rho_{B \rightarrow E}(r)$:   **select** A, B, C
    into A, E, C
    from r

$\square$

Many relational queries are so-called *select-project-join*-queries. Tuples are first selected from participating relations. They are then joined, and the uninteresting attributes are projected out. SQL makes expressing such queries very convenient, since a single select statement is often sufficient.

Ordinary set operations have a slightly more verbose representation in SQL. To begin with, the union operation has a corresponding **union-***expression* in SQL. The arguments of the expression are not simply relations, but relations produced by select statements; thus, for $r \cup s$ one has to write

select   *

from r

union

select   *

from s

By adding the keyword **all** after **union**, duplicates are retained; the default is that duplicates are pruned out. In the case of projection, either **all** or **distinct** can be added after **select**. In this case, however, **all** is the default: duplicates are not eliminated, unless explicitly requested by using **distinct**.

Set intersection and difference can be expressed just like union. The keywords used are **intersection** and **minus**, respectively. However, these two operations often appear in contexts where the argument tables have only a single column. Then the **in** predicate provides a convenient way for expressing intersection; by preceding the predicate with the keyword **not** the operation turns into set difference. More exactly, suppose A is an attribute in the schemas of both r and s. Then $r[A] \cap s[A]$ can be expressed by writing

select A

from r

where A **in**

         (**select** A

           from s)

To interpret this, it is useful to know how the select statements are executed in general. The from clause defines implicit *range variables*, one for each participating relation, that step through the tuples in the relations. This corresponds to several nested loops, one level for each range variable. (The range variables can also be made explicit by writing the name of the variable after the name of the corresponding relation; this is useful if the same relation appears in several roles in the query.)

The body of the loop then tests the conditions of the where clause using the current values of the range variables.

Returning to the **in** predicate above, it simply tests that the value for the A attribute in the current tuple (the one that is the value of the range variable) does appear in the one-column relation specified by the second select statement. Effectively, this corresponds to intersection.

Example 4.12 Consider again the queries expressed in relational algebra in Example 4.6 (page 43). Here are the same queries expressed in SQL.

(1) 'Give the titles of the papers that are longer than ten pages.'

>   **select**   Title
>   **from**   Paper, FinalCopy
>   **where**   #OfPages > 10 **and**
>   FinalCopy.Paper_Number = Paper.Paper_Number

(2) 'Give a list of the first authors of the papers whose final copy is still missing.'

>   **select**   Author_Name
>   **from**   AuthoredBy, AcceptedPaper
>   **where**   Position = 1 **and**
>   AuthoredBy.Paper_Number =
>   AcceptedPaper.Paper_Number **and**
>   AcceptedPaper.Paper_Number **not in**
>   (**select** Paper_Number
>   **from** FinalCopy)

(3) 'Which program committee members did not evaluate any papers?'

>   **select**   PCMember_Name
>   **from**   PCMember
>   **where**   PCMember_Name **not in**
>   (**select** Reviewer_Name
>   **from** Evaluation)

□

SQL contains lots of other features not covered here. These include statements for updating the database, aggregate functions, and the ability to partition a table into several 'groups'. Integrity constraints are expressed in the definition of the database; they are discussed in Chapter 7.

4.4   Implementing the relational model

Implementation of a database management system is a complicated task. In this section we discuss some parts of the implementation of the relational model that influence the database design process: the data structures used for storing relations, indices, and query evaluation and optimization. We bypass totally many important issues, such as transaction management.

4.4.1   Files and indices

We use a simplified model of the storage of relations. We assume that one relation is stored in one file, with all the rows of the relation stored sequentially.

Typically, a disk file is organized into *database pages*, the unit which is read or written in one I/O-operation. Each page of the file used for storing the relation r has a *page identifier*. After the page has been read to main memory, a given tuple within the page can be found fairly quickly by a sequential search.

Inserting a row into a relation is done by first finding a block with free space for the row within the file. Then the block is read into main memory, it is updated, and written back to disk. Deletion of a row is usually done just by marking the row as free in the block. Modification can be done either as a combination of a deletion and an insertion, or by modifying the row in place. The latter alternative is usually possible only if the modification does not lengthen the file.

An *index* of a relation r over relation schema R is a data structure which helps in locating rows of r faster under some conditions. An index I is *based on* some *index attributes* $\{A_1, \ldots, A_n\} \subseteq R$. Conceptually, one can consider an index to be a data structure containing pairs $((a_1, \ldots, a_n), b)$, where $(a_1, \ldots, a_n)$ is a tuple of values for the attributes $A_1, \ldots, A_n$ and b is the address of the tuples in r with these values, that is, a pointer to the set $\sigma_{A_1=a_1,\ldots,A_n=a_n}(r)$. If this set contains at most one element, b can be a page identifier. Otherwise b is a set of page identifiers implemented in some standard manner, such as a linked list.

An alternative way is to think of an index based on $A_1, \ldots, A_n$ as an $n+1$ attribute relation over the attributes $A_1, \ldots, A_n, B$, where the values of attribute B are page identifiers or pointers to sets of page identifiers.

Example 4.13 In Example 4.1 (page 37) we considered the relation schema Paper (*Paper_Number*, Title). To speed up searches based on the name of the paper we might want to use an index based on the attribute Title. For combining the information in Paper with data in other rows one usually uses joins based on the Paper_Number attribute. Hence an index based on this attribute could be useful.   □

An index can make queries faster. The price that has to be paid is that indices require space and that updates get slower, since the data structures of the index have to be updated.

Denoting by ψ the condition $A_1 = a_1 \wedge \ldots \wedge A_n = a_n$, the index supports fast retrieval of the rows in the relation $\sigma_\psi(r)$. Suppose the index contains a pair $((a_1, \ldots, a_n), b)$; after b has been found, the rows with the given A-values can be obtained from r with at most one disk operation per row.

The relevant pages have to be fetched into main memory. There are basically two types of indices depending on how the structure of the file relates to the index.

In a *clustering index* rows in the subrelation $\sigma_\psi(r)$ are stored more or less consecutively. That is, for the index entry $((a_1, \ldots, a_n), b)$ the pages in b contain (almost) only rows satisfying the condition ψ. If an index is not clustering, it is called *nonclustering*. Then the rows satisfying ψ can be scattered around the file.

Indices are usually implemented using either B-trees or hashing. A *B-tree* is a generalization of a balanced binary search tree.

A B-tree is used as an index by storing the page identifiers at the leaves (or internal nodes) of the tree. A search for some value begins from the root and is guided by the values stored at the nodes. Thus the height of the tree determines how many nodes have to be examined to find the relevant page identifiers.

B-trees offer fairly fast retrieval. The data structure is also fully dynamic: its properties are not influenced by insertions and deletions. A B-tree index based on $A_1, \ldots, A_n$ supports also retrieval of all the rows with values $A_1 = a_1, \ldots, A_k = a_k$ for $k < n$; such searches are called *prefix queries*. Hence a B-tree index based on $A_1, \ldots, A_n$ can also be used as an index based on $A_1, \ldots, A_k$.

Hash indices use an array to store the page identifiers. To find the pages corresponding to the values of the index attributes, a *hash function* is used to compute a pointer to some location of the array. For example, if attribute A has numeric values, a hashing index might compute the value of $A \bmod k$, where k is the size of the hash table. For a given array location h, all page identifiers corresponding to rows with $A \bmod k = h$ are stored into the location h (or some location easily accessible from h).

Hash indices offer very fast retrieval of rows under normal conditions. Typically, only one or two disk accesses are needed to retrieve any row of any relation. The first access is needed for large relations to find the relevant location of the hash table, and the second disk access retrieves the actual row. Also the CPU processing needed for using a hash index is simple.

On the other hand, hash indices have some drawbacks. If the hash function is badly chosen or the hash table becomes full, then many attribute values are mapped onto the same location. Such *collisions* slow down the use of the index.

In the worst case the page identifiers of all rows are stored into a single location of the hash table, and the index does not speed up searches significantly. If the hash table is too small, collisions are frequent; if the table is too large, space is wasted. The efficient use of a hash index requires that fairly accurate information about the size of the relation is available. Also, if the size of the relation increases or decreases significantly, the size of the hash table should be modified. An additional drawback of hash indices is that they do not normally support prefix searches.

The *primary index* is an index based on the attributes of the primary key of the relation schema. Such an index can avoid one level of indirection: instead of the index containing page identifiers at the leaves of the B-tree, the leaves can directly be disk blocks of the relation. Similarly, for a primary index implemented using hashing the value of the hash function can be the page identifier. A *secondary index* is an index that is not primary.

The choice of indices is one of the main problems in physical design. The first stage of index selection is usually easy. One creates indices for the primary keys of each relation corresponding to (strong) entity types. For relation schemas corresponding to weak entity types, indices can be based on the key attributes.

For relation schemas corresponding to relationship types, indices can be based on the key attributes, or the components of the key, depending on the functionality of the relationship type and the query profile. Some small relations can be left without any indices. Also, if a large relation is always processed sequentially, no index is necessary.

The choice of the possible secondary indices is typically harder. One has to study the expected queries and weigh the gains in query times against the loss in update times and in space usage.

4.4.2   Implementing the relational algebra

In this section we describe the basic methods for implementing the operations of relational algebra.

Projection

A projection operation $r[X]$ is simple to implement: just read each block of r, and for each row t in a block output the row $t[X]$. After this has been done, sort the rows according to their attribute values and eliminate possible duplicates. Usually projection is done in conjunction with other operations from the query.

Selection

A selection $\sigma_\phi(r)$ can be implemented in several different ways. Perhaps the simplest alternative is to read every row of r and check whether condition ϕ holds.

If the condition ϕ is of the form $A = d$, where d is a constant, we can use an index I defined on A to locate the rows satisfying the condition.

A B-tree index can also be used for selections of the form $\sigma_{A \leq d}(r)$, or for similar comparison predicates between one attribute and a constant. The parts of the B-tree corresponding to the condition can be found quickly. A hashing index is usually not suitable for fast implementation of such selections.

If the condition ϕ is a conjunction, say $\phi = \phi_1 \wedge \phi_2$, there are several possibilities. The simplest is to use the identity $\sigma_\phi(r) = \sigma_{\phi_1}(\sigma_{\phi_2}(r))$ by first computing the selection with respect to one subcondition and then looking at the other part of ϕ. The operation $\sigma_{\phi_2}(r)$ can be implemented by using an index.

An alternative way of evaluating $\sigma_{\phi_1 \wedge \phi_2}(r)$ can be applied if both ϕ_1 and ϕ_2 are conditions of the form A_i op d_i and if indices suitable for the evaluation of both conditions are available. Then one can find the set S_i of identifiers of the pages containing rows satisfying condition ϕ_i, for $i = 1$ and $i = 2$, and compute the intersection $S_1 \cap S_2$. The pages with identifiers in $S_1 \cap S_2$ are read and the rows in them are checked against the selection condition. Thus there is no need to read all the pages corresponding to a subselection: it is sufficient to read the pages that for each subcondition contain at least one row satisfying it.

A selection with a disjunctive condition $\sigma_{\phi_1 \vee \phi_2}(r)$ is usually harder to evaluate efficiently than a conjunctive selection. One can use the equality $\sigma_{\phi_1 \vee \phi_2} = \sigma_{\phi_1}(r) \cup \sigma_{\phi_2}(r)$ to reduce the problem to evaluating a simpler selection. However, this is possibly wasteful, since rows satisfying both conditions ϕ_1 and ϕ_2 may be read twice. An alternative is to use the form $\sigma_{\phi_1 \vee c_2} = \sigma_{\phi_1}(r) \cup \sigma_{\phi_2 \wedge \neg \phi_1}(r)$ and to hope that the conjunctive condition in the latter selection can be used to avoid reading all the rows satisfying ϕ_1 again.

Union and difference

Implementing the union operation would be extremely simple if duplicate rows were allowed.[1] Then $r \cup s$ could be formed just by writing the rows of

---

[1] Most implementations of the relational model allow duplicates in relations.

r and the rows of s to disk. Since duplicates are not allowed in relations, one has to take care that they are removed.

A solution for this is to sort r and s according to some sequence of attributes and then merge the sorted relations, writing each row at most once.

However, this solution is not optimal if the sizes of r and s are different. If, for example, s is very small and an index based on a key of r exists, one can first eliminate duplicates by removing those rows of s that appear in r and then write the result. The advantage of this solution is that the larger relation r need not be sorted at all.

The result of a difference operation $r \setminus s$ can be computed in a similar way as the result of $r \cup s$. The first alternative is to sort r and s independently and then merge them, producing output only from rows that occur in r but not in s. The second alternative is to check for each row t of r whether t occurs in s using an index. If r is small, this is faster than the first alternative.

Join

The join operation $\bowtie$ is needed in every query combining data from different relations and hence it is very common. Typically most of the time needed for evaluating queries is spent in computing joins.

There are several alternative methods for computing joins. We discuss three of these, trying to illustrate the basic techniques. As an example we consider the problem of computing the natural join $r \bowtie s$, when r and s are relations over $R(AB)$ and $S(BC)$, respectively.

A trivial method for computing $r \bowtie s$ is to compute the Cartesian product $r \times s$ and then select the rows satisfying the join condition. Since $r \times s$ can be much larger than $r \bowtie s$, this method is very slow.

A better alternative can be found by considering the decomposition of $r \bowtie s$ into smaller joins:

$$r \bowtie s = \bigcup_{t \in r} \left(\{t\} \bowtie \sigma_{B=t[B]}(s) \right).$$

That is, the result $r \bowtie s$ can be computed by considering each row t of r separately. For each t we compute the small join $\{t\} \bowtie s$ by selecting the rows $u \in s$ with $u[B] = t[B]$. This method can be called *selection join* because of the underlying identity, or *index join* because it is typically implemented using an index on s.

If both r and s have indices based on attribute B, the index join can be improved by noticing that

$$r \bowtie s = \bigcup_{b \in r[B]} \left(\sigma_{B=b}(r) \bowtie \sigma_{B=b}(s) \right).$$

The third method is called the *sort join*. In sort join, the result of $r \bowtie s$ is computed by sorting both r and s on the basis of B-values and then going through r and s simultaneously, producing the desired output.

4.4.3   Query optimization

A (semi)declarative language like SQL is not easy to implement efficiently. There are often many possible ways to execute a given query. The query optimizer tries to find an efficient evaluation method. The optimization of relational queries can be divided into two parts: transformation of the query on the level of the query language to a simpler or more efficiently implementable form, and choice of the implementation method for each basic operation in the query.

Query optimizers in commercial database management systems differ widely in power. If the query optimizer does not function properly, the user or the database administrator has to try to force the system into a faster way of evaluating certain crucial queries. This can be done by writing the query in a new form.

One should, however, be wary of transforming queries unnecessarily. It can introduce errors. It can also fool a good query optimizer into producing worse solutions than those produced from the straightforward way of expressing the query.

Query optimizers use as their input the structure of the query and the database schema. Some optimizers also use dynamic information about the sizes of the relations. This makes it possible, for instance, to choose the method for computing joins by considering the relative sizes of the relations.

Exercises

Exercise 4.1 Prove the following properties.

(a) $\sigma_{\phi \wedge \psi}(r) = \sigma_\phi(r) \cap \sigma_\psi(r)$.

(b) $\sigma_{\phi_1}(\sigma_{\phi_2}(r)) = \sigma_{\phi_1 \wedge \phi_2}(r)$.

(c) $\sigma_\phi(r \cup s) = \sigma_\phi(r) \cup \sigma_\phi(s)$.

(d) $\pi_Y(\pi_X(r)) = \pi_Y(r)$, if $Y \subseteq X$.

(e) $\pi_X(\sigma_\phi(r)) = \sigma_\phi(\pi_X(r))$, if ϕ mentions only attributes in X.

(f) $\sigma_\phi(r \bowtie s) = \sigma_\phi(r) \bowtie s$, if ϕ mentions only attributes in R (the schema of r).

Exercise 4.2 Suppose that the Cartesian product is chosen as one of the basic operations in relational algebra, and that the join operation is defined on the basis of the Cartesian product. Prove Theorem 4.1 using this definition for join.

Exercise 4.3 Consider the conference database. Express the following queries in relational algebra and in SQL.

(a) 'Which program committee members submitted papers to the conference?'

(b) 'List the titles of those papers for which all authors were program committee members.'

(c) 'Which program committee members chaired a session where their own paper was presented?'

Exercise 4.4 Give an English interpretation of the following queries.

(a) $\pi_{Title}(\sigma_{Position=4}(\text{AuthoredBy} \bowtie \text{Paper}))$

(b) **select distinct** Reviewer_Name
 from   Evaluation
 where   Reviewer_Name **not in**
            (**select** Reviewer_Name
            from Evaluation
            where Score > 6)

Exercise 4.5 Design relation schemas for the database described in Exercise 3.2 (page 32). Use your database schema to express in relational algebra the following queries.

(a) When is the Los Angeles Philharmonic playing a symphony by Sibelius?

(b) List forthcoming concerts conducted by Esa-Pekka Salonen.

(c) When is the Los Angeles Philharmonic giving a concert that is conducted by the composer of one of the symphonies played?

Exercise 4.6 Several relation schemas presented in Example 4.1 (page 37) are subsets of some other relation schemas. What is the use of such schemas in general? Could (or should) some schemas be combined in Example 4.1 without making the use of the database more difficult?

Exercise 4.7 Transform the ER-diagram produced in Exercise 3.4 (page 32) into relation schemas and create a small database using a database management system based on SQL.

Exercise 4.8 Let r be a relation over $R(A, B, C)$. Express in SQL a query that could be used for testing whether A could serve as a key of r. That is, your query should help in deciding whether there exist two distinct tuples in r that have the same A-value.

Exercise 4.9 SQL provides a predicate called **exists** for testing the existence of a particular tuple in a relation. The typical use of **exists** is

```
select      ...
from        r
where       exists
            ( select *
            from s
            where ... )
```

The where clause of the latter query is used for stating conditions that relate the tuples in r to the tuples in s.

How could the **exists** predicate be used for expressing the intersection of two relations?

Exercise 4.10 The join operation leaves in its result no trace of those tuples in the argument relations for which a matching tuple was not found. Sometimes it would be useful to retain all the tuples in both relations. This operation is called the *outer join*. If a matching tuple does not exist, then the values for the attributes that originate from the other relation should be filled with suitable padding – such as the **null** value, which in general represents unknown information in SQL.

Write an SQL query for computing the outer join of two relations. To insert a constant value into a tuple resulting from a select statement, simply list that constant value in the correct position in the select clause.

Exercise 4.11 Consider a relation r over (Person, Parent, Sex) used for storing information about parents. Attribute Sex is used to distinguish mothers and fathers. Express the following queries in SQL.

(a) Who is the father of John Smith?

(b) Who are the grandfathers of John Smith?

(c) List all the ancestors of John Smith found in the database.

Exercise 4.12 Generate random relations over a single-attribute schema and compare the time needed to output the relation in arbitrary order and in sorted order.

Exercise 4.13 Compare the efficiency of B-tree indices and hash indices in your database management system for numeric and character-valued attributes, and for queries of the form $\sigma_{A=a}(r)$ and $\sigma_{A\leq a}(r)$.

Exercise 4.14 Investigate the algorithms used by your database management system for computing joins.

Bibliographic notes

The foundations of the relational data model were laid in a series of papers by Codd [Cod70, Cod72, Cod74]. Several proposals have been made to extend the model, mainly to add its descriptive power to capture more accurately the semantics of the universe of discourse being modelled [Cod79, Cod90]. The core of the model is, however, fairly stable; see [FV86, Var88, Ull88, PDGV89, Kan90] for some up-to-date expositions.

The question of what constitutes 'the relational model' is, in fact, somewhat polemic. Relational database management systems abound, and each vendor may have its own conception of some details of the model. Codd presents in [Cod86] his view of the minimum requirements that every relational database management system should satisfy. The theory community probably considers some other aspects, such as the richness of integrity constraints, more important.

Several surveys and tutorials of query systems that go beyond the relational algebra have been published recently [BR86, Ull88, CGT89].

The SQL standard is defined in [SQL86]. The version of SQL used in this book conforms to the standard with minor exceptions, such as the **intersection** and **minus** operations, which are not defined by the standard but are supported by most vendors. Critique of the standard can be found in [Dat87, Dat90b]. A new standard [SQL92] has recently been approved.

A thorough treatment of file structures can be found in [Wie87]. B-trees and hashing are described in various data structures textbooks, including [Meh84, AHU74]. Evaluation methods for the operations of relational algebra are treated in detail in [Ull88], as is query optimization. The elimination of duplicate tuples is studied in [BD83].

Chapter 5

Object-Oriented Data Models

The ER-model provides two basic concepts, entities and relationships, for describing the structure of data. The relational model uses only one structure, a relation, for representing all types of data. The models are also parsimonious in their approach to data manipulation operations: the ER-model ignores this aspect altogether, and the relational model has a small collection of powerful operations.

In data models the maxim 'small is beautiful' is generally accepted. However, after the relational model gained acceptance, some problems emerged. New application domains, such as computer-aided design, demanded considerably more modelling power and more complex operations than the relational model provided.

The suggested solution to these problems is the use of object-oriented data models, which provide constructs for building arbitrarily complex data objects, and where also the set of data manipulation operations can be extended. Object-oriented data models have been under extensive research during the latter half of the 1980s. They are expected to become a commercially important technology in the first half of the 1990s.

In this chapter we describe the basic concepts of these data models and discuss their connection to the relational model. The area is still developing rapidly and no single model has yet been generally accepted. We concentrate therefore on the most common issues in object-oriented data models.

The reasons that have led to the development of object-oriented data models are discussed in detail in Section 5.1. The subsequent sections are devoted to various characteristic issues of object-oriented data models: a type facility that can be used to define complex objects; the concept of object identity that makes sharing a natural concept; the inheritance of definitions, a paradigm for modular database definition; and the definition of operations together with the definition of the structure of the data.

5.1   Why more data models?

There are at least four reasons why the relational model is not sufficient or adequate for some data management tasks:

- New applications of database technology require improved data modelling facilities.

- In addition to the type and form of the data, one should also be able to define the operations on the data at the same time.

- The relational data model does not support modular design of database schemas.

- The interface between a programming language and a relational query language is low-level.

We next discuss these points in more detail.

Several new applications requiring the storage of massive amounts of complex data have arisen in the last few years. A typical example is computer aided design (CAD), where one stores and manipulates the designs of complex structures, such as equipment, machinery, or VLSI chips. This application requires the manipulation of large chunks of data as a unit: for example, one wants to be able to rotate the whole picture of an overhead projector on the screen. A relational database system is usually ill suited for such applications, since the data describing the projector is fragmented among several relations and hence retrieving it can take a lot of time.

Other applications requiring more modelling power include office information systems, decision support systems, scientific and statistical database management, and computer supported cooperative work.

Another motivation for developing a new data model is that operations cannot be defined in the relational model. The ability to structure the data is useful in itself, but one would additionally want to be able to define operations on the data. Consider for example the simple data type for describing a date. This data type consists of probably three parts: the day, the month, and the year. Operations defined for dates might include checking whether a three-component value describes a valid date, computing the day of the week represented by a date, computing the number of days between two dates, and so on. These operations are in some sense a part of the definition of the data type, and hence it should be possible to define them at the same time as the data type is defined.

In a relational system such operations have to be defined separately, either in all applications or, if application development is carried out systematically, in some library of utility operations. In any case the operation definitions are separate from the data definition.

One could argue that such operations should be part of the data manipulation language. In fact, some database languages include built-in operations for manipulating dates. However, it is impossible to be prepared for all possible data types or operations that the users' applications may need. Continuing the date example, consider the operation of deciding whether a given date is a holiday or not. This operation varies from country to country, movable feasts make it vary from year to year, and still other variations are possible. Thus it certainly cannot be part of a fixed set of operations. Similarly, CAD applications need complex user-defined operations on the data.

Yet another motivation for improving the relational data model is modularity of database design. Suppose we have, for example, designed a database schema for processing questionnaires sent to individuals. This schema probably contains some relation schemas identifying the individuals (within the study), giving their addresses, and then the schemas for storing the answers to the questions in the form. The attributes identifying the individuals probably appear in the schemas for storing the answers.

If we afterwards want to produce a schema for processing questionnaires sent to corporations, the original schema has to be modified: the identifying attributes of a corporation are probably subtly different from those of an individual. Thus we have to modify many schemas slightly.

One could envision a data model where the definition of a relation schema could be parameterized: instead of having two schemas with subtle differences, we could have a generic definition of a questionnaire schema and then just instantiate this in two different ways by giving the identifying attributes of individuals and corporations, respectively.

The last reason we consider for introducing new data models concerns the interface of a database and an application program. The *impedance mismatch* problem arises when one accesses a relational database using an embedded language, say SQL, from a C program. The answer to a relational query is a set of tuples. However, conventional programming languages are badly equipped for manipulating sets of tuples. For efficiency reasons one cannot express the whole answer to the query as a data structure of C. Rather, the embedded languages use the additional notion of a *cursor* to point to the current record of the answer to the query. This largely destroys the advantages of using a fairly declarative, set-oriented query language like SQL. Object-oriented data models and systems try to achieve a reasonably seamless connection between the query language and a general-purpose programming language.

5.2   Structured values

The relational model contains two ways of forming complex or structured values. The first mechanism is tuples. A tuple is an aggregated value: a person can be represented by name and birth date, and a book can be represented by its ISBN number, title, author, publisher, and purchase price.

The second mechanism in the relational model is that of a relation. Tuples of similar type can be collected together to form a set.

Apart from these two concepts, the relational model contains no direct way of defining more complex objects. One can say that the relational model is *flat*: a relational database is a set of relations, each relation is a set of tuples, and each tuple is a fixed-length list of values.

New applications require the ability to define more complex types, such as tuples containing sets as their elements, sets of sets, lists of sets of tuples, and many others. Programming languages have traditionally had rich type structures for defining such complex types, but the classical data models have not allowed the definition of more complex structures. Object-oriented data models have such mechanisms; the concepts and the terminology are taken from programming languages.

A *type* in an object-oriented data model can be a primitive type like integer or string, or it can be formed from existing types by using constructors such as aggregation, set formation, list formation, and so on.

Example 5.1 Consider the conference example already treated in Example 2.2 (page 15) and in Figure 3.6 (page 31). We can define types corresponding to the data in a Pascal-like notation as follows.

> **type** PaperType =
>   [Paper_Number: integer; Title: string;
>   authors: **list of** string;
>   evaluations: **set of** EvaluationType];
> **type** EvaluationType = [score: ScoreType; comments: string;
>   PCMember: MemberType];
> **type** MemberType = [Name: string; Address: string]

Here the notation [a: t; b: s] means an aggregate or record type with two components named a and b. Component a has type t and component b has type s.

With these type definitions, information about one paper could be stored in a variable defined by

   var p: PaperType;

□

The *schema* of an object-oriented database consists of the type definitions and some variables defined to be sets of some type. These special set variables are called *class variables* and they correspond to the relation schemas of the relational model; the value of a class variable is a *class* and it corresponds to a relation.

Example 5.2 Continuing the example, information about all the papers could be stored using a class variable c defined by

   class c: **set of** PaperType;

Note how this fairly natural description already exceeds the number of levels in the relational model. Class c is a set of tuples, each of which contains a list of authors and a set of evaluations.   □

A relational schema $R(A_1, \ldots, A_n)$ corresponds to a type definition of the form

   type $t = [A_1 : t_1, \ldots, A_n : t_n]$;

where each type t_i is a primitive type corresponding to the domain of attribute A_i. The value of class variable r defined by

   class r: **set of** t;

corresponds to a relation over the schema.

A database defined by type and class definitions can be accessed using an extension of SQL, where components of structured entities are accessed using the dot notation.

Example 5.3 We can search for all the evaluation comments written by a program committee member named Beeri using the following query.

   select   p.Title, e.comments
   from   p in c, e in p.evaluations
   where   e.PCMember.Name = 'Beeri'

Expressing this query using normal SQL would require the use of a join condition.   □

One difficulty in the development of object-oriented data models is obtaining a strong declarative query language. The dynamic type system of object-oriented models makes this task much harder than in the relational model.

5.3   Object identity

An important distinction in object-oriented data models is the difference between *objects* and *values*. The idea is that a database describes (some part of) the target of the database. The target consists of objects that can be identified, that is, from objects that have a unique identity different from any other object. This identity of an object stays the same even though the values of the attributes of the object may vary.

For example, a person stays the same person even if his/her name changes; a car remains the same even if its license number is changed; a conference paper stays the same even though the authors decide to change its title.

Thus an object represented in the database has its identity, which stays the same during the whole lifetime of the object. Additionally, the object has a *state*, representing the collection of attribute values for the object.

The state of an object can contain *atomic values* (such as integers), structured values, and also references to other objects. The values of the components of the state can change drastically during the lifetime of the object.

Every object has a type. Object types are defined by giving the type of the states of objects of that type.

Example 5.4 Continuing Example 5.1 we can decide to make objects out of program committee members. Hence we define an object type by

> **otype** MemberObj: **state** = MemberType

and modify the definition of EvaluationType to be

> **type** EvaluationType = [score: ScoreType; comments: string;
> PCMember: MemberObj];

The queries written for these types remain unchanged. Only the representation of the data about program committee members has changed: they are now represented using objects, not just structured values.   □

An advantage of using objects with unmodifiable identity is that it makes *sharing* of information easy to model. By sharing of information between two objects or entities o_1 and o_2 we mean that some component of o_1 and some component of o_2 are always the same, no matter how the database is updated. If o_1 and o_2 share information t, this is represented in a relational database by the fact that some rows corresponding to o_1 and o_2 have the same values, probably the values for the key attribute identifying t. Now if the values of the key attributes of t change, maintaining sharing requires that the references to t in both o_1 and o_2 are changed. This places a burden on the applications.

In a database with object identity, sharing of t is implemented by having the object identifier of t appear as a component of both o_1 and o_2. Since the object identifier cannot change, changes to the state of t are automatically reflected in o_1 and o_2.

Example 5.5 An evaluation of a paper can be thought of as an object shared by the paper and the program committee member. To achieve this, we could modify the type definitions given above as follows.

> **otype** MemberObj: **state** = MemberType;
> **type** MemberType = [Name: string; Address: string;
>   evaluations: **set of** EvaluationObj];
> **otype** EvaluationObj: **state** =
>   [score: ScoreType; comments: string];
> **otype** PaperObj: **state** =
>   [Paper_Number: integer; Title: string;
>   authors: **list of** string;
>   evaluations: **set of** EvaluationObj];   □

The immutability of the object identifier has important advantages. Some methods for relational database design require that the keys of relations should not be modified. A way of ensuring this is to use artificial keys, often called surrogates. In object-oriented models the immutability of object identifiers is built into the data model; surrogates in the relational model are something of a late addition that is not completely integrated with the rest of the data model.

5.4   Inheritance

In defining a database schema, several objects or types often resemble each other closely. The target of the database contains several classes of objects that are similar. For example, the database might contain information about students and faculty. The elements of both classes are persons and presumably share some attributes, such as last name, first name, address, and so on. Duplication of this information on the schema level is useless and it can even be harmful, if the database design has to be changed. The database designer should not be forced to repeat the common parts of the definitions.

Inheritance of type definitions and operations is one of the basic features of the object-oriented data models. The ER-model contains inheritance in the notion of an **isa**-relationship. In object-oriented data models inheritance is given a more central position.

Example 5.6 Continuing Example 5.1, we could define a type for accepted papers as follows:

>   **type** AcceptedPaperType **inherits** PaperType
>   **add** [AssignTo: SessionObj];

This would mean that a variable of type AcceptedPaperType contains the same fields as a variable of type PaperType, and an additional field of type SessionObj, representing the session where the paper will be presented.

$\square$

The example above is the simplest type of inheritance, a static propagation of attributes from one schema to another. The type that inherits the attributes is called a *subtype* of the *supertype* containing the smaller set of attributes. There are several other notions of inheritance, and the concepts used vary from one data model to another.

5.5   Operations

The final and perhaps most important new idea of object-oriented data models is the integration of operation definitions into the definition of the structure of data.

Example 5.7 Continuing Example 5.1, assume that the scores for papers range from 0 to 10. Then one would like to have an operation for computing the average score of a paper. This operation will most probably not be implemented by the database management system; rather, it must be supplied by the user. In an object-oriented model we could define

>   ScoreType = '10' | '10–' | '9+' | '9' | ... | '0' ;
>   **function** ScoreAverage(S: **set of** ScoreType): ScoreType;
>   ...
>   **end** ScoreType;

$\square$

Defining certain operations with the schema collects dependent information together and hence makes maintenance easier. It also improves the modularity of the database schema: queries or applications do not necessarily have to know the exact structure of the individual types or classes; they can just use the operations.

The usability of operations increases if subtypes can inherit them.

Example 5.8 The function ScoreAverage could be applied to any entity of type ScoreType, so we could write in extended SQL

> **select**   p.evaluations.ScoreAverage
> **from**   p in Papers
> **where**   p.Paper_Number = 1

The expression p.evaluations has type **set of** EvaluationObj, which can be considered to be a subtype of **set of** ScoreType. Hence inheritance of operations makes it possible to apply the function ScoreAverage to the expression.   □

Exercises

Exercise 5.1 Transform the type definitions of Example 5.1 into definitions of relation schemas.

Exercise 5.2 Outline an algorithm for transforming type and class definitions into definitions of relation schemas.

Exercise 5.3 Complete the transformation of the ER-diagram of Example 2.2 to type definitions.

Exercise 5.4 Outline a transformation from ER-diagrams to type definitions.

Exercise 5.5 Rewrite the query given in Example 5.3 using the modified type definitions of Example 5.5.

Exercise 5.6 Investigate the following formal definition of sharing. Objects o_1 and o_2 share information, if for some queries Q_1 and Q_2 with one free variable (from an appropriate query class) we have

$$Q_1(o_1)(\mathbf{r}) = Q_2(o_2)(\mathbf{r})$$

for all allowed database states $\mathbf{r}$.

Exercise 5.7 The Postgres database system includes a basic type which can contain expressions of the query language. Explain how fields based on such a type can be used to implement sharing.

Exercise 5.8 Consider the definitions

      otype OrderType: **state** = [Name: string; Address: string;
         Items: **set of** ItemType];
      otype ItemType: **state** = [Number: integer; Name: string];
      otype WeightItemType **inherits** ItemType
         add [Weight: integer];
      otype QuantityItemType **inherits** ItemType
         add [Quantity: integer];

Write the corresponding relation schemas.

Exercise 5.9 A VLSI chip contains a collection of gates, connected to each other using wires. The chip also contains pins, which are connected to some gates. Each gate is located somewhere in the chip, and it has a width and length. Write type definitions for modelling a chip.

Bibliographic notes

A large number of different object-oriented data models exists. Beeri [Bee90] has given a clear description of different concepts used in object-oriented databases. In particular, Section 5.3 is based on [Bee90].

    Object-oriented data models have borrowed some concepts from semantic data models; a collection of material related to semantic data models can be found in [BMS84, MB89, HK87]. The relationship of the entity-relationship model and the object-oriented data models is discussed in [NP89], while a description of how an object-oriented model can be derived from the relational model is given in [SS90].

    Collections of material on object-oriented data models and systems are [ZM90, KL89]. A comprehensive bibliography has been prepared by Vossen [Vos91]. Object-orientation is not the only direction that current database research is studying; the manifestos published by the competing camps are rather entertaining [The89, ABD+90, The90, Mai91].

    Discussions of existing object-oriented database management systems can be found in [D+91, LLOW91, BOS91, SK91, LLPS91, Hor91, Ban92, BDK92].

Chapter 6
Design Principles

Database design aims at a database schema that can be used to store and process the users' data simply and efficiently. Different data models can be used to describe the structure of the database, and a data model often provides several ways of representing the same information. Some of the possible solutions are, however, better than others.

In this chapter we consider the question: What is a good ER-schema, a good relation schema, or a good database schema? That is, can anything general be said about the database schemas that good database design practice should produce? Here our goal is to provide intuitive motivation for some general design principles that to a certain degree are applicable always, no matter what data model is used. Formal definitions and methods for producing schemas with these properties are considered in later chapters.

For the ER-model and the relational model, the setting of the above questions is simple. In using the ER-model the basic question is what entity types and relationship types are used and how they are connected together. The basic issue in designing a relation schema is what attributes should appear together in a schema.

We begin in Section 6.1 by considering the required correspondence between the database schema and the target of the database. In Section 6.2 we discuss the important principle of representing each fact only once, and show by example that violating this principle causes difficulties in updates. These problems are usually called anomalies. The use of null values may sometimes seem an easy solution, especially to avoid deletion anomalies. In Section 6.3 we discuss in detail the questions related to the

69

occurrences of null values.

Null values are a special form of attribute values. Other questions related to the domains of attributes are considered in Section 6.4. Implementing a complex domain may require the use of an entity type instead of an attribute. In contrast, Section 6.5 discusses requirements that the modelling of relationships places on attributes, and especially on the naming of attributes.

Section 6.6 considers various solutions that can be used for modelling hierarchical constructs, one of the most frequent trouble spots in conceptual modelling. Finally, Section 6.7 considers the problems related to schemas where extensive modification of rows takes place.

6.1   What should be modelled?

A basic requirement for a database schema is that it should model the target of the database correctly. The entity types and relationship types of the schema should have counterparts in the real world. Similarly, each relevant object or concept or relationship in the target of the database should be modelled in the schema.

There are, however, usually several correct models of the target: the schema can have varying degrees of detail. A suitable level of detail is such that writing the queries and applications accessing the database is as easy as possible. Both a too detailed description and a too general description of the target can be harmful.

A typical case occurs when one has to decide whether to use one or several entity types to represent some real-world objects. For example, if a company manufactures 17 different products, we do not want to model this in the database schemas. This would make application development difficult, and a change in the product line would require extensions to the schema. Since there are 17 different products, it can be expected that the products will change. Rather than using a different schema for each product, we want to use a generic entity type for modelling products. This entity type might have subentity types for products with different properties.

What if the company manufactures not 17, but 2 different products? Should this be visible in the model? Here the choice of what to represent in the model and what to leave out is more difficult. If the company has a very stable product line with exactly these products, then representing this information in the schema can be useful and even mandatory. If one product is a television and the other a radio, their attributes are so different that both products should be represented by an entity of their own. If this is not done, then all applications have to differentiate between the products at run time. Still, the two products have something in common and hence it can be useful to have an entity type representing all products, with subentity types for televisions and for radios.

If, on the other hand, the number of products is more or less random, it just happens to be currently 2, then the schema should probably not contain the information about what the products now are. In general, the database schema should contain only information that is fairly stable. Frequently changing facts should be stored in the database instance.

A similar situation often occurs when one has to decide whether using an entity type or an attribute is more appropriate. This choice is considered in the sequel.

One can summarize the above discussion into two claims:

- Too detailed schemas make application development difficult.

- Too general schemas make application development difficult.

6.2   Unique representation of facts

In addition to a correct representation of the target, perhaps the main requirement for an ER-schema or relational schema is *simplicity*. Each entity, relationship, or schema should represent a simple collection of information. It should be possible to explain to the users of the database the meaning and use of each entity. On the relational level, the meaning of a single row should be simple to describe, and similarly the collection of all the rows in a relation should have some fairly clear and intuitive meaning. The simplicity and clarity of the entities is reflected in the structure of application programs.

Simplicity is related to the representation of information. The basic principle in database design is that each fact should be represented only once. While an attribute value can and will occur several times, the association of two or more values, describing a fact, should occur only once. For example, the address of a program committee member should be represented in only one entity, not in all entities representing evaluations written by that member. Similarly, the chairperson of a session should be reported in only one place, not with all the papers given in that session.

Another way of looking at the unique representation principle is to consider updates to the database. A database schema where the relation schemas are too large makes it necessary to use a single tuple for storing several facts. Such a schema is said to suffer from *anomalies*. It is customary to distinguish three different forms of anomalies: *insertion anomalies*, *deletion anomalies*, and *update anomalies*. These concepts are easiest to explain using an example.

Example 6.1 Consider the conference database, and assume that the relation schema

Talk (*Paper_Number*, Session_Number, Chairperson_Name)

is used to record information about the assignment of accepted papers to sessions.

The corresponding relation would contain two kinds of facts: associations between papers and sessions, and information about session chairpersons. If we know only one fact but not the other, for instance that paper number 13 has been scheduled for session 2 which is still without a chairperson, we are faced with an insertion anomaly: what value should we put in the Chairperson_Name column?

One possibility is to use the value **null** for that purpose. But suppose the opposite is true, that is, we know the chairperson of a session before any papers have been assigned to the session. Storing this fact by using the value **null** for Paper_Number is not possible, since Paper_Number is a key of the schema. A **null** value in a key attribute would make it impossible to identify a tuple, at least if the relation has several such tuples. Each tuple, and similarly each entity in the ER-model, must be identifiable using values in the appropriate domain, not using a null value. This principle is called *entity integrity*.

A deletion anomaly is the inverse of an insertion anomaly. Suppose that after the conference program has been completed, one of the chairpersons calls and says that he cannot make it to the conference. How can we delete the chairperson information from the tuples for the papers in his session without destroying the information about paper assignments? A solution would be to use null values, but this is often unsatisfactory. We return to the null value problem in more detail in the following section.

An update anomaly occurs when we wish to change a session chairperson. The information about the chairperson is now stored once for each paper that is assigned to his session; consequently, we must update several tuples to maintain the consistency of the database. In a well-designed database schema, updating one fact should be possible by updating just one tuple.   □

Still another way of looking at the topic of representing each fact only once is to consider shared information. The address of the PC member is shared between all evaluations written by that member: any change in the address should be reflected in all these evaluations. The principle 'one fact in one place' can be reformulated by saying that for shared information there should be an abstraction representing that information. In our example, the information about PC members is shared between evaluations, and hence a corresponding abstraction (an entity type or a relation schema representing PC members) should exist.

6.3   Null values

Above we saw that entity integrity requires key attributes to have non-null values. It is tempting to allow **null** as a legal value of the non-key attributes to make updates easier. However, our third design principle is that *all* attributes of each entity or tuple should have non-null values. If this is not the case, then all the entities in the entity set do not have all the properties described in the entity type. This indicates that the design has not found the correct way of modelling the entities. This rule is, however, not strict: in many cases allowing nulls leads to natural database designs.

Example 6.2 Consider again the schema of Example 6.1 and the problem that arises when a chairperson cancels his participation in the conference. Replacing the name of the chairperson by **null** would leave us with a tuple like (47, 3, **null**), indicating that Paper 47 has been scheduled for presentation in Session 3. The fact that such an incomplete tuple is interesting and worth retaining in the database indicates that the original schema was too large: it combined several entities in the same schema. □

There are also various technical reasons for trying to avoid null values altogether. First, there may be many different reasons why some information is missing and cannot be stored in the database, but in SQL the same value, **null**, has to be used in all such cases, even though their semantics can be quite different. Two of the most common reasons for using the value **null** are that information is applicable but not known, or that information is inapplicable.

Example 6.3 Suppose we use the schema

   AssignedTo (*Paper_Number*, Session_Number)

for recording not only the assignment of papers to sessions, but also the acceptance information by storing the value **null** in the Session_Number attribute of those papers that have not been accepted. Those nulls are examples of information that is inapplicable. To make the interpretation of the relation unambiguous, they cannot be mixed with 'applicable but not known' nulls. Therefore a paper should be associated with some session immediately it is accepted. Thus, mere acceptance information could not be recorded as such. □

In the case of information that is applicable but not known, we still might know something about the missing information. For instance, if in Example 6.1 two chairpersons cancel their participation, we must store the same **null** in all tuples where their names appeared. It is impossible to indicate that the papers in the same session still all have the same chairperson, possibly different from the chairperson of the other session.

Finally, query interpretation becomes difficult if null values appear in the tuples. How should nulls behave in joins? Two null values might or might not match; either solution is not good for all situations. Indeed, to properly handle joins in the presence of null values, the definition of the join operation should be extended to produce not only those tuples that certainly belong to the result, but also those tuples that may belong to the result (if the null values participating in the join happen to match).

Another problem caused by null values is that two complementary queries cannot any more be assumed to cover all possible cases, as the following example indicates.

Example 6.4 Consider again the schema of Example 6.3, but suppose now that only the 'value applicable but not known' nulls are used. Suppose we wish to find the papers that are presented during the first, the second, and the third day of the conference. A natural way to express these queries is to use selection operations with selection conditions like 'Session_Number < 5', '5 ≤ Session_Number ≤ 8', and 'Session_Number > 8', respectively. How should we handle the papers whose Session_Number is **null**? Either they belong to the result of all three queries or to the result of none of the three queries. Both solutions are problematic: in the first case, a paper might be processed several times, whereas in the second case it might be forgotten altogether. Again, the proper solution would be to extend the definition of the selection operation by a maybe-answer. □

On the other hand, the rule of avoiding null values is by no means indisputable. The desire to avoid too small relation schemas, usually to improve the efficiency of query evaluation, may still lead to a decision where null values are allowed. For instance, what if 90 % of the PC members have fax numbers? Can we still have an attribute of PCMember representing the fax number? Or should we have a separate entity type for fax numbers and a relationship type connecting this type and the PCMember entity type? (An alternative also avoiding null values would be to have a subtype of PC members, say PCMemberWithFax, and an **isa**-relationship type connecting this subtype to the entity type PCMember.) Such solutions may put too much emphasis on an unessential attribute that is never used in join or selection operations, and unnecessarily complicate the design.

Detailed guidelines are hard to give. A possible way of looking at missing information is to consider the difference between *structural null values* and *occasional null values*. If the value for some attribute is null for a well-defined subtype of an entity type, and if the lack of the attribute value has some relevance to the manipulation and use of the database, then the null values can be called structural. For example, consider the representation of employees and their offices. A possible solution is to treat Office as an attribute of the Employee entity. If the salesmen of the company do not have offices, then the null values for salesmen's offices would be structural nulls.

On the other hand, if the missing values are more or less random, and the entities with missing values do not form any specific subtype of the entity type, then the null values might be called occasional. If all employees have an office, except that some new employees have not yet been assigned an office, the null values in their Office attribute are occasional nulls. Similarly, the missing fax numbers could be called occasional nulls, since we probably will not treat the PC members with no fax numbers in any basically different way than those members with fax numbers.

One attempt at a formulation of the null value problem is to say that structural null values are not allowed, but occasional nulls are. Thus the fax numbers could be represented as an attribute of the entity type PCMember, even though all members do not have a fax number.

6.4   Object types and attributes

In conceptual design one should be able to find the relevant entity types, relationship types and attributes. In some cases this poses no problems; for instance, it is hard to imagine concrete objects (such as cars) as relationship types. But should a car be represented as an entity type or as an attribute? And what about more abstract objects, such as managers; should they be represented as an attribute of employees, or as a separate entity type, or perhaps as a binary relationship type with two participants, both of whom are employees (one being the manager of the other)?

If sample queries produced by requirements analysis are available, a simple syntactic analysis of the sample queries can be helpful: often the verbs in the queries correspond to relationship types in the ER-diagram, whereas nouns correspond to entity types or attributes. However, this rule must be applied with care: the queries may use nouns that are derived from verbs. Moreover, sometimes the verbs or nouns have no direct counterpart in the ER-diagram.

Example 6.5 Consider the sample queries in Example 2.2 (page 15). In addition to technical verbs (such as 'list'), the only non-technical verbs that can be found are 'differ' and 'accept'. Some nouns ('paper', 'score', 'grade', 'program committee member', 'percentage') cannot possibly be interpreted as verbs, whereas others ('arrival', 'rejection') could just as well be replaced by verbs had the queries been formulated differently.

Comparing this with Figure 2.2 (page 18), we notice that 'paper' and 'program committee member' are modelled as entity types, whereas 'score' and 'grade' have been unified into one attribute. The final indisputable noun, 'percentage', as well as the verb 'differ' have no direct counterparts in the ER-diagram – the answers to the queries will be computed, not stored. Of the remaining nouns, 'arrival' is essentially modelled using the Number attribute which makes computing the desired answer possible. Finally, 'rejection' and 'accept' are both modelled using the weak entity type AcceptedPaper.

In summary, the example illustrates that the noun/verb-analysis can at best serve only as the starting point of the design, and sound modelling requires deeper analysis.   □

However, in many cases there is no simple set of queries that the database should be able to support. Instead, one has to search for the object types by consulting the experts on the target of the database, by studying forms and other existing documentation, imagining the types of actions the application will perform, and so on.

The difference between attributes and entity types depends on the intended application. An attribute is something with no discernible structure that would interest the application. That is, attribute values are atomic from the viewpoint of the applications. If the components of an attribute must be accessed, then the attribute should really be replaced by several attributes or by an entity type having the components as its attributes.

Typical cases where an attribute is changed to an entity type are: (i) the value of the attribute can be missing, (ii) the value of the attribute consists of several parts, (iii) the domain of the attribute is important and hard to specify, or (iv) the attribute can have several values.

Missing values have already been discussed above. As an example of the second case, consider an address. If treating an address as an atomic string is sufficient, then an address can be modelled as an attribute or as several attributes. Often, however, it is useful to treat addresses as an entity type with attributes like Street, City, and Zip. In fact, if we wish to express in the ER-diagram everything we know about the dependencies between these attribute values, it may even be necessary to replace the single entity type by several entity types.

Another example about the attribute versus entity type problem was discussed in Example 2.2 (page 15): whether to model the authors of a paper as an attribute or as an entity type.

Even when a value is clearly atomic, there may be various reasons for using an entity type instead of an attribute. A typical instance is connected to the storage of addresses: if we want to be able to check that the Zip codes in an address list are correct, a simple way is to form a relation for Zip codes and require that the values occurring in a Zip code field of an address also occur in this separate relation. (In the terminology of Chapter 7, we require that an appropriate inclusion dependency holds.) Basically, this is a way of implementing the complex domain of an attribute. It is also an example of a property that is generally called *referential integrity*: the values found in one relation must also appear in another to be valid.

The fourth common reason for replacing an attribute by an entity type is that the attribute can have several values. As an example, most people have only one telephone number for their office, but some have several numbers. How should this be modelled?

The term 'multivalued attribute' refers to the idea that the attribute Phone has as its value a set of phone numbers, not a single number. But then it is impossible to access the individual numbers in our data model.

Another possibility is to use several attributes, such as Phone1, Phone2, and so on. But where should one stop; what is the maximum number of phone numbers a person can have? Moreover, we required that an object should have a valid value for all its attributes. What is the second phone number of a person who has only one phone? The only sound solution in this approach is to use several object types: person with one phone, person with two phones – and indeed, person with no phone at all. Clearly, this is cumbersome and unintuitive.

In our version of the ER-model, the recommended solution for this situation is to model phone numbers as an entity type, and to have a relationship type between persons and phone numbers. This way a person can have any number of phones, and both entity types are quite natural.

6.5   Naming of attributes

Recall that while all object types were required to have unique names in an ER-diagram, several attributes could share the same name. If houses and phones are two object types that both have an attribute called Number, no one will assume that the attributes have the same meaning.

A reason for favoring short names is ease of maintenance. It is common to see ER-diagrams where the name of an entity type is used as a prefix of the name of an attribute (for example, entity type Session could have attribute SessionNumber instead of plain Number in Figure 2.2 (page 18)). But suppose that the name of the entity type is changed. Then all attribute names that are based on the name of the entity type must also be changed to keep the naming of attributes consistent. In a way, such names would violate our principle of unique representation of facts on the schema level. Just as redundant information should be avoided in the database instance, it should also be avoided in the database schema.

Another reason for not using names of entity types as prefixes of attribute names is that when the ER-diagram is transformed into a relational database schema, the names of the attributes also get transformed. For reasons explained in Chapter 11, it may be necessary to attach the name of an entity type or a role name into the name of a relational attribute. If this is already done in the ER-diagram, the resulting names (such as ChairedSession_SessionNumber) can seem unnatural.

On the other hand, long names, with entity types as prefixes, can make it easier to read the queries and applications that access the database: the origins of the attributes are always visible.

Thus it is not necessary to avoid name clashes for attributes with a different meaning. If, however, two entity types have attributes that *do* mean exactly the same thing, then that attribute should be replaced by an entity type and connected via two relationship types into the entity types. In other words, while several attributes can have the same name, each attribute in an ER-diagram should have a unique meaning.

This rule may cause some seemingly unrelated object types to become connected in an ER-diagram. For instance, if it is necessary to store various dates in the database, then Date should be represented as an entity type in the ER-diagram. The entity type should participate in relationship types with all those entity types that need a date.

If the correctness of dates is very important and the entity type is essentially used for implementing a complex domain, there is nothing wrong with this solution. However, if one is satisfied with treating dates as strings, then forbidding the use of a date as an attribute may seem too harsh. After all, the use of a single entity type for dates will certainly clutter the ER-diagram and make the more important connections harder to spot.

Just as in the case of null values, this rule should also be applied with deliberation. For instance, one can imagine that the different occurrences of dates really have different meanings – such as start date, finish date, order date – and then they could be modelled as attributes.

The bottom line here is that attribute names should not be used to represent relationships in the ER-model. Returning to Figure 2.2 (page 18), one could imagine that program committee members could be modelled as an entity type with three attributes: Name, PaperNumber and Score, and that the relationship type Evaluation could be omitted. But then the connection to papers would be via the value of attribute PaperNumber. While this is exactly the way used for representing relationships in the relational model, it is *not* the way that should be used in the entity-relationship model. All relationships should be explicit and represented

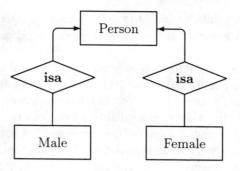

Figure 6.1   An entity-relationship diagram for men, women, and persons.

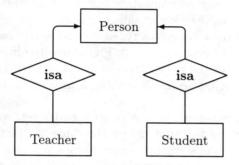

Figure 6.2   An entity-relationship diagram for faculty members, students, and persons.

using relationship types as in Figure 2.2.

6.6   Representing hierarchical structures

The entity-relationship model has two existential relationship types: **isa**-relationship types and **id**-relationship types. They are typically used for modelling various hierarchical structures. In this section we study the modelling of three hierarchical concepts: generalization, instantiation, and specialization.

Generalization refers to the case where one entity set encompasses all the entities found in entity sets that occur on a lower level in a hierarchy.

Example 6.6 Figure 6.1 shows how persons can be modelled as a generalization of men and women. Another example of generalization occurs in Figure 6.2, which repeats a fragment of Figure 3.4 (page 30).   □

In Figure 6.1, the entity sets on the lower levels are disjoint. This is often considered to be a necessary property of generalization, but in our

ER-model the disjointness of entity sets cannot be specified. Figure 6.2 is an example of generalization where the lower level entity sets are not disjoint.

Generalization hierarchies often extend over several levels; the conference database of Figure 3.6 (page 31) contains one simple hierarchy of submitted papers, accepted papers, and papers where a final copy has been received. Notice that a generalization need not be a superset of several entity sets; one entity type on the lower level is sufficient. This still conveys useful information: those submitted papers that are not accepted papers have been rejected.

Why is it useful to model generalizations explicitly in the ER-diagram? One reason is that the generalization may be of interest in its own right. Moreover, the generalization usually participates in relationship types, and using the lower level entity types instead would cause the need for several similar relationship types. In Figure 6.1 it is likely that Person is the entity type with the most attributes, and in most relationship types (if any) we are not interested in making a distinction between men and women.

In generalization, both the lower level entity sets and their generalization consist of entities that are on the same abstraction level. In the second hierarchical construction, *instantiation*, a higher level entity type is used as a starting point for specifying various instance sets on a different level of abstraction.

Example 6.7 Figures 6.3 and 6.4 show two examples of instantiation. In the first, cars are modelled as instances of car models, and in the second individual episodes are considered as instances of a series of TV-shows. (Figure 6.4 (already shown as Figure 3.3 (page 28)) is repeated here for ease of comparison.)

In Figure 6.3, instantiation is modelled using a standard relationship type, since cars can be uniquely identified using their own attributes (Licence#). In Figure 6.4, however, the name of the show is needed in addition to the number of an episode for identifying individual episodes. Therefore an **id**-relationship type must be used.   □

The third concept used in the modelling of hierarchies, *specialization*, can occur both with generalization and with instantiation. It resembles the type/subtype concept in programming languages: we say that entity type $\mathcal{E}$ is a specialization of another entity type $\mathcal{P}$, if the $\mathcal{E}$ entities inherit all the attributes of $\mathcal{P}$, and if they additionally have some attributes of their own. All hierarchies modelled using **id**-relationship types are examples of specialization, whereas **isa**-relationship types model specialization only when the child entities have some attributes of their own. Thus, in Figure 3.6 (page 31) entity type Paper is a generalization of both

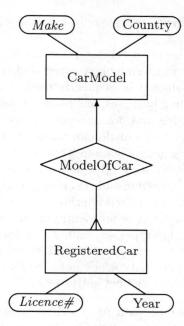

Figure 6.3   An entity-relationship diagram for models of cars and their instances.

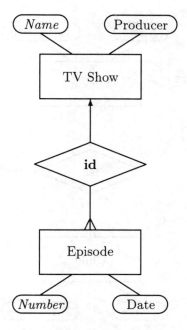

Figure 6.4   An entity-relationship diagram for TV-shows and their episodes.

AcceptedPaper and FinalCopy, but only FinalCopy is a specialization of Paper.

A more complex case of specialization occurs later in Example 7.4.

We have discussed the terminology associated with the modelling of hierarchies at length, since it is frequently used in the literature on the ER-model. For modelling purposes, one need not consciously classify the hierarchies as specializing and non-specializing, as long as the target is modelled correctly. As a rule of thumb, **isa**-relationship types are most often used for modelling generalization, whereas **id**-relationship types are used for modelling instantiation. But as we saw in Figure 6.3, standard relationship types can be used in addition to existential relationship types. The decision on which kind of relationship type to use depends only on which attributes we want to use for identifying the child entities.

Existential relationship types are mainly used for organizing the information about one entity in a manageable and logical way, and for avoiding duplication of data. They are typically *not* used for representing relationships between two or more distinct entities.

Example 6.8 Suppose we wish to model the relationship between fathers and children. When presented as a homework problem in a small university on the west coast, one proposed solution was the one shown in Figure 6.5.

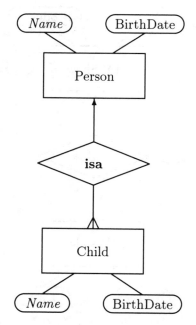

Figure 6.5   Incorrect modelling of children and father.

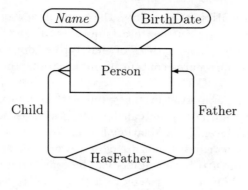

Figure 6.6   Correct modelling of children and father.

The idea behind the solution was that the relationship type should model the 'is child of' relationship between children and father. The **isa**-relationship type, however, simply serves the purpose of partitioning the person entities into two sets: those who are children and those that are not (probably meaning that their parent is unknown). But for those persons whose father is known, the ER-diagram provides no means of accessing the data about the father.

A correct way to model the child/father relationship is shown in Figure 6.6.   □

6.7   Surrogates and modifications

The key attributes of entity types should be such that their values do not change. Changing the values of key attributes can be harmful. Assume that we have an entity from entity type $\mathcal{E}$, and that we want to modify the value of attribute $\mathcal{A}$ of the entity. If $\mathcal{A}$ is an identifying attribute of the entity type, then the values of $\mathcal{A}$ are used for referring to entities of type $\mathcal{E}$ when the ER-diagram is transformed into a relational database. If the value of $\mathcal{A}$ changes, several relations must therefore be updated.

Another fact influencing the choice of attributes is that if the key of an entity type contains many attributes, queries become cumbersome to write.

If no natural attribute set forms a key with constant values, or if the set of key attributes contains many attributes, a possible solution is to use *surrogate attributes*, which correspond closely to the object identifiers in object-oriented models.

Surrogates are internal identifiers of objects or rows, and the users of the database do not see their values. Also, the value of the surrogate contains no information, at least from the point of view of the application. If an entity type has a surrogate attribute as an identifying attribute, then each reference to the entities of that type is done by means of the surrogate. Since surrogates contain no information, there is no need to change them.

Surrogates are supported by many but not all database management systems. If they are not, they can be introduced as normal attributes either on the ER-level or the relational level. In fact, many entity types naturally contain attributes that are close to surrogates. For example, in an Order entity the attribute Number can be considered to be a surrogate attribute, even though it can achieve a status of a 'real' attribute. If surrogates are to be used in all schemas, it is probably best to introduce them at a single stage of the design.

Heavy modification of attribute values causes also some technical difficulties. If an attribute has values of different length, then typically database management systems reserve space only for the original value of a row. If the fields of the row are later changed so that the length of the row increases, a new position must be found for the row.

Modifications of attribute values can be almost totally avoided by designing the database so that a modification can be represented as an insertion. This can, however, lead to problems with the use of space and also to slow queries. Consider again the example of storing information about persons and their addresses. One way of representing this information is to have an entity type with a person's name and address. Whenever the address is changed, the corresponding entity is also modified. An alternative way is to store for each person a collection of addresses, together with the time when the address became effective. In this solution, the modification of an address can be implemented by adding the new address; no modification of rows is necessary.

One advantage of this method is that the historical information about the old addresses is preserved. A disadvantage is, naturally, that more space is used and also that the retrieval of the current address of a person can be more costly than in the case of the first representation.

Exercises

Exercise 6.1 Suppose the relation schema Descendant(*Parent, Child*) is used for storing parental information, and that the value **null** is used in those tuples where the parents are unknown. Are these nulls structural or occasional? Do they cause any problems in the use of the database?

Exercise 6.2 Explain how the database considered in Exercise 6.1 could be implemented if null values were not allowed.

Exercise 6.3 Give some more examples of generalization and instantiation.

Exercise 6.4 Suppose the generalizations in Figures 6.1 and 6.2 are used in the same ER-diagram. Would this cause any conceptual problems? In general, can an entity type simultaneously serve as a generalization of several different subentity types?

Exercise 6.5 Consider the AssignedTo and ChairedBy relationship types in Figure 3.6 (page 31). Do they represent any of the three hierarchical constructs (generalization, instantiation, or specialization)? Discuss their similarities to and differences from the diagrams in Example 6.6 (page 79).

Exercise 6.6 Consider the two methods given in Section 6.7 for representing the addresses of persons. Compare the methods using a test program and a relational database management system. Store a collection of addresses using both methods and measure the time and space needed for an address change, retrieval of a single address, and retrieval of all addresses. Make reasonable assumptions about the number of address modifications per person.

Exercise 6.7 Section 6.7 shows how updates can be replaced by insertions. Explain how the same idea can be applied to transform even deletions into insertions. Discuss the pros and cons of this approach.

Bibliographic notes

The book by Fleming and von Halle [FvH89] is a practical guide to database design. It includes detailed instructions and checklists for relational design.

Codd [Cod90] discusses extensively the handling of missing information in the relational model. Lipski and Imieliński [Lip79, IL84] and Reiter [Rei84] study the semantics of missing information and the consequences this should have on the operations of relational algebra. This problem has since given rise to numerous research papers, indicating how difficult it is to solve in a satisfactory manner.

Kent's book [Ken78] is a classic study of the problems of modelling data. Smith and Smith [SS77a, SS77b] discuss many of the constructs considered in Section 6.6. Sciore [Sci91] studies generalization and specialization in the framework of the relational model.

Chapter 7

Integrity Constraints and Dependencies

A database is used to store and manipulate data representing the target of the database. The relation schemas as such allow also the storage of data that does not represent any possible state of the target. The relation instances can be almost arbitrary: only the requirement that the components of a row must belong to the corresponding domains restricts the instances.

This is not an acceptable state of affairs, and therefore data models provide ways of expressing conditions on the allowed instances of the database. Such conditions are called *integrity constraints*. The restrictions are common to all applications using the database and form an integral part of the specification of the database.

In the ER-model we already encountered two types of restrictions, keys and the cardinality of a relationship type. Implicitly, an ER-diagram also requires that the entities participating in a relationship must belong to the corresponding entity sets. Also on the relational level we need formalisms for expressing such constraints.

In this chapter we introduce two basic classes of constraints: functional dependencies and inclusion dependencies. We also discuss various classifications of integrity constraints, present some more general classes of constraints, and consider how different constraints can be expressed in the ER-model. In addition to providing ways of ensuring the correctness of data, integrity constraints have a central role in the design of relational databases. We shall see in later chapters how the desired properties of database schemas can be defined in terms of the functional and inclusion dependencies that hold in the schema.

7.1   Functional dependencies

Functional dependencies formalize and generalize the notion of a key. They are the most important class of dependencies.

A functional dependency $X \to Y$ states that for a given value combination for the attributes in X there exists at most one corresponding value combination for the attributes in Y. Another way of expressing this is that values for the attributes in X determine unique values for the attributes in Y. The dependency is therefore often read as 'X (functionally) determines Y'.

Example 7.1 In the conference example of Chapter 3 the entity Paper had two attributes. When the ER-diagram is transformed to a relational schema, we obtain the schema

Paper (*Paper_Number*, Title).

In this schema the functional dependency

Paper_Number $\to$ Title

holds. It means that each paper has at most one title.   □

Formally, let $R(A_1, \ldots, A_n)$ be a relation schema. A *functional dependency* (FD) over R is an expression

$R : X \to Y,$

where X and Y are subsets of R. If r is a relation over R, then $R : X \to Y$ *holds* in r if and only if for all tuples $t, t' \in r$ we have:

if $t[X] = t'[X]$, then $t[Y] = t'[Y]$;

we also say that r *satisfies* $R : X \to Y$.

We use the notation $r \models X \to Y$ to denote that $R : X \to Y$ holds in r. The functional dependency $R : X \to Y$ is *standard*, if X is not empty; if X is empty, the dependency is *nonstandard*. The dependency is *trivial*, if $Y \subseteq X$; otherwise the dependency is *nontrivial*. If R is obvious or irrelevant, it is omitted, and we write $X \to Y$. Throughout the book we assume that all functional dependencies are standard, unless otherwise mentioned.

The satisfaction of a functional dependency was defined above for a given relation r. Some of the dependencies that a relation instance satisfies may be accidental: they hold at the moment, but they could well be violated when the relation is updated. Some dependencies, on the other hand, are such that we wish them to hold always, no matter how the relation is changed. These are the dependencies that the database designer must find and specify. We say that the functional dependency $R : X \rightarrow Y$ *holds in relation schema* R if any relation instance over r must satisfy $R : X \rightarrow Y$. The task of the database management system is to make sure that this requirement is fulfilled; this is called *dependency enforcement of.*

A functional dependency has a double role: it indicates that attribute sets X and Y are associated, and it also shows the type of the association. The same association can be represented in different ways, as the following result indicates.

Theorem 7.1 The dependency $X \rightarrow Y$ holds in relation r if and only if for all $A \in Y$, the dependency $X \rightarrow A$ holds in r.
   Proof. Exercise 7.1.   □

Theorem 7.1 tells us that it is sufficient to consider only functional dependencies with one attribute on the right-hand side of the dependency; longer right-hand sides can be expressed by a collection of dependencies. A collection of functional dependencies where each dependency has a single attribute on the right-hand side is said to be in *canonical form*. Such representations can be useful in proofs. Still, it is often more intuitive to write several attributes on the right-hand side of a dependency.

We can now define formally the concept of a key using functional dependencies. First, an attribute set $X \subseteq R$ is a *superkey* of R, if the dependency $X \rightarrow R$ holds. A *key* of R is a superkey Y such that no $X \subset Y$ is a superkey of R. Keys and superkeys are important concepts: most functional dependencies occurring in practice arise from the specification of keys. Furthermore, one aim of design theory is to obtain a database schema where basically all nontrivial functional dependencies have a superkey as their left-hand side. This topic is considered in Chapter 8.

Example 7.2 In the above example, the attribute Paper_Number is a key of the schema Paper (*Paper_Number*, Title). The two attributes together form a superkey of Paper.   □

7.2   Inclusion dependencies

A functional dependency is defined for a single relation schema and relation. Constraints that state conditions on the occurrence of values from one relation in another relation are also important in database design.

These constraints arise in two ways in the ER-model. An **isa**- or **id**-relationship corresponds directly to such a constraint. The ER-model requires also that in an ER-diagram where a relationship type $\mathcal{R}$ connects two entity types $\mathcal{E}_1$ and $\mathcal{E}_2$, the entities participating in a relationship in $\mathcal{R}$ must also be in the entity sets that correspond to $\mathcal{E}_1$ and $\mathcal{E}_2$. This section explains how similar constraints can be expressed in the relational model.

Let **R** be a database schema. An *inclusion dependency* (IND) over **R** is an expression $R[X] \subseteq S[Y]$, where R and S are relation schemas of **R**, and X and Y are equal-length sequences of attributes of R and S, respectively.

Suppose **r** is a database over **R**, and let r and s be the relations corresponding to R and S, respectively. Consider the inclusion dependency $R[X] \subseteq S[Y]$, where $X = \langle A_1, \ldots, A_n \rangle$ and $Y = \langle B_1, \ldots, B_n \rangle$. The inclusion dependency *holds* in **r** if for every tuple $t \in r$ there exists a tuple $t' \in s$ such that $t[A_i] = t'[B_i]$ for $1 \leq i \leq n$. Recalling from page 40 the extended definition of projection as an operation that produces sets of sequences, the condition can be formulated equivalently as $t[X] = t'[Y]$.

An inclusion dependency $R[X] \subseteq S[Y]$ is *trivial*, if $R = S$ and $X = Y$. A trivial inclusion dependency holds vacuously, and naturally we are mainly interested in nontrivial inclusion dependencies.

Example 7.3 In the conference example we had entity types Paper and PCMember connected by the relationship type Evaluation. These give the following relation schemas:

> Paper (*Paper_Number*, Title),
> PCMember (*PCMember_Name*, Address), and
> Evaluation (*Paper_Number*, *Reviewer_Name*, Score, Comments).

Between these the nontrivial inclusion dependencies

> Evaluation[Paper_Number] $\subseteq$ Paper[Paper_Number] and
> Evaluation[Reviewer_Name] $\subseteq$ PCMember[PCMember_Name]

hold.   □

An inclusion dependency is a condition stating that if some combination of values occurs in one part of the database, it must occur also in a certain other part of the database. Such conditions are fairly common in practical databases: most of the data is interconnected. The general form of inclusion dependencies that arise when one transforms ER-diagrams to relational schemas is described in Chapter 11.

The concept of *referential integrity* was mentioned in Section 6.4. It has been widely used from the inception of the relational model. Briefly, it means that if an attribute A is a key of relation schema R and A appears in another relation schema S, the inclusion dependency $S[A] \subseteq R[A]$ holds. In this case A is a *foreign key* of S.

Inclusion dependencies are quite general, and the algorithmic problems related to them are fairly complex. Thus several subclasses of the class of inclusion dependencies have been defined. In general, a *class* of dependencies is the set of all possible dependencies of a certain type. We use calligraphic symbols to denote classes of dependencies. The class of functional dependencies is denoted by $\mathcal{F}$ and the class of inclusion dependencies by $\mathcal{I}$.

An inclusion dependency $R[X] \subseteq S[Y]$ is *unary*, if X (and hence Y) contains only one attribute. Most inclusion dependencies (but not all) occurring in practice seem to be unary. Moreover, often the dependencies are also *typed*: an inclusion dependency $R[X] \subseteq S[Y]$ is typed if $X = Y$.

The dependency $R[X] \subseteq S[Y]$ is *key-based*, if Y is a key of S. Such a dependency is close to the idea of referential integrity. Again, most inclusion dependencies arising in practice are key-based. In transforming an ER-schema to a relational schema all the inclusion dependencies one obtains are key-based.

Example 7.4 Consider a company manufacturing complex pieces of equipment. The company has several products. Each product has a set of possible properties, such as color, weight, and size, and each property of a product has a set of allowed values.

Several products can be ordered together. Each item in the order must specify the required product in sufficient detail. Thus, an item in' the order might be '100 steel bolts whose diameter is half an inch and whose length is 2 inches'. Here the product is bolt, and its properties are material, diameter, and length.

A crude ER-diagram for this application is given in Figure 7.1. A property is identified by using the product, and the allowed values associated with a property are similarly identified using the property. Only a couple of attributes are shown.

The example produces the following schemas:

> Product (*Product_Number*, Description),
> Property (*Product_Number*, *Property_Number*, Remarks),
> AllowedValue (*Product_Number*, *Property_Number*, *Value*),
> ItemValues (*Item_Number*, *Product_Number*, *Property_Number*,
>   *Value*), and
> Item (*Item_Number*, Quantity).

To comply with our conventions of attribute naming, the ER-attributes with the same names have been prefixed with the names of the relation schemas.

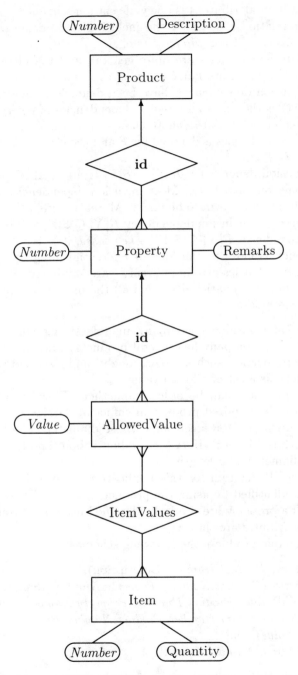

Figure 7.1   An entity-relationship diagram for products and their properties.

The inclusion dependencies between the schemas are

> Property[Product_Number] ⊆ Product[Product_Number],
> AllowedValue[Product_Number, Property_Number] ⊆
> Property[Product_Number, Property_Number],
> ItemValues[Product_Number, Property_Number, Value] ⊆
> AllowedValue[Product_Number, Property_Number, Value], and
> ItemValues[Item_Number] ⊆ Item[Item_Number].

Note how the **id**-relationship types lead quite naturally to long inclusion dependencies. All the inclusion dependencies are key-based and typed.

In this example, the keys and the inclusion dependencies do not express all constraints. An ordered item should be associated only with values of a single product. For instance, if one relationship in ItemValues talks about the material of bolts and another about the length of nails, these should be associated with different ordered items. Another constraint that is still missing is that a particular property of an ordered item should be associated with only one value. These constraints are hard to express in the ER-diagram. They can, however, be expressed in the relational schema using the functional dependencies

> ItemValues : Item_Number → Product_Number and
> ItemValues : Item_Number Property_Number → Value.   □

In an inclusion dependency $R[X] \subseteq S[Y]$ the symbols X and Y denote sequences of attributes in R and S. Thus one attribute can occur several times in a sequence. For example, if the dependency $R[AA] \subseteq S[BC]$ holds in a database (r, s), then for each A-value occurring in r, relation s must contain a row with that value in both the B- and the C-columns. The practical value of such a dependency seems limited.

The case where the right-hand side of an inclusion dependency has repeated attributes is slightly more useful. The dependency $R[AB] \subseteq S[CC]$ means that for each $t \in r$ we have $t[A] = t[B]$ and $t[B] \in s[C]$. Thus for a relation r over R all A- and B-values must be identical. This indicates a design problem in the R schema.

Functional dependencies and inclusion dependencies are the two most important classes of integrity constraints for database design. From here on, we shall include them as an integral part of a database schema. Thus a database schema is not just a set of relation schemas **R**, but a triple $(\mathbf{R}, F, I)$, where F and I are the functional dependencies and inclusion dependencies that hold in **R**.

In addition to being crucial in logical database design, inclusion dependencies can also provide hints for physical design. For instance, the left-hand side of an inclusion dependency is a typical attribute set for which an index might be useful.

7.3   Other classes of dependencies

Several other classes of dependencies have been defined and studied extensively. Many of these do not seem to have a large effect on database design.

Multivalued dependencies are in some sense a generalization of functional dependencies. Let R be a relation schema and let A and B be attributes of R. A functional dependency $A \rightarrow B$ states that at most one B-value corresponds to each A-value. A *multivalued dependency* $A \twoheadrightarrow B$ states that each A-value has an associated *set* of B-values, and this set is independent of the values of the other attributes.

Formally, the dependency $X \twoheadrightarrow Y$ holds in a relation r if for all $t, t' \in r$ with $t[X] = t'[X]$ there exist rows $u, u' \in r$ such that

$$
\begin{aligned}
&u[X] = t[X], && u'[X] = t'[X]; \\
&u[Y] = t[Y], && u'[Y] = t'[Y]; \text{ and} \\
&u[R \setminus XY] = t'[R \setminus XY], && u'[R \setminus XY] = t[R \setminus XY].
\end{aligned}
$$

Example 7.5 As an example of multivalued dependencies, consider information about courses and their teachers. Suppose that the attributes are Teacher, Assistant, Course_Number, Time, and Room. Assuming that each course is taught by one faculty member, we could state that the dependency Course_Number $\rightarrow$ Teacher holds. Each course can have several assistants, which can be expressed as Course_Number $\twoheadrightarrow$ Assistant. Finally, each course can meet several times a week in different places, giving rise to the dependency Course_Number $\twoheadrightarrow$ Time Room. This dependency *cannot* be replaced by two dependencies (Course_Number $\twoheadrightarrow$ Time and Course_Number $\twoheadrightarrow$ Room), since Time and Room are not independent.   □

An alternative representation of the meaning of a multivalued dependency $R : A \twoheadrightarrow B$ is the following table.

	A	B	$R \setminus AB$
$t:$	a	b	x
$t':$	a	b'	x'
$u:$	a	b	x'
$u':$	a	b'	x

The meaning of the four rows in the table is that if there exist two rows t and t' with the values shown, then the other two rows u and u' must also be present in the relation.

The intuitive notion behind a multivalued dependency is fairly clear. One wants to express the fact that although X does not determine Y functionally, there nevertheless exists an association between X and Y: any X-value has an associated set of Y-values. The formal semantics of a multivalued dependency is, however, rather unintuitive. One reason for this is that in the cases where a (nontrivial) multivalued dependency holds in a relation, the meaning of the schema is obscure.

Multivalued dependencies are further generalized by the following class of dependencies. Let $\mathbf{R}$ be a set of relation schemas, and denote by U the set of all attributes occurring in $\mathbf{R}$. Let X_i be a subset of U for $i = 1, \ldots, k$, and denote by X the union of the sets X_i. A *join dependency* over the sets X_i is denoted by

$$X_1 \bowtie X_2 \bowtie \cdots \bowtie X_k$$

or, alternatively, by $\bowtie \{X_1, \ldots, X_k\}$. Let r be a relation over X. Then r satisfies the join dependency, if

$$r = \pi_{X_1}(r) \bowtie \pi_{X_2}(r) \bowtie \cdots \bowtie \pi_{X_k}(r).$$

If $X = U$, the join dependency is called a *full join dependency*.

The most common class of join dependencies consists of those full join dependencies where the X_i sets are exactly the relation schemas of $\mathbf{R}$. Such a join dependency expresses the fact that given a relation r over the set of all attributes, no information is lost by storing r using its projections $\pi_{R_i}(r)$; the relation r can be retrieved by computing the join of the projections. In database design one often strives for a database schema $(\mathbf{R}, F, I)$ such that the full join dependency over its relation schemas holds. This notion, known as *lossless join*, is considered further in Section 8.5.

Join dependencies are a generalization of multivalued dependencies: a multivalued dependency $X \twoheadrightarrow Y$ in a relation schema $R = XYZ$ is equivalent to the join dependency $XY \bowtie XZ$. The proof is left as an exercise.

Next we discuss a large class of dependencies that has two equivalent definitions: algebraic dependencies or extended embedded implicational dependencies.

An inclusion dependency $R[X] \subseteq S[Y]$ can be thought of as an expression: 'the projection of R on X is a subset of the projection of S on Y'. *Algebraic dependencies* are obtained by generalizing this idea by allowing arbitrary project-join expressions instead of only projections. Thus an algebraic dependency is of the form

$$E_1 \subseteq E_2,$$

where E_1 and E_2 are project-join expressions over a database schema. A project-join expression is an expression of relational algebra where only the projection and the join operations are used. Moreover, the arguments in the expressions are names of relation schemas, not relations. The names act as variables that are replaced by the corresponding relations when the value of such an expression is evaluated for a particular database instance. The expressions can contain several occurrences of the same relation schema. The dependency holds in a database $\mathbf{r}$, if the value of E_1 on $\mathbf{r}$ is included in the result of E_2 on $\mathbf{r}$.

Example 7.6 In Example 7.4 additional functional dependencies were required. We shall see in Chapter 8 that these dependencies make the ItemValues schema violate so-called normal forms. An alternative design would be to replace ItemValues by two schemas, as follows:

> ItemProduct (*Item_Number*, Product_Number), and
> ItemValues2 (*Item_Number*, *Property_Number*, Value).

However, this transformation leads to the inability to express the three-attribute inclusion dependency

> ItemValues[Product_Number, Property_Number, Value] $\subseteq$
> AllowedValue[Product_Number, Property_Number, Value],

since the attributes on the left-hand side are no longer grouped together. The dependency could be replaced by the algebraic dependency

> (ItemProduct $\bowtie$ ItemValues2)[X] $\subseteq$ AllowedValue[X],

where X is the attribute sequence $\langle$Product_Number, Property_Number, Value$\rangle$.   □

In algebraic dependencies the possibility of using the same relation schema several times is necessary for expressing equality, which is needed for functional dependencies. A functional dependency $R : X \to A$ can be expressed as

$$\sigma_{R_1.X=R_2.X}(R_1 \times R_2) \subseteq \sigma_{R_1.XA=R_2.XA}(R_1 \times R_2).$$

Here R_1 and R_2 denote two copies of R, and the selections should be understood as join conditions. The dot notation $(R.X)$ is used to disambiguate attribute names that appear in several relation schemas.

An equivalent definition of algebraic dependencies is based on the use of first-order predicate logic. The atomic formulas used are either equations between variables or of the form $R(z_1, \ldots, z_k)$, where R is a relation schema with k attributes and z_i is a variable for $i = 1, \ldots, k$. The sentences are basically implications.

Let $R(AB)$ and $S(CD)$ be two schemas, and consider the inclusion dependency $R[A] \subseteq S[C]$. It can be expressed as

$\forall a, b (R(a, b) \Rightarrow \exists d S(a, d)).$

The functional dependency $R : A \rightarrow B$ can be expressed as

$\forall a, b, b' (R(a, b) \wedge R(a, b') \Rightarrow b = b').$

Generally, an *extended embedded implicational dependency* or XEID is a sentence of the form

$\forall x_1, \ldots, x_m ((A_1 \wedge \cdots \wedge A_n \Rightarrow \exists y_1, \ldots, y_r (B_1 \wedge \cdots \wedge B_s)).$

Each A_i is a relational formula and each B_i is a relational formula or an equality between two variables. Additionally, the formula $A_1 \wedge \cdots \wedge A_n$ is *typed*: a single variable cannot occur in two distinct attributes of one relation schema.

Showing that an XEID can be expressed as an algebraic dependency and vice versa is fairly easy. Given an XEID, one constructs two expressions corresponding to the left- and right-hand sides of the implication; the inclusion in the algebraic dependency corresponds to the implication.

7.4   Implication of dependencies

The dependencies holding in a database are usually not independent. For example, if $A \rightarrow B$ and $B \rightarrow C$ hold in a relation, also $A \rightarrow C$ holds.

Let d be a dependency and D a set of dependencies. Recall that for a database $\mathbf{r}$, the notation $\mathbf{r} \models d$ means that d holds in $\mathbf{r}$. Similarly, $\mathbf{r} \models D$ means that $\mathbf{r} \models d$ holds for every $d \in D$.

A single dependency d *follows* from D, denoted by $D \models d$, if d holds in every database that satisfies all the dependencies in D. That is, if $\mathbf{r} \models D$, then also $\mathbf{r} \models d$. We also say that D *semantically implies* d, or just that D *implies* d. Hence the above example can be stated as

$\{A \rightarrow B, B \rightarrow C\} \models A \rightarrow C.$

Similarly, if E is a set of dependencies, the notation $D \models E$ means that $D \models e$ for each $e \in E$.

Let $(\mathbf{R}, F, I)$ be a database schema. We shall see in Chapter 9 that $F \cup I$ may imply new functional dependencies that are not implied by F alone. Since we often need to refer to the functional dependencies that hold in a relation schema, it is useful to introduce the following notation. For a relation schema $R \in \mathbf{R}$, denote by F_R the set of functional dependencies over R implied by $F \cup I$. That is,

$F_R = \{X \rightarrow Y \mid X, Y \subseteq R, F \cup I \models R : X \rightarrow Y\}.$

The above definition of semantic implication can be said to be too general, since we consider every database in the definition. Would it not be better to consider only finite databases? The corresponding version of implication is known as *finite implication*, and it is defined as follows. Given a set of dependencies D and a dependency d, we say that D *finitely implies* d (denoted by $D \models_f d$) if for all *finite* databases $\mathbf{r}$ such that $\mathbf{r} \models D$ we have $\mathbf{r} \models d$. Usually finite implication and normal implication are the same notion, but for the combined class of functional and inclusion dependencies they differ. This is shown later in Example 9.6.

Using the notion of semantic implication one can define the notion of equivalence between sets of integrity constraints. Sets D and E are *equivalent*, denoted $D \equiv E$, if $D \models E$ and $E \models D$. If D and E are equivalent sets, one can also say that D is a *cover* of E (and vice versa). Equivalent sets of dependencies express the same restrictions. However, their intuitiveness and size can be widely different.

Example 7.7 If $F = \{A \to B, B \to C, C \to A\}$ and $G = \{A \to BC, B \to A, C \to A\}$, then F and G are equivalent.   □

The problem of deciding whether two collections of integrity constraints are equivalent is considered in Chapter 10.

7.5   Projection of integrity constraints

So far, we have only considered the case where the database schema is fixed. In the design of a database the schema often evolves in many ways, for example when a problem in the suggested design is found. When the schema is changed, one has to be able to find out what the given integrity constraints mean for the modified schema.

For example, suppose we have considered a relation schema $R(ABC)$ and the integrity constraint $A \to BC$, and assume that the schema is subsequently changed to $R'(AB)$. The original dependency implies the dependency $A \to B$, which should be associated with R'. Next we define formally the impact of a set of integrity constraints on a smaller schema.

Let $\mathbf{R} = (R_1, \ldots, R_k)$ and $\mathbf{S} = (S_1, \ldots, S_k)$ be sequences of relation schemas. We say that $\mathbf{S}$ is *contained in* $\mathbf{R}$, denoted $\mathbf{S} \subseteq \mathbf{R}$, if every relation schema of $\mathbf{S}$ is contained in the corresponding relation schema of $\mathbf{R}$. In other words, $S_i \subseteq R_i$ for each $i = 1, \ldots, k$.

Let $\mathcal{D}$ be the class of dependencies considered, let $\mathbf{R}$ and $\mathbf{S}$ be sequences of relation schemas such that $\mathbf{S} \subseteq \mathbf{R}$, and let $D \subseteq \mathcal{D}$ be a set of integrity constraints over $\mathbf{R}$. Then the *projection* of D over $\mathbf{S}$ (denoted $D[\mathbf{S}]$) is the set

$\{d \mid d \in \mathcal{D} \text{ is a dependency over } \mathbf{S} \text{ and } D \models d\}.$

Example 7.8 A simple example is obtained by considering a database schema that consists of a single relation schema. Consider the schema $R(ABC)$ and the dependency set $F = \{A \rightarrow B, B \rightarrow C\}$. Letting S be the schema $S(AC)$, the projection $F[S]$ is equivalent to the set $\{A \rightarrow C\}$.   □

The concept of a projection of a dependency set is most useful for functional dependencies, but it can be applied to any integrity constraints.

Example 7.9 Let $\mathbf{R} = (R(AB), S(CE))$, and let the set of dependencies be $D = \{R[AB] \subseteq S[CE]\}$. Then $\mathbf{S} = (R'(A), S(CE))$ is contained in $\mathbf{R}$, and $D[\mathbf{S}]$ is equivalent to the set $\{R[A] \subseteq S[C]\}$.   □

Computing the projection of a dependency set is a difficult problem. We return to it in Chapter 10.

7.6 Classifications of constraints

Integrity constraints can be classified in many ways. One way is to study what parts of the database one has to investigate simultaneously to determine whether the constraint holds or not. This gives the following classification.

- Constraints whose truth can be checked by looking at the values in one row at a time. Domain restrictions are of this type.

- Constraints whose truth can be checked by looking at several rows from one relation at the same time. Functional, multivalued, and join dependencies are of this type.

- Constraints whose truth can be checked by looking at several rows from several relations at the same time. Inclusion dependencies are of this type.

Another classification of dependencies arises from their logical form. Functional dependencies are of the form 'if something exists in the database, then two values must be equal'. Hence they are called *equality-generating dependencies*. Inclusion dependencies, multivalued dependencies, and join dependencies all have the general form 'if something exists in the database, then something else must also exist'. Thus these dependencies can be called *tuple-generating dependencies*.

We have considered only constraints that say something about the allowed *states* of the database. A *dynamic constraint* is one that restricts the allowed changes of the database state. An example is the requirement that the salary of an employee can only be raised in an update.

This particular constraint reflects the policy of the company that uses the database. It is questionable to what extent such constraints should be considered in database design, since the policies are often subject to change, which may cause a need for an expensive reorganization of the database. The constraints that are 'laws of nature' are stable and thus more important. An example of this type of dynamic constraint is marital status, which can only change from married to widowed, married to divorced, or from single, widowed, or divorced to married.

A further classification of integrity constraints is based on the behavior of the constraint under renamings of the values. Some restrictions depend on the meaning of individual values. Domain definitions are of this type. For example, we can require that each value stored for attribute Length is less than 2.5 meters. The truth of such constraints is not preserved if we permute the values in an arbitrary manner.

Some constraints depend only on the equality and inequality of individual values; the dependency types we have considered are of this type. Such constraints are called *domain-independent constraints*. An extension of algebraic dependencies can, in fact, be used to define all such domain-independent constraints.

7.7   Specifying constraints in the ER-model

The entity-relationship model offers only limited possibilities for expressing constraints. Only three constructs are available for this purpose: (a) a subset of the attributes of an entity type can be defined as the key (the set of identifying attributes) of that type, (b) existential relationship types can be used for expressing existence constraints, and (c) the functionality of standard relationship types can be specified.

It is noteworthy that the latter two forms of constraints involve object types, not individual attributes. Contrast this with the relational model, where the most common constraints, functional dependencies, are expressed using attribute names. To be able to express the same constraints in the ER-model, it may be necessary to replace entity types by smaller entity types containing exactly the desired attributes – and sometimes even this is not sufficient: all constraints that can be expressed in the relational model simply cannot be expressed within the ER-model. Although the ER-model is generally considered to be on a higher abstraction level and in some sense 'more powerful' than the relational model, in the area of integrity constraints this is not true.

Example 7.10 The modelling of zip codes is an often used example in database design. We shall treat it here in some detail – not as a typical problem encountered by database designers, but rather to illustrate the meaning of different constraints in the ER-model.

Suppose that we wish to build a catalog with three fields: street address, city, and zip code. As discussed in Section 6.4, the least we must do is to create an entity type having three attributes: Street, City, and Zip. The entities should obey two rules.

(1) Street address and name of city should uniquely determine zip code. In other words, two houses on the same street in the same city should have the same zip code.

(2) Zip code should uniquely determine city. In other words, two addresses with the same zip code should be in the same city.

We have on purpose expressed the rules so that they could easily be represented within the relational model: they correspond to the functional dependencies Street City → Zip and Zip → City. But how could the rules be expressed in the ER-model?

If all the attributes are associated with the same entity type, then the only tool that we have available is specifying various keys. The attributes {Street, City} are one possibility, and the set {Street, Zip} is an alternative. In relational terms, these correspond to the functional dependencies Street City → Zip and Street Zip → City. Thus the second rule is not correctly represented.

The fundamental problem with this approach is that by specifying keys we can only express constraints where a set of attributes functionally determines all the other attributes of the same entity type. The second rule is not of this form (it does not mention one of the attributes at all), and it cannot be specified using this technique.

Since associating all the attributes with the same entity type does not work, let us try an opposite approach: we could create three one-attribute entity types, and a relationship type involving all three entity types, as in Figure 7.2. Then we could try to define the functionalities of the relationship type so that the diagram correctly represents the two rules.

How should the functionalities be defined? Street and city uniquely determine zip code, so the relationship type should be functional with respect to ZipCode. Similarly, street and zip code uniquely determine city, so the relationship type should be functional with respect to City as well. We see that we are faced with exactly the same problem as before: how to model a constraint that does *not* involve all three attributes?

Since the individual attributes are available in the distinct entity types, it is tempting simply to add a second relationship type as in Figure 7.3. At first glance, this seems to do the job nicely: both rules are now properly represented. However, the rules are expressed using *two*

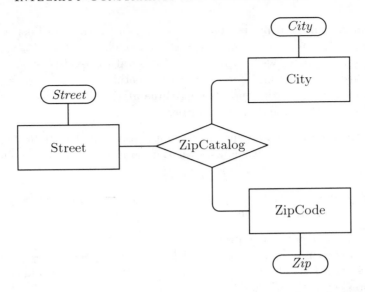

Figure 7.2   An entity-relationship diagram for a catalog of zip codes.

different relationship types. By thinking about the instance level, we see that this will not do: the rules might not be obeyed simultaneously as they should be.

Figure 7.4 shows a very small database instance that corresponds to the diagram in Figure 7.3. It is still incorrect, because a zip code can be associated with two different cities in the two relationship types. The constraints that pertain to a standard relationship should always be expressed using one, and only one relationship type.

We still could try the third possibility for expressing constraints: the use of existential relationship types. Figure 7.5 shows one reasonable solution. It correctly expresses the second constraint, and it also implies that street address and zip code together form a meaningful piece of data. But even this solution fails to model the first rule correctly.

We shall later see that when an ER-diagram is transformed into a relational database schema, the result is a 'dependency preserving BCNF schema' (these terms will be defined in Chapter 8). Example 8.13 shows that for the set of dependencies considered here, there does not exist any dependency preserving BCNF schema. Knowing this we can deduce that there cannot possibly exist any ER-diagram that simultaneously represents both of the rules given at the beginning of this example.

The problems considered above seem to be rare in real database design. Moreover, here the problems arose because for the sake of the example we wanted to model everything we know about zip codes and addresses. For real applications it may not be of extreme importance that

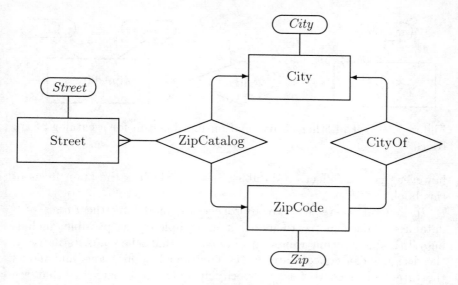

Figure 7.3   Another entity-relationship diagram for a catalog of zip codes.

both of the above rules are checked automatically; rather, it may be much more important that address data is accessible fast and in a convenient form, favoring the simple solution where all three attributes are grouped into the same entity type. If it is crucial that the database satisfies both of the rules given above, at least one of them must be checked procedurally on the application level.   □

Some versions of the ER-model provide more possibilities for expressing constraints than our version; for instance, it is rather common that *all* entities in an entity set can be required to participate in some relationship type which has the entity type as a participant. These relationship types are said to have *mandatory* participation. Such constraints do not,

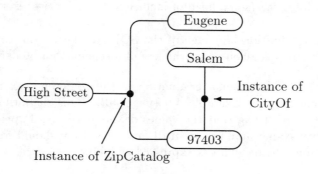

Figure 7.4   A database instance.

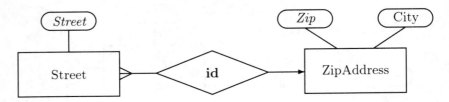

Figure 7.5   Yet another entity-relationship diagram for a catalog of zip codes.

however, have an effect on database design, which is the main focus of this book.

In general, there are two approaches to modelling the target of a database. One can try to model it as completely as possible, including all the known constraints into the conceptual schema. Alternatively, the designer can concentrate on the envisioned applications and model the target on a coarser scale, specifying only the constraints that are important for the applications. The former approach makes the adding of new applications easy, whereas the latter approach probably produces more efficient applications. This is one of the many issues where the database designer must use personal judgment and experience to arrive at the proper solution.

7.8   Integrity constraints in database management systems

Database management systems give varying support for expressing and enforcing integrity constraints. Domains of attributes can usually be defined, at least by giving their type (such as character or numeric). Several systems support keys either directly or by definition of indices with no duplicate values. General functional dependencies are seldom supported. Referential integrity (some form of inclusion dependencies) is sometimes supported.

The data definition language of the SQL standard requires that the type of attributes is given. Also the key of a schema can be defined.

Example 7.11 The schema Evaluation of the conference example was defined using SQL in Example 4.9 (page 46). This definition can be augmented by requiring that the values of the attributes Paper_Number and Reviewer_Name may not be **null**, and that they should form a key of the relation schema. This is expressed as follows.

> **create table** Evaluation (
> Paper_Number **decimal**(3) **not null**,

> Reviewer_Name **char**(20) **not null**,
> Score **decimal**(2),
> Comments **char**(255),
> **unique** (Paper_Number, Reviewer_Name)
>)

Entity integrity requires that the attributes mentioned in the unique clause must have the specifier **not null**: they may not contain null values.

□

The new SQL standard (often referred to as SQL2) supports a larger class of integrity constraints, including a general form of inclusion dependencies. Also supported are row constraints, which are conditions that can be evaluated by looking at one row at a time, and assertions, which are general integrity constraints.

Example 7.12 According to the SQL2 standard, the inclusion dependency Evaluation[Paper_Number] ⊆ Paper[Paper_Number] could be written in the definition of the Evaluation schema as follows:

> **foreign key** (Paper_Number)
> **references** Paper (Paper_Number)

An alternative formulation for the same constraint but now expressed as a general constraint would be

> **check** (Paper_Number **in**
> (**select** Paper_Number **from** Paper)).

□

We discuss next how a database management system can enforce the various constraints discussed in this chapter.

A key dependency $X \rightarrow R$ for schema R can be enforced by keeping an index based on the attributes in X, and specifying the index to be such that no duplicate values are allowed. The enforcement of such a functional dependency is done by keeping the index up-to-date. Deletions cause no problems for functional dependencies.

An arbitrary functional dependency $R : Y \rightarrow A$ is much harder to enforce. When a row t is added to relation r corresponding to R, we have to check that in the subrelation $\sigma_{Y=t[Y]}(r)$ all the A-values are equal. In other words, we have to implement a selection. Unless there is an index on attributes in Y, we have no better choice than reading through relation r.

A key-based inclusion dependency $R[X] \subseteq S[Y]$ is fairly easy to enforce. If a row t is added to relation r corresponding to R, then one has to check that $t[X] \in s[Y]$, where s is the relation corresponding to S. This can be done by checking whether the selection $\sigma_{Y=t[X]}(s)$ is nonempty. Since the dependency is key-based, there probably is an index on Y in S, and hence the selection can be implemented efficiently.

The other problematic situation for the inclusion dependency $R[X] \subseteq S[Y]$ is deleting a row u from relation s. Again, one has to check whether there are any rows in r with X-attributes having value $u[Y]$, and this can be done in the same way as any selection. The difference from the case of insertions is that the left-hand side attributes X are more likely not to have an index based on them.

Inclusion dependencies that are not key-based are much harder to enforce. The same idea of checking whether the appropriate selection is nonempty still holds, but performing the selection can require considerably more processing, if there is no index for the right-hand side attributes of the dependency.

For other integrity constraints, domain restrictions can in some cases be implemented directly by the database management system. For example, domains like 'strings of at most 20 characters' are often enforced by the system. Complex domains like the set of valid zip codes have to be implemented by making them into entity types and by adding appropriate inclusion dependencies.

Integrity constraints can be enforced either at *update time* or at *commit time*. Enforcement at update time means that each time a relation is modified, all relevant constraints are verified. Commit time checking means that the constraints are checked only when the user or the application executes a commit operation. This is typically done at the end of a *transaction*, which is a collection of operations that should always be executed together (or, in case of errors, cancelled together).

For small updates, update time checking is usually much more efficient than commit time checking, since at update time the database management system has a lot of information about what has just happened to the relations. For example, enforcing an inclusion dependency $R[X] \subseteq S[Y]$ at update time proceeds as described above: for each insertion or deletion one has to perform a check on appropriate rows in the other relation. Commit time checking of an inclusion dependency means that the entire relations r and s have to be examined: they may have been modified in such a way that the constraint no longer holds.

However, if relations r and s change drastically in one transaction, it is probably more efficient to do all the updates first and check the inclusion dependency afterwards, at commit time. Then the condition $r[X] \subseteq s[Y]$ can be checked by computing $r[X]$ and $s[Y]$ and by comparing them, whereas update time checking would require many small selections.

Some types of integrity constraints cannot be enforced at update time. An example is a circular set of inclusion dependencies. For example, if we have the dependencies $R[X] \subseteq S[Y]$ and $S[Y] \subseteq R[X]$, inserting a row into r with new X-values necessarily violates the first dependency. The updates to a schema with a circular set of inclusion dependencies have to happen in batches, and the constraints hold only after each batch.

If an update operation violates an integrity constraint, there are three possibilities for proceeding. The simplest one is to reject such an operation. A more complicated approach uses cascading operations that attempt to restore the validity of the constraints. For instance, suppose that the inclusion dependency $R[A] \subseteq S[B]$ should hold, and a tuple is deleted from the relation over the S schema in such a way that the dependency is violated. Then all the violating tuples in the relation over R could also be deleted to satisfy the dependency. These deletions may cause a need for additional deletions (if there are inclusion dependencies where R appears on the right-hand side); hence the need for cascading operations. Finally, the third possibility for enforcing a dependency is to change some values in the violating tuples. For instance, if A is not the primary key of R, then all violations of the inclusion dependency $R[A] \subseteq S[B]$ could be handled by replacing those A-values that do not appear as B-values by **null**.

Ideally, a database management system should allow the database designer to choose the policy for dependency enforcement. This is often not the case, and the designer should take the policy into account when specifying the constraints.

Exercises

Exercise 7.1 Prove Theorem 7.1.

Exercise 7.2 What nontrivial functional dependencies hold in the following relation?

A	B	C	D
0	0	0	1
2	1	2	0
1	1	2	0
0	0	1	2

Exercise 7.3 What is the intuitive meaning of a nonstandard functional dependency $R : \emptyset \rightarrow A$? Is it reasonable to assume that in a well-designed database schema all functional dependencies are standard?

Exercise 7.4 Give an expression for deciding whether $r \models A \rightarrow B$ using:

(a) the concepts of projection and superkey,

(b) selection, projection, and the predicate $|s| \leq c$, where s is a relation and c is a constant.

Exercise 7.5 Estimate the size of the relation produced by the expressions $\sigma_{A=a}(r)$ and $r[A]$, if

(a) nothing is assumed about A; or

(b) A is a key of r.

Exercise 7.6 Consider the relation schemas $R(AB)$ and $S(BC)$ and relations r and s over R and S, respectively. Estimate the size of the natural join $r \bowtie s$, when

(a) no dependencies hold in the database schema;

(b) B is a key of S; or

(c) B is a key of S and the inclusion dependency $R[B] \subseteq S[B]$ holds.

Exercise 7.7 Is it true that if $R[A] \subseteq S[C]$ and $R[B] \subseteq S[D]$, then $R[AB] \subseteq S[CD]$?

Exercise 7.8 Give an example of two relational database schemas $(\mathbf{R}, F, I)$ and $(\mathbf{R}, F, I')$ such that I and I' are equivalent, but still I is nonredundant and key-based, while I' is redundant and not key-based.
   Hint. Don't think too hard, this is easy.

Exercise 7.9 If a relationship type is represented as a relation schema, what types of functional dependencies correspond to the functionality of the relationship type?

Exercise 7.10 Complete the transformation of Exercise 5.1 (page 67) by listing the integrity constraints that the resulting database schema should satisfy.

Exercise 7.11 Extend the algorithm of Exercise 5.2 (page 67) to produce also the integrity constraints for the resulting database schema.

Exercise 7.12 Show that join dependencies are a generalization of multivalued dependencies, meaning that a multivalued dependency $X \twoheadrightarrow Y$ over relation schema $R = XYZ$ holds in an relation r over R if and only if the join dependency $XY \bowtie XZ$ holds in r.

Exercise 7.13 Recall that a functional dependency $R : X \to A$ can be expressed as the following algebraic dependency:

$$\sigma_{R_1.X=R_2.X}(R_1 \times R_2) \subseteq \sigma_{R_1.XA=R_2.XA}(R_1 \times R_2).$$

(a) How does the meaning of the algebraic dependency change, if set inclusion is replaced by equality? (The resulting expression does not belong to the class of algebraic dependencies.)

(b) How does the meaning of the algebraic dependency change, if the join condition on the right-hand side $(R_1.XA = R_2.XA)$ is replaced by the condition '$R_1.A = R_2.A$'?

(c) How does the meaning of the algebraic dependency change, if both of the above changes are made?

Exercise 7.14 Show that finite and infinite implication are the same for sets of functional dependencies: if D is a set of functional dependencies and d is a single functional dependency, then $D \models d$ if and only if $D \models_f d$.

Exercise 7.15 Consider the *two-tuple implication* $F \models_2 f$ between a set F of functional dependencies and a functional dependency f, defined by $F \models_2 f$ if and only if for all relations r with two rows and $r \models F$ we also have $r \models f$. Show that $F \models_2 f$ if and only if $F \models f$ for all F and f.

Exercise 7.16 Show that finite and infinite implication are the same for sets of inclusion dependencies: if D is a set of inclusion dependencies and d is a single inclusion dependency, then $D \models d$ if and only if $D \models_f d$.

Exercise 7.17 As an example of a dynamic integrity constraint consider the schema

　　　　Order (Number, Name, Status),

where the allowed values of the Status attribute are 'current', 'completed', and 'cancelled'. An integrity constraint could state that an order cannot change from completed to cancelled or current, neither can it change from cancelled to completed or current. How could you store the same information and constraints without using dynamic integrity constraints? What are the static constraints replacing the dynamic one?

Exercise 7.18 Consider a database of ship voyages. We assume that a voyage consists of a sequence of events where one ship picks up a single cargo and delivers it to a sequence of ports. A ship can visit only one port in a single day.

　　　Construct an ER-diagram for this database. Discuss the various possibilities and problems in representing the above informal constraints in the ER-diagram.

Exercise 7.19 Would it be useful to have different notations for the cases 'each A-value is associated with exactly one B-value' and 'each A-value is associated with at most one B-value'? Consider the applicability of these concepts both in the relational model and in the ER-model.

Exercise 7.20 Consider the enforcement of the functional dependency $R : X \to A$. Evaluate the number of disk accesses needed when (a) one, (b) 10 000 rows are inserted into the relation over R. What kind of index structures are useful?

Exercise 7.21 Investigate what types of integrity constraints your database management system supports. How can the enforcement of the constraints be controlled?

Bibliographic notes

Functional dependencies were already present in Codd's early work [Cod70, Cod72, Cod74]. Inclusion dependencies have occurred in the disguise of referential integrity since the invention of the relational model. Formally they were defined by Casanova, Fagin, and Papadimitriou [CFP84]. They have received some theoretical attention [Mit83b, Mit83a, CK86, CKV90], but papers considering the use of inclusion dependencies in database design are rare [CV83, CAdS83, CAdS84, MR86b, Sci86]. Fagin [Fag81] considers explicit domain dependencies.

Multivalued dependencies were defined by Fagin [Fag77]. They have been studied extensively (see [Mai83]). The tabular form used in the definition of multivalued dependencies can be generalized; this gives the class of *template dependencies* [SU82, FMUY83]. Join dependencies were defined by Rissanen [Ris77]; they are also expressible as template dependencies. Extended embedded implicational dependencies are defined in [Fag82b] and algebraic dependencies in [YP82], where the equivalence of the two classes of constraints is also shown. Tuple-generating dependencies and equality-generating dependencies were defined by Beeri and Vardi [BV84a].

The role of dependencies in database design is discussed by Beeri and Kifer [BK86]. The usual approach is that the database designer specifies a set of constraints, which restrict the set of allowed transactions. An alternative would be that the designer specifies the classes of allowed transactions and the constraints are deduced from the specification. This approach has been studied by Abiteboul and Vianu [AV88, AV89].

Ginsburg and Zaiddan [GZ82] show that a set of functional dependencies can imply some constraints on projections that are not expressible as functional dependencies. Our definition of projection does not deal with such constraints.

A lucid discussion of the role of domains and foreign keys in database schemas is given by Date in [Dat90b]; he discusses referential integrity in [Dat81]. The effect of referential integrity constraints on data manipulation is studied in [Mar91].

The SQL language is described in [SQL86] and the SQL2 standard in [SQL92].

Nicolas [Nic82] and McCune and Henschen [MH89] give methods for the efficient enforcement of constraints. Exercise 7.15 is from [SDPF81]. Exercise 7.18 is from [Ull88].

Chapter 8

Properties of Relational Schemas

Database design aims at database schemas that can be used for storing the required data about an application. We saw in Chapter 6 that there are some general principles that should be observed when designing database schemas. The goal of this book is to develop a database design method that can produce such schemas using automated tools. For this end, we need a more formal treatment of the desired properties of schemas: the principles presented in Chapter 6 were informal and hence not particularly suitable for use in automated tools.

The last chapter discussed what type of conditions on database instances are needed to guarantee the consistency of the data. Inclusion dependencies and functional dependencies emerged as two important classes of constraints. It turns out that one can formalize the desired properties of database schemas given in Chapter 6 by considering what integrity constraints hold in the database schema. In this chapter we give such formal definitions, based on the functional and inclusion dependencies of the schema.

The basic issue in designing a relational database schema is what attributes should appear together in a schema. A database schema where the relation schemas are too large makes it necessary to use a single tuple for storing several facts, and anomalies occur. On the other hand, the splitting of information in a database schema should not be carried too far. In the extreme case we could use a separate relation schema for every attribute. Surely all attribute values could then be stored in the

113

database without any problems. But it is not the values *per se* that are of interest. Rather, the database should maintain the *connections* between the values: a fact is typically composed of several attribute values, not a single value. In producing a database schema one has to achieve a proper compromise between these two competing goals: splitting the data into smaller units (so that smaller facts can be stored in the database) and grouping the data into larger units (so that sufficient connections between the attribute values are maintained).

Section 8.1 discusses the role of attribute names from a formal point of view. We define in Section 8.2 a series of increasingly restrictive *normal forms*, with the intent that a highly normalized schema is free from anomalies. Simple examples show that if a schema is *not* normalized, it does suffer from anomalies. We show this in a slightly more formal way in Section 8.3. The normal forms also aim at reducing the possibility of redundancy, since redundancy and update anomalies go hand in hand. Section 8.4 describe how the normal form concepts can be formulated for object-oriented data models.

Normal forms favor small relation schemas: the smaller the schema, the less chance it has of violating the normal form conditions. A condition that discourages the use of too small relation schemas is called *losslessness* and defined in Section 8.5. Intuitively, it is intended to guarantee that by using several tables to store the data, we do not lose any important connections between the attributes.

Normal forms are defined using the functional dependencies holding in the relation schemas. Functional dependencies can, however, be formulated also in global terms, without reference to particular relation schemas. Section 8.6 considers the meaning of such dependencies, and presents the so-called weak instance model. It also studies how such dependencies could be enforced while studying only single schemas; the condition is called *independence*. A related condition, *dependency preservation*, is discussed in Section 8.7; it has meaning even if no global functional dependencies are considered. Like the lossless join property, dependency preservation works in the opposite direction to normal forms: the more attributes we group together, the easier it is to make sure that all dependencies are preserved.

Section 8.8 considers the properties of inclusion dependencies that hold in a database schema. We motivate the key-basedness condition already given in Section 7.2 by the desire to avoid redundancy and anomalies. We also introduce the noncircularity condition for the set of inclusion dependencies.

8.1   Attribute names

In previous chapters we have on many occasions discussed the importance of attribute names. In the ER-model, the same attribute name could be used in several places, but each attribute was still supposed to have a unique meaning. When an ER-diagram is mapped into a relational schema, each occurrence of an attribute in the ER-diagram generates a new attribute name in the relational schema. Therefore, if an attribute name appears in several relation schemas, all the attributes denote the same concept. For instance, an attribute like Name should refer to the same kind of names everywhere – not to names of persons in one schema and to names of companies in another schema.

Databases with this property are said to satisfy the *Universal Relation Schema Assumption* (URSA). The assumption means that attributes have a global meaning in a database schema, and that it makes sense to connect the data stored in the individual relations using a natural join. The assumption is fundamental to the theory of relational database design, though it is not always explicitly stated.

The universal schema assumption should not be confused with the *universal relation assumption*, which states that the relations in a database instance are always projections of some relation (the 'universal relation') over the universal relation schema U, which contains all the attributes that appear in the database. The universal relation assumption caused much controversy in the early years of relational database research – understandably, since it is totally unrealistic: the reason for decomposing the universal schema into a collection of smaller schemas is just the desire to record facts that could not be stored in tuples over the universal schema. The universal schema assumption is much weaker and easily acceptable.

By the above discussion, $\mathbf{R} = (U)$ is usually a poor choice for a set of relation schemas. Instead, we shall use a collection of smaller schemas, $(R_1, \ldots, R_k)$. Then $\mathbf{R} = (R_1, \ldots, R_k)$ is called a *decomposition* of U.

8.2   Normal forms based on functional dependencies

We shall define a sequence of increasingly demanding normal forms: first normal form (1NF), second normal form (2NF), third normal form (3NF), and Boyce-Codd normal form (BCNF).

First normal form is not really a condition for well-designed relation schemas. Rather, it states an implicit assumption in the relational model, namely that values in attribute domains are atomic. It is not possible to

group several values together into a set and store that set as the value
of some attribute in one tuple – at least if the individual values in the
set should be accessible from within the database management system.
Therefore relations in 1NF are often called *flat relations*.

Example 8.1 Consider again the schema

Talk (Paper_Number, Session_Number, Chairperson_Name)

in Example 6.1 (page 72). Suppose that the numbers of papers presented
in a session are grouped together, so that a relation instance would look
like this:

Paper_Number	Session_Number	Chairperson_Name
16 86	4	Daniel J. Rosenkrantz
33 28 75	5	Catriel Beeri

Then changing the chairperson of a session would be easy, and there
would not be any redundancy in the relation. However, adding one paper
to a session or deleting one paper from a session would be impossible
within the relational model.   □

The possibility of removing this restriction from the relational model
has been studied extensively. Relations like the one in Example 8.1 are
called *non-first-normal-form relations* (abbreviated NFNF or NF^2) or
nested relations. They are not yet supported by commercial database
management systems, and in this book we only deal with 1NF relations.

Second normal form is the first really to prevent the storing of different
types of facts in one relation. To define it formally, let R be a set of
attributes and F a set of functional dependencies over R. An attribute
$A \in R$ is *prime*, if there exists a key X of R (with respect to F) such that
$A \in X$. An attribute is *nonprime* if it is not a member of any key of R.

Relation schema R is in second normal form with respect to F if for
every nonprime attribute $A \in R$ we have: whenever $F \models X \to A$ such
that $A \notin X$, X is not a proper subset of any key of R. A dependency
$X \to A$ violating this property is called a *partial dependency* (since X
forms a part of some key).

Intuitively, a nonprime attribute A captures some data about a concept identified by the key attributes. If X, a part of some key, functionally
determines A, this indicates that the XA-values together describe some
fact; and since additional attributes are needed to form the key of the
schema, those additional attributes are used for describing some other
fact. Thus, the relation is used for storing several kinds of facts – a
source of the anomalies we discussed before.

Example 8.2 Suppose

Evaluation (*Paper_Number*, Title, *Reviewer_Name*, Score)

is used for storing evaluations of papers. Then the partial dependency Paper_Number → Title holds in the schema, violating 2NF. It is obvious that the schema is used for two unrelated facts: the title of a paper and the score it has received from a reviewer.[1]   □

Example 8.3 The schema

Talk (*Paper_Number*, Session_Number, Chairperson_Name)

in Example 6.1 is in 2NF, assuming that the dependencies are

Paper_Number → Session_Number and
Session_Number → Chairperson_Name.

The only key is Paper_Number, so there cannot be any standard partial dependencies.   □

Since we saw in Example 6.1 that the schema considered in Example 8.3 is not well-designed, the definition of 2NF does not capture all poorly designed schemas.

Third normal form restricts the allowed schemas further. Consider the definition of second normal form and a dependency $X \to A$ that does *not* violate the 2NF property. There are two possibilities: either X is a superkey of R, or it is not, in which case for any key Z of R we have $Z \to X$, $X \to A$, and $X \not\to Z$. This is called a *transitive dependency*. Third normal form forbids transitive dependencies in addition to not allowing partial dependencies.

Formally, relation schema R is in third normal form if for every non-prime attribute $A \in R$ we have: whenever $F \models X \to A$ such that $A \notin X$, X is a superkey of R.

By the above discussion, it is clear that every relation schema that is in 3NF is also in 2NF.

Example 8.4 Consider once more the schema

Talk (*Paper_Number*, Session_Number, Chairperson_Name)

of Examples 6.1 and 8.3. Since Session_Number is not a key of the schema, the dependencies Paper_Number → Session_Number and Session_Number → Chairperson_Name form a transitive dependency, violating 3NF.   □

---

[1]Even if the facts *are* related, surely the relationship cannot be described by a functional dependency – or by any domain-independent constraint.

Finally, *Boyce-Codd normal form*, abbreviated BCNF, drops the requirement that only nonprime attributes are considered on the right-hand side of the dependencies that may violate the normal form conditions. Similar anomalous situations may occur in the case of prime attributes as well, and BCNF seeks to prevent them. Thus a relation schema R is in Boyce-Codd normal form if for every $A \in R$ we have: whenever $F \models X \to A$ such that $A \notin X$, X is a superkey of R. This is the design goal stated in Section 7.1: all nontrivial functional dependencies should have a superkey as their left-hand side.

Example 8.5 Suppose that we use the schema

Session_Persons (Session_Number, Chairperson_Name, Author)

for storing information about session chairpersons and the authors presenting a paper in their session – useful for establishing contacts between chairpersons and speakers before the session. Let us assume that each person can chair at most one session, implying that the dependency Chairperson_Name $\to$ Session_Number should hold (in addition to the dependency Session_Number $\to$ Chairperson_Name). Then Session_Persons is in 3NF but not in BCNF: the keys of the schema are {Session_Number, Author} and {Chairperson_Name, Author}. Both of the functional dependencies have a proper subset of the key on the left-hand side and a prime attribute on the right-hand side.   □

Boyce-Codd normal form guarantees that the relation schema represents facts about a single concept: no functional dependencies between components of the schema are allowed, except the ones connected to keys.

Since the requirements are increasingly stronger, why are we interested in the normal forms that are weaker than Boyce-Codd normal form? Indeed, second normal form is only of historical interest. But even though BCNF prevents more anomalies than 3NF, it is still not always advisable to strive for a schema that is in BCNF: in doing so, it may become impossible to satisfy some of the other properties that a well-designed database schema should have. We shall return to this question in Section 8.7.

Some even more restrictive normal forms have been proposed, too, but such normal forms are based on some other forms of integrity constraints, not functional dependencies. For instance, the *fourth normal form* (4NF) is defined using multi-valued dependencies, and the *project-join normal form* (PJ/NF) using functional dependencies and join dependencies.

The relationship between BCNF and the higher normal forms can to some extent be expressed using only functional dependencies. Namely, a relation schema that is in BCNF is in 4NF if it has at least one key that consists of a single attribute; and a relation schema that is in 3NF is in PJ/NF if it has only keys that consist of a single attribute. We shall, however, not analyse the higher normal forms in more detail.

8.3 Anomalies and normal forms

In this section we show that Boyce-Codd normal form is a necessary condition for the absence of anomalies. To achieve the result, we need a formal definition of anomalies. We concentrate on insertion anomalies, since the extensions to deletion and update anomalies are straightforward.

An insertion u can be thought to consist of a set of pairs

$$\{(A_i, v_i) \mid i = 1, \ldots, n\},$$

where A_i is an attribute and v_i is an element of $Dom(A_i)$ for each $i = 1, \ldots, n$. The insertion is *implemented* in a database state $\mathbf{r}$, if there exists a relation r and a row $t \in r$ such that

$$t[A_1, \ldots, A_n] = (v_1, \ldots, v_n).$$

The set $\{A_1, \ldots, A_n\}$ is called an *insertion set* for the database schema.

Let $(\mathbf{R}, F, I)$ be a database schema, and let $\mathcal{Z}$ be the collection of all insertion sets for $\mathbf{R}$. The schema $(\mathbf{R}, F, I)$ is *free from insertion anomalies*, if $\mathbf{R}$ contains for each $Z \in \mathcal{Z}$ a schema R such that $Z \subseteq R$ and Z is a superkey of R. In this case the insertion can be done in relation r corresponding to R without violating entity integrity. If the condition does not hold, entity integrity is violated.

Example 8.6 In the schema

  Talk (*Paper_Number*, Session_Number, Chairperson_Name)

of Example 8.4, the insertion sets are {Paper_Number, Session_Number} and {Session_Number, Chairperson_Name}: we want to be able to store facts about the session of a paper, and about the chairperson of a session. Since the key of the schema is Paper_Number, an insertion anomaly may occur: the information about the chairperson of a session cannot be inserted if no information about papers for that session is present.   □

Assume then that each nontrivial functional dependency $X \to A$ holding in $\mathbf{R}$ means that XA is a possible insertion set. This assumption can be justified as follows. Since the functional dependency means that at most one A-value is associated with any X-value, the dependency in particular implies that a connection exists between X-values and A-values. Hence the set XA is a possible insertion set: one may want to insert into the database a fact that consists of values for the XA attributes.

Theorem 8.1 Let $(\mathbf{R}, F, I)$ be a database schema. Assume that for each schema $R \in \mathbf{R}$ and for each nontrivial functional dependency $X \to A$ in

F_R the set XA is an insertion set. Then $(\mathbf{R}, F, I)$ is free of insertion anomalies only if each schema of $\mathbf{R}$ is in Boyce-Codd normal form.

Proof. Assume $R \in \mathbf{R}$ is not in Boyce-Codd normal form. Then R satisfies a functional dependency $X \to A$ with $A \notin X$ such that X is not a superkey of R. This implies that XA is an insertion set for $\mathbf{R}$. An insertion specifying the values of XA cannot be done without violating entity integrity. $\square$

The converse of the theorem holds under the assumption that insertion sets are exactly the sets XA resulting from a functional dependency plus the schemas of the database.

8.4   Normal forms for other data models

In this section we discuss briefly how the normal form conditions apply to the ER-model and to object-oriented data models. The preceding desirable conditions, such as normal forms, have been defined using the concepts of the relational model. However, the motivation for these concepts is largely independent of the data model that is being used. Hence the conditions can be partly adapted to apply also to other data models.

Third normal form and Boyce-Codd normal form were motivated by the desire to avoid redundancy in the representation of the data. The normal forms are based on the notion of a functional dependency. In addition to the relational model, this concept can equally well be applied to the ER-model, and the treatment of normal forms for relation schemas can be applied to entity types and relationship types.

The normal form concepts can also be applied equally well to object-oriented data models. The formal definitions are slightly different, since in object-data models the attribute is not the only basic concept. The concept corresponding to the set of attributes of a relation schema is the set of operations of a type. The set of operations includes, of course, the operations for selecting the value of each of the attributes in the type, but it can also include some other functions.

To define the normal forms for object-oriented data models we can use a generalization of functional dependencies. Consider a type definition C and a class c corresponding to C. Given two functions f and g defined on objects of type C, we say that f determines g in c, if for all $x, y \in c$ we have: if $f(x) = f(y)$, then $g(x) = g(y)$. If f determines g in c, we denote $c \models f \to g$.

As the terminology and notation suggest, the notion of a function determining another is a generalization of functional dependencies: a dependency $X \to Y$ holding in a relation r corresponds to the expression $r \models \pi_X \to \pi_Y$.

The concept of a function determining another can also be formalized by considering the equivalence classes defined by the functions. If $f \to g$ holds, then the partition defined by f is a refinement of the partition defined by g.

We say that two functions f and g are equivalent with respect to a class c, if $c \models f \to g$ and $c \models g \to f$ both hold. The functions are equivalent with respect to a class definition C, if they are equivalent for any allowed value of the class corresponding to the class definition.

Now the normal form conditions can be defined in the same way as for relation schemas. Denote by id the identical function, that is, the function satisfying $\mathrm{id}(x) = x$ for all x. A class definition is in Boyce-Codd normal form, if for all allowed instances c of the class and for all functions f and g explicitly defined in the definition of the class we have: if $f \to g$, and f and g are not equivalent, then $f \to \mathrm{id}$.

If the class definition has only attributes, but no other defined operations, then it is in Boyce-Codd normal form with respect to the above definition exactly when it is in Boyce-Codd normal form with respect to the original definition.

An alternative way of defining normal forms for object-oriented data models is to consider a mapping of object-oriented schemas to relational database schemas and then say that that the object oriented schema is in normal form if and only if the corresponding relational schema is in normal form.

In the case treated above, this would mean that to a class definition C we associate a relation schema $R(C)$ consisting of one attribute A_σ for each operation σ of C. Given a class c corresponding to C, a relation $r(c)$ over $R(C)$ is defined by letting $r(c)$ to contain one row t_o for each object o in c; the values of attributes of t_o are the values of the corresponding operation when applied to o, that is, $t_o[A_\sigma] = \sigma(o)$.

While normal forms generalize easily to other data models, the other conditions defined in this chapter are more specific to the relational model.

8.5   Lossless joins

Let $(\mathbf{R}, F, I)$ be a database schema over U, where $\mathbf{R} = (R_1, \ldots, R_k)$. Suppose we wish to store in the database a fact involving some attributes X such that $X \not\subseteq R$ for any $R \in \mathbf{R}$. Then that fact has to be split into parts, each part belonging to some relation. The database should be designed so that the fact can be reconstructed by combining the individual parts. The operation offered by relational algebra for combining data from several relations is the join operation.

With this motivation in mind, we say that $(\mathbf{R}, F, I)$ has the *lossless join property* or that $(\mathbf{R}, F, I)$ is a *lossless database schema*, if for all relations r over U that satisfy F_U, the equality

$$r = r[R_1] \bowtie \cdots \bowtie r[R_k]$$

holds.

Example 8.7 Let $U = ABC$ and $\mathbf{R} = (AB, BC)$, and let $F = I = \emptyset$.
Let r be the following relation:

A	B	C
1	3	5
1	3	6
2	3	6
2	4	6

Then the projections of r and their join are as follows:

A	B
1	3
2	3
2	4

B	C
3	5
3	6
4	6

A	B	C
1	3	5
1	3	6
2	3	5
2	3	6
2	4	6

r_1 r_2 $r_1 \bowtie r_2$

We have one more tuple in $r_1 \bowtie r_2$ than in r. Thus $(\mathbf{R}, F, I)$ is not a lossless database schema over U.   □

In Example 8.7 we have $r \subseteq r_1 \bowtie r_2$. Recall that in Theorem 4.1 (page 45) this was shown to hold in general. Therefore, if r is projected on r_1 and r_2 which are then joined back together using a join that is not lossless, this does not mean that we would lose some data values in relation r by projecting it. Instead, we lose the knowledge about the existing connections between the values in r: the result may have too many tuples. A join that is not lossless is called *lossy*.

An alternative way of formulating the lossless join condition is to require that the dependency set D of $\mathbf{R}$ implies the join dependency (see Section 7.3) $\mathbf{R} \equiv R_1 \bowtie R_2 \bowtie \ldots \bowtie R_k$.

The lossless join property is quite fundamental. It is usually satisfied by natural database schemas. However, the accidental omission of a relation schema can easily cause a lossy join; for database schemas with a large number of relation schemas such omission can occur. In automated design tools it is therefore useful to test whether the join is lossless. An algorithm for this is given in Section 10.7.

8.6   Global functional dependencies and independence

The universal relation schema assumption presented at the beginning of this chapter means that attributes have a global meaning in a database schema, and that it makes sense to connect the data stored in the individual relations using a natural join. Given the universality of attribute names, why did we carefully define functional dependencies only with respect to a particular relation schema, and not as global constraints for the entire database schema?

The foremost reason is that defining the semantics of functional dependencies in a more general setting is far from trivial. Next we explore the various possibilities and extend our previous definition so that we are able to talk about the satisfaction of functional dependencies by a database, not only by a relation.

When is a functional dependency satisfied by a database? To find a sound answer, let us first recall our current definition of dependency satisfaction. Let $R(A_1, \ldots, A_n)$ be a relation schema and r a relation over R. A functional dependency $R : X \rightarrow Y$, where X and Y are subsets of R, holds in r if and only if for all tuples $t, t' \in r$ we have: if $t[X] = t'[X]$, then $t[Y] = t'[Y]$.

Now, let U be the set of all the attributes that appear in a set of relation schemas $\mathbf{R} = (R_1, \ldots, R_k)$. Let $X \rightarrow Y$ (where $X \subseteq U$ and $Y \subseteq U$) be a *global functional dependency*, a functional dependency where the name of the relation schema is omitted. When does $X \rightarrow Y$ hold in a database $\mathbf{r}$ over $\mathbf{R}$?

Suppose that there exists a relation schema $R \in \mathbf{R}$ such that $X \subseteq R$ and $Y \subseteq R$, and let $r \in \mathbf{r}$ be the relation over R. Clearly, if $R : X \rightarrow Y$ does not hold in r, it is intuitively impossible for $X \rightarrow Y$ to hold in $\mathbf{R}$: if a dependency is violated by one relation, then it cannot be satisfied by the database that contains the relation. Perhaps this necessary condition could also be sufficient? We could try the following definition for dependency satisfaction.

> *Satisfaction by Projections.* Database $\mathbf{r}$ over $\mathbf{R}$ satisfies a set of global functional dependencies F if and only if the projected set of dependencies $F[R]$ holds for each $r \in \mathbf{r}$, where R is the relation schema over which r is defined.

This suggestion is, however, too simplistic. It does not capture our intuitive notion of a functional dependency, as the following example shows.

Example 8.8 Consider a database schema with two relation schemas:

AssignedTo (*Paper_Number*, Session_Number) and
ChairedBy (*Session_Number*, Chairperson_Name).

Suppose the set of global functional dependencies is

$$F = \{\text{Paper\_Number} \rightarrow \text{Chairperson\_Name}\}.$$

The projection of this set of dependencies is empty for both relation schemas. Therefore *any* database instance would satisfy F, implying that we could just as well use an empty set of dependencies instead of F. This cannot be the correct way of defining dependency satisfaction.

Intuitively, it would appear that the database instance shown below should not satisfy F, because there are two different chairpersons associated with paper number 16 (through session number 4). If the last tuple in the second relation was omitted, then only one chairperson would be associated with each paper, and this corresponds to what we intuitively understand by a functional dependency.

Paper_Number	Session_Number
47	3
16	4

Session_Number	Chairperson_Name
3	Carlo Zaniolo
4	Daniel J. Rosenkrantz
4	Catriel Beeri

□

Since replacing the global set of dependencies by smaller relation specific sets does not work, we might try the opposite approach: leave the global set of dependencies as it is, but combine the data in the database into a single large relation, where we could then apply our standard definition for dependency satisfaction in one relation. The usual method for combining relations is to use the natural join. This suggests the next possible definition for satisfaction of global dependencies.

Satisfaction by Join. Database $\mathbf{r} = (r_1, \ldots, r_k)$ satisfies a set of global functional dependencies F if and only if $r_1 \bowtie r_2 \bowtie \cdots \bowtie r_k$ satisfies F.

It is not difficult to see that neither of the preceding definitions implies the other (cf. Exercise 8.8). Because Satisfaction by Projections was considered a necessary requirement for global satisfaction, Satisfaction by Join cannot alone be taken as our definition for dependency satisfaction. But perhaps the two conditions together would represent all the requirements that we wish the definition to capture? Unfortunately, even this is not sufficient, as Example 8.9 shows.

Example 8.9

This time, suppose the two relation schemas in the database schema are Chairperson (Paper_Number, Session_Number, Chairperson_Name) and Schedule (Paper_Number, Session_Number, Time), and let the set of global functional dependencies be $F = \{$Paper_Number $\to$ Session_Number$\}$. Consider the following database.

Paper_Number	Session_Number	Chairperson_Name
16	4	Daniel J. Rosenkrantz

Paper_Number	Session_Number	Time
16	3	W 13:30–14:45

This database satisfies F according to Satisfaction by Projections (since every relation with at most one tuple satisfies all dependencies among its attributes) and also according to Satisfaction by Join (since the join is empty). And yet our intuition says that the dependency should not be satisfied, since two session numbers are associated with paper number 16 (albeit in different relations). □

The problem with Satisfaction by Join is that although it tries to check the validity of dependencies over connections that exist in the database, some of the connections disappear in the process of joining the relations together. The conclusion from this is that joining the relations cannot be the right approach for defining the satisfaction of dependencies.

Since the two connections appear between Paper_Number and Session_Number in Example 8.9, they should appear in the relation that combines the data in the individual relations, no matter how the combined relation is constructed. This motivates the following concept.

Let $\mathbf{r} = (r_1, \ldots, r_k)$ be a database over $\mathbf{R} = (R_1, \ldots, R_k)$, and suppose that U is the set of attributes appearing in $\mathbf{R}$. A relation r over U is a *containing instance* for $\mathbf{r}$ if $r_i \subseteq r[R_i]$ for $1 \le i \le k$.

Whenever a connection or several connections among some attributes appears in the database, all the connections have to be present in the containing instance – otherwise they could not be present in the projections. Although the individual relations could satisfy a functional dependency in different ways (using different 'functions'), this is not possible when all the connections are collected into the containing instance. We therefore define dependency satisfaction as follows.

Satisfaction by Containing Instance. A database $\mathbf{r}$ satisfies a global set of functional dependencies F if and only if $\mathbf{r}$ has a containing instance that satisfies F.

This definition is generally accepted as a sound definition of dependency satisfaction. Note that a database can have any number of containing instances. In the *weak instance model* we are interested in one particular containing instance. A relation r is a *weak instance* for $\mathbf{R}$, if r is a containing instance for $\mathbf{R}$, and if for any containing instance s we have $r \subseteq s$. Thus r is the smallest possible containing instance. The weak instance model forms the basis of so-called *universal relation interfaces*, which we, however, shall not treat in this book.

Independence is a notion related to global functional dependencies. The idea behind independence is that although global dependencies are sometimes useful, checking that a containing instance exists is generally too hard. One would like to maintain the global dependencies by checking only functional dependencies in individual schemas. A schema is called independent if this is possible.

Let $(\mathbf{R}, F, I)$ be a database schema. A database $\mathbf{r}$ over $\mathbf{R}$ is *locally consistent*, if it satisfies I and each relation r of $\mathbf{r}$ over relation schema R satisfies the set F_R. The database schema $(\mathbf{R}, F, I)$ is *independent*, if each locally consistent database $\mathbf{r}$ also satisfies the set $G = \cup_{R \in \mathbf{R}} F_R$ in the sense of Satisfaction by Containing Instance.

Example 8.10 The database schema in Example 8.9 with $F = \{\text{Paper\_Number} \rightarrow \text{Session\_Number}\}$ and $I = \emptyset$ is not independent, since the example database considered is locally consistent, but does not satisfy the functional dependency.

However, if F is as above, but I contains the inclusion dependency

Chairperson[Paper_Number, Session_Number] $\subseteq$
Schedule[Paper_Number, Session_Number],

the schema is independent. □

Note that attribute naming is a crucial factor affecting independence. If all functional dependencies are defined within schemas, and no two schemas have common attributes, then the database schema is automatically independent.

Independence is a general concept; it can be compared to correctness notions in distributed systems, where one wants to ensure global correctness of a system by checking only local conditions.

8.7 Preservation of dependencies

A simpler condition related to independence is preservation of dependencies. Let U be a set of attributes and $(\mathbf{R}, F, I)$ a database schema over U, where $\mathbf{R} = (R_1, \ldots, R_k)$. Recall from Section 7.5 (page 98) that $F[R_i]$

denotes the functional dependencies among the attributes of R_i implied by F. Clearly,

$$F \models \bigcup_{i=1}^{k} F[R_i].$$

Database schema $(\mathbf{R}, F, I)$ is *dependency preserving* if also the converse holds, that is, if

$$\bigcup_{i=1}^{k} F[R_i] \models F.$$

Note that dependency preservation does not require that each dependency in F belongs to some projection $F[R_i]$; it only requires that the union of the projections *implies* all the dependencies.

Example 8.11 Let $U = ABC$ and $F = \{A \to B, B \to C, C \to A\}$. The database schema $(\mathbf{R}, F, \emptyset)$ where $\mathbf{R} = (AB, BC)$ does not appear dependency preserving at first glance, since A and C do not appear together in any relation schema. However, it is sufficient that all the dependencies in F are implied by the projected dependencies. This indeed is the case for $\mathbf{R}$: $F[AB] = \{A \to B, B \to A\}$, $F[BC] = \{B \to C, C \to B\}$, and $F[AB] \cup F[BC] \models C \to A$. □

If a database schema does not preserve dependencies, then maintaining the constraints requires more effort than in the case when the dependencies can be checked by investigating individual relations. It can be shown that dependency preservation is a necessary condition for independence. It is not a sufficient condition, however.

Example 8.12 The database schema in Example 8.9 with $F = \{\text{Paper\_Number} \to \text{Session\_Number}\}$ and $I = \emptyset$ was not independent, even though the dependency in F was preserved. In fact, the dependency is present in two projections of F. □

Actually a dependency preserving database schema with only key dependenciesis independent if and only if each dependency is preserved in a unique way. Let $(\mathbf{R}, F, \emptyset)$ be a database schema with all relation schemas in Boyce-Codd normal form, and denote

$$K_R = \{X \to R \mid X \text{ is a key of } R\}.$$

Since F contains only key dependencies, we have that $\cup_{R \in \mathbf{R}} K_R \models F$. We say that F is *uniquely represented* in $\mathbf{R}$, if for each $R, S \in \mathbf{R}$ and each $W \subseteq S$ such that W includes as a proper subset a key of S we have $F \setminus K_S \not\models R \to W$. That is, the non-key attributes of any schema S can be derived using only the dependencies associated with S.

Theorem 8.2 Let **R** and F be as above. Then **R** is independent if and only if F is uniquely represented in **R**. □

The following example is already a classical case of interfering design goals.

Example 8.13 Consider again the database containing zip codes (attribute Zip), names of cities (City) and names of streets (Street) already discussed in Section 7.7. Consider the relation schema

Address (Street, City, Zip).

The functional dependencies that Address should satisfy are Zip → City and City Street → Zip. Clearly, with these dependencies Address is a dependency preserving database schema over {Street, City, Zip}. The keys of Address are {City, Street} and {Zip, Street}. Thus every attribute in Address is prime, and the schema is trivially in 3NF. It is not in BCNF, since the dependency Zip → City has a subset of a key as the left-hand side.

The attributes of Address could be represented as a lossless database schema by the two relation schemas {Zip, City} and {Zip, Street}. Both schemas are in BCNF. However, the database schema is not dependency preserving, since City Street → Zip is not preserved. In fact, this holds for *any* database schema that does not contain the Address schema.

For this example we can thus obtain either a 3NF, lossless, dependency preserving database schema, or a BCNF, lossless database schema, but BCNF and dependency preservation are goals that cannot be reached simultaneously. □

The conclusion of Example 8.13 can be generalized. It is customary to regard the lossless join property as a fundamental property that a database schema should always have. After that, we have a choice between 3NF and dependency preservation, or BCNF, possibly without dependency preservation. Schemas with either set of properties are always reachable. We shall in Chapter 12 give an algorithm for producing 3NF, dependency preserving database schemas, and an algorithm for producing BCNF database schemas.

8.8 Properties of inclusion dependencies in a schema

Normal forms were defined using functional dependencies. The basic message was that the only functional dependencies that should remain in a well-designed schema are key dependencies. In this section we consider what should be required of the inclusion dependencies holding in a database schema. We review the key-basedness condition presented in Section 7.2 (page 91), and show how it can be motivated by the desire to avoid anomalies and redundancy. We also introduce the concept of a noncircular set of inclusion dependencies. This condition makes updates easier. The transformation in Chapter 11 that produces a relational database schema from an ER-diagram creates schemas with these properties.

Recall that an inclusion dependency $R[X] \subseteq S[Y]$ is *key-based*, if Y is a key of S. If this is not the case, there are two possibilities: either Y contains a key as a proper subset, or Y is not a superkey.

In the first case, let $Y = WZ$, where W is a key and Z is nonempty. We can break X into two parts in the same way: $X = VT$. Then it can be argued that storing the T-attributes in schema R is unnecessary: their values are uniquely determined by the other values. Namely, if (r, s) is a pair of relations satisfying $R[X] \subseteq S[Y]$, then for a given row $t \in r$, the value of $t[T]$ must be equal to $u[Z]$, where $u \in s$ is any row such that $u[W] = t[V]$. Hence the attributes in T could be removed from schema R, since R contains redundant information.

Example 8.14 Consider the schemas

> Employee (*EmpName*, DeptName) and
> ManagedBy (DeptName, *Manager*),

where the first schema is used to store information about the department of each employee, and the second schema is used to store information about the managers of departments. It can be sensible to require that the inclusion dependency

> ManagedBy[Manager, DeptName] $\subseteq$
> Employee[EmpName, DeptName]

holds, since it expresses the natural constraint that each manager is an employee of the department he manages. The inclusion dependency is not key-based, and the attribute set on the right-hand side includes a key as a proper subset. We notice that the DeptName attribute is not needed in the ManagedBy schema, since the inclusion dependency guarantees that the same information can be found from the Employee schema.   □

The second possibility for a non-key-based inclusion dependency $R[X] \subseteq S[Y]$ was that Y is not a superkey. Consider then an insertion of row t into the relation r over R. To check that such an insertion does not violate the inclusion dependency, one has to locate the row u of relation s with $t[X] = u[Y]$. This can be slow, as Y is not a superkey. If an insertion violates an inclusion dependency, a reasonable course of action is to insert an additional row so that the dependency holds. In this situation this is almost impossible, since entity integrity for schema S would be violated.

We now move to another property of inclusion dependencies, noncircularity. Let $(\mathbf{R}, F, I)$ be a database schema. We define the *inclusion dependency graph* $ind(\mathbf{R}, I)$ as a directed multigraph $(\mathbf{R}, E)$. There is an arc from R to S in E if and only if I contains a nontrivial dependency of the form $R[X] \subseteq S[Y]$. We say that I is *noncircular* if $ind(\mathbf{R}, I)$ is acyclic. Otherwise, I is *circular*.

Circular sets of inclusion dependencies seem to generate difficulties in updating the relations.

Example 8.15 Suppose we have a schema Personnel containing the attributes Manager and EmpName, and assume we want to express the fact that every manager is also an employee. This can be done by introducing the inclusion dependency

Personnel[Manager] $\subseteq$ Personnel[EmpName].

But then it is difficult to store information about the CEO of the company; we have to make him his own manager, or use a null value for that field.

An alternative design would be to have the schemas PersonData (*EmpName*) and ManagerData (*EmpName*, Manager), and the inclusion dependencies

ManagerData[Manager] $\subseteq$ PersonData[EmpName] and
ManagerData[EmpName] $\subseteq$ PersonData[EmpName].   □

Circular sets of inclusion dependencies can also cause loops in insertions. If we insert a row into a database and some inclusion dependency is violated, then we can try to remedy the situation by adding rows. A circular set can, in principle, cause an infinite set of such correcting insertions.

The transformations of ER-schemas to relational schemas described in Chapter 11 produce noncircular sets of inclusion dependencies, since the inclusion dependencies go from schemas representing relationships to schemas representing entity types. An exception to this is the case where two entity types are connected by an existential relationship type (an **isa**-relationship type or an **id**-relationship type). These generate inclusion dependencies between relation schemas corresponding to entity types. But the **isa**- and **id**-relationship types cannot cause circularities, since the relationships cannot form a cycle in the ER-diagram: the reference graph of the ER-diagram was assumed to be acyclic (see page 29).

Figure 8.1   An entity-relationship diagram for departments and managers.

Some variants of the ER-model contain relationship types, where the cardinality constraints can have a minimum cardinality. That is, one can for example state that for a relationship type $\mathcal{R}$ between entity types $\mathcal{E}_1$ and $\mathcal{E}_2$, each $\mathcal{E}_1$ entity participates in *exactly* one relationship in $\mathcal{R}$. Such a requirement transforms to a circular set of inclusion dependencies, but the circularity can be removed by combining schemas.

Example 8.16 Consider the ER-schema in Figure 8.1. Transformed to relational schemas, this design gives the following.

Department (*DeptName*),
Manager (*Name*), and
ManagedBy (*DeptName*, Name).

The inclusion dependencies are

ManagedBy[DeptName] $\subseteq$ Department[DeptName] and
ManagedBy[Name] $\subseteq$ Manager[Name].

If we required that the participation of departments in the ManagedBy relationship type is obligatory, this would mean that also the inclusion dependency

Department[DeptName] $\subseteq$ ManagedBy[DeptName]

holds, and this would give a circular set of inclusion dependencies. In this case this is easy to avoid by including the attribute Manager into the Department schema. In general, for instance if the relationship type is not functional, the situation is more difficult.   □

Exercises

Exercise 8.1 Familiarize yourself with the database schema of an existing database application. Do the attribute names satisfy the universal relation schema assumption?

Exercise 8.2 Show that the database schema $((AB, BC), \{B \rightarrow A\}, \emptyset)$ is lossless.

Exercise 8.3 What are natural insertion sets for the relation schemas of Example 4.1 (page 37)?

Exercise 8.4 In Section 8.3 we argued that one obtains insertion sets from functional dependencies. Give an example of a relation schema with insertion sets that do not arise from functional dependencies.

Exercise 8.5 Consider the set of attributes $R = ABCDEGH$ and the set of functional dependencies $F = \{AB \rightarrow C, AC \rightarrow B, AD \rightarrow E, B \rightarrow D, BC \rightarrow A, E \rightarrow G\}$. For each of the following attribute sets X, (i) compute a cover of $F[X]$, and (ii) name the strongest normal form not violated by X and $F[X]$. Here are the sets:

(a) $X = ABC$

(b) $X = ABCD$

(c) $X = ABCEG$

(d) $X = ABCH$

(e) $X = ABCDEGH$

Exercise 8.6 Let r be a relation over R and let F be the set of functional dependencies satisfied by r. Assume that R is in BCNF. Prove that r is nonredundant in the sense that for all $t \in r$ and any $A \in R$, the value of $t[A]$ cannot be deduced using F even if all the other values in r are known. (Essentially this proves that BCNF helps to avoid all redundancy in so far as redundancy is related to functional dependencies.)

Does the converse hold? That is, if R violates BCNF, does there exist a relation r where at least one of the values can be deduced if the other values are known?

Exercise 8.7 ** Give an axiomatization for the concept of a function determining another outlined in Section 8.4.

Exercise 8.8 Find databases $\mathbf{r}_1$ and $\mathbf{r}_2$ and sets of global functional dependencies F_1 and F_2 with the following properties.

- Database $\mathbf{r}_1$ satisfies F_1 according to Satisfaction by Projections, but does not satisfy F_1 according to Satisfaction by Join.

- Database $\mathbf{r}_2$ satisfies F_2 according to Satisfaction by Join, but does not satisfy F_2 according to Satisfaction by Projections.

Exercise 8.9 Do Satisfaction by Projections and Satisfaction by Join together imply Satisfaction by Containing Instance? Does the converse hold?

Exercise 8.10 Consider the set of functional dependencies $F = \{A \to C, B \to C, CD \to E, CD \to F, EF \to A\}$. Does this set of dependencies hold in the following database?

A	D	E
0	0	0
1	2	0

A	B
0	3
1	4

C	E	F
0	0	0

B	D	F
3	0	0
4	2	0

Exercise 8.11 Let R and F be as in Exercise 8.5. Which of the following decompositions are dependency preserving?

(a) $\{AB, BC, ABDE, EG\}$,

(b) $\{ABC, ABDEG\}$, and

(c) $\{ABC, ACDE, ADG\}$.

Exercise 8.12 Let $(\mathbf{R}, F, \emptyset)$ be a dependency preserving database schema over U. Prove that the database schema has the lossless join property if and only if $F \models R \to U$ for some $R \in \mathbf{R}$.

Exercise 8.13 Compare empirically the efficiency of maintaining a functional dependency $A \to C$ in a relation over relation schema $R(ABC)$, and in a database with the relation schemas $R_1(AB)$ and $R_2(BC)$. The latter database schema is not dependency preserving.

Bibliographic notes

The underlying assumptions of the relational data model are discussed extensively in [Mai83, MUV84, MRS85, Sci86, MRW86]. Criticism of the assumptions and responses to the criticism can be found in [Ken79, BG80, Ken81, Ull83, Ken83b].

The normal forms discussed in Section 8.2 were defined in the early papers by Codd [Cod70, Cod72]. Additional normal forms have been defined by Fagin [Fag77, Fag79, Fag81]. Kent [Ken83a] gives a nontechnical comparison of the various normal forms, and Date and Fagin [DF91] characterize some higher normal forms in terms of functional dependencies. Exercise 8.6 is from [Ull88]. Boyce-Codd normal form and object-oriented concepts are compared by Biskup [Bis89], who extends the study to inclusion dependencies in [BD91].

Treatments of non-first-normal-form relations are given in [AB86, OY87, RK87, RKS88, AFS89, PDGV89].

Formal treatments of anomalies can be found in [BG80, LP82, Vos88, Cha89]. The insertion sets in a database schema are studied in [DGS87].

Normal forms are applied to the ER-model in [BCN92].

The material about dependency satisfaction and containing instances, including Exercise 8.10, is based on the work of Honeyman [Hon82]. Notions of dependency satisfaction for other classes of dependencies have been studied by Graham, Mendelzon, and Vardi [GMV86]. Some early papers on independence are [Sag83, GY84]. Testing for independence in the presence of inclusion dependencies is studied in [AC91]. Theorem 8.2 is from [Sag83]. The related concept of *separability* is studied in [CM87].

A further notion related to independence is *constant-time maintainability*. It means that one can check in constant time whether a new database resulting from the insertion of a tuple satisfies the constraints of the database schema. Constant-time maintainability is studied in [GW86, Wan89, WG92]. Chan and Hernández [CH88, CH91, HC91] and Wang [Wan90] study the relationships of these and some additional concepts.

Exercise 8.12 is from [LT83]; see also [BDB79, Var84].

Chapter 9

Axiomatizations for Dependencies

Integrity constraints are important in ensuring that the data stored in the database is correct. The previous chapter showed how integrity constraints, and especially functional and inclusion dependencies, can be used to define properties a well-designed schema should have. To develop methods and tools for computer-aided database design, we thus need to be able to manipulate integrity constraints and to decide whether sets of constraints satisfy the desired properties.

In this chapter we start the analysis of functional and inclusion dependencies by considering how one can axiomatize these dependency classes. Using the axiomatizations, Chapter 10 develops concepts and algorithms for manipulating collections of dependencies.

The properties defined in Chapter 8 made heavy use of the notion of a dependency set D implying a single dependency d. To be able to check whether some desired property holds, we often have to be able to decide if D implies d, that is, if $D \models d$ holds. For example, in dependency preservation we have to check whether $\cup_i F[R_i] \models f$ for all $f \in F$, and Boyce-Codd normal form requires that for all $R : X \to A$ implied by F attribute set X contains a key of R.

This problem of deciding whether a dependency set D implies a single dependency d is called the *implication problem*. The definition of $D \models d$ gives little support for solving the implication problem: it is hardly feasible to investigate every database.

In this chapter we present axiomatizations for some dependency types.

An axiomatization is a collection of formal rules that can be used to derive a dependency from a set. The axiomatizations are sound and complete, meaning that such a derivation exists if and only if the dependency is implied by the set. Thus the formal rules give a characterization of semantic implication, and they give possibilities for developing algorithms for solving the implication problem.

Section 9.1 presents the basic concepts about axiomatizations. A simple set of axioms for functional dependencies is given in Section 9.2, while Section 9.3 gives an axiomatization for inclusion dependencies. Even though functional and inclusion dependencies both have fairly simple properties, they can interact in unexpected ways. The interaction is studied and the axiomatization for functional and inclusion dependencies is given in Section 9.4.

9.1   Basic concepts

Recall first some definitions and notation introduced in Chapter 7.

- $\mathbf{r} \models d$ means that d holds in $\mathbf{r}$.

- $\mathbf{r} \models D$ means that $\mathbf{r} \models d$ holds for every $d \in D$.

- A single dependency d *follows* from D, denoted by $D \models d$, if d holds in every database that satisfies all the dependencies in D. That is, if $\mathbf{r} \models D$, then also $\mathbf{r} \models d$.

- For a set E of dependencies, the notation $D \models E$ means that $D \models e$ for each $e \in E$.

An *axiomatization* of a class of dependencies (for instance, functional dependencies or inclusion dependencies) gives a collection of rules that can be used to derive new dependencies from a given set of dependencies. An axiomatization is purely syntactic. Thus one has to prove separately that it has a sensible relationship with the intended meaning of the dependencies. In other words, if a new dependency can be derived from a set of dependencies using the axiomatization, the derived dependency should not be arbitrary: it must follow from the set of dependencies in the above sense, otherwise the axiomatization is of no use. The converse must also hold. We shall soon define these properties more formally.

Given a class of dependencies $\mathcal{D}$, an *axiomatization* for $\mathcal{D}$ consists of *axiom schemas* and *inference rules*. Informally, an axiom schema tells which dependencies of $\mathcal{D}$ hold in every database, and the inference rules indicate how new valid dependencies can be derived from known dependencies. Inference rules are often also called axioms. For example, for functional dependencies we have the axiom schema stating that for a relation schema R and attribute sets $X, Y \subseteq R$ with $Y \subseteq X$ the dependency $X \to Y$ holds in R. An example of an inference rule is: if $X \to Y$ and $Y \to Z$ hold, then $X \to Z$ also holds.

Suppose we have an axiomatization for $\mathcal{D}$, and let D be a set of dependencies from $\mathcal{D}$ and d a single dependency also from $\mathcal{D}$. A *derivation* of d from D is a finite sequence $e_1, \ldots, e_m$ of dependencies, where $e_m = d$, and each e_i is either a member of D, an instance of an axiom schema, or obtained from the previous dependencies $e_1, \ldots, e_{i-1}$ in the derivation by using an inference rule. If a derivation of d from D exists, we say that d can be *derived* from D and denote $D \vdash d$. This relation is also called *proof-theoretic implication*.

For example, from $D = \{X \to AB\}$ we can derive the dependency $d = X \to A$ using the above axiom schema and inference rule. The derivation contains three dependencies:

$$X \to AB,$$
$$AB \to A, \text{ and}$$
$$X \to A.$$

The first dependency is a member of D, the second is an instance of the axiom schema, and the third (that is, d), has been obtained from the first and the second using the inference rule.

Note that a subsequence $e_1, \ldots, e_k$ of a derivation $e_1, \ldots, e_m$ is also a derivation; hence $D \vdash e_k$ for all $k = 1, \ldots, m$.

Two important properties of an axiomatization are soundness and completeness. Soundness states that each derived dependency really holds, and completeness means that each valid dependency can be derived from a given set of dependencies using the axiomatization. Formally, the system is *sound*, if for all D and d we have: if $D \vdash d$, then also $D \models d$. *Completeness* means the converse: if $D \models d$, then also $D \vdash d$.

The dependencies given by a database designer describe the target of the database. Their semantic consequences should also be true propositions about the target. A sound and complete axiomatization for a class of dependencies gives a way of knowing the consequences of a set of dependencies without considering all (finite) databases; rather, it is sufficient to consider only the possible derivations. (Even this may not be very easy.)

An axiomatization is also indicative of the general properties of a class of dependencies. A simple sound and complete axiomatization can be considered to be evidence for the usefulness of the class.

9.2   Axioms for functional dependencies

The following three rules constitute an axiomatization of functional dependencies. Let R be a relation schema and $X, Y, Z \subseteq R$.

F1 If $Y \subseteq X$, then $X \to Y$.

F2 If $X \to Y$, then $XZ \to YZ$.

F3 If $X \to Y$ and $Y \to Z$, then $X \to Z$.

Axiom schema F1 says that values for attributes in X determine unique values for Y, if $Y \subseteq X$. Rule F2 is slightly less intuitive. It asserts that if values for X determine values for Y, then values for XZ determine values for YZ. Rule F3 is the transitivity rule, stating that if X determines Y and Y determines Z, then X determines Z.

Example 9.1 Assume we are given the set F consisting of the three dependencies

> (1) $A \to B$,
> (2) $BC \to D$, and
> (3) $BDE \to J$.

Then we can derive the dependency $ACE \to J$ from F as follows:

> (4) $ACE \to BCE$ (1) and F2 ($Z = CE$)
> (5) $BBCE \to BDE$ (2) and F2 ($Z = BE$)
> (6) $BCE \to BDE$ simplification of (5)
> (7) $BCE \to J$ (6), (3), and F3
> (8) $ACE \to J$ (4), (7), and F3. $\square$

The axioms F1, F2, and F3 are fairly natural, and their soundness is not difficult to prove.

Theorem 9.1 (Soundness) Let F be a set of functional dependencies, and assume $X \to Y$ is derived from F using the above axioms. Let r be a relation with $r \models F$. Then $r \models X \to Y$.

Proof. By induction on the length of the derivation. Let $e_1, \ldots, e_m$ be a derivation of $X \to Y$ from F, and assume the theorem holds for all shorter derivations. Consider $e_m = X \to Y$. It is either a member of F, an instance of F1, or obtained from some previous dependencies e_i and e_j by using F2 or F3, where $i, j < m$. If e_m is an instance of F1 or a member of F, it holds trivially in r.

Next assume e_m is obtained from e_i by using rule F2; then e_i has the form $X' \to Y'$, where X' and Y' are such that $X = X'Z$ and $Y = Y'Z$ for some Z. We know (by the induction assumption) that $r \models e_i$. Let $t, t' \in r$ and $t[X'Z] = t'[X'Z]$. Then $t[X'] = t'[X']$, and thus $t[Y'] = t'[Y']$. But this implies that $t[Y'Z] = t'[Y'Z]$; in particular, $t[Y] = t'[Y]$. Hence e_m holds in r.

The final case is that e_m is obtained from e_i and e_j by using F3. Let $e_i = X \to W$ and $e_j = W \to Y$ for some W. Again, by the induction assumption, we have $r \models e_i$ and $r \models e_j$. Let $t, t' \in r$ and $t[X] = t'[X]$. Since $r \models e_i$, we have $t[W] = t'[W]$. But as $r \models e_j$, we have $t[Y] = t'[Y]$, proving that e_m holds in r. $\square$

Now that soundness has been established, we turn to the other desirable property, completeness. For this we need some additional rules showing how functional dependencies behave.

Lemma 9.1

(i) $\{X \to Y, X \to Z\} \models X \to YZ$.
(ii) $\{X \to Y, WY \to Z\} \models XW \to YZ$.
(iii)   If $Z \subseteq Y$ and $X \to Y$, then $X \to Z$.

Proof. Exercise 9.2. $\square$

Let F be a set of functional dependencies over R and let $X \subseteq R$. The *closure* of X with respect to F, denoted by X_F^+, is the set of all attributes $A \in R$ such that $X \to A$ can be derived using axioms F1, F2, and F3. (In fact, axioms F1 and F3 would be sufficient for computing the closure.) Often the dependency set F is obvious from the context, and then we write simply X^+ instead of X_F^+.

Example 9.2 Consider the schema $R(ABCDE)$ and the dependency set $F = \{A \to B, BC \to D, DE \to A, E \to D\}$. Then the closure of the set AE is $ABDE$, and the closure of CE is $ABCDE$. $\square$

The following lemma shows the importance of the concept of closure of an attribute set.

Lemma 9.2 Let F be a set of functional dependencies and let X and Y be attribute sets. Then $X \to Y$ can be derived from F using axioms F1, F2, and F3 if and only if $Y \subseteq X^+$.

Proof. Exercise 9.3. $\square$

The notion of closure can be related to keys as follows. If for a dependency set F the closure X^+ of X contains all the attributes of the schema R, then we have that $X \to R$ by Lemma 9.2. By the soundness results of Theorem 9.1, then $F \models X \to R$. Hence X is a key of R.

We can now prove the completeness of the axiomatization of functional dependencies.

Theorem 9.2 (Completeness) Let F be a set of functional dependencies over R and $X \to Y$ a functional dependency. If $F \models X \to Y$, then $X \to Y$ can be derived from F using axioms F1, F2, and F3, that is, $F \vdash X \to Y$.

Proof. Consider a two-row relation $r = \{t, t'\}$ over R, where $t[X^+] = t'[X^+]$ and $t[A] \neq t'[A]$ for all $A \in R \setminus X^+$. We show that $r \models F$; by the assumption $F \models X \to Y$ this implies $r \models X \to Y$. Since $X \subseteq X^+$ and $t[X^+] = t'[X^+]$, we therefore have $t[Y] = t'[Y]$ and thus $Y \subseteq X^+$. By the above lemma, this shows that $F \vdash X \to Y$.

Thus it remains to show that $r \models F$. Let $V \to W \in F$. If $V \not\subseteq X^+$, then $t[V] \neq t'[V]$ and $V \to W$ holds vacuously in r. Otherwise $V \subseteq X^+$. Hence $F \vdash X \to V$, and since $V \to W \in F$, an application of F3 gives us $F \vdash X \to W$. Thus $W \subseteq X^+$, and $t[W] = t'[W]$. This shows that $V \to W$ holds in r, proving the theorem. $\qquad\square$

The proof of the completeness theorem does not directly tell us how to obtain a derivation of $X \to Y$ from F, given that $F \models X \to Y$. Efficient methods for deciding whether $F \models X \to Y$ are considered in Chapter 10.

9.3   Axioms for inclusion dependencies

Inclusion dependencies have a fairly simple axiomatization with four axioms.

I1 $R[A_1, \ldots, A_n] \subseteq R[A_1, \ldots, A_n]$.

I2 If $R[A_1, \ldots, A_n] \subseteq S[B_1, \ldots, B_n]$, then $R[A_{\sigma_1}, \ldots, A_{\sigma_m}] \subseteq S[B_{\sigma_1}, \ldots, B_{\sigma_m}]$, where $\sigma_1, \ldots, \sigma_m$ are members of $\{1, \ldots, n\}$.

I3 If $R[A_1, \ldots, A_n] \subseteq S[B_1, \ldots, B_n]$ and $S[B_1, \ldots, B_n] \subseteq T[C_1, \ldots, C_n]$, then $R[A_1, \ldots, A_n] \subseteq T[C_1, \ldots, C_n]$.

I4 If $R[AB] \subseteq S[CC]$ holds and d is an inclusion dependency that also holds and contains an occurrence of A of the form $R[\ldots, A, \ldots]$, then d' holds, where d' is a dependency obtained from d by substituting B for A in one or more occurrences of A as an attribute of the schema R.

Axiom I1 asserts that an identical dependency holds always. Axiom I2 says that one can permute the attributes, leave some out and take multiple copies of attributes, as long as the same transformation is applied to both sides of a dependency. Axiom I3 is the transitivity axiom, similar to axiom F3 for functional dependencies. Axiom I4 asserts that if an attribute appears twice on the right-hand side of a dependency, the left-hand side attributes must have the same values on every row.

Example 9.3 Consider the set of inclusion dependencies $\{R[AB] \subseteq S[CC], R[AD] \subseteq T[EF]\}$. Using axiom I4 we can derive from these in one step the dependency $R[BD] \subseteq T[EF]$.   □

Theorem 9.3 The axioms I1–I4 are sound and complete for inclusion dependencies.

   Proof. Soundness can be proved much like the soundness of the axioms for functional dependencies. The main difference comes from axiom I4, the soundness of which is considered in Exercise 9.10. For the proof of completeness it is convenient to use some concepts that are introduced in Chapter 10. Theorem 10.9 proves completeness when the inclusion dependencies do not contain repeated attributes (in which case axiom I4 is not needed). The general case is somewhat tedious and the proof is omitted.   □

9.4   An axiomatization of functional and inclusion dependencies

While the complete axiomatizations for functional and inclusion dependencies are simple and intuitive, these classes of dependencies have fairly complex interaction. In this section we first give some examples of this interaction and introduce some concepts which are needed for the axiomatization of the combined dependency class.

   The first example shows how an inclusion dependency and a functional dependency imply a functional dependency.

Example 9.4 Let $R(AB)$ and $S(DE)$ be two schemas. Suppose $R[AB] \subseteq S[DE]$ and $S : D \to E$ hold in a database (r, s) over (R, S). Then $R : A \to B$ holds, too. To prove this, let $t, t' \in r$, and assume $t[A] = t'[A]$. There exist rows $u, u' \in s$ such that $t[AB] = u[DE]$ and $t'[AB] = u'[DE]$. Since $u[D] = t[A] = t'[A] = u'[D]$ and $S : D \to E$, we have $u[E] = u'[E]$. But this means $t[B] = t'[B]$.   □

   Thus for an inclusion dependency $R[X] \subseteq S[Y]$ the functional dependencies holding in Y are reflected also among the corresponding attributes of X. The new dependencies are called the *pullback* dependencies.

   If the inclusion dependency is unary, then the situation in Example 9.4 cannot arise. This is one reason why the properties of unary inclusion dependencies are simpler than those of general inclusion dependencies.

   The next example shows how a new and longer inclusion dependency can be implied by two inclusion dependencies and a functional dependency.

Example 9.5 Let $R(ABC)$ and $S(DEF)$ be two schemas. Suppose $R[AB] \subseteq S[DE]$, $R[AC] \subseteq S[DF]$ and $S : D \to E$ hold in a database (r, s) over (R, S). Then $R[ABC] \subseteq S[DEF]$ holds.

Let $t \in r$. We have to find $v \in s$ such that $t[ABC] = v[DEF]$. The two inclusion dependencies imply that there are rows $u, u' \in s$ such that $t[AB] = u[DE]$ and $t[AC] = u'[DF]$. Since $S : D \to E$ holds and $u[D] = t[A] = u'[D]$, we have $u[E] = u'[E]$. Because $t[B] = u[E]$, this means $t[ABC] = u'[DEF]$, as required. □

Again this phenomenon is possible only because the inclusion dependencies are not unary.

For inclusion dependencies alone and for functional dependencies alone finite and infinite implication are the same. For the combined class these notions are different.

Example 9.6 Let $R(AB)$ be a relation schema and let $D = \{R[A] \subseteq R[B], R : A \to B\}$. Then $D \models_f R[B] \subseteq R[A]$, but $D \not\models R[B] \subseteq R[A]$.

We show first that $D \not\models R[B] \subseteq R[A]$. Let r be the infinite relation $\{(i + 1, i) \mid i = 0, 1, \ldots\}$. Then r satisfies the dependencies in D, but $R[B] \subseteq R[A]$ does not hold in r, since the value 0 occurs in the B-column, but it does not occur in the A-column.

Let then r be a finite relation satisfying the dependencies in D. Then $r[A] \subseteq r[B]$ and hence $|r[A]| \leq |r[B]|$. On the other hand, the dependency $A \to B$ means that $|r[B]| \leq |r[A]|$. Therefore $|r[A]| = |r[B]|$ and $r[A] = r[B]$, and hence $R[B] \subseteq R[A]$ holds in r. □

In the above example the inclusion dependencies were unary, but they formed a circular set. For functional dependencies and noncircular sets of inclusion dependencies finite and infinite implication are the same notion. The proof is omitted.

An axiomatization of functional and inclusion dependencies consists of the axioms F1, F2, and F3 for functional dependencies, axioms I1, I2, I3, and I4 for inclusion dependencies and four new axioms F4, FI1, FI2, and FI3, given below.

The first new rule F4 is not exactly an axiom, rather, it introduces formally some notation already implicitly used. It describes the transformation from attribute sets, as used in functional dependencies, to attribute sequences, as required for inclusion dependencies.

The axioms FI1 and FI2 are generalizations of the examples presented above. The last new axiom is slightly more complicated.

F4 Let X' and Y' be attribute sets, and let X and Y be attribute sequences containing exactly the same attributes as X' and Y', respectively. The notation $X \to Y$ denotes the functional dependency $X' \to Y'$.

FI1 If $R[UV] \subseteq S[XY]$, $|X| = |U|$, and $S : X \to Y$, then $R : U \to V$.

FI2 If $R[UV] \subseteq S[XY]$, $R[UW] \subseteq S[XZ]$, and $S : X \to Y$, then $R[UVW] \subseteq S[XYZ]$.

FI3 If $R[U] \subseteq S[V]$ and $S : V \to A$, then $R'[UB] \subseteq S[VA]$, where B is a new attribute and $R' = R \cup \{B\}$.

To explain axiom FI3 we need some additional concepts. Given a relation r over R, a relation r' over $R \cup \{B\}$ is a *B-variant* of r, if $r'[R] = r$. Intuitively, r' is the same as r, except that r' contains a new column for B and some values in that column.

Axiom FI3 means that if (r, s) satisfies $R[U] \subseteq S[V]$ and $S : V \to A$, then r has a B-variant r' such that $R'[UB] \subseteq S[VA]$ holds in (r', s).

If we use FI3 in a derivation, the attribute B must be new in the sense that it does not appear in the original dependency set, in the relation schemas or in any previous step of the derivation. Attribute B serves as an auxiliary attribute that is used to derive dependencies among the original attributes: it should not appear in the final dependency of any interesting derivation. Axiom FI3 can be used in derivations only as a tool to show that some attributes are in fact equal, that is, they satisfy a dependency of the form $R[DE] \subseteq S[CC]$.

Some intuition about axiom FI3 can be obtained by considering the use of inclusion dependencies in queries. An inclusion dependency $R[D] \subseteq S[C]$ forms an access path between the schemas R and S. Suppose this inclusion dependency and the functional dependency $S : C \to A$ hold in a database (r, s). Then for each D-value x of r, relation s contains a unique A-value. This value is found by locating the tuples of s with the value x in the C-column, and by looking up the value in their A-columns. This value is unique, since $C \to A$ holds in s. Hence one can view R as containing an additional attribute, say B, which stores for each D-value the corresponding A-value.[1]

Example 9.7 Consider the relation schema $R(ABCD)$ and the dependencies

$$D = \{C \to D, R[AB] \subseteq R[CD], R[BA] \subseteq R[CD], R[B] \subseteq R[A]\},$$

and the single dependency $d = R[AB] \subseteq R[BA]$. Now one can show that d cannot be derived from D without using FI3. However, the dependency d holds in every database satisfying D, and d can also be derived from D using all the axioms. □

---

[1] Actually the soundness of the axiom would be preserved even without the assumption that a functional dependency holds in the upper schema. However, without the functional dependency axiom FI3 cannot be applied in proving the equivalence of any two attributes.

The axiomatization consisting of axioms F1–F4, I1–I4, and FI1–FI3 is sound and complete for the class of dependencies consisting of functional and inclusion dependencies. Some indication of the proof is given in Chapter 10. Thus for a set D of functional and inclusion dependencies and a single dependency d we have $D \models d$ if and only if $D \vdash d$ using this axiomatization. However, the implication problem (given D and d, decide if $D \models d$) is algorithmically unsolvable. The complete axiomatization cannot be used to solve this problem, since the derivation of d from D can be arbitrarily long.

Exercises

Exercise 9.1 Consider the set F containing the functional dependencies

$$ABC \rightarrow E,$$
$$DB \rightarrow A,$$
$$IC \rightarrow B.$$

Derive from F the dependency $ICD \rightarrow E$.

Exercise 9.2 Prove Lemma 9.1.

Exercise 9.3 Prove Lemma 9.2.

Exercise 9.4 We saw in Chapter 7 that functional and inclusion dependencies can be expressed as statements in the first-order predicate calculus. Why do we need separate axiomatizations for dependencies?

Exercise 9.5 ** Assume a class of dependencies has a sound and complete axiomatization with a recursive set of axioms. Show that the implication problem is recursively enumerable.

Exercise 9.6 ** Show that the relation '$D \not\models_f d$' is recursively enumerable.

Exercise 9.7 ** Show that if a class of dependencies has a sound and complete axiomatization and if finite and unrestricted implication coincide, the implication problem is solvable.

Exercise 9.8 Prove that for the dependency set D and the dependency d given in Example 9.7 we have $D \not\models d$.

Exercise 9.9 Show that for the set D and dependency d in Example 9.7 we cannot derive d from D without using axiom FI3. Show how to derive d from D using axiom FI3.

Exercise 9.10 Show that axiom I4 is sound. That is, if $R[AB] \subseteq S[CC]$ and d hold in a database $\mathbf{r}$ and d contains an occurrence of A of the form $R[\ldots, A, \ldots]$, then d' holds in $\mathbf{r}$, where d' is a dependency obtained from d by substituting B for A in one or more occurrences of A as an attribute of the schema R.

Exercise 9.11 Show that the following analogue of I4 can be derived from the axiomatization of functional and inclusion dependencies: if $R[AB] \subseteq S[CC]$ and $R : X \rightarrow Y$ hold in a database $\mathbf{r}$, then $R : X' \rightarrow Y'$ holds in $\mathbf{r}$, where X' and Y' are obtained from X and Y by substituting B for A in one or more occurrences of A.

Exercise 9.12
Consider the schemas $R(A', B', E', F', G')$ and $S(A, B, H, E, F)$, and the dependency set D that consists of the following dependencies:

$R[A'B'] \subseteq S[AB]$,
$R[A'E'F'] \subseteq S[AEF]$,
$R[B'E'G'] \subseteq S[BEF]$,
$S : A \rightarrow H$,
$S : B \rightarrow H$, and
$S : EH \rightarrow F$.

Prove that (i) $D \models R[F'G'] \subseteq S[FF]$, (ii) $R[F'G'] \subseteq S[FF]$ cannot be derived from D without using axiom FI3, and (iii) $R[F'G'] \subseteq S[FF]$ can be derived from D using axiom FI3.

Exercise 9.13 Show that for any set D of functional and inclusion dependencies there exists a database $\mathbf{r}$ with nonempty relations such that $\mathbf{r} \models D$.

Hint. The exercise is easy.

Exercise 9.14 Consider cardinality constraints of the form $R[X] \leq c$, where c is a constant. Investigate their properties and their interaction with functional and inclusion dependencies.

Exercise 9.15 Suppose $R[X] \subseteq S[Y]$ holds. We saw in axiom FI1 that the functional dependencies holding in $S[Y]$ hold also in $R[X]$. Generalize this observation: what kind of dependencies between the attributes of Y are reflected to attributes in X?

Bibliographic notes

The axiomatization of functional dependencies was given by Armstrong [Arm74]; the formulation above is the one used by several authors, including Ullman [Ull88].

The axiom system for inclusion dependencies was essentially suggested by Casanova, Fagin, and Papadimitriou [CFP84]. They did not include the last rule handling multiple occurrences of the same attribute. It was introduced by Mitchell [Mit83a].

The axiomatization of functional and inclusion dependencies was given by Mitchell [Mit83a]. Example 9.7 is also from [Mit83a].

Chapter 10

Algorithms for Design Problems

Integrity constraints can be used to define the properties of a good database schema. The previous chapter showed how the relationships of integrity constraints can be characterized by giving sound and complete axiomatizations. Our goal is to obtain methods and tools for producing schemas with certain properties. While a sound and complete axiomatization gives an exact characterization of the implications of a set of integrity constraints, the characterization is hard to use, since it is nonconstructive. This chapter shows how sets of constraints can be analyzed and manipulated. The methods are heavily based on the understanding of the dependency classes provided by the axiomatizations.

Since functional and inclusion dependencies are natural classes of dependencies, and since using the ER-model leads naturally to these types of integrity constraints, we concentrate on some fundamental algorithms for functional and inclusion dependencies.

We present an algorithm for the implication problem of functional dependencies in Section 10.1. In Section 10.2 we show how it can be implemented to operate in linear time. The main idea of the fast implementation is used in several other areas of computer science; related problems are described in the exercises. Section 10.3 considers different types of covers for sets of functional dependencies. These concepts are used in producing schemas in normal form.

Section 10.4 considers the problem of computing the projection of a dependency set; this is a fairly difficult problem, but it has to be solved in some phases of database design.

Section 10.5 defines the chase concept, which is a way of modifying a database so that it satisfies a given set of dependencies. The chase will be used heavily in the sequel.

Normal forms were defined in Chapter 8. In Section 10.6 we consider the complexity of deciding whether a given schema is in third normal form or in Boyce-Codd normal form. Section 10.7 gives an algorithm for testing whether a database schema is lossless. Section 10.8 proves the completeness of the axiomatization of inclusion dependencies using the chase concept. Section 10.9 lists several results about the complexity of the implication problem for various subclasses of functional and inclusion dependencies. The implication problems turn out to be quite hard.

We saw in Chapter 9 that functional and inclusion dependencies can in general have fairly complicated interaction. Section 10.10 shows, however, that in the situations arising in database design functional and inclusion dependencies do not have interaction.

10.1 Computing closures of attribute sets

Let R be a relation schema and F a set of functional dependencies. For an attribute set $X \subseteq R$ the closure X^+ was defined to be the set

$$\{A \in R \mid F \vdash X \to A\}.$$

By the soundness and completeness of the axiomatization of functional dependencies this is equivalently

$$\{A \in R \mid F \models X \to A\}.$$

Next we give an algorithm for computing X^+.

Algorithm 10.1 Computation of the closure of a set of attributes.
Input. A set R of attributes, a set F of functional dependencies over R, and a set $X \subseteq R$.
Output. The closure X^+ of X with respect to F.
Method. Compute sets of attributes $X_0, X_1, \ldots$ as follows:

1. $X_0 = X$.

2. For $i = 0, 1, 2, \ldots$ compute

$$X_{i+1} = X_i \cup \{A \mid \text{for some } Y \to Z \in F \text{ we have} \\ Y \subseteq X_i \text{ and } A \in Z\}.$$

The iteration stops when $X_{i+1} = X_i$. The output is X_i. □

Example 10.1 Let $R = ABCDEGHI$ and $F = \{CE \rightarrow ACH, BC \rightarrow AD, ACH \rightarrow ADG, ADG \rightarrow GI\}$. The closure of BCE is computed as follows.

1. $X_0 = BCE$;

2. $X_1 = BCE \cup ACH \cup AD = ABCDEH$;

3. $X_2 = ABCDEH \cup ACH \cup AD \cup ADG = ABCDEGH$;

4. $X_3 = ABCDEGH \cup GI = ABCDEGHI = R$.

Then the iteration stops, and thus $(BCE)^+ = R$, and BCE is a superkey.
$\square$

Theorem 10.1 Algorithm 10.1 computes X^+ correctly.

Proof. The algorithm stops after at most $|R|$ iterations, since it computes a finite set and the iteration terminates after the set does not grow any more. Denote by W the result of the algorithm. We show that $W \subseteq X^+$ and $X^+ \subseteq W$.

To prove $W \subseteq X^+$ it suffices to show by induction that $X_i \subseteq X^+$ for all i. For $i = 0$ this is immediate. Assume then $X_i \subseteq X^+$ and let $A \in X_{i+1} \setminus X_i$. Then for some $Y \rightarrow Z \in F$ we have $Y \subseteq X_i$ and $A \in Z$. By the induction assumption $X \rightarrow Y$ can be derived from F; hence $X \rightarrow Z$ can be derived (by F3) and $X \rightarrow A$ can be derived (by F1 and F3). This means that $A \in X^+$.

Next we show that $X^+ \subseteq W$. Define a two-tuple relation $r = \{t, t'\}$ by letting $t[A] = t'[A]$ for all $A \in W$ and $t[B] \neq t'[B]$ for all $B \in R \setminus W$. We shall show that $r \models F$. Then, let C be an arbitrary element of X^+. Since we have $F \models X \rightarrow C$ by completeness, we get $r \models X \rightarrow C$. As $X \subseteq W$, we must have $t[C] = t'[C]$ and hence $C \in W$. Thus it remains for us to prove that $r \models F$.

Let $Y \rightarrow Z$ be an arbitrary dependency of F. If $Y \not\subseteq W$, then $t[Y] \neq t'[Y]$, and the dependency holds vacuously. If $Y \subseteq W$, we have $Z \subseteq W$, since the iteration in the algorithm terminated at W. But $Z \subseteq W$ implies $t[Z] = t'[Z]$, and the dependency holds in r. $\square$

One may wonder why it is sufficient to consider a small two-tuple relation r in the proof of Theorem 10.1. The reason is that r is not used as a representative of an arbitrary relation. Rather, it is explicitly constructed so that it in some sense corresponds to the result of the algorithm for computing X^+ (where X, in turn, may be arbitrary). Thus the relation serves only as a technical tool that helps in the proof. Because the structure of the relation is known, it allows us to draw conclusions about the connection between semantic implication and the result of the algorithm.

A similar construction was used to prove the completeness of the ax-iomatization of functional dependencies (Theorem 9.2). We shall later see yet another application of the same technique in the proof of Theorem 10.9.

10.2   Linear-time algorithm for closures

Consider now a naive implementation of Algorithm 10.1. The iteration is performed at most $|R|$ times. Each iteration scans through all the dependencies $Y \rightarrow Z$ once, and checks for each whether $Y \subseteq X_i$. Thus the time taken is

$$O(|R||F||R|) = O(|R|^2|F|).$$

This is not the best possible implementation of the algorithm; it repeat-edly performs the tests $Y \subseteq X_i$ from scratch, even though X_i changes only slightly from one iteration into another. The algorithm can be im-plemented to run in time $O(\|F\|)$, where $\|F\|$ is the number of attributes appearing in F (with repetitions counted), that is, the sum of the lengths of the dependencies in F.

This speed-up is achieved as follows. Maintain for each dependency $f = Y \rightarrow Z$ of F a counter $\text{count}(f)$ of the number of attributes of Y that are not in X_i. Also, for each attribute A build a list $L(A)$ of the dependencies in F where A occurs on the left-hand side.

When an attribute A is added to X_i, scan through the list $L(A)$ and decrement the counter $\text{count}(f)$ for each dependency in the list. When the count for $Y \rightarrow Z$ is 0, we have $Y \subseteq X_i$, and attributes in Z can be added to X_{i+1}.

In more detail, the algorithm is as follows.

Algorithm 10.2 Fast computation of the closure of a set of attributes.
Input. A set R of attributes, a set F of functional dependencies over R, and a set $X \subseteq R$.
Output. The closure X^+ of X with respect to F.
Method. Compute the set CL by the following algorithm. When the computation stops, $CL = X^+$.

1.   unmark all members of R;
2.   **for** each $f = Y \rightarrow Z \in F$ **do**
3. $\text{count}(f) := |Y|$;
4.   **for** each $A \in Y$ **do**
5.   add f to the list $L(A)$;
6.   **od**;
7.   **od**;

8. $CL := X$;

9.   **while** CL contains an unmarked element A **do**

10.   mark A;

11.   **for** each $f \in L(A)$ **do**

12. $\text{count}(f) := \text{count}(f) - 1$;

13.   **if** $\text{count}(f) = 0$ **then**

14.   let $f = Y \to Z$;

15. $CL := CL \cup Z$;

16.   **fi**;

17.   **od**;

18. **od**;   □

Theorem 10.2 Algorithm 10.2 computes X^+ correctly.

Proof. The algorithm halts for all inputs, since attributes are never unmarked after they have been marked, and the number of attributes is finite.

Consider the following conditions:

1. All marked elements are in CL.

2. $CL \subseteq X^+$.

3. For all $f = Y \to Z \in F$ we have
   $\text{count}(f) = |\{A \in Y \mid A \text{ not marked }\}|$.

Assume these conditions hold at the end of the algorithm. Then all elements of CL are marked, and $CL \subseteq X^+$. To prove that $CL = X^+$, it remains to show that $X^+ \subseteq CL$. Suppose this is not true. Then X^+ contains an attribute A that does not belong to CL. Consider the derivation of $X \to A$. The correctness of Algorithm 10.1 implies that the derivation can be organized so that it consists only of applications of axioms F1 and F3, where F3 is always applied to the previous dependency in the derivation and to a dependency in F. Let $X \to Z$ be the first dependency in the derivation such that the left-hand side of the dependency is X and $Z \not\subseteq CL$. Then $X \to Z$ has been derived by axiom F3 from dependencies $X \to Y$ and $Y \to Z$, where $Y \to Z \in F$. Because $X \to Z$ is the first dependency with $Z \not\subseteq CL$, we have $Y \subseteq CL$. Therefore all attributes in Y are marked, and $\text{count}(Y \to Z) = 0$. But then the Z attributes are added to CL on line 15 of the algorithm, contradicting the assumption that $Z \not\subseteq CL$. Thus we have proved that $X^+ \subseteq CL$.

Next we show that the invariant holds at every iteration. The first condition is clear, since only elements in CL are ever marked. Condition 2 holds in the first iteration, since $CL = X \subseteq X^+$. For subsequent iterations, we have to show that an element B added to CL belongs to X^+. In this case $B \in Z \setminus CL$ for some dependency $f = Y \to Z \in F$

such that $\text{count}(f) = 0$. This means that all elements of Y are marked, and hence $Y \subseteq CL$. Since $CL \subseteq X^+$, we have $Y \subseteq X^+$, and therefore $B \in Z \subseteq X^+$.

Condition 3 holds in the first iteration by the initialization of the counts. Whenever an attribute is marked, we update the counts accordingly, and thus condition 3 is preserved. $\qquad\square$

Theorem 10.3 Algorithm 10.2 computes X^+ in time $O(|R| + \|F\|)$.

Proof. The initialization takes time $O(|R| + \|F\|)$. To analyze the while loop, we first note that each element is marked only once. Altogether, the counts are decremented at most $\|F\|$ times. The innermost loop goes through all the right-hand sides of dependencies once, and once more the time needed is $O(\|F\|)$. $\qquad\square$

Recall that the implication problem for functional dependencies is as follows: given a set F of dependencies and a dependency $Y \to Z$, determine whether $F \models Y \to Z$. By the above result, this problem is solvable in time $O(|R| + \|F\|)$.

Since in most cases $|R| < \|F\|$, we often say that the running time of the fast algorithm for closure computation is $O(\|F\|)$.

Algorithm 10.2 occurs in different contexts in computer science. The exercises list several of its applications and predecessors.

10.3   Covers for sets of dependencies

Given sets of functional dependencies F and G, recall that F is a *cover* of G if $F \models G$ and $G \models F$, that is, if the dependency sets hold in exactly the same databases. We also say that F and G are *equivalent*. Equivalent sets are equally expressive, but their size and intuitiveness can differ.

Example 10.2 The set

$$F = \{A \to BC, B \to AD, CD \to E, E \to CD\}$$

and the set

$$G = \{A \to BE, B \to A, CD \to E, E \to CD\}$$

are equivalent. To prove this, we need to show that $F \models G$ and $G \models F$. For those dependencies that belong to both sets this is obvious. The nontrivial cases are showing that $F \models A \to E$ and $G \models \{A \to C, B \to D\}$. This is an easy exercise using the axiomatization of functional dependencies. $\qquad\square$

In general, testing whether F and G are equivalent can be done by testing for every $X \rightarrow Y \in F$ whether $G \models X \rightarrow Y$ and vice versa. Using Algorithm 10.2, the time needed is $O(|F|\|G\| + |G|\|F\|)$.

A dependency set G is *nonredundant*, if for all $d \in G$ we have $G \backslash \{d\} \not\models d$. A nonredundant set G equivalent to F is a *nonredundant cover* of F. Such a set can be found in time $O(|F|\|F\|)$.

Algorithm 10.3 Computing a nonredundant cover.
Input. A schema R and a set F of functional dependencies over R.
Output. A nonredundant set G equivalent to F.
Method.

1. $G := F$;
2.   **for** each $f \in G$ **do**
3.   **if** $G \backslash \{f\} \vdash f$ **then**
4. $G := G \backslash \{f\}$;
5.   **fi**;
6.   **od**;   □

A dependency set G is *minimum*, if there does not exist a set F such that F is a cover of G and $|F| < |G|$. That is, a minimum set contains the smallest possible number of dependencies. A minimum cover is necessarily nonredundant, but the converse does not hold: for example, $\{A \rightarrow B, A \rightarrow C\}$ is nonredundant, but not minimum.

Several other classes of covers have been introduced. A set G is *optimum*, if there does not exist an equivalent set F with $\|F\| < \|G\|$. Thus the length of G is as small as possible. The set G is *L-minimum*, if for every $X \rightarrow Y$ in G and for all $X' \subset X$ we have $G \not\vdash X' \rightarrow Y$. A *canonical cover* is an L-minimum cover such that the right-hand side of each dependency consists of just one attribute. Further, G is *LR-minimum*, if it is L-minimum and if for every $X \rightarrow Y$ and for all $Y' \subset Y$ we have that the set $(G \backslash \{X \rightarrow Y\}) \cup \{X \rightarrow Y'\}$ is not equivalent to G. The left-hand sides of an L-minimum set do not contain any unnecessary attributes, and for an LR-minimum set this holds also for the right-hand sides.

As an example of an algorithm for forming covers of functional dependencies, we consider the problem of computing a nonredundant L-minimum cover.

Algorithm 10.4 Computing a nonredundant L-minimum cover.
Input. A schema R and a set F of functional dependencies over R.
Output. A nonredundant L-minimum set G equivalent to F.
Method. Compute first a nonredundant cover G for F. Then modify the dependencies of G so that they are L-minimum, as follows.

```
1.    for all X → Y ∈ G do
2.        Z := X;
3.        for all A ∈ Z do
4.            if G ⊢ Z \ {A} → Y then
5.                Z := Z \ {A};
6.            fi;
7.        od;
8.        G := (G \ {X → Y}) ∪ {Z → Y};
9.    od;                                                    □
```

The complexity of finding different types of covers is considered in the exercises.

10.4   Projection of functional dependencies

Suppose we are given a set F of functional dependencies over a schema R and a subset $X \subseteq R$. This set X can, for example, be a new schema. How do we compute the set of functional dependencies among the attributes of X implied by F? This turns out to be a computationally difficult problem. It can be avoided in the design algorithms; nevertheless, even if the algorithms do not need this information, it may be very useful to the database designer. Therefore the problem is worth considering from the algorithmic viewpoint.

Recall from Section 7.5 (page 98) that the projection of a dependency set was defined to be

$$F[X] = \{Y \to Z \mid F \models Y \to Z \wedge YZ \subseteq X\}.$$

We want to compute a cover for this set.

Example 10.3 Let the schema be $R(ABC)$ and consider the functional dependencies $F = \{A \to B, B \to C, C \to A\}$. Then $F[AB] \equiv \{A \to B, B \to A\}$ and $F[AC] \equiv \{A \to C, C \to A\}$.   □

Example 10.3 shows that for computing projections it is not sufficient just to eliminate some of the dependencies in the original set; dependencies with new left-hand sides may need to be introduced. The trivial method for computing $F[X]$ is to consider each possible left-hand side, as follows.

Algorithm 10.5 Computation of the projection of a set of functional dependencies.

Input. A set F of functional dependencies over R and a subset $X \subseteq R$.
Output. A cover for $F[X]$.
Method.

1.   **for** each $Y \subseteq X$ **do**
2. $Z := Y_F^+$;
3.   output $Y \to Z \cap X$;
4.   **od**;   □

The complexity of the trivial algorithm is $O(\|F\|2^{|X|})$, since X has $2^{|X|}$ subsets and for each we perform one computation of the closure, using time $O(\|F\|)$.

The trivial algorithm is somewhat unsatisfactory. However, it seems difficult to give an improvement resulting in a superior worst-case time bound. The following algorithm, however, seems to operate fast in practical situations.

Algorithm 10.6 Faster computation of the projection of a set of functional dependencies.
Input. A set F of functional dependencies over R and a subset $X \subseteq R$.
Output. A cover for $F[X]$.
Method.

1. $G :=$ canonical cover of F;
2. $W := R \setminus X$;
3.   **while** $W \neq \emptyset$ **do**
4.   let $A \in W$ be arbitrary;
5. $W := W \setminus \{A\}$;
6. $H := \{ZY \to B \mid$ there exist dependencies
7. $ZA \to B$ and $Y \to A$ in $G\}$;
8.   remove trivial dependencies from H;
9. $G := G \setminus \{f \in G \mid A$ occurs in $f\} \cup H$;
10.   **od**;
11.   output G;   □

Example 10.4 Consider the set

$$F = \{C \to D, E \to J, I \to J, J \to K, K \to J, DK \to L\}.$$

Suppose Algorithm 10.6 is applied to F to compute $F[CEIL]$. Then $G = F$ and initially $W = DJK$. Assuming that the attributes in W are handled in alphabetical order, we first choose $A = D$. The only possible choices in the definition of H are the dependencies $DK \to L$ and $C \to D$, producing $H = \{CK \to L\}$. The dependencies containing D are

removed from G, and after the first execution of the while loop we have
$G = \{E \rightarrow J, I \rightarrow J, J \rightarrow K, K \rightarrow J, CK \rightarrow L\}$.

Next we have $A = J$. Now H gets three dependencies: $\{E \rightarrow K, I \rightarrow K, K \rightarrow K\}$. Since $K \rightarrow K$ is trivial, the four dependencies containing J are replaced by the remaining two dependencies in H, and we have $G = \{E \rightarrow K, I \rightarrow K, CK \rightarrow L\}$.

Finally $A = K$. This produces two dependencies into H, and since all dependencies of G contain K, the set G is essentially replaced by H. Therefore the final iteration produces the set $G = \{CE \rightarrow L, CI \rightarrow L\}$.

□

Theorem 10.4 Algorithm 10.6 works correctly.

Proof. The procedure stops after $|R \setminus W|$ iterations. For the correctness of the output, consider the invariant

> G is a set of dependencies over attributes WX and $G \equiv F[WX]$.

If the invariant holds at the end of the while loop in the algorithm, the result of the algorithm is correct. The invariant holds trivially at the first iteration. Consider an arbitrary iteration of the while loop. Denote by G_0 the set G before the iteration and by G_1 the set G after the iteration. Then

$$G_1 = G_0 \setminus \{f \in G \mid A \text{ occurs in } f\} \cup H.$$

The induction assumption says that $G_0 \equiv F[WX]$, and we have to show that $G_1 \equiv F[WX \setminus \{A\}]$.

Let $f \in G_1$. If $f \in G_0$, then by the induction assumption $F[WX] \models f$. If $f \notin G_0$, then f has been added to H because of two dependencies f_1 and f_2 in G_0. The induction assumption asserts that $F[WX] \models \{f_1, f_2\}$, and axiom F3 implies that again $F[WX] \models f$. Since A does not occur in f, we have $F[WX \setminus \{A\}] \models f$. Thus

$$F[WX \setminus \{A\}] \models G_1.$$

For the converse, assume $V \rightarrow C$ is an arbitrary dependency from $F[WX \setminus \{A\}]$. Since $F[WX \setminus \{A\}] \subseteq F[WX]$, we have by the induction assumption that $G_0 \models V \rightarrow C$. Consider the computation of $V_{G_0}^+$ using Algorithm 10.1; the algorithm produces a sequence

$$V = V_0 \subseteq V_1 \subseteq \cdots \subseteq V_k.$$

We show by induction on i that $V_i \cap WX \subseteq V_{G_1}^+$. For $i = 0$ the claim is clear. Assume then $V_i \cap WX \subseteq V_{G_1}^+$, and let $f \in G_0$ be the dependency applied to obtain V_{i+1} from V_i. If $f \in G_0$, the claim holds immediately.

If f contains A on the right-hand side, the same is true. So assume f has the form $ZA \rightarrow B$. Then $ZA \subseteq V_i$. Since $A \in V_i$, some nontrivial dependency of the form $Y \rightarrow A$ must have been applied to get V_i. Thus $Y \subseteq V_{i-1}$. By the induction assumption $Y \subseteq V_{G_1}^+$. Since f can be applied, $ZA \subseteq V_i$ and $Z \subseteq V_{G_1}^+$. The dependency $ZY \rightarrow B$ is in H and therefore also in G_1, and hence $B \in V_{G_1}^+$. □

Exercise 10.18 gives a method that can be used to further improve the efficiency of Algorithm 10.6.

10.5   The chase procedure

Suppose we are given a set F of functional dependencies over R, and a relation r, also over R. Assume r does not satisfy all the dependencies in F. We describe a way of applying the dependencies in F to r so that the modified relation r will then satisfy F. Later, we describe a similar technique for inclusion dependencies.

The process of modifying a relation or a database to obey some constraints is known as the *chase*. It has several applications in dependency manipulation and query optimization. We use this concept extensively in this and subsequent chapters.

10.5.1   The chase for functional dependencies

We start with the formal description of the chase for functional dependencies, or *fd-chase*, for short.

Algorithm 10.7 The chase for functional dependencies.
Input. A set F of functional dependencies and a relation r, both over a schema R.
Output. A modified relation r that satisfies F.
Method. Apply the following rule as long as possible.
FD rule: If F contains a dependency $X \rightarrow Y$ and if for some rows $t, t' \in r$ it holds that $t[X] = t'[X]$ but $t[A] \neq t'[A]$ for some $A \in Y$, change each occurrence of the larger of the values $t[A]$ and $t'[A]$ to be equal to the smaller one.[1] □

We denote by chase(r, F) the result of the chase of r by F. The order of applying different dependencies was not specified in the algorithm. Assuming r and F are ordered, we can state that the rule is applied first to the earliest possible rows t and t', and with the first applicable

---

[1]We assume that the attribute values in a relation can be ordered according to some criterion.

dependency from F. The order of the applications turns out to have no effect, however.

Similarly, the condition that larger values are replaced by smaller values is not essential. Later, however, we shall apply the chase to relations that contain variables in addition to the normal constant values. Variables are treated as being larger values than any of the constants; therefore the ordering is important in order to replace variables by constants, when the constant value is implied by the functional dependencies.

It is also important to note that when a value is replaced by another one, this is done everywhere in the relation – even in different columns. This simplifies some proofs, although it has the seemingly unpleasant effect of modifying r more than necessary. In the next section we shall extend the chase to work also with inclusion dependencies, and then it becomes essential that the FD rule is applied globally. An example of this can be found in Example 10.6.

Example 10.5 Consider the schema R and the dependency set F from Example 10.1 (page 149). Let r be the following relation.

A	B	C	D	E	G	H	I
1	2	3	4	5	6	7	8
9	2	3	12	5	14	15	16
17	18	3	20	5	22	23	24

When computing the value of chase(r, F), we first consider the two top rows. The first applicable dependency is $CE \rightarrow ACH$, causing the value 9 to be changed to 1 and the value 15 to 7. Then we apply the dependency $BC \rightarrow AD$, causing the change of the value 12 to 4. After that, the dependency $ACH \rightarrow ADG$ can be applied, and it causes the change of 14 to 6. Now the relation looks as follows:

A	B	C	D	E	G	H	I
1	2	3	4	5	6	7	8
1	2	3	4	5	6	7	16
17	18	3	20	5	22	23	24

Still one dependency, $ADG \rightarrow GI$, can be applied to the two first rows; it causes the change of 16 to 8. This makes the two first rows identical, and we are left with a two-tuple relation. To it we can again apply the dependency $CE \rightarrow ACH$, causing the change of 17 to 1 and of 23 to 7. Again, we can apply $ACH \rightarrow ADG$, causing the change of 20 to 4 and of 22 to 6. Applying the dependency $ADG \rightarrow GI$ forces us to change 24 to 8. After this, no further changes have to be made, and thus the chase stops. The result is shown below.

A	B	C	D	E	G	H	I
1	2	3	4	5	6	7	8
1	18	3	4	5	6	7	8

□

Theorem 10.5 (i) The fd-chase stops for all dependency sets F and all finite relations r. (ii) The result chase(r, F) satisfies the dependencies of F.

Proof. (i) Each application of the FD rule reduces the number of different values occurring in the relation. Since the original relation has only a finite number of different values, the process must terminate.

(ii) If there were a dependency $X \rightarrow Y \in F$ not satisfied by chase(r, F), the FD rule could still be applied. □

The chase procedure can be used to compute the closure of a set of attributes. Suppose we are given a set of functional dependencies F over R and a subset $X \subseteq R$, and we want to compute the closure of X. This can be done by constructing a two-row relation $r_X = \{t, t'\}$, where no value appears in two different columns, $t[X] = t'[X]$, and $t[A] \neq t'[A]$ for all $A \in R \setminus X$. Then perform the chase on r_X. The result has still two rows (unless X is a superkey of R). Assume the procedure takes k applications of the FD rule, and denote by X_i the set of attributes for which the rows of the relation agree after i applications of the rule. Thus $X_0 = X$, and for all i we have $X_i \subseteq X_{i+1}$. One can easily show by induction that $X \rightarrow X_i$ follows from F for each i. Hence we have $X_i \subseteq X^+$ for all i.

The relation chase(r, F) satisfies the dependencies in F, but violates each dependency $X \rightarrow B$, where $B \in R \setminus X_k$. This means $R \setminus X_k \subseteq R \setminus X^+$, and hence $X^+ \subseteq X_k$. Thus we have shown $X_k = X^+$.

If X is a superkey of R, at some point during the chase the two rows become equal and we get a relation with a single row. This tells us that $X^+ = R$.

10.5.2   The chase for functional and inclusion dependencies

We now turn to the definition of the chase for functional and inclusion dependencies. We need another rule for handling inclusion dependencies; they can force us to add new rows to the database.

Algorithm 10.8 The chase for functional and inclusion dependencies.
Input. A database schema $(\mathbf{R}, F, I)$ where $\mathbf{R} = (R_1, \dots, R_k)$, and a database $\mathbf{r}$ over $\mathbf{R}$.
Output. A modified database $\mathbf{r}$.
Method. Apply the following rules as long as possible.

IND rule: If I contains a dependency $R_i[X] \subseteq R_j[Y]$ and for some row $t \in r_i$ it holds that $t[X] \notin r_j[Y]$, then add row s to r_j, where $s[Y] = t[X]$ and the other values of s are values from $Dom(R_j)$ greater than all current values occurring in $\mathbf{r}$.

FD rule: If F contains a dependency $R_i : X \to Y$ and for some rows $t, t' \in r$ it holds that $t[X] = t'[X]$ but $t[A] \neq t'[A]$ for some $A \in Y$, change each occurrence (in any of the relations of $\mathbf{r}$) of the larger of the values $t[A]$ and $t'[A]$ to be equal to the smaller one. □

The result of the chase of $\mathbf{r}$ by F and I is denoted by chase$(\mathbf{r}, F, I)$. As described above, the chase is a nondeterministic procedure. It can be made deterministic by specifying the order of application of rules.

When tuple s is constructed in the IND rule, the values in $t[X]$ are padded with new, unused values to complete the tuple. The reason for using such values is that we want the new tuple to interfere as little as possible with the existing tuples: the new tuple should not unnecessarily become a target for the FD rule.

Example 10.6 Let $R(A, B, C)$ and $S(D, E)$ be relation schemas, and suppose the dependencies $I = \{R[A, B] \subseteq S[D, E]\}$ and $F = \{D \to E\}$ hold. Consider the following database:

A	B	C
1	3	5
1	3	6
2	3	6
2	4	6

r

D	E
7	10
8	11
9	11

s

If we perform the chase, the IND rule requires that we add the tuples $(1, 3)$, $(2, 3)$, and $(2, 4)$ to s. But then the functional dependency $S : D \to E$ is violated, so the value 4 has to be changed everywhere to 3. Note the importance of making global changes when the FD rule is applied. If only values in column E were changed, relation r would remain intact, and the IND rule could be applied again. The process would never terminate. □

Theorem 10.6 (i) The chase for functional and inclusion dependencies stops, if the set of inclusion dependencies is noncircular. (ii) The result of the chase, chase$(\mathbf{r}, F, I)$, is a database satisfying the dependencies of $F \cup I$. □

For noncircular sets of inclusion dependencies the chase can be organized as follows.

Algorithm 10.9 Computing chase($\mathbf{r}, F, I$) for a noncircular set I.
Input. A database schema $(\mathbf{R}, F, I)$ where $\mathbf{R} = (R_1, \ldots, R_k)$, and a database $\mathbf{r}$ over $\mathbf{R}$.
Output. A modified database $\mathbf{r}$.
Method. Assume the relation schemas $R_1, \ldots, R_k$ are numbered so that if $R_i[X] \subseteq R_j[Y]$ is in I, then $i < j$. Denote the rows constructed in the application of the IND rule by pad($t[X], Y, R_j$), and denote the result of applying the FD rule to all relations r_i of $\mathbf{r}$ with dependency set F as many times as possible by chase($\mathbf{r}, F$).

```
1.     for j := 1 to k do
2.          for all Rᵢ[X] ⊆ Rⱼ[Y] ∈ I do
3.               for all t ∈ rᵢ do
4.                    if t[X] ∉ rⱼ[Y] then
5.                         rⱼ := rⱼ ∪ {pad(t[X], Y, Rⱼ)};
6.                    fi;
7.               od;
8.          od;
9.          chase(r, F);
10.    od;                                                    □
```

The functional dependency chase could also be done only once, after the outermost for loop.

10.6   Recognizing normal form schemas

Third normal form and Boyce-Codd normal form define the desired properties of individual relation schemas. How does one obtain schemas in normal form? A simple answer is that if one makes an ER-diagram and transforms it to relation schemas, the resulting schemas will be in 3NF, or in Boyce-Codd normal form, as will be shown in Chapter 11.

This is not, however, sufficient. In two-level design some integrity constraints are found only on the relational level. One has to be able to test whether a schema satisfies the desired normal form; if not, it is replaced by a collection of smaller schemas. We shall give algorithms for normalizing a relation schema R in Chapter 12.

Therefore the following decision problems are of interest. For testing the normal form properties we define two versions of the problem: one where the relation schema itself is tested, and another where a subset of the schema is tested. In the first case the set of dependencies may be used as such, whereas in the second case we may need to know which dependencies hold in the subset. This has an effect on the complexity of the problems.

PRIMALITY Given a relation schema R, a set of functional dependencies F over R, and an attribute $A \in R$, is A a prime attribute of R?

3NFTEST Given a relation schema R and a set of functional dependencies F over R, is R in third normal form with respect to F?

3NFTEST **for subschema** Given a relation schema R, a set of functional dependencies F over R, and a proper subset X of R, is X in third normal form with respect to F?

BCNFTEST Given a relation schema R and a set of functional dependencies F over R, is R in Boyce-Codd normal form with respect to F?

BCNFTEST **for subschema** Given a relation schema R, a set of functional dependencies F over R, and a proper subset X of R, is X in Boyce-Codd normal form with respect to F?

Unfortunately, most of these decision problems are computationally hard (assuming $P \neq NP$).

Theorem 10.7

(i)   PRIMALITY is NP-complete.
(ii)   3NFTEST is NP-complete.
(iii) 3NFTEST for subschema is NP-hard.
(iv)   BCNFTEST can be solved in polynomial time.
(v)   BCNFTEST for subschema is coNP-complete.

$\square$

Note in particular the difference in the complexities of 3NFTEST and BCNFTEST. Testing whether a given R is in BCNF with respect to a set of dependencies F is fast: simply check that the left-hand side of each dependency in F is a superkey of R by computing the closure of the left-hand side with respect to F. The fundamental reason for the complexity of 3NFTEST is the difficulty of deciding which attributes are prime. 3NFTEST for subschema is naturally no easier than 3NFTEST.

In BCNFTEST for subschema the complexity is essentially caused by the difficulty of computing the projection of F on X.

We should not be discouraged by Theorem 10.7. Although testing the normal form properties is computationally hard, it may still be possible to find an efficient normalization algorithm by avoiding an explicit test of the normal form properties. In fact, such algorithms do exist, as we shall see in Chapter 13. Also, the proofs of the completeness results tell something about the worst case of the problems. It is possible to develop methods that use exponential time only in pathological cases, but work quite well for the schemas occurring in practice. These will be treated in later chapters.

10.7   Testing for lossless join

Recall from Section 8.5 (page 121) that a database schema $(\mathbf{R}, F, I)$ over attribute set U has the lossless join property, if for any relation r over U satisfying F_U the equality

$$r = r[R_1] \bowtie \cdots \bowtie r[R_n]$$

holds. In this section we present an algorithm for testing whether this property holds in the case I is empty. The algorithm is (once again) based on the chase. If I is nonempty, lossless join testing is much more difficult and largely unstudied.

Functional dependencies in general make it easier for a database schema to have a lossless join: they prevent arbitrary connections from being present in the original relation. In Example 8.7 (page 122) the relation r does not satisfy any nontrivial functional dependencies. It is not surprising that if we join the two projected relations using attribute B, then to get a lossless join, B should determine at least one of A and C. Otherwise arbitrary connections between A and C are possible, and the join produces all of them, no matter whether they are present in r or not.

In general, we have the following result.

Theorem 10.8 Let $(\mathbf{R}, F, \emptyset)$ be a database schema over U, such that $\mathbf{R} = \{R_1, R_2\}$. Then $(\mathbf{R}, F, \emptyset)$ is lossless if and only if $F \models R_1 \cap R_2 \to R_1$ or $F \models R_1 \cap R_2 \to R_2$.

Proof. *If.* Assume without loss of generality that $F \models R_1 \cap R_2 \to R_1$. Let r be a relation over U and denote $s = r[R_1] \bowtie r[R_2]$. Let $t \in s$; we claim that $t \in r$.

By the definition of s, there exist tuples u and v in r such that $u[R_1] = t[R_1]$, $v[R_2] = t[R_2]$, and $u[R_1 \cap R_2] = v[R_1 \cap R_2] = t[R_1 \cap R_2]$. Because $F \models R_1 \cap R_2 \to R_1$, it follows that $u[R_1] = v[R_1]$, and therefore $t = v$.

Only if. Assuming that $R_1 \cap R_2 \not\to R_1$ and $R_1 \cap R_2 \not\to R_2$ we must show that $(\mathbf{R}, F, \emptyset)$ is lossy. Denote $X = (R_1 \cap R_2)_F^+$. Construct the following relation r over U:

X	$R_1 \setminus X$	$R_2 \setminus X$
$aa \cdots a$	$aa \cdots a$	$bb \cdots b$
$aa \cdots a$	$bb \cdots b$	$aa \cdots a$

It is easy to check that $r \models F$. Moreover, since $R_1 \cap R_2 \not\to R_1$ and $R_1 \cap R_2 \not\to R_2$, both $R_1 \setminus X$ and $R_2 \setminus X$ are nonempty. Therefore both $r[R_1]$ and $r[R_2]$ contain two tuples, and their join contains four tuples – more than r.   □

Theorem 10.8 gives a simple and efficient condition for testing the losslessness of a database schema that contains two relation schemas. What about the general case where a database schema has more than two relation schemas? One might imagine that if such a database schema is to be lossless, there has to exist some sequence of binary joins, each of which is lossless, eventually joining together all the schemas in the database. In this case Theorem 10.8 could be applied repeatedly to test the losslessness of each binary join, and the main problem would be finding a suitable order for joining the relations. However, the following example shows that this need not be the case: in some cases the join of several relations can be lossless, although the join of any two relations is lossy.

Example 10.7 Let $(\mathbf{R}, F, \emptyset)$ be a database schema over $U = ABCD$, where $\mathbf{R} = \{AB, BCD, ACD\}$ and $F = \{A \to C, B \to D\}$. Theorem 10.8 can be used to check that for any two schemas $R_1, R_2 \in \mathbf{R}$, we can find two relations r_1 and r_2 over R_1 and R_2 such that the relations satisfy $F[R_1]$ and $F[R_2]$, respectively, but their join is lossy.

Next we show that $(\mathbf{R}, F, \emptyset)$ has the lossless join property. Consider a tuple $t \in (r[AB] \bowtie r[BCD]) \bowtie r[ACD]$, where r is a relation over U such that $r \models F$. This means that there are tuples $v \in r[AB]$, $w \in r[BCD]$ and $u \in r[ACD]$ such that

(i) $v[A] = u[A] = t[A]$,
(ii) $v[B] = w[B] = t[B]$, and
(iii) $w[CD] = u[CD] = t[CD]$.

Extending the projected tuples u, v and w into corresponding tuples u', v' and w' over U, we can summarize our knowledge about these tuples with the following relation:

	A	B	C	D
t:	a	b	c	d
v':	a	b	x_1	x_2
w':	x_3	b	c	d
u':	a	x_4	c	d

Since u', v' and w' all come from the original relation r, the corresponding subrelation must satisfy F. Because $A \to C$, tuples u' and v' imply that $x_1 = c$. And because $B \to D$, tuples v' and w' imply that $x_2 = d$. Therefore v', a tuple in r, is equal to t, a tuple in the three-way join of the three projections. Since t was arbitrary, this proves the claim. □

Example 10.7 indicates that we need a general test for the losslessness of a database schema: applying Theorem 10.8 repeatedly is not sufficient. Fortunately, Example 10.7 also suggests how the general test can be carried out. Notice how the values in the tuples u', v' and w' that are known to match the values in t correspond to the attributes of the relation schemas in the database schema. This observation leads to Algorithm 10.10.

Algorithm 10.10 Testing the losslessness of a database schema.
Input. A database schema $(\mathbf{R}, F, \emptyset)$ over U, such that $\mathbf{R} = (R_1, \ldots, R_k)$.
Output. 'Yes' if $(\mathbf{R}, F, \emptyset)$ has the lossless join property, 'no' otherwise.
Method.

1. Construct a relation r over U. The relation r consists of tuples t_i, one for each R_i in $\mathbf{R}$, such that $t_i[A] = a$ if $A \in R_i$, and otherwise $t_i[A] = b_i^A$.

2. Compute chase(r, F). In changing the values in r, all b-values should be treated as greater than any a-values.

3. If chase(r, F) contains a tuple with no b-values, output 'yes', otherwise output 'no'.   □

The correctness proof of Algorithm 10.10 generalizes the arguments used in Example 10.7. We omit the details.

10.8   Completeness of axiomatizations

In this section we first show that the axiomatization of inclusion dependencies given in Chapter 9 is complete. This is the first example of a complicated proof based on a study of the chase process.

Inclusion dependencies were defined so that the attribute sequences could contain several occurrences of one attribute. This extension is needed when the interaction of functional and inclusion dependencies is considered. For the proof of completeness of the axiomatization of inclusion dependencies, we can ignore such dependencies (if they do not appear in the given set of dependencies). An inclusion dependency $R[A_1, \ldots, A_n] \subseteq S[B_1, \ldots, B_n]$ contains no *repeated attributes*, if $A_i \neq A_j$ and if $B_i \neq B_j$ for all i and j with $1 \leq i < j \leq n$.

Theorem 10.9 The axiomatization consisting of axioms I1, I2, and I3 is complete for inclusion dependencies with no repeated attributes.
   Proof. Consider a set of relation schemas $\mathbf{R} = (R_1, \ldots, R_k)$, a set I of inclusion dependencies over $\mathbf{R}$ and inclusion dependency d such that $I \models d$, and assume d and the dependencies of I contain no repeated attributes. We want to show that d can be derived from I using axioms I1, I2, and I3. Let $d = R_a[A_1, \ldots, A_n] \subseteq R_b[B_1, \ldots, B_n]$. Denote by

$\mathbf{r} = (r_1, \ldots, r_k)$ the database where all relations except r_a are empty, and r_a contains one row t, with $t[A_i] = i$ for each $i = 1, \ldots, n$ and $t[B] = 0$ for $B \notin \{A_1, \ldots, A_n\}$.

We use a modification of the chase procedure, where the rows added by the IND rule contain 0 for the attributes not in the right-hand side of the current inclusion dependency. Denote this chase by chase_0 and let $\mathbf{r}' = \text{chase}_0(\mathbf{r}, \emptyset, I)$, with $\mathbf{r}' = (r_1', \ldots, r_k')$. Note that $\mathbf{r}'$ is finite: the relations of $\mathbf{r}$ have only a finite number of possible tuples, because the modified chase procedure does not introduce any new values. Also $\mathbf{r}' \models I$.

Consider the following claim:

> If $u \in r_c'$ and for some attributes $C_1, \ldots, C_h$ of R_c we have $u[C_i] = g_i > 0$ for each $i = 1, \ldots, h$, and $g_i \neq g_j$ for $i \neq j$, then the dependency $R_a[A_{g_1}, \ldots, A_{g_h}] \subseteq R_c[C_1, \ldots, C_h]$ can be derived from I.

The theorem follows easily from this claim. Since $\mathbf{r} \subseteq \mathbf{r}'$, we have $t \in r_a$. As $\mathbf{r}' \models I$, relation r_b contains a row u such that $u[B_i] = t[A_i] = i$ for each $i = 1, \ldots, k$. By the claim d can be derived from I.

Proof of claim. We use induction on the number of rows in the database when the tuple u was inserted into the database. For the base case we have $u = t$, and as $u[C_i] = g_i$ for each $i = 1, \ldots, h$, we have $C_i = A_{g_i}$. Thus the dependency

$$R_a[A_{g_1}, \ldots, A_{g_h}] \subseteq R_c[C_1, \ldots, C_h]$$

can be deduced using axiom I1.

Assume then the claim holds for all rows inserted before u, and assume u was inserted because of a dependency

$$R_e[E_1, \ldots, E_q] \subseteq R_c[D_1, \ldots, D_q] \tag{10.1}$$

and a tuple $v \in r_e$; here $q \geq h$. For each $i = 1, \ldots, h$ we have $C_i = D_{j_i}$ for some j_i with $1 \leq j_i \leq q$, since $u[D] = 0$ for $D \in R_c \setminus \{D_1, \ldots, D_q\}$. Now for $i = 1, \ldots, h$ we have

$$0 < g_i = u[C_i] = u[D_{j_i}] = v[E_{j_i}].$$

By the induction assumption the dependency

$$R_a[A_{g_1}, \ldots, A_{g_h}] \subseteq R_e[E_{j_1}, \ldots, E_{j_h}] \tag{10.2}$$

can be derived from I. Using axiom I2, we obtain from inclusion dependency 10.1 the dependency

$$R_e[E_{j_1}, \ldots, E_{j_h}] \subseteq R_c[D_{j_1}, \ldots, D_{j_h}].$$

Applying axiom I3 to this and inclusion dependency 10.2 we get

$$R_a[A_{g_1}, \ldots, A_{g_h}] \subseteq R_e[D_{j_1}, \ldots, D_{j_h}],$$

and, remembering that $C_i = D_{j_i}$ for all $i = 1, \ldots, h$,

$$R_a[A_{g_1}, \ldots, A_{g_h}] \subseteq R_c[C_1, \ldots, C_h]. \qquad \square$$

The above is a typical proof of a completeness result. Assuming $D \models d$, one wants to show $D \vdash d$. Starting from a small database corresponding to d in some sense, the chase procedure is used to generate a database satisfying D. Since $D \models d$, the result of the chase satisfies d as well. The structure of the result is known, and the proof of d from D can be extracted from it.

The completeness proof for the axiomatization of functional and inclusion dependencies follows these lines, but it is technically more complicated. One has to consider dependencies containing more than one occurrence of an attribute, and also the new attributes introduced by axiom FI3. We omit the proof.

10.9   Complexity of implication problems ·

In this section we give some results about the complexity of the implication problems for certain subclasses of functional and inclusion dependencies. The proofs are mostly considered in the exercises.

Given a dependency set D and a dependency d, the efficiency of an algorithm for deciding whether $D \models d$ is measured in terms of the lengths of D and d. We have already obtained some results about functional dependencies in Section 10.2.

Theorem 10.10 The implication problem for sets of functional dependencies is solvable in linear time.

   Proof. In Section 10.2 we showed that the closure of an attribute set can be computed in linear time. Given a set of functional dependencies F and a functional dependency $X \to Y$, testing whether $F \models X \to Y$ can be done by computing X^+ and checking whether $Y \subseteq X^+$. The computation of the closure takes linear time. $\square$

Thus functional dependencies behave rather well computationally. For inclusion dependencies the implication problem is much harder.

Theorem 10.11 The implication problem for sets of inclusion dependencies is PSPACE-complete.

   Proof. Exercises 10.28 and 10.29. $\square$

Hence the implication problem is hard already for inclusion dependencies alone. The interaction with functional dependencies makes the problem much harder still, in fact, it is undecidable.

Theorem 10.12 The implication problem for sets of functional dependencies and inclusion dependencies is undecidable. □

Thus no algorithm can for arbitrary sets F and I of functional and inclusion dependencies decide whether $F \cup I \models d$, where d is a functional or inclusion dependency. The implication problems for inclusion dependencies seem hopeless. However, the intractability results are obtained by considering contrived dependency sets, which are extremely unlikely to occur in practice. If we consider only restricted classes of inclusion dependencies occurring in practice, the implication problems are much easier.

We start by considering the effect of noncircularity. It was one of the conditions for the set of integrity constraints required on semantical grounds. We have already seen that if circular sets of inclusion dependencies are considered, finite and infinite implication do not coincide. This is a sign that requiring noncircularity might have a good effect on the complexity of the algorithmic problems.

Theorem 10.13 The implication problem for noncircular sets of inclusion dependencies is NP-complete.
Proof. Exercise 10.30 gives some advice for proving that the problem is in NP. □

Theorem 10.14 The implication problem for functional dependencies and noncircular sets of inclusion dependencies is decidable. The problem requires exponential time.
Proof. Decidability can be proved by showing that finite and infinite implication are the same concept for such sets of dependencies. □

Most inclusion dependencies occurring in practice are unary. If one is willing to consider only such dependencies, the implication problems can be solved in polynomial time.

Theorem 10.15 (i) The implication problem for unary inclusion dependencies is solvable in linear time.

(ii) The implication problem for functional dependencies and unary inclusion dependencies is solvable in polynomial time.

(iii) The implication problem for functional dependencies and noncircular sets of unary inclusion dependencies is solvable in linear time.
Proof. Exercise 10.31. □

INCLUSION DEPENDENCIES	FUNCTIONAL DEPENDENCIES	
	none	standard
none	—	linear time
unary and noncircular	linear time	linear time
unary	linear time	polynomial time
noncircular	NP-complete	exponential time
k-ary with no repeated attributes	polynomial time	undecidable
unrestricted	PSPACE-complete	undecidable

Table 10.1 Complexity of the implication problem.

A natural generalization of unary inclusion dependencies is the class of *k-ary inclusion dependencies*, where each side of a dependency may contain at most k attributes. This restriction makes the implication problem of inclusion dependencies polynomial for fixed k.

Theorem 10.16 The implication problem for k-ary inclusion dependencies with no repeated attributes can be solved in time $O(m^k)$, where m is the number of attributes in the database.
   Proof. Exercise 10.32.   □

If functional dependencies are also present the restriction to k-ary dependencies does not help: already the implication problem for functional dependencies and binary inclusion dependencies is undecidable.

Table 10.1 summarizes the results about the complexity of the implication problem for various classes of dependencies.

10.10 Interaction of functional and inclusion dependencies

Examples 9.4 (page 141), 9.5 (page 142), and 9.7 (page 143) and the results in Section 10.9 showed that arbitrary sets of functional and inclusion dependencies can have complicated interaction which can considerably slow down the algorithms needed in database design. Here we try to find subclasses for which dependencies of different types would have no effect on each other.

Given a database schema $(\mathbf{R}, F, I)$, we say that F and I have *no interaction*, if for each functional dependency f we have

$$F \cup I \models f \text{ if and only if } F \models f$$

and for each inclusion dependency d we have

$$F \cup I \models d \text{ if and only if } I \models d.$$

That is, if F and I have no interaction, the consequences of $F \cup I$ can be obtained by considering F and I separately.[2] Of course, if I implies d, then $F \cup I$ implies d, and similarly if F implies f, then $F \cup I$ implies f. Thus to show that F and I have no interaction, one has to show that if $F \cup I$ implies something, then it is already implied by F or I. Or, in other words, we have to show that if F does not imply f, adding I does not change the situation, and similarly, if I does not imply d, neither does $F \cup I$.

Our aim in this section is to show that in the situations arising in database design, functional and inclusion dependencies have no interaction. In particular, we show that (i) if I is a noncircular set of unary inclusion dependencies, then I and an arbitrary F have no interaction, and (ii) if I is a noncircular set of key-based inclusion dependencies and F is such that all schemas of $\mathbf{R}$ are in Boyce-Codd normal form, then F and I have no interaction.

We first prove a result showing that if $\mathbf{r}$ in a very strong sense (soon to be defined formally) satisfies no nontrivial inclusion dependencies, then chase($\mathbf{r}, F, I$) satisfies exactly the dependencies implied by $F \cup I$. We need some additional concepts.

The set of *values* val(t) of tuple $t = (v_1, \ldots, v_n)$ is the set $\{v_1, \ldots, v_n\}$, for a relation r the set val(r) of its values is $\cup\{\text{val}(t) \mid t \in r\}$ and for a database $\mathbf{r}$ the set val($\mathbf{r}$) is $\cup\{\text{val}(r) \mid r \text{ is a relation of } \mathbf{r}\}$. Two databases $\mathbf{r}$ and $\mathbf{s}$ (relations r and s) are *disjoint* if val($\mathbf{r}$) $\cap$ val($\mathbf{s}$) $= \emptyset$ (val(r) $\cap$ val(s) $= \emptyset$). A database $\mathbf{r}$ has *disjoint columns*, if all relations in $\mathbf{r}$ are disjoint, and if for all relations $r \in \mathbf{r}$ and all attributes A and B we have $r[A] \cap r[B] = \emptyset$ when $A \neq B$. A *mapping* between databases $\mathbf{r}$ and $\mathbf{s}$ is a mapping $g : \text{val}(\mathbf{r}) \to \text{val}(\mathbf{s})$. It is extended to tuples by $g(t) = (g(v_1), \ldots, g(v_n))$ for $t = (v_1, \ldots, v_n)$, and to relations by $g(r) = \{g(t) \mid t \in r\}$.

Theorem 10.17 Let $(\mathbf{R}, F, I)$ be a database schema, where I is a noncircular set of inclusion dependencies and $\mathbf{R} = (R_1, \ldots, R_k)$. Let $\mathbf{r} = (r_1, \ldots, r_k)$ be a database over $\mathbf{R}$ such that $r_i \neq \emptyset$ for all $i = 1, \ldots, k$. Assume that $\mathbf{r}$ has disjoint columns. Then chase($\mathbf{r}, F, I$) satisfies an inclusion dependency d if and only if $F \cup I \models d$.

Proof. Denote chase($\mathbf{r}, F, I$) by $\mathbf{r}'$. We have $\mathbf{r}' \models F \cup I$ by Theorem 10.6.

---

[2]Here f and d must be dependencies over $\mathbf{R}$, that is, they cannot contain any auxiliary attributes produced by Axiom FI3.

It remains to show that the only inclusion dependencies that hold in $\mathbf{r}'$ are the consequences of $F \cup I$. Suppose $\mathbf{r}'$ satisfies some dependency $R_c[X] \subseteq R_e[Y]$ that is not a consequence of $F \cup I$. That is, there exists a database $\mathbf{s} = (s_1, \ldots, s_k)$ such that $\mathbf{s} \models F \cup I$ and $\mathbf{s} \not\models R_c[X] \subseteq R_e[Y]$. We can assume that $s_i \neq \emptyset$ for all $i = 1, \ldots, k$, as all functional dependencies are standard: if some relation s_i is empty, we can add a row to it with new values and then complete the database by chasing. Let $t \in s_c$ be such that $t[X] \neq u[Y]$ for all $u \in s_d$.

Choose a mapping $g : \text{val}(\mathbf{r}) \to \text{val}(\mathbf{s})$ such that $g(r_c) = \{t\}$ and that $g(r_j) \subseteq s_j$ for all $j = 1, \ldots, k$. Such a mapping g exists, since the relations r_j are disjoint and values in their different columns are different. For instance, g could collapse every relation in $\mathbf{r}$ into a single tuple.

We shall extend g to a mapping $\text{val}(\mathbf{r}') \to \text{val}(\mathbf{s})$ such that $g(r'_j) \subseteq s_j$ holds for all j. After this has been shown, the theorem is obtained as follows. Because $g(r_c) = \{t\}$, we have $g(r_c)[A] = \{t[A]\}$ for all $A \in R_c$. If new rows are added to r'_c by the IND rule, these rows can never be used together with the original rows of r_c in an application of the FD rule. This is because the inclusion dependencies are noncircular and $\mathbf{r}$ has disjoint columns. Therefore the original rows in r_c may be modified only by applications of the FD rule to two such rows. No matter what changes are made, r'_c must still contain at least one row w composed of the values in r_c; that is, $w[A] \in r_c[A]$ for all $A \in R_c$. Now

$$g(w[A]) \in g(r_c[A]) = g(r_c)[A] = \{t[A]\} \text{ for all } A \in R_c,$$

and therefore $g(w[X]) = \{t[X]\}$. Thus

$$\{t[X]\} = g(w[X]) = g(w)[X] \in g(r'_c)[X] = g(r'_c[X]).$$

Since $R_c[X] \subseteq R_e[Y]$ holds in $\mathbf{r}'$, we have

$$r'_c[X] \subseteq r'_e[Y],$$

and hence

$$g(r'_c[X]) \subseteq g(r'_e[Y]) = g(r'_e)[Y] \subseteq s_d[Y].$$

Thus we get

$$t[X] \in s_d[Y],$$

a contradiction.

It remains to show that g can indeed be extended to a mapping from $\text{val}(\mathbf{r}')$ to $\text{val}(\mathbf{s})$ so that the condition

$$g(r'_j) \subseteq s_j \tag{10.3}$$

continues to hold for all j. Consider a step in the chase that produces $\mathbf{r}'$ from $\mathbf{r}$. Assume condition 10.3 holds for all j until this step.

Suppose we apply the IND rule. Let $d = R_a[W] \subseteq R_b[V] \in I$, $u \in r_a$, and assume $u[W] \notin r_b[V]$. Then we add the row $u' = \text{pad}(u[W], V, R_b)$ to r_b (see Algorithm 10.9 (page 161)). Since by condition 10.3 $g(u) \in s_a$ and $\mathbf{s} \models d$, relation s_b contains a row v such that $g(u)[W] = v[V]$. For each new value $b = u'[B]$ introduced by pad, where $B \in R_b \setminus V$, define $g(b) = v[B]$. Then $g(u') = v \in s_b$, and 10.3 continues to hold.

Consider then an application of the FD rule. Let $u, v \in r_a$. Assume $Z \to B \in F$ and $u[Z] = v[Z]$, but $u[B] \neq v[B]$. Then the FD rule forces us to change each occurrence of, say, $v[B]$ to $u[B]$. As condition 10.3 holds before the change, the rows $g(u)$ and $g(v)$ belong to s_a. Further, $\mathbf{s} \models F$, and $g(u)[Z] = g(v)[Z]$. Thus we have $g(u)[B] = g(v)[B]$, that is, $g(u[B]) = g(v[B])$. This means that changing all the occurrences of $v[B]$ to $u[B]$ does not modify the image of $\mathbf{r}$ under g, and hence condition 10.3 continues to hold.   □

Note that a relation with disjoint columns satisfies no nontrivial inclusion dependencies. According to Theorem 10.17, the chase of such a relation satisfies only the inclusion dependencies implied by the sets of dependencies. Thus it gives a method for computing the inclusion dependencies implied by a set of functional and inclusion dependencies: one generates the chase of a database with disjoint columns, and then checks which inclusion dependencies hold in the result. However, the method can be very inefficient, since the result of the chase can be of exponential size compared to the original database.

As a corollary we also obtain a way of testing the equivalence of two sets of dependencies of the form $F \cup I$ and $F' \cup I$.

Corollary 10.1 Let $\mathbf{R}, F, I$, and $\mathbf{r}$ be as above, and let F' be a set of functional dependencies. If $\text{chase}(\mathbf{r}, F, I) = \text{chase}(\mathbf{r}, F', I)$, then the inclusion dependencies implied by $F \cup I$ are the same as those implied by $F' \cup I$. In particular, if $\text{chase}(\mathbf{r}, F, I) = \text{chase}(\mathbf{r}, \emptyset, I)$, then $F \cup I$ and I imply exactly the same inclusion dependencies.   □

We now move to the subclasses of inclusion dependencies and show that in some cases the FD rule cannot be applied in the chase.

Theorem 10.18 Let F be a set of functional dependencies, and suppose I contains only unary inclusion dependencies. Suppose the relations of $\mathbf{r}$ satisfy the dependencies of F. Then in computing $\text{chase}(\mathbf{r}, F, I)$ the FD rule is not applied and hence $\mathbf{r} \subseteq \text{chase}(\mathbf{r}, F, I)$.[3]

---

[3] That is, each relation of $\mathbf{r}$ is a subset of the corresponding relation of $\text{chase}(\mathbf{r}, F, I)$.

Proof. Assume the contrary, and consider the first application of the FD rule. As the original relations satisfied F, the application must inspect some row $u = \text{pad}(t[X], Y, R_j)$ added to r_j. Since I contains only unary dependencies, Y contains only one attribute, say B. The value $u[B]$ does not occur in r_j, since otherwise u would not be added to r_j. The values $u[C]$ for $C \neq B$ do not occur in r_j by the definition of pad. Hence u contains only values which did not previously occur in r_j, and no functional dependency can be applied to it. The original relation r_j satisfied F, so no changes are caused by it. $\square$

Theorem 10.19 Let $(\mathbf{R}, F, I)$ be a database schema such that each relation schema in $\mathbf{R}$ is in Boyce-Codd normal form. Suppose that I contains only key-based dependencies, and that the relations of $\mathbf{r}$ satisfy F. Then in computing $\text{chase}(\mathbf{r}, F, I)$ the FD rule is not applied and hence $\mathbf{r} \subseteq \text{chase}(\mathbf{r}, F, I)$.

Proof. Suppose this is not the case, and let the first application be to tuples u and u' in relation r_j. Assume first that u belonged to the original relation r_j. Then u' must have been added to r_j and is therefore of the form $\text{pad}(t'[X], Y, R_j)$ for some inclusion dependency $R_i[X] \subseteq R_j[Y]$ in I. Denote

$$\text{ag}(u, u') = \{A \in R_j \mid u[A] = u'[A]\}.$$

Then $\text{ag}(u, u')$ is a proper subset of Y, since pad produces new values for the other attributes and the row would not have been added, if a row u'' with $u''[Y] = u'[Y]$ was already in r_j. Since I is key-based, Y is a key for R_j. But as R_j is in BCNF, this means $\text{ag}(u, u')$ cannot determine functionally any attribute outside itself, so no dependency can be applied to u and u'.

If u and u' have both been added to r_j, they are of the form $u = \text{pad}(t[X], Y, R_j)$ and $u' = \text{pad}(t'[X'], Y', R_j)$. Now $\text{ag}(u, u')$ is again a proper subset of Y and Y', and hence no functional dependency can be applied to rows u and u'. $\square$

The above theorems showed that the FD rule cannot be applied in certain situations. This means that no additional functional dependencies are introduced by the chase; this observation is formulated as the following lemma.

Lemma 10.1 Let F be a set of functional dependencies and let I be a set of inclusion dependencies. Assume $F \not\models X \rightarrow Y$, and let $\mathbf{r}$ be a database satisfying F but not $X \rightarrow Y$. Suppose $\mathbf{r} \subseteq \text{chase}(\mathbf{r}, F, I)$. Then $F \cup I \not\models X \rightarrow Y$.

Proof. By Theorem 10.6 we have $\text{chase}(\mathbf{r}, F, I) \models F \cup I$. Since $\mathbf{r} \subseteq \text{chase}(\mathbf{r}, F, I)$, we have $\text{chase}(\mathbf{r}, F, I) \not\models X \rightarrow Y$. $\square$

Now we can prove the results showing that in certain cases functional and inclusion dependencies have no interaction.

Theorem 10.20 Let I be a noncircular set of unary inclusion dependencies and F a set of functional dependencies. Then F and I have no interaction.

Proof. Consider a functional dependency $X \to Y$ not implied by F, and let $\mathbf{r}$ be a database satisfying F but not $X \to Y$. By Theorem 10.18 we have $\mathbf{r} \subseteq \text{chase}(\mathbf{r}, F, I)$ and by Lemma 10.1 it follows that $F \cup I \not\models X \to Y$.

Let then $\mathbf{r}$ be a database with disjoint columns consisting of one-row relations. By Theorem 10.18 no functional dependencies are applied in computing $\text{chase}(\mathbf{r}, F, I)$ and hence $\text{chase}(\mathbf{r}, F, I) = \text{chase}(\mathbf{r}, \emptyset, I)$. By Corollary 10.1 this means that the inclusion dependencies implied by $F \cup I$ are exactly those implied by I.   □

Theorem 10.20 relies on the assumption that all functional dependencies are standard; nonstandard functional dependencies have some (very weak) interaction even with unary inclusion dependencies (see Exercise 10.36).

Theorem 10.21 Let $(\mathbf{R}, F, I)$ be a database schema such that I is a noncircular set of key-based inclusion dependencies and each relation schema in $\mathbf{R}$ is in Boyce-Codd normal form. Then F and I have no interaction.

Proof. The proof is exactly the same as in Theorem 10.20, except that instead of Theorem 10.18 we use Theorem 10.19.   □

Exercises

Exercise 10.1 Simulate the operation of Algorithm 10.2 on the input of Example 10.1.

Exercise 10.2 Let $G = (V, E)$ be a directed graph. The *reachability problem* is as follows: given a node $v \in V$, find all nodes reachable from v. Show that this problem can be solved using Algorithm 10.2 by letting $R = V$ and $F = \{A \to B \mid A, B \in R \wedge (A, B) \in E\}$. Show that the closure of $\{v\}$ contains the reachable nodes. The complexity of the algorithm is $O(|R| + \|F\|) = O(|V| + |E|)$, the familiar optimal bound.

Exercise 10.3 What kind of an algorithm does one obtain for the reachability problem by the approach in Exercise 10.2? Is it depth-first or breadth-first, or neither?

Exercise 10.4 Given a context-free grammar $G = (V, T, P, S)$, a symbol $M \in V \cup T$ is *reachable*, if M occurs in some sentential form derivable from S. Show that reachable symbols can be found by letting $R = V \cup T$ and $F = P$, and by computing the closure of the set $\{S\}$.

Exercise 10.5 A symbol M is *useful*, if M occurs in some derivation of a terminal string from S. A useful symbol is reachable. Useful symbols can be computed by first removing all non-reachable symbols from the grammar. Then let R and G be as in Exercise 10.4, and let

$$F' = \{N \to K \mid K \to N \in P\}.$$

Compute the closure of T with respect to F'. Show that the symbols belonging to this set are useful.

Exercise 10.6 ** A *propositional Horn formula* is an expression

$$A :- B_1, \ldots, B_n,$$

where $n \geq 0$. Given a collection of such formulas and a query $C_1, \ldots, C_k$, the satisfiability problem asks whether an empty resolvent can be derived from the query using the resolution rule. Show that this problem can be solved using Algorithm 10.2 by letting F consist of dependencies of the form $B_1, \ldots, B_n \to A$, and by then computing the closure of the attribute set $\emptyset$.

Exercise 10.7 Can you improve the running time of Algorithm 10.2 to $O(\|F\|)$?

Exercise 10.8 Give an optimum cover for the set

$$B_1 A \to C_1 C_2,$$
$$C_1 C_2 \to B_1 A,$$
$$B_2 A \to C_3 C_4,$$
$$C_3 C_4 \to B_2 A, \text{ and}$$
$$DC_1 C_2 C_3 C_4 \to E.$$

Exercise 10.9 Give an algorithm for checking whether for a dependency $X \to Y \in F$ there exists some set $X' \subset X$ such that $F \vdash X' \to Y$. What is the complexity of your algorithm?

Exercise 10.10 Show that Algorithm 10.4 works correctly.

Exercise 10.11 Give an algorithm for producing a canonical cover for a set F of functional dependencies. What is the complexity of your algorithm?

Exercise 10.12 Give an algorithm for producing an LR-minimum cover for a set F of functional dependencies. What is the complexity of your algorithm?

Exercise 10.13 Give an algorithm for producing an optimum cover for a set F of functional dependencies. What is the complexity of your algorithm?

Exercise 10.14 ** Show that an optimum set of functional dependencies is also minimum.

Exercise 10.15 ** Show that for any constant $c > 0$ there exists an LR-minimum set of functional dependencies F and an optimum cover G of F such that $\|F\|/\|G\| \geq c$.

Exercise 10.16 ** Show that if F is a nonredundant set of functional dependencies over R and if G is a cover of F, then $|F|/|G| \leq |R| - 1$ and $\|F\|/\|G\| \leq |R|(|R| - 1)$.

Exercise 10.17 Let

$$R = \{A_1, \ldots, A_n, B_1, \ldots, B_n, C_1, \ldots, C_n, D\},$$
$$F = \{A_i \rightarrow C_i, B_i \rightarrow C_i \mid 1 \leq i \leq n\} \cup \{C_1 \cdots C_n \rightarrow D\}, \text{ and}$$
$$X = \{A_1, \ldots, A_n, B_1, \ldots, B_n, D\}.$$

What is the size of the smallest cover for $F[X]$?

Exercise 10.18 Given $X \subseteq R$, define the *antecedents* of X, denoted by X_F^-, to be the set of all attributes of R that can be used to derive a dependency where some set of attributes determines an attribute in X. This set is defined iteratively as follows:

1. $X_0 = X$;

2. $X_{i+1} = X_i \cup \{B \mid B \in Y \text{ for some } Y \rightarrow Z \in F$
   such that $Z \cap X_i \neq \emptyset\}$.

The iteration stops after a finite number of iterations when $X_{i+1} = X_i$. The set X_i for which this holds is denoted by X_F^-. It can be shown that for computing a cover of $F[X]$ it suffices to consider only dependencies of the form $Y \rightarrow B$ such that for some Z we have $B \in Z$ and $Y \rightarrow Z \in F$, and furthermore

$$YB \subseteq X_F^+ \cap X_F^-.$$

Prove this.

Using this result a possibly large proportion of the dependencies in F can be omitted in the computation of $F[X]$.

Exercise 10.19 Show that the definition of X_F^- can be formulated as the computation of the closure of X with respect to a suitably constructed set of functional dependencies.

Exercise 10.20 How would you implement the fd-chase in an SQL-based database system? Assume that the values occurring in different columns are disjoint.

Exercise 10.21 What is the worst case complexity of the fd-chase algorithm as a function of the sizes of F and r?

Exercise 10.22 Show that in order to check whether a schema is in Boyce-Codd normal form it suffices to consider only the dependencies in the given dependency set. That is, prove that if R is a relation schema and F is a nonredundant, canonical set of dependencies over R such that R is not in BCNF, then F contains a dependency $X \to A$ such that X is not a superkey (and $A \notin X$). This in fact shows that the problem BCNFTEST for subschema can be solved in polynomial time.

Exercise 10.23 Continuing the previous exercise, show that if F is a nonredundant, canonical set of dependencies over R and R is not in third normal form, F contains a dependency $X \to A$ violating the conditions of 3NF: X is not a superkey, $A \notin X$, and A is not prime. Why does this not imply the polynomial time solvability of 3NFTEST?

Exercise 10.24 Let $(\mathbf{R}, F, \emptyset)$ be a database schema over U. Give an algorithm for deciding whether $(\mathbf{R}, F, \emptyset)$ is dependency preserving. Your algorithm should run in polynomial time with respect to $\|F\|$ and $|U|$; thus it should avoid computing the projections of F.

Exercise 10.25 Let $R = ABCDEG$ and let F be as in Exercise 8.5 (page 132). Which of the database schemas in Exercise 8.11 (page 133) are lossless?

Exercise 10.26 ** Let $\mathbf{r} = (r_1, \ldots, r_k)$ be a database over $(\mathbf{R}, \emptyset, \emptyset)$, where $\mathbf{R} = (R_1, \ldots, R_k)$. The database $\mathbf{r}$ is *join consistent* if

$$(r_1 \bowtie r_2 \bowtie \cdots \bowtie r_k)[R_i] = r_i$$

for $1 \leq i \leq k$. Show that the problem of testing a database for join consistency is NP-complete.

Exercise 10.27 Apply the proof of Theorem 10.9 to obtain a derivation of $R[BC] \subseteq R[AD]$ from the set $\{R[AB] \subseteq R[DA], R[CBA] \subseteq R[ABC]\}$ using axioms I1, I2, and I3.

Exercise 10.28 ** Show that the implication problem for inclusion dependencies is in PSPACE.

Hint. Prove that in the proof of Theorem 10.9 the existence of a row in $\mathbf{r}' = \text{chase}_0(\mathbf{r}, \emptyset, I)$ can be nondeterministically verified in polynomial space, and use Savitch's theorem.

Exercise 10.29 ** Show that the implication problem for sets of inclusion dependencies is PSPACE-hard.

Hint. Show that the PSPACE-complete problem of linear bounded automaton acceptance can be reduced to the problem of checking whether a set of inclusion dependencies implies a single inclusion dependency. The transition function of the automaton is modelled using inclusion dependencies.

Exercise 10.30 ** Show that the implication problem for noncircular sets of inclusion dependencies is in NP.

Hint. Prove that in the proof of Theorem 10.9 each row appears in $\mathbf{r}' = \text{chase}_0(\mathbf{r}, \emptyset, I)$ after a polynomial number of applications of the IND rule, given that I is a noncircular set. Thus the existence of a row in $\mathbf{r}'$ can be checked by guessing a derivation of polynomial length and then verifying the guess.

Exercise 10.31 Prove parts (i) and (iii) of Theorem 10.15.

Exercise 10.32 Prove Theorem 10.16.

Exercise 10.33 Recall that an inclusion dependency $R[X] \subseteq S[Y]$ is typed, if $X = Y$. Show that the implication problem for typed inclusion dependencies can be solved in polynomial time.

Exercise 10.34 Prove or disprove: if F is a set of functional dependencies and I is a set of typed inclusion dependencies, then F and I have no interaction.

Exercise 10.35 Give an example of a database schema $(\mathbf{R}, \emptyset, I)$, where I is a noncircular set of inclusion dependencies, and a database $\mathbf{r}$ such that $\text{chase}(\mathbf{r}, \emptyset, I)$ has exponential size compared to the sizes of $\mathbf{r}$ and I.

Exercise 10.36 What dependencies are implied by the set $\{\emptyset \rightarrow A, S[B] \subseteq R[A]\}$ over the relation schemas $R(A)$ and $S(B)$?

Bibliographic notes

The linear time algorithm for computing closures is by Beeri and Bernstein [BB79]. A basic paper for different notions of covers is Maier [Mai80], and a lot of material is covered in [Mai83]. Exercise 10.14 is also by Maier [Mai80]. Exercise 10.15 is from [MR83]. Exercise 10.16 is from [Got87b].

Algorithm 10.6 and Exercises 10.18 and 10.19 are from [Got87a]. Exercise 10.17 is from [FJT83].

The basic properties of the chase procedure are from [MMS79, ASU79]. The formulation for functional and inclusion dependencies is by Johnson and Klug [JK84]. The chase defined is actually the *R-chase* of [JK84]: only the tuples needed to satisfy an inclusion dependency are added to the relations. A thorough study of the chase can be found in [BV84b].

The book by Garey and Johnson [GJ79] is a good introduction to the complexity classes needed in Section 10.6. The complexity results of Theorem 10.7 are by Lucchesi and Osborn [LO78] (PRIMALITY), Jou and Fischer [JF82] (3NFTEST) and Beeri and Bernstein [BB79] (BCNFTEST for subschema).

The results about lossless joins are by Aho, Beeri and Ullman [ABU79]. More efficient tests for the lossless join property are given in [LD80, DST80]. Exercise 10.26 is from [HLY80].

The completeness of the axiomatization of inclusion dependencies and the PSPACE-completeness of their implication problem was shown in [CFP84], and the undecidability of the implication problem for functional and inclusion dependencies independently in [Mit83a, CV85]. Theorem 10.14 is from [CK85]. Many results for unary inclusion dependencies are given in [CKV90], where also the interaction of unary inclusion dependencies, unary functional dependencies, and domain dependencies is considered. Exercise 10.36 is also from [CKV90]. The NP-completeness for the case of noncircular sets of inclusion dependencies was proved in [CK86, Man84].

Section 10.10 follows [MR88]. Results resembling Theorems 10.19 and 10.21 can also be found in [AC91]. Exercise 10.33 is from [CV83].

Chapter 11

Mappings between ER-diagrams and Relational Database Schemas

The iterative approach to database design described in Chapter 2 creates a need for two mappings between data models: one for mapping an ER-diagram into a relational database schema, and another for mapping a relational database schema into an ER-diagram. We call the former mapping the *relational mapping*, and the latter mapping the *ER-mapping*. The previous chapters have described how the properties of relation schemas can be defined using integrity constraints, and how dependency sets can be analyzed. We now have sufficient machinery available to allow the mappings to be defined formally and their results analyzed.

This chapter is devoted to a description of the mappings. We start in Section 11.1 by describing the relational mapping; the correctness of the mapping is discussed in Section 11.2. Then in Section 11.3 we define an entity-relationship normal form (ERNF) and show that every relational database schema produced by the relational mapping is in ERNF. A weaker form of ERNF is discussed in Section 11.4; this form allows some null values. Finally, in Section 11.5 we show how every relational schema that is in ERNF can be mapped into an ER-diagram.

The entity-relationship normal form is an important concept: it completely characterizes the relational schemas that can be handled by the mappings defined in this chapter. Chapter 12 deals with the problem of transforming an arbitrary relational database schema into ERNF.

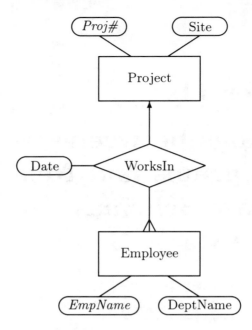

Figure 11.1   An entity-relationship diagram for employees and projects.

11.1   The relational mapping

The structure of the relational database schema obtained from an ER-diagram using the relational mapping is specified in Section 11.1.1. Assigning names to the attributes in the relational schema is a surprisingly complicated problem; the name assignment algorithm is studied in detail in Section 11.1.2.

11.1.1   Structure of the relational database schema

The following example illustrates possible choices in the mapping of ER-diagrams into relational schemas.

Example 11.1 Consider the ER-diagram shown in Figure 11.1. To avoid the name assignment problems, we abandon our normal policy of naming the ER-attributes and use unique attribute names in the ER-diagram.

It is natural to produce one relation schema for each entity type and for each relationship type. Alternatively, one could include the WorksIn information into the Employee relation schema. The rationale behind this is that since each employee works in a unique project, the information about the project can just as well be stored with the employee information. This would produce a database schema with two relation schemas:

Employee (*EmpName*, DeptName, Proj#, Date) and
Project (*Proj#*, Site).

The result is compact, but it suffers from an insertion anomaly: it is not possible to record employee information without knowing the project that the employee works in or without using null values.

If the relationship type is represented by a relation schema of its own, we get three relation schemas:

Employee (*EmpName*, DeptName),
WorksIn (*EmpName*, Proj#, Date), and
Project (*Proj#*, Site).

The anomaly has been removed, but the relational schema still does not carry all the information present in the ER-diagram. For instance, it is possible to store in the WorksIn relation a project number that is not found in the Project relation. This contradicts the ER-diagram, which states that WorksIn relationships are possible only between *existing* projects and employees.

The fix for this problem is to use more integrity constraints (in addition to the key dependencies indicated above by italicizing). The following two inclusion dependencies will do the job:

WorksIn[EmpName] $\subseteq$ Employee[EmpName] and
WorksIn[Proj#] $\subseteq$ Project[Proj#].   □

We now describe the structure of the resulting relational database schema in detail. Allowing null values can sometimes lead to simpler schemas and better performance. Therefore we give two versions of the mapping from ER-diagrams to relational schemas. The first one produces a relation schema from each object type, and the second one (described in Section 11.4) combines some relationship types with entity types. The attribute naming problem will be treated in detail later; now we just introduce notation that takes care of the naming.

The attributes that appear in an ER-diagram occur in two different contexts in the relational schema: locally, in a schema generated for the object type to which the ER-attribute is directly connected; and remotely, when the attribute is needed for identifying a relationship. These two different contexts may require that different names be used for the relational attributes, although they originate from the same ER-attribute.

We define two functions that map attribute names in the ER-diagram into attribute names in the relational schema. The first function, denoted $l(\mathcal{O}, \mathcal{A})$, produces the *local name* for attribute $\mathcal{A}$ occurring in object type $\mathcal{O}$.

The second part of the naming concerns an attribute $\mathcal{A}$ of an entity type $\mathcal{E}$ that appears outside the schema E created for $\mathcal{E}$. Then $\mathcal{A}$ must be part of the primary key of $\mathcal{E}$. There are three cases when this can happen, and for two of them we need a special *foreign name* mapping:

- In a schema E_1 created for a weak entity type $\mathcal{E}_1$, with $\mathcal{E}_1$ **isa** $\mathcal{E}$. Then $\mathcal{A}$ appears in E_1 with the same name as in E.

- In a relationship type $\mathcal{R}$, where $\mathcal{E}$ is the ith participant of $\mathcal{R}$. The name of $\mathcal{A}$ in the schema corresponding to $\mathcal{R}$ is denoted by $f(\mathcal{R}, i, \mathcal{A})$.[1]

- In a schema created for a weak entity type $\mathcal{E}_1$, with $\mathcal{E}_1$ **id** $\mathcal{E}$. The name of $\mathcal{A}$ in the schema corresponding to $\mathcal{E}_1$ is denoted by $f(\mathcal{E}_1, \mathcal{E}, \mathcal{A})$.

The local and foreign name mappings are extended to sets and sequences of attributes in the obvious way. Thus, if $\mathcal{W}$ is a set of ER-attributes of object type $\mathcal{O}$, then the set of local names for the attributes in $\mathcal{W}$ is defined as

$$l(\mathcal{O}, \mathcal{W}) = \{l(\mathcal{O}, \mathcal{A}) \mid \mathcal{A} \in \mathcal{W}\}.$$

Similarly, sets of foreign names are denoted by $f(\mathcal{R}, i, \mathcal{W})$ and $f(\mathcal{E}, \mathcal{E}', \mathcal{W})$. In particular, the set of local names of all ER-attributes of an object type $\mathcal{O}$ is denoted by $l(\mathcal{O}, \mathcal{O})$. An expression like $l(\mathcal{O}, \mathcal{W})$ can also be used to denote a sequence, for example in an inclusion dependency.

The set of primary key attributes of an entity type $\mathcal{E}$ is denoted by $\mathcal{K}_\mathcal{E}$.

In the relational mapping, a relation schema is created for each object type. The name of the relation schema is identical to the name of the corresponding object type. The mapping defines the attributes, keys, and the leaving inclusion dependencies for each schema. The keys are the only form of functional dependencies produced by the mapping.

The attributes of the relation schema are the local names of the attributes of the object type, plus the foreign names of any attributes inherited from other schemas.

The keys of the schemas corresponding to strong entity types are obtained directly from the ER-diagram. For schemas corresponding to weak entity types, the keys are obtained from keys of the parent types; we say that the schema for a weak entity type *inherits* the key attributes of the schema corresponding to its source entity type. For schemas corresponding to relationship types, the keys are determined by the functionality of the relationship type.

---

[1] This somewhat awkward notation is necessary to make it possible for an entity type to participate in a relationship type in multiple roles.

We shall denote the relational mapping defined in this and the following section by the symbol *Rel*. The mapping is described in detail in Figure 11.2. An example of the application of the mapping has already been given: the final relational schema in Example 11.1 was obtained by applying *Rel* to the ER-diagram in Figure 11.1.

11.1.2   Attribute naming

The following example illustrates why attribute naming is not straightforward.

Example 11.2 Consider the ER-diagram shown in Figure 11.3. It can immediately be seen that some attributes have to be renamed in the schemas resulting from the transformation of the previous section; otherwise Name would be an attribute loaded with different roles.   □

The problem is caused by the difference in naming conventions between the ER-model and the relational model with the universal relation schema assumption. Therefore one has to enforce the universal relation schema assumption when the local names of attributes are defined. The function $l(\mathcal{O}, \mathcal{A})$ is defined as

$$l(\mathcal{O}, \mathcal{A}) = \begin{cases} \mathcal{A}, \text{ if in the ER-diagram } \mathcal{O} \text{ is the only object type} \\ \qquad \text{that has an attribute that is called } \mathcal{A}, \text{ and} \\ \mathcal{O}\_\mathcal{A}, \text{ otherwise.} \end{cases}$$

For the foreign names we need a more complicated naming rule. The following example shows that prefixing attribute names with schema names is not always enough.

Example 11.3 By the renaming rule we get the following two relation schemas for the ER-diagram in Example 11.2:

Teacher (Teacher_Name) and
Course (Number, Course_Name).

If the Teacher_Name and Course_Name attributes were used everywhere to represent the corresponding ER-attributes, the transformation of the previous section would produce the following schemas and dependencies in addition to the ones found above.

Assists (Teacher_Name, Number)
Assists : Teacher_Name → Number
Assists[Teacher_Name] ⊆ Teacher[Teacher_Name]
Assists[Number] ⊆ Course[Number]

Strong entity set $\mathcal{E}$

    Schema $E = l(\mathcal{E}, \mathcal{E})$.

    Keys $l(\mathcal{E}, \mathcal{K})$, where $\mathcal{K}$ is a key of $\mathcal{E}$.

    Leaving inclusion dependencies None.

Weak entity set $\mathcal{E}$, with parents $\mathcal{E}$ **isa** $\mathcal{E}_1$, ..., $\mathcal{E}$ **isa** $\mathcal{E}_h$ and $\mathcal{E}$ **id** $\mathcal{E}_{h+1}$, ..., $\mathcal{E}$ **id** $\mathcal{E}_k$. Let the corresponding relation schemas be $E_1, \ldots, E_k$.

    Schema

$$\begin{aligned} E &= l(\mathcal{E}, \mathcal{E}) \cup l(\mathcal{E}_1, \mathcal{K}_{\mathcal{E}_1}) \cup \cdots \cup l(\mathcal{E}_h, \mathcal{K}_{\mathcal{E}_h}) \cup \\ & \quad f(\mathcal{E}, \mathcal{E}_{h+1}, \mathcal{K}_{\mathcal{E}_{h+1}}) \cup \cdots \cup f(\mathcal{E}, \mathcal{E}_k, \mathcal{K}_{\mathcal{E}_k}). \end{aligned}$$

    Keys

$$l(\mathcal{E}_i, \mathcal{K}_{\mathcal{E}_i}), \quad i = 1, \ldots, h, \text{ and}$$
$$l(\mathcal{E}_i, \mathcal{K}_{\mathcal{E}_i}) l(\mathcal{E}, \mathcal{W}_i), \quad i = h+1, \ldots, k,$$

where $\mathcal{W}_i$, for $i = h+1, \ldots, k$, is the set of attributes of $\mathcal{E}$ needed for identifying the entities of $\mathcal{E}$ in addition to the key of $\mathcal{E}_i$.

    Leaving inclusion dependencies

$$E[l(\mathcal{E}_i, \mathcal{K}_{\mathcal{E}_i})] \subseteq E_i[l(\mathcal{E}_i, \mathcal{K}_{\mathcal{E}_i})], \quad i = 1, \ldots, h, \text{ and}$$
$$E[f(\mathcal{E}, \mathcal{E}_i, \mathcal{K}_{\mathcal{E}_i})] \subseteq E_i[l(\mathcal{E}_i, \mathcal{K}_{\mathcal{E}_i})], \quad i = h+1, \ldots, k.$$

Relationship set $\mathcal{R}$, with participating entity types $\mathcal{E}_1, \ldots, \mathcal{E}_k$, and corresponding relation schemas $E_1, \ldots, E_k$.

    Schema $R = l(\mathcal{R}, \mathcal{R}) \cup f(\mathcal{R}, 1, \mathcal{K}_{\mathcal{E}_1}) \cup \cdots \cup f(\mathcal{R}, k, \mathcal{K}_{\mathcal{E}_k})$.

    Keys If $\mathcal{R}$ is functional with respect to $\mathcal{E}_j$, then

$$f(\mathcal{R}, 1, \mathcal{K}_{\mathcal{E}_1}) \cdots f(\mathcal{R}, k, \mathcal{K}_{\mathcal{E}_k}) \setminus f(\mathcal{R}, j, \mathcal{K}_{\mathcal{E}_j})$$

    else

$$f(\mathcal{R}, 1, \mathcal{K}_{\mathcal{E}_1}) \cdots f(\mathcal{R}, k, \mathcal{K}_{\mathcal{E}_k}).$$

    Leaving inclusion dependencies
$$R[f(\mathcal{R}, i, \mathcal{K}_{\mathcal{E}_i})] \subseteq E_i[l(\mathcal{E}_i, \mathcal{K}_{\mathcal{E}_i})], \quad i = 1, \ldots, k.$$

Figure 11.2   The *Rel* mapping.

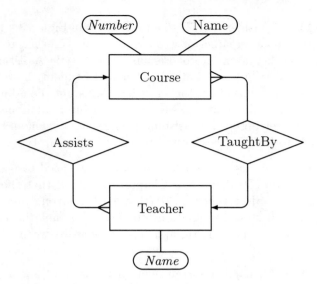

Figure 11.3   An entity-relationship diagram for teachers and courses.

TaughtBy (Number, Teacher_Name)
TaughtBy : Number → Teacher_Name
TaughtBy[Number] ⊆ Course[Number]
TaughtBy[Teacher_Name] ⊆ Teacher[Teacher_Name]

In fact, this would be an acceptable database schema. However, our goal is to use global functional dependencies. That is, we would like to drop the specification of a relation schema from the functional dependencies. But that would produce two functional dependencies,

Teacher_Name → Number and
Number → Teacher_Name,

indicating that Number and Teacher_Name are in a one-to-one correspondence: something that is in no way implied by the ER-diagram.

The problem arises because the multiple *roles* played by the entity type Teacher are lost if schema names are omitted from dependencies. Faculty members teach courses but also serve as teaching assistants of courses. These roles must be reflected in names chosen for the attributes in the relation schemas used for representing relationship types.   □

The key idea will be to break multiple connections between a pair of attributes in the relational database schema by using suitable renamings. On the other hand, there may exist multiple connections that should *not* cause renamings, as the following example shows.

Example 11.4 Consider the ER-diagram shown in Figure 3.4 (page 30). The relation schemas created for weak entity types Teacher and Student both inherit the key attribute of Person. Entity type Assistant should inherit the key attributes of both Teacher and Student; however, since both of these entity types have the *same* key, Assistant should not inherit the key twice (with different names). Besides being redundant, it would create a perfect setting for inconsistency. The renaming should therefore be careful not to break cycles caused by **isa**-relationship types.   □

For defining the mapping for foreign names, we need to use the connection graph $conn(\mathcal{D})$ defined in Chapter 3. Recall that the nodes of $conn(\mathcal{D})$ are the object types in $\mathcal{D}$ (that is, the strong and weak entity types, and all standard relationship types, but not the **id**- or **isa**-relationship types). The multigraph has an edge between $\mathcal{O}_1$ and $\mathcal{O}_2$ if

- entity type $\mathcal{O}_1$ participates in relationship type $\mathcal{O}_2$, or

- $\mathcal{O}_1$ and $\mathcal{O}_2$ are connected by an **id**-relationship type, or

- $\mathcal{O}_1$ and $\mathcal{O}_2$ are connected by an **isa**-relationship type.

The first two kinds of edges are called *strong* edges and the third kind of edges are called *weak* edges. Because an entity type can participate in a relationship set in multiple roles, there may be several strong edges between two nodes in $conn(\mathcal{D})$, and hence $conn(\mathcal{D})$ is a multigraph.

Next, we are going to find from $conn(\mathcal{D})$ the cycles that might cause referencing conflicts in the mapping from the ER-diagram into a relational schema. The conflicts are resolved by marking some edges in $conn(\mathcal{D})$; the mapping that produces foreign names will use the marks as an indication that a longer name is necessary.

Initially, all edges in $conn(\mathcal{D})$ are unmarked. Then repeatedly do the following:

- Find a cycle in $conn(\mathcal{D})$ that uses only unmarked edges and contains at least one strong edge.

- Let a strong edge in the cycle be between nodes $\mathcal{O}$ and $\mathcal{E}$. Mark it. Ask the designer to provide a role name for the corresponding connection in the ER-diagram, unless the designer has done so already.

The repetition stops when there are no such cycles in $conn(\mathcal{D})$.

The foreign names are now defined as follows:

$$f(\mathcal{R}, i, \mathcal{A}) = \begin{cases} N\_A, & \text{if the } i\text{th participant } \mathcal{E}_i \text{ of relationship} \\ & \text{type } \mathcal{R} \text{ has role name } N \text{ attached to it, and} \\ l(\mathcal{E}_i, \mathcal{A}), & \text{otherwise} \end{cases}$$

and

$$f(\mathcal{E}_1, \mathcal{E}, \mathcal{A}) = \begin{cases} N\_A, \text{ if the \textbf{id}-relationship type between} \\ \quad \mathcal{E}_1 \text{ and } \mathcal{E} \text{ has role name } N \text{ attached to it, and} \\ l(\mathcal{E}, \mathcal{A}), \text{ otherwise} \end{cases}$$

Since role names are unique, we have that if an attribute name $f(\mathcal{R}, i, \mathcal{A})$ occurs more than once in a database schema, then the edge from $\mathcal{R}$ to the ith participant of $\mathcal{R}$ must be unmarked.

Example 11.5 Let us apply *Rel* to the ER-diagram shown in Figure 3.6 (page 31). To begin with, the following structures are produced for the strong entity types by *Rel*.

> Session (*Session_Number*, Time)
> PCMember (*PCMember_Name*, Address)
> Paper (*Paper_Number*, Title)
> Author (*Author_Name*)

For finding the names of the attributes in the remaining schemas, the multigraph *conn*($\mathcal{D}$) is constructed. The graph has one cycle, formed by the nodes AcceptedPaper, Paper, Evaluation, PCMember, ChairedBy, Session, and AssignedTo. All edges in this cycle are strong, except the edge from AcceptedPaper to Paper. One of the strong edges is chosen, say the edge between Evaluation and PCMember. It is marked, and the role name Reviewer is given by the designer.

Then the following parts are added to the relational database schema.

> AcceptedPaper (*Paper_Number*)
> FinalCopy (*Paper_Number*, #OfPages)
> Evaluation (*Paper_Number*, *Reviewer_Name*, Score, Comments)
> ChairedBy (*Session_Number*, Chairperson_Name)
> AssignedTo (*Paper_Number*, Session_Number)
> AuthoredBy (*Author_Name*, *Paper_Number*, Position)

> AcceptedPaper[Paper_Number] $\subseteq$ Paper[Paper_Number]
> FinalCopy[Paper_Number] $\subseteq$ AcceptedPaper[Paper_Number]
> ChairedBy[Session_Number] $\subseteq$ Session[Session_Number]
> ChairedBy[PCMember_Name] $\subseteq$ PCMember[PCMember_Name]
> Evaluation[Paper_Number] $\subseteq$ Paper[Paper_Number]
> Evaluation[Reviewer_Name] $\subseteq$ PCMember[PCMember_Name]
> AssignedTo[Paper_Number] $\subseteq$ AcceptedPaper[Paper_Number]
> AssignedTo[Session_Number] $\subseteq$ Session[Session_Number]
> AuthoredBy[Paper_Number] $\subseteq$ Paper[Paper_Number]
> AuthoredBy[Author_Name] $\subseteq$ Author[Author_Name]   □

Figure 11.4   An entity-relationship diagram for hotels and rooms.

The *Rel* mapping can be extended to produce a suggested set of indices for the relation schemas. One choice is to create an index for each key of a relation schema created for an entity type. For schemas representing (functional) relationship types, one can create indices based on the key attributes of all (but one) of the participating entity types.

11.2   Properties of the relational mapping

What properties should a relational mapping have? A mapping that is in some intuitive sense natural would certainly be desirable. Such a property cannot be proved, merely argued upon. Sometimes the result may seem less than optimal; consider the ER-diagram shown in Figure 11.4.

The *Rel* mapping produces the following three relation schemas for this ER-diagram.

>   Hotel (*Name*)
>   Room (*Number*)
>   HotelRoom (*Name, Number*)

A list of room numbers is in all likelihood not very interesting (unless it is important that some room numbers – such as those on the thirteenth floor – are not used). The designer would probably be satisfied with the two other schemas – possibly with HotelRoom alone.

Note, however, that the problem here lies in the ER-diagram, not in the mapping. Since the ER-diagram makes it possible to store information about room numbers without connecting the rooms to particular hotels, the same must be true in the relational schema. If strong entity types with one attribute appear in the ER-diagram, corresponding relation schemas with one attribute must appear in the relational database schema. In this case a more natural ER-diagram would define HotelRoom as a weak entity type and Hotel as a parent of HotelRoom.

This argument can be generalized: we say that a relational mapping is *correct* for an ER-diagram $\mathcal{D}$, if for every object (entity or relationship) in a database instance over $\mathcal{D}$ it is true that

Figure 11.5   An entity-relationship diagram for departments and managers.

(1) the object can be represented in the relational database stored according to $Rel(\mathcal{D})$, and

(2) the object can be uniquely identified in the relational database stored according to $Rel(\mathcal{D})$.

Thus correctness means that not only is there a correspondence between an ER-diagram and a relational schema, but the same holds also for the instances. The same data can be stored using both representations. The correctness of the Rel mapping follows directly from the construction.

Whenever $\mathbf{S}_1$ and $\mathbf{S}_2$ are two database schemas (not necessarily in the same data model) such that $\mathbf{S}_2$ can be used to represent all database instances that can be represented using $\mathbf{S}_1$, we say that the *information capacity* of $\mathbf{S}_2$ is larger than or equal to the information capacity of $\mathbf{S}_1$. The correctness of the Rel mapping means that the information capacity of $Rel(\mathcal{D})$ is larger than or equal to the information capacity of $\mathcal{D}$.

The correctness criteria should be read carefully. They say that we can recover all the information in an ER-database from the corresponding relational database, *once we know how to interpret the data in the relational database.* In fact, there may be several possible interpretations, as the following example shows.

Example 11.6 Compare the ER-diagrams shown in Figure 11.5 and Figure 11.6. The Rel mapping produces for these diagrams isomorphic[2] relational database schemas.   □

The following simple observation follows from the definition of the Rel mapping.

Lemma 11.1 Let $\mathcal{D}$ be an acyclic ER-diagram and $Rel(\mathcal{D}) = (\mathbf{R}, F, I)$. Then $ref(\mathcal{D})$ and $ind(\mathbf{R}, I)$ are isomorphic.[3]   □

---

[2]Isomorphism of two structures (here two relational database schemas) means that one can be obtained from the other by renaming the basic components (here attributes) in a one-to-one fashion.

[3]Recall that $ref(\mathcal{D})$ is the reference graph for $\mathcal{D}$, defined in Section 3.2, and that $ind(\mathbf{R}, I)$ is the inclusion dependency graph defined in Section 8.8.

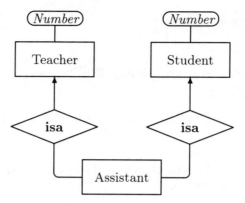

Figure 11.6   An entity-relationship diagram for teachers, assistants, and students.

11.3   Entity-relationship normal form ERNF

In this section we define the key concept of *entity-relationship normal form*, abbreviated ERNF. The normal form specifies the structure of the relational database schema resulting from the *Rel* mapping.

Let R be a relation schema and let $R[X_1] \subseteq S_1[Y_1], \ldots, R[X_n] \subseteq S_n[Y_n]$ be the inclusion dependencies leaving R. Denote

$$Z = \bigcup_{i=1}^{n} X_i$$

and let V be the set of attributes in R that do not belong to Z. We define three different classes of relation schemas that can result from applying *Rel* to an ER-diagram.

- R is a *relationship schema* if it satisfies the following conditions:

  (1) R has no entering inclusion dependencies.

  (2) R has at least two leaving inclusion dependencies, and the left-hand sides of the leaving inclusion dependencies are pairwise disjoint.

  (3) Either Z is a key of R, or there exists a j ($1 \leq j \leq n$) such that $Z \setminus X_j$ is a key of R.

- R is a *strong entity schema* if it has no leaving inclusion dependencies.

- R is a *weak entity schema* if it satisfies the following conditions:

(1) R has at least one leaving inclusion dependency.

(2) For any inclusion dependency $R[X] \subseteq S[Y]$ one of the following holds.

  (a) The set X is a key of R, or

  (b) X is a proper subset of a key W of R, and the attributes in $W \setminus X$ do not belong to Z.

A relational database schema $(\mathbf{R}, F, I)$ is in *entity-relationship normal form* (ERNF, for short), if

(1) I is an acyclic and nonredundant set of inclusion dependencies.

(2) All inclusion dependencies in I are key-based.

(3) All relation schemas are in Boyce-Codd normal form with respect to the functional dependencies implied by $F \cup I$.

(4) The relation schemas in $\mathbf{R}$ can be partitioned into relationship schemas, strong entity schemas, and weak entity schemas.

The following theorem gives an exact characterization of the schemas produced by *Rel*.

Theorem 11.1 Let $(\mathbf{R}, F, I)$ be a relational database schema. There exists an acyclic ER-diagram $\mathcal{D}$ such that $(\mathbf{R}, F, I)$ is isomorphic with $Rel(\mathcal{D})$ if and only if $(\mathbf{R}, F, I)$ is in entity-relationship normal form.

The proof of Theorem 11.1 is somewhat involved. We first present some notation and lemmas needed for showing that the schemas produced by *Rel* are in Boyce-Codd normal form.

Recall the multigraph $conn(\mathcal{D})$ from the description of the *Rel* mapping. The nodes are the object types, and a strong edge exists between $\mathcal{O}_1$ and $\mathcal{O}_1$ if either $\mathcal{O}_1$ participates in the relationship type $\mathcal{O}_2$, or if $\mathcal{O}_1$ **id** $\mathcal{O}_2$ holds. The multigraph has a weak edge between $\mathcal{O}_1$ and $\mathcal{O}_2$ if $\mathcal{O}_1$ **isa** $\mathcal{O}_2$ holds. In finding the attribute names, some of the strong edges in this graph were marked and labelled, so that no cycle in $conn(\mathcal{D})$ contains an unmarked strong edge.

Next we form a compressed version $compr(\mathcal{D})$ of $conn(\mathcal{D})$ by repeatedly applying the following: if $\mathcal{O}_1$ **isa** $\mathcal{O}_2$ holds, combine the nodes corresponding to $\mathcal{O}_1$ and $\mathcal{O}_2$. The edges adjacent to these nodes are moved to be adjacent to the new node. This merging operation is repeated until all edges corresponding to **isa** relationship types have been removed.

In the resulting graph all edges are strong, and hence there are no cycles consisting of only unmarked edges in $compr(\mathcal{D})$. We identify the nodes of $compr(\mathcal{D})$ with the corresponding relation schemas. If a node T of $compr(\mathcal{D})$ has been formed by collapsing several nodes, then we consider the node to consist of the union of the schemas corresponding to these nodes. For a node T, the notation F_T denotes the set of functional dependencies generated for schema T by Rel. If T has been created by merging several nodes, then F_T stands for the union of the sets of functional dependencies generated for these nodes. Denote by F the set of all functional dependencies generated by Rel.

The next series of lemmas consider the set of relation schemas $\mathbf{R}$ obtained by applying the Rel mapping to an ER-diagram.

A *path* in $compr(\mathcal{D})$ is a sequence $(e_1, \ldots, e_n)$ of edges such that the end point of e_i is the starting point of e_{i+1} for $i = 1, \ldots, n-1$. The path is *unmarked*, if all edges in it are unmarked.

Lemma 11.2 If two schemas R and S have common attributes, then $compr(\mathcal{D})$ contains an unmarked path from R to S. Each schema on this path contains all the attributes of $R \cap S$.

Proof. By a straightforward case analysis. Without weak entity types, such paths are very short: if both R and S are relation schemas created for relationship types, the length of the path is 2; if one of them was created for an entity type, the length of the path is 1. Because weak edges were pruned from $compr(\mathcal{D})$, the existence of **isa**-relationship types in the ER-diagram does not affect this property. Only the use of **id**-relationship types can create longer paths. The only potentially difficult case arises when two weak entity types have the same source and also participate in two relationship types. However, this creates a cycle in $conn(\mathcal{D})$, and the foreign name mapping prevents R and S from inheriting common attributes from multiple sources. $\square$

If we consider the graph $conn(\mathcal{D})$ instead of $compr(\mathcal{D})$, then the first part of Lemma 11.2 still holds. However, the schemas on the path from R to S may not contain all the attributes of $R \cap S$, as the following example shows.

Example 11.7 Denote by $\mathcal{D}$ the ER-diagram shown in Figure 11.7. It has an acyclic reference graph but a cyclic connection graph. When Rel is applied to this diagram and the graph $conn(\mathcal{D})$ is constructed, it contains two paths between E and F. Now $E \cap F = AB$, and yet the intermediate node on each path excludes one of the common attributes. In $compr(\mathcal{D})$ all four nodes are collapsed into a single node. $\square$

Lemma 11.3 The graph $compr(\mathcal{D})$ contains at most one unmarked path between any two nodes. $\square$

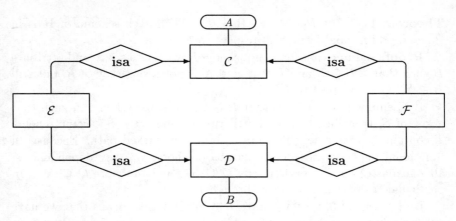

Figure 11.7   An entity-relationship diagram with several similar inheritance paths.

Lemma 11.4 If relation schemas R and S are nodes connected by an unmarked edge in $compr(\mathcal{D})$, and $R \cap S \neq \emptyset$, then $R \cap S$ is either a key of R and a subset of a key of S, or a key of S and a subset of a key of R.

Proof. By Lemma 11.3 at most one unmarked path exists between R and S. The claim follows by inspecting the definition of the Rel mapping. □

Lemma 11.5 If $X \rightarrow Y \in F_T$ and $B \in Y \setminus X$, then T is the only relation schema that contains both X and B.

Proof. Assume the contrary: for some schema $R \neq T$ we have $XB \subseteq R$. Since R and T have common attributes, there is by Lemma 11.2 an unmarked path between R and T, and all the schemas on this path contain the set XB. Hence we can assume that R and T are adjacent. But then $XB \subseteq R \cap T$, contradicting Lemma 11.4. □

Lemma 11.6 (i) Let R be a schema and $X \subseteq R$. Then

$$X^+ = S_1^+ \cup \cdots \cup S_k^+,$$

where $S_1, \ldots, S_k$ are the schemas such that some key of S_i is included in X.

(ii) If $T \subseteq X^+$, then $compr(\mathcal{D})$ contains an unmarked path from S_i to T for some i ($1 \leq i \leq k$), and the path includes only schemas Q with $Q \subseteq X^+$.

Proof. (i) All dependencies generated by Rel are key dependencies, and the elimination of unmarked cycles means that for no schema Q can the key of Q be included in $(S_1 \cup \cdots \cup S_k)^+$, but not in some S_i^+. (ii) Part (i), and induction on the computation of S_i^+. □

Theorem 11.2 Let $Rel(\mathcal{D}) = (\mathbf{R}, F, I)$. Then each schema of $\mathbf{R}$ is in Boyce-Codd normal form with respect to F.

   Proof. Assume that for some schema R we have a set X and attribute B such that $XB \subseteq R$ and $B \notin X$ and X is not a superkey of R, but still $B \in X^+$ (with respect to F).

   By Lemma 11.6, we have that $B \in S_i^+$ for some schema S_i such that a key of S_i is included in X. Furthermore, since $B \in S_i^+$, some schema T containing B is reachable from S_i by an unmarked path. Because all functional dependencies in the database schema are key dependencies, all schemas Q on this path satisfy $Q \subseteq S_i^+$, and therefore $Q \subseteq X^+$. In particular, this path cannot go through R.

   By Lemma 11.5, we must have $T \neq S_i$. But this means that we have an unmarked cycle in $compr(\mathcal{D})$ consisting of the edges from R to S_i (a subset of X is shared by R and S_i), from S_i to T (obtained above), and from T to R (B belongs to both T and R). The existence of an unmarked cycle is a contradiction.   □

   Proof of Theorem 11.1. *Only if.* Let $\mathcal{D}$ be an acyclic ER-diagram and let $(\mathbf{R}, F, I)$ be isomorphic with $Rel(\mathcal{D})$. We must show that $(\mathbf{R}, F, I)$ is in entity-relationship normal form.

   The definition of entity-relationship normal form does not rely on attribute naming: if $(\mathbf{R}, F, I)$ is in entity-relationship normal form then every relational database schema that is isomorphic with $(\mathbf{R}, F, I)$ is in entity-relationship normal form. Therefore we can without loss of generality assume that $(\mathbf{R}, F, I) = Rel(\mathcal{D})$.

   The acyclicity of I follows from Lemma 11.1, and the key-basedness of the inclusion dependencies follows directly from their construction.

   Theorem 11.2 showed that the schemas produced by Rel are in BCNF, when only the keys generated by Rel are considered. There are, however, also inclusion dependencies present in the database schema, and thus we have to check that the complicated interaction of functional and inclusion dependencies is not possible. But this is easy: all the inclusion dependencies are key-based and they form an acyclic set, and each relation schema is in BCNF with respect to the functional dependencies. Hence Theorem 10.21 applies to this case.

   Therefore the only nontrivial functional dependencies between the attributes of a relation schema are those explicitly generated by Rel, and the relation schemas are in BCNF.

   For the fourth condition, we claim that relationship types produce relationship schemas, strong entity types produce strong entity schemas, and weak entity types produce weak entity schemas.

   Consider a relationship type $\mathcal{R}$. Let R be the corresponding relation schema in $\mathbf{R}$; we claim that R is a relationship schema.

Relationship types have at least two participants, and each participant gives rise to a leaving inclusion dependency. Moreover, inclusion dependencies always enter schemas that correspond to entity types.

The leaving inclusion dependencies have on their left-hand sides attribute sequences that are inherited from the keys of the schemas created for the participating entity types. If one entity type participates many times (in different roles) in $\mathcal{R}$, the connection graph has a cycle and the attribute sequences are renamed using different role names. If, on the other hand, two different relation schemas E_1 and E_2 that correspond to participating entity types $\mathcal{E}_1$ and $\mathcal{E}_2$ have identical (or overlapping) key attributes, they must have inherited the attributes from the same source $\mathcal{E}_3$. Hence the connection graph contains the cycle $\mathcal{R}-\mathcal{E}_1-\mathcal{E}_3-\mathcal{E}_2-\mathcal{R}$. Therefore the attributes are renamed before they are used in R.

It follows that the attribute sequences on the left-hand sides of leaving inclusion dependencies must be pairwise disjoint.

The third condition required from relationship schemas is obvious by the definition of the *Rel* mapping.

Entity types can be handled in a similar manner; we leave the straightforward details for the exercises.

If. Let $(\mathbf{R}, F, I)$ be a relational database schema in entity-relationship normal form. We must show that there exists an ER-diagram $\mathcal{D}$ such that $Rel(\mathcal{D})$ is isomorphic with $(\mathbf{R}, F, I)$.

We prove this by constructing explicitly the ER-diagram $\mathcal{D}$. This construction will actually serve as the inverse of the *Rel* mapping. The objects in the diagram correspond to the classification of the relation schemas. Since our goal is isomorphism, not equality, we shall not consider in detail how the attribute names are handled. From the theoretical point of view, they can be transferred as such from the relational schema to the ER-diagram. In practice, particularly if R has been created using *Rel*, it is advisable to drop the prefixes from attribute names in the ER-diagram.

Each relationship schema R gives rise to a relationship type $\mathcal{R}$. The attributes of $\mathcal{R}$ correspond to those attributes of R that do not appear on the left-hand side of any inclusion dependency leaving R. Since inclusion dependencies cannot enter relationship schemas, an inclusion dependency from R to E must enter a strong entity schema or a weak entity schema. An entity type will be created for such a schema, and it will be made a participant of $\mathcal{R}$. Moreover, if R has a key that does not contain the left-hand side attributes of the inclusion dependency, the relationship type is functional with respect to E. Since the schema is in Boyce-Codd normal form, it can contain only key dependencies. Each key of R corresponds to a key of $\mathcal{R}$.

Strong entity schemas simply produce a corresponding strong entity type, with a one-to-one correspondence between the key attributes of the relation schema and the entity type. Since the schema is in Boyce-Codd normal form, it can contain only key dependencies. If there are several key dependencies, the entity type has several keys.

Weak entity types are created for weak entity schemas. The attributes of the weak entity type correspond to those attributes of the relation schema that do not appear on the left-hand side of any leaving inclusion dependency. Every inclusion dependency from a key of E to some schema E' produces an **isa**-relationship set between the corresponding entity types. Each left-hand side of such an inclusion dependency produces a key for the corresponding weak entity type. Similarly, each inclusion dependency from a proper subset X of a key of E produces an **id**-relationship type between the corresponding entity types. The key attributes of the starting point of the **id**-relationship type consist of the attributes in W, where XW is a key of the weak entity schema, and X is the left-hand side of the inclusion dependency leaving the schema. Again, there may be several keys.

We have considered all the information in the relational database schema $(\mathbf{R}, F, I)$ and constructed an ER-diagram $\mathcal{D}$ where every piece of that information is explicitly represented. From the construction it is clear that all the information is preserved in $Rel(\mathcal{D})$. Moreover, since every relation schema, every functional dependency and every inclusion dependency has a counterpart in the ER-diagram, $Rel(\mathcal{D})$ cannot contain any components that were not present in $(\mathbf{R}, F, I)$. Thus $Rel(\mathcal{D}) = (\mathbf{R}, F, I)$ up to a renaming of attributes, meaning that $Rel(\mathcal{D})$ and $(\mathbf{R}, F, I)$ are isomorphic. $\square$

Theorem 11.1 characterizes the Rel mapping completely: it describes the structure of $Rel(\mathcal{D})$, and it also says that every relational database schema in entity-relationship normal form represents some ER-diagram. In other words, Rel is a surjective mapping from acyclic ER-diagrams to relational schemas in entity-relationship normal form.

11.4   Weak ERNF

Entity-relationship normal form is a strong condition. Some fairly natural schemas do not satisfy it.

Example 11.8 Consider the following relational database schema.

> Department (*DeptName*, Floor)
> Employee (*EmpName*, DeptName, Salary)

> Employee[DeptName] $\subseteq$ Department[DeptName]

The database schema is not in ERNF, since the Employee schema is not of any of the three types: it has exactly one leaving inclusion dependency, so the only possibility would be that it is a weak entity schema. However, the left-hand side of the inclusion dependency, DeptName, is not a key or part of a key.

The schema suffers from an insertion anomaly. One can argue that this schema is correct, if an employee cannot exist without a department. However, since employees and departments have an independent existence in the database schema, ERNF is not satisfied.   □

Generalizing the example, we notice that any foreign key that is not part of the key of the schema leads immediately to a violation of ERNF. Such foreign keys are, however, rather common: if the information in the database is fragmented among very many relations, performance can suffer.

Example 11.9 Consider the use of the two relation schemas

> Employee (*EmpName*, Salary) and
> WorksIn (*EmpName*, DeptName)

as opposed to the single schema

> Employee (*EmpName*, DeptName, Salary).

An experiment compared the performance of the query 'find the average salary in a given department' using these two designs. For three different database management systems, the ratios of execution times (two schemas versus one schema) were approximately 1.5, 2, and 5. For some other performance statistics (like lock usage) the ratios were even larger.   □

Next we relax the definition of ERNF to allow the use of foreign keys in entity schemas. This makes it possible to eliminate some relationship schemas. This relaxation is a simple form of denormalization.

Again, we begin with the classification of individual relation schemas. For relationship schemas the condition is the same as in the case of ERNF, but for the other two classes we allow more freedom. Let R be a relation schema and let $R[X_1] \subseteq S_1[Y_1], \ldots, R[X_n] \subseteq S_n[Y_n]$ be the inclusion dependencies leaving R. Denote

$$Z = \bigcup_{i=1}^{n} X_i$$

and let V be the set of attributes in R that do not belong to Z.

- R is a *relationship schema* if it satisfies the following conditions:

(1) R has no entering inclusion dependencies.

(2) R has at least two leaving inclusion dependencies, and their left-hand sides X_i are pairwise disjoint.

(3) Either Z is a key of R, or there exists a j $(1 \leq j \leq n)$ such that $Z \setminus X_j$ is a key of R.

- R is a *strong entity schema with foreign keys* if it has no leaving inclusion dependencies $R[X] \subseteq S[Y]$ such that X intersects a key of R.

- R is a *weak entity schema with foreign keys* if it satisfies the following conditions:

  (1) R has at least one leaving inclusion dependency whose left-hand side intersects a key of R.

  (2) For any inclusion dependency $R[X] \subseteq S[Y]$ where X intersects a key of R, one of the following holds.

    (a) The set X is a key of R, or

    (b) X is a proper subset of a key W of R, and the attributes in $W \setminus X$ do not belong to Z.

A relational database schema $(\mathbf{R}, F, I)$ is in *weak entity-relationship normal form*(WERNF, for short), if

(1) I is an acyclic and nonredundant set of inclusion dependencies.

(2) All inclusion dependencies in I are key-based.

(3) All relation schemas in $\mathbf{R}$ are in Boyce-Codd normal form with respect to the functional dependencies implied by $F \cup I$.

(4) The relation schemas in $\mathbf{R}$ can be partitioned into relationship schemas, strong entity schemas with foreign keys, and weak entity schemas with foreign keys.

Example 11.10 The database schema in Example 11.8 is in weak ERNF, since the offending schema Employee can be classified as a strong entity schema with a foreign key. □

Example 11.11 The first database schema in Example 11.1 is in weak ERNF, but not in ERNF. □

Example 11.12 A schema can simultaneously satisfy the requirements for a relationship schema and for a weak entity schema with foreign keys. Consider the schemas $R(AB)$, $S(A)$ and $T(B)$, with the functional dependency $A \rightarrow B$ and the inclusion dependencies $R[A] \subseteq S[A]$ and $R[B] \subseteq T[B]$. Now R is a relationship schema, but it can also be considered to be a weak entity schema with foreign keys. Namely, if $\mathcal{R}$ **isa** $\mathcal{S}$, and if $\mathcal{R}$ and $\mathcal{T}$ are connected by a relationship type that is functional with respect to $\mathcal{T}$, then the set of relation schemas (R, S, T) could be obtained from $\mathcal{R}$, $\mathcal{S}$, and $\mathcal{T}$ by including the relationship type into R. □

Next we describe an additional step to the *Rel* mapping. Suppose that the database schema $(\mathbf{R}, F, I)$ is in ERNF, and let R be a schema that corresponds to a binary relationship type $\mathcal{R}$ with participating entity types $\mathcal{E}_1$ and $\mathcal{E}_2$, and assume the relationship type is functional with respect to $\mathcal{E}_2$. Let K_1 and K_2 be the primary keys of E_1 and E_2, the relation schemas that correspond to $\mathcal{E}_1$ and $\mathcal{E}_2$. Then the attribute set of R is $K_1 K_2 V$, and the key of R is K_1. The schema R can be removed from the database schema by adding the foreign key K_2 and the attributes in V to the attribute set of E_1, and by adding the inclusion dependency $E_1[K_2] \subseteq E_2[K_2]$ to the set of constraints of the schema.

This step can be applied if the connections between $\mathcal{R}$ and $\mathcal{E}_1$ and between $\mathcal{R}$ and $\mathcal{E}_2$ are both unmarked in the connection graph $conn(\mathcal{D})$ used in producing the database schema, and if the addition of an inclusion dependency from E_1 to E_2 does not make the set of inclusion dependencies circular.

Example 11.13 Continuing Example 11.5, we notice that in the ER-diagram shown in Figure 3.6 there are two binary functional relationship types, namely AssignedTo and ChairedBy. The schemas corresponding to these relationship types and the associated inclusion dependencies can be removed using the above transformation, and the result has the modified schemas

> AcceptedPaper (*Paper_Number*, Session_Number) and
> Session (*Session_Number*, Time, PCMember_Name)

and the new inclusion dependencies

> AcceptedPaper[Session_Number] ⊆ Session[Session_Number] and
> Session[PCMember_Name] ⊆ PCMember[PCMember_Name].

The SQL definition corresponding to these schemas would allow the columns Session_Number and PCMember_Name to contain nulls. Ordinarily (if the relationship types are represented by separate schemas) nulls are always forbidden. □

A database schema in weak ERNF can be transformed to ERNF just by replacing all foreign keys by schemas representing binary relationships. A foreign key of a schema R is recognized as the left-hand side X of an inclusion dependency such that X does not intersect any key of R.

Weak ERNF allowed the elimination of some binary relationship schemas at the expense of allowing null values. In a similar way, weak entity schemas representing children of **isa**-relationship types can be combined with their parent schemas. Again the penalty is the possible occurrence of null values.

Let $(\mathbf{R}, F, I)$ be a relational database schema, and let $E, F \in \mathbf{R}$ be two relation schemas resulting from entity types $\mathcal{E}$ and $\mathcal{F}$, where $\mathcal{E}$ **isa** $\mathcal{F}$. Let K be the primary key of $\mathcal{F}$; then K is a key of $\mathcal{E}$ and $K = E \cap F$. Schema E can be removed by replacing F with the schema $E \cup F$. Each inclusion dependency entering or leaving E is modified to enter or leave F. The keys of the new schema $E \cup F$ are the keys of E and the keys of F.

The transformation does not cause any cycles in the set of inclusion dependencies, and all modified inclusion dependencies are key-based. Also, if the original schemas are in Boyce-Codd normal form, so are the new ones. The resulting schemas are entity schemas in our classification.

Thus if $(\mathbf{R}, F, I)$ is in ERNF, so is the schema $(\mathbf{R}', F', I')$ where some weak entity schemas have been combined with their parents. The difference between the schemas is that in the new schema one has to use null values to convey information about the membership of objects in different types.

Example 11.14 Continuing Examples 11.5 and 11.13, we consider mapping the ER-diagram of Figure 3.6 to a relational database schema. The state of the database schema after Example 11.13 is such that it contains two relation schemas corresponding to weak entity types, namely AcceptedPaper and FinalCopy. Combining first AcceptedPaper with Paper and then also FinalCopy with Paper, we obtain a new schema

Paper (*Paper_Number*, Title, Session_Number, #OfPages).

If a row in the corresponding relation contains a null value for the attribute Session_Number, then the row represents an entity in the entity set Paper, but not in the weak entity set AcceptedPaper. In this case the value of the #OfPages attribute must also be null, although this cannot be specified in SQL! Therefore the state of the denormalized database may be such that it does not correspond to any instance of the ER-database, and this is one of the reasons why null values and denormalization should be used only for a very good reason.

Similarly, a row with a nonnull value in Session_Number and a null value in #OfPages represents an entity from the set AcceptedPaper, but outside the set FinalCopy.

With these optimizations, the resulting relational database schema is as follows.

Session (*Session_Number*, Time, PCMember_Name)
PCMember (*PCMember_Name*, Address)
Paper (*Paper_Number*, Title, Session_Number, #OfPages)
Author (*Author_Name*)
Evaluation (*Paper_Number*, *Reviewer_Name*, Score, Comments)
AuthoredBy (*Author_Name*, *Paper_Number*, Position)

Paper[Session_Number] $\subseteq$ Session[Session_Number]
Evaluation[Paper_Number] $\subseteq$ Paper[Paper_Number]
Evaluation[Reviewer_Name] $\subseteq$ PCMember[PCMember_Name]
AuthoredBy[Paper_Number] $\subseteq$ Paper[Paper_Number]
AuthoredBy[Author_Name] $\subseteq$ Author[Author_Name]
Session[PCMember_Name] $\subseteq$ PCMember[PCMember_Name] $\square$

One can also consider combining some nonfunctional relationship schemas with entity schemas; this is a radical denormalization technique, since it introduces redundancy. Hence using it requires great care in the application development.

11.5   Mapping entity-relationship normal form schemas into ER-diagrams

Our goal in this section is to find the correct inverse of the *Rel* mapping: an ER-mapping *Ent* from entity-relationship normal form schemas into ER-diagrams.

The first observation that can be made is that in a mathematical sense, such an inverse is not obtainable. Though we saw that *Rel* is surjective, it is not injective, as Example 11.6 shows.

Therefore the mapping *Ent* does not necessarily yield a single ER-diagram, but a set of ER-diagrams. The designer's task is to choose the correct diagram from the set.

What does it mean for *Ent* to be correct? Surely it should not produce too large a set of diagrams for the designer to choose from. Ideally, each $\mathcal{D}$ in $Ent(\mathbf{R}, F, I)$ should be such that $Rel(\mathcal{D})$ is isomorphic with $(\mathbf{R}, F, I)$. Another requirement is that *Ent* should not omit any diagrams that can be mapped to $(\mathbf{R}, F, I)$: the set $Ent(Rel(\mathcal{D}))$ should contain a diagram that is isomorphic with $\mathcal{D}$.

Clearly, these two requirements taken together with the correctness of the relational mapping also imply that Ent preserves the information capacity of its input schema.

In practice, we need not construct the entire set $Ent(\mathbf{R}, F, I)$; it is sufficient to find one ER-diagram that correctly represents $(\mathbf{R}, F, I)$. In the proof of Theorem 11.1 we actually presented the method for constructing ER-diagrams: classify the relation schemas into the four types, using the classification form an object type of an appropriate type from each schema, and connect the object types using the inclusion dependency information. This is described in more detail in Algorithm 11.1.

Algorithm 11.1 Mapping relational database schemas into ER-diagrams.
Input. A relational database schema $(\mathbf{R}, F, I)$ in ERNF.
Output. An ER-diagram $\mathcal{D}$ such that $Rel(\mathcal{D})$ and $(\mathbf{R}, F, I)$ are isomorphic.
Method.

1.   classify each schema of $\mathbf{R}$ as a strong entity schema,
2.   a weak entity schema, or a relationship schema;
3.   **for** each strong entity schema E in $\mathbf{R}$ **do**
4.   create an entity type $\mathcal{E}$ into $\mathcal{D}$;
5.   **for** each $A \in E$ **do**
6.   create an ER-attribute $\mathcal{A}$ for $\mathcal{E}$;
7.   **od**;
8.   **od**;
9.   **for** each weak entity schema E in $\mathbf{R}$ **do**
10.   create a weak entity type $\mathcal{E}$ into $\mathcal{D}$;
11.   let the inclusion dependencies leaving E be
12.   of the form $E[X_i] \subseteq F_i[Y_i]$, for $i = 1, \ldots, k$;
13.   **for** $i = 1, \ldots, k$ **do**
14.   **if** X_i is a key of E **then**
15.   create an **isa**-relationship type between $\mathcal{E}$ and $\mathcal{F}_i$;
16.   **else** X must be a subset of a key Y of E;
17.   create an **id**-relationship type between $\mathcal{E}$ and $\mathcal{F}_i$;
18.   let the ER-attributes corresponding to $Y \setminus X$
19.   be the attributes needed for identifying
20.   the entities of $\mathcal{E}$ in addition to
21.   the key of $\mathcal{F}_i$;
22.   **fi**;
23.   **for** each $A \in E$ **do**
24.   **if** $A \notin \cup_{i=1}^{n} X_i$ **then**

```
25.                    create an ER-attribute 𝒜 for ℰ;
26.              fi;
27.         od;
28.   od;
29.   for each relationship schema R in R do
30.         create a relationship type ℛ into 𝒟;
31.         let the inclusion dependencies leaving R be
32.               of the form R[X_i] ⊆ F_i[Y_i], for i = 1, ..., k;
33.         for i = 1, ..., k do
34.               make ℱ_i one of the participants of ℛ;
35.               if X_1 ⋯ X_{i−1}X_{i+1} ⋯ X_k is a key of R then
36.                     make ℛ functional with respect to ℱ_i;
37.               fi;
38.         od;
39.         for each A ∈ E do
40.               if A ∉ ∪_{i=1}^n X_i then
41.                     create an ER-attribute 𝒜 for ℰ;
42.               fi;
43.         od;
44.   od;                                                □
```

In the proof of Theorem 11.1 we were satisfied with an arbitrary classification satisfying the requirements. In real life we shall ask the designer to classify the schemas that could be classified in various ways. Typically, this means that the designer may need to decide between the choice of a relationship type and a weak entity type, as illustrated by Figures 11.5 and 11.6.

Example 11.15 Let us apply *Ent* to the relational schema given in Example 11.5. Most of the relation schemas are uniquely classified in the correct way. The ChairedBy and AssignedTo schemas could be either relationship schemas or subset schemas; designer interaction is needed for classifying them so that the result corresponds to reality.   □

In the cases where interaction with the designer is needed, most schemas should correspond to relationship types. If one is willing to rely on guesswork and to let the designer fix the wrong decisions manually, ties could be broken simply by giving relationship schemas precedence over other possible interpretations.

By the proof of Theorem 11.1 it is obvious that the correctness criteria we laid out for *Ent* are satisfied. One may question whether it is sufficient that *Ent* is able to find an ER-diagram that corresponds to a relational schema; is that diagram necessarily the natural one? If this is not the

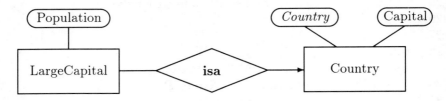

Figure 11.8   An entity-relationship diagram for countries and large capitals.

case, the problem is usually in the original relational schema, not in the ER-mapping.

Example 11.16 Consider the following relational schema.

> Country (*Country*, Capital)
> LargeCapital (*Capital*, Population)
>
> Capital → Country
>
> LargeCapital[Capital] ⊆ Country[Capital]

Our algorithm would classify Country as a strong entity schema and LargeCapital as a weak entity schema, producing the diagram shown in Figure 11.8. The result seems unnatural: certainly 'large capitals are not countries'.

The problem here is twofold. First, the unnatural result reflects a poor choice of names: the name of the Country schema should indicate that it actually represents a relationship between countries and their capitals. If the name CountryCapital was used instead, the result would already be better; 'large capitals are country capitals' is understandable (though poor English).

The second problem is that two entity types and one relationship type have actually all been represented with the Country schema. One might argue that *Ent* should notice this and produce a diagram with entity types for countries and capitals and a one-to-one relationship between them. However, if we insist on maintaining the same information capacity in both the relational schema and the ER-diagram, then surely a similar transformation must be done on the relational level. Thus this is really a problem with relational normalization, not with the ER-mapping.   □

The simple technique we have presented covers completely the mapping of database schemas that are in entity-relationship normal form. The next chapter deals with the problem of transforming relational database schemas into ERNF.

Exercises

Exercise 11.1 Apply the *Rel* mapping to the ER-diagram given in Figure 11.9.

Exercise 11.2 Apply the *Rel* mapping to the ER-diagram given in Figure 11.10.

Exercise 11.3 Implement the *Rel* mapping using a high-level language, such as LISP or PROLOG. The program should ask for role names from the user.

Exercise 11.4 Prove Lemmas 11.2 and 11.3.

Exercise 11.5 Complete the proof of the 'Only if'-part of Theorem 11.1.

Exercise 11.6 Compare the performance of some queries based on the two database schemas considered in Example 11.9.

Exercise 11.7 Prove or disprove: if R is a schema produced by *Rel*, A is an attribute of R and A is the foreign name of an ER-attribute, then A belongs to a foreign key of R.

Exercise 11.8 Compare the efficiency of representing entity types $\mathcal{E}_1$ and $\mathcal{E}_2$, where $\mathcal{E}_1$ **isa** $\mathcal{E}_2$, by using one or two relation schemas.

Exercise 11.9 ** Under what conditions is the relational database schema produced by the *Rel* mapping independent?
    Hint. Consider multiple inheritance.

Exercise 11.10 Denormalize the relational database schema produced in Exercise 11.1.

Exercise 11.11 Denormalize the relational database schema produced in Exercise 11.2.

Exercise 11.12 Consider the following relational schema.

> Teacher (*Teacher_Name*, Office)
> Course (*Course_Number*, Course_Name)
> TaughtBy (*Teacher_Name*, *Course_Number*, Term)
>
> TaughtBy[Teacher_Name] $\subseteq$ Teacher[Teacher_Name]
> TaughtBy[Course_Number] $\subseteq$ Course[Course_Number]

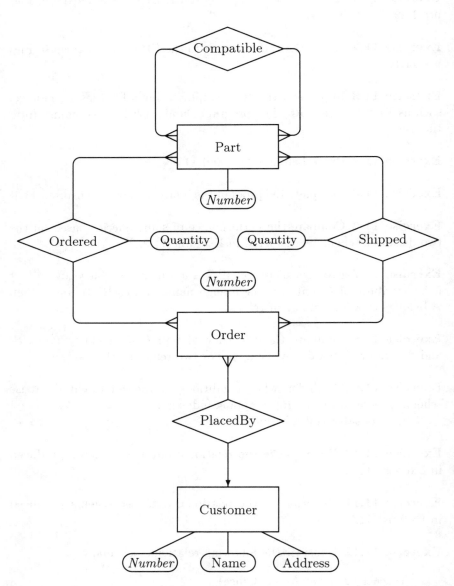

Figure 11.9   An entity-relationship diagram for orders and shipments.

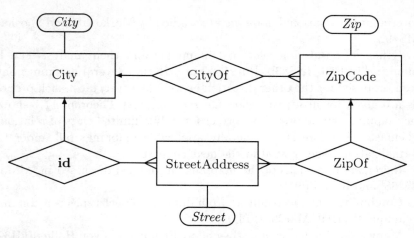

Figure 11.10 An entity-relationship diagram for zip codes, city names, and street names.

(a) Construct the ER-diagram created for the schema by the *Ent* mapping.

(b) How would adding the functional dependency Teacher_Name → Course_Number affect the ER-diagram?

(c) Suppose we wish to express the constraint 'Every teacher must teach at least one course (sometime).' How could this be expressed in the relational schema? How would it affect the behavior of *Ent*?

Bibliographic notes

Many of the ideas in this and the following chapter appeared in some form in the early work by Casanova and Amaral de Sá [CAdS83, CAdS84]. The techniques have since been developed further, most notably in a series of papers by Markowitz, Shoshani and Makowsky. Section 11.1 is based on their work. Section 11.1.1 follows [MS89b]. The algorithm in Section 11.1.2 is a simplified version of the one originally proposed in [MS89a]. Other papers dealing with these mappings are [MMR86, MM86]. The problems caused by loops in the ER-diagram are discussed in [JNS83a].

The entity-relationship normal form concept is originally due to Casanova and Amaral de Sá [CAdS83, CAdS84] (see also [CNC83]). The definition given in Section 11.3 is, however, different. The information capacity concept is due to Hull [Hul86] (see also [Lie82]). The correctness criteria for the relational mapping are studied by Markowitz and Shoshani [MS89b].

Other proposals for relational mappings and their analysis can be found in [TYF86, JNS83b, Put91, Kal91, JK89]. Several mappings have been proposed for the other direction as well; however, most such proposals are given for arbitrary relational schemas. As Theorem 11.1 shows, the mapping can be provably correct for only a limited class of relational schemas. Therefore such generally applicable mappings fall under the normalization issue treated in the next chapter.

Incremental versions of the mappings have been discussed in [MM87, MM88] and in [CTL91].

Combining schemas resulting from different object types is a common technique [FvH89, Mar90, CTL91].

Many guide books, such as the one by Fleming and von Halle [FvH89], propose also more radical denormalizations.

Chapter 12

Schema Transformations

In a database design method that uses both ER-schemas and relational database schemas one has to be able to map a description in one data model to the other. Mapping ER-schemas to relation schemas is fairly straightforward, at least in principle, as Chapter 11 showed. There we also showed how a relational database schema that is in entity-relationship normal form can be mapped to an ER-diagram. In this chapter we are going to extend that mapping so that it can be applied to arbitrary relational database schemas. This is achieved by giving methods that transform a relational database schema by replacing it with another relational database schema, preferably in ERNF. Often this cannot be done automatically, but rather using interaction with the designer.

Such a mapping is needed in iterative database design in two cases. The first case occurs when changes done to the schema on the relational level lead to a result violating ERNF. The second case occurs when the design starts from the relational level, for example, if an existing database is to be modified. Then the database schema has to be replaced by one in ERNF before an ER-schema can be formed using the *Ent* mapping presented in the previous chapter.

The starting point of the transformation is a schema not in ERNF. The definition of entity-relationship normal form listed four conditions, each of which could be violated. We shall tackle the conditions one by one and show how schemas that violate a particular condition can be transformed. In all cases, we try to find a reasonable interpretation of the original schema and maintain as much as possible of its structure.

What are typical problems in a relation schema? Some attributes of

211

the entity type or the relationship type may be missing. This is easy to remedy. More problematic is the case when several object types have been represented using a single schema. Our strategy will typically be to split such relation schemas into smaller parts, trying to separate the representations of various object types.

The first two sections of this chapter consider how an arbitrary relation schema can be transformed to a database schema in third normal form or Boyce-Codd normal form. We start in Section 12.1 with an algorithm that produces schemas in third normal form, so that the resulting decomposition preserves dependencies and has the lossless join property. However, for ERNF we need the stronger Boyce-Codd normal form property. Section 12.2 considers how we can obtain schemas in BCNF.

Section 12.3 shows how inclusion dependencies can be modified to become key-based, while Section 12.4 shows how circular sets of inclusion dependencies are modified so that cycles are broken. Section 12.5 shows how schemas not in any of the three allowed classes of ERNF can be modified to conform to the requirements. Section 12.6 presents a larger example of the transformations.

12.1   Producing 3NF schemas

The first transformation starts with a relation schema R and a set of functional dependencies over it. It produces a representation of R as a dependency preserving database schema with the lossless join property and individual schemas in 3NF. The basic idea is to produce a relation schema for each functional dependency in a canonical cover of the original set.

Algorithm 12.1 Computation of a 3NF, dependency preserving, lossless decomposition.
Input. A set R of attributes and a set F of functional dependencies over R.
Output. A decomposition $\mathbf{R} = (R_1, \ldots, R_k)$ of R such that $\mathbf{R}$ is lossless and dependency preserving, and each R_i is in 3NF.
Method.

1. Find a nonredundant canonical cover G for F.

2. Combine the right-hand sides of the dependencies that have the same left-hand side in G. That is, replace all the dependencies $X \rightarrow A_1, \ldots, X \rightarrow A_h$ in G with the dependency $X \rightarrow A_1 \cdots A_h$.

3. For each dependency $X \rightarrow Y$ in G, add a relation schema XY into $\mathbf{R}$ (unless it already contains the schema XY).

4. If **R** is not a lossless decomposition of R, add a schema X to **R**, where X is some key of R. ☐

Example 12.1 In the zip code example with attributes Street, City, and Zip, and dependencies Zip → City and City Street → Zip, the dependency set is already a nonredundant canonical cover. The algorithm would then produce schemas {Zip, City} and {City, Zip, Street}. ☐

Because the essential step in Algorithm 12.1 is the creation of a schema XY for a dependency $X \rightarrow Y$, the algorithm is often called the *synthesis* algorithm.

The algorithm produces a schema for each connection between attributes that has been represented by a functional dependency. A problem with blind use of the synthesis algorithm is that a many-to-many connection between two attributes cannot be represented using a functional dependency, and hence step 3 of the algorithm cannot produce a schema like $R(AB)$, where AB is the key. This can be formally avoided by adding a dummy attribute D and adding the dependency $AB \rightarrow D$; this forces the algorithm to produce the schema $R'(ABD)$, and then the attribute D can be removed.

Almost all the work in the algorithm is done in the computation of a suitable cover for the original dependency set. The properties of the cover lead to desired properties for the resulting database schema.

Theorem 12.1 Given a set R of attributes and a set F of functional dependencies over R, Algorithm 12.1 produces a lossless and dependency preserving decomposition of R into schemas in third normal form.

Proof. The resulting decomposition preserves dependencies, since for the nonredundant canonical cover G of F and for each dependency $X \rightarrow Y$ in G the decomposition has at least one schema that contains XY.

Showing that each relation schema is in third normal form relies heavily on the properties of canonical covers. Assume the algorithm produces a schema S that is not in 3NF. Let S be formed from dependencies with right-hand side X, that is, let $S = XA_1 \cdots A_h$. Then F contains a dependency $X \rightarrow A_i$ for each $i = 1, \ldots, h$. Let $V \rightarrow C$ be the offending dependency, so that V is not a superkey of R, C is not prime, and $C \notin V$.

We show first that X is a key of S. By the construction we have that X determines S functionally. If X is not a key, then for some $D \in X$ we would have $F \vdash X \setminus \{D\} \rightarrow S$. Then the dependencies with left-hand side X would not satisfy the condition of L-minimality.

Since X is a key, we have $C \notin X$, and hence $C = A_i$ for some i. Assume first $V \subset X$. Then the dependency $X \rightarrow A_i$ would contradict the definition of L-minimality, since $F \vdash V \rightarrow A_i$.

Consider then the case where $V \not\subset X$. Then $V = YW$ for some $Y \subset X$ and $W \subseteq A_1 \cdots A_{i-1} A_{i+1} \cdots A_h$, with $W \neq \emptyset$. The dependency $X \to A_i$ was part of the canonical nonredundant cover; we deduce a contradiction by showing that it can be derived from the set $G = F \setminus \{X \to A_i\}$.

Since V is not a superkey and X is a key, we have $X \not\subseteq V_F^+$; hence $V_F^+ = V_G^+$, since in the computation of the closure of V the dependency $X \to A_i$ cannot be used. We assumed that $F \vdash V \to A_i$; hence this implies $G \vdash V \to A_i$.

The dependencies $X \to A_j$ belong to G for $j \neq i$. Thus we have $W \subseteq X_G^+$. Since $Y \subseteq X$, we have $V = YW \subseteq X_G^+$ and hence (since $G \vdash V \to A_i$) it follows that $A_i \in X_G^+$ and $G \vdash X \to A_i$. Thus $F \setminus \{X \to A_i\} \vdash F$, and F is redundant.

Showing that the resulting database schema has the lossless join property is based on the use of Algorithm 10.10 (page 165). We leave the details as Exercise 12.3.   □

Algorithm 12.1 is based on the assumption that the set of attributes and dependencies of the database is known before any relation schema is formed. This is probably an unrealistic assumption, and the algorithm is not sufficient by itself for database design. It can, however, be used to find reasonably good solutions for small complicated subtasks in the design, as in Example 12.1.

12.2   Decomposition into Boyce-Codd normal form

The previous section showed how we could produce a decomposition of a schema consisting of third normal form schemas. Now we consider producing schemas in Boyce-Codd normal form. The basic idea is to start with a relation schema and divide it into two parts on the basis of a functional dependency that violates Boyce-Codd normal form. This division step is continued recursively until all resulting parts satisfy the normal form condition.

We describe the decomposition algorithm in two phases. First, Section 12.2.1 gives a decomposition algorithm for a set of attributes such that each relation schema in the resulting decomposition is in Boyce-Codd normal form. Thus Section 12.2.1 only deals with functional dependencies. Section 12.2.2 considers how inclusion dependencies have to be modified when the schema is decomposed.

12.2.1   Restructuring of the database schema

We assume that the set of functional dependencies considered contains also the dependencies possibly implied by the interaction of functional and inclusion dependencies. Suppose U is a relation schema that is not in Boyce-Codd normal form with respect to a set of functional dependencies F over U. We should replace U by its lossless decomposition $\mathbf{R}$ such that each $R \in \mathbf{R}$ is in BCNF.

Theorem 10.8 (page 163) is useful for creating binary decompositions. It showed that a decomposition of a schema into two parts is lossless if and only if the intersection of the parts determines functionally at least one of the parts. Though Example 10.7 (page 164) shows that there exist lossless decompositions that cannot be expressed as a sequence of lossless binary decompositions, it is also true that we can always find *some* lossless decomposition by decomposing a schema repeatedly on the basis of Theorem 10.8.

The details of the decomposition algorithm are given in Algorithm 12.2.

Algorithm 12.2 Computation of a BCNF decomposition.
Input. A set U of attributes and a set F of functional dependencies over U.
Output. A collection of relation schemas $\mathbf{R}$ over U such that $\mathbf{R}$ is lossless and each $R \in \mathbf{R}$ is in BCNF.
Method. Call Decompose(U, F), where Decompose is the following algorithm.

1.	**if** U is in BCNF with respect to F **then** output U
2.	**else**
3.	let $X \rightarrow Y$ be a nontrivial dependency such that
4.	$F \models X \rightarrow Y$ and X is not a superkey of U;
5.	Decompose($XY, F[XY]$);
6.	Decompose($U \setminus (Y \setminus X), F[U \setminus (Y \setminus X)]$);
7.	**fi**; □

Note that Algorithm 12.2 does not specify how the dependency on lines 3–4 is chosen. Different choices may lead to different decompositions.

Since Algorithm 12.2 calls itself recursively, it is convenient to represent its execution using a tree where each node corresponds to the U parameter of a call to the algorithm. The tree is called the *decomposition tree*. The relation schemas that form the output of Algorithm 12.2 appear in the leaves of the decomposition tree.

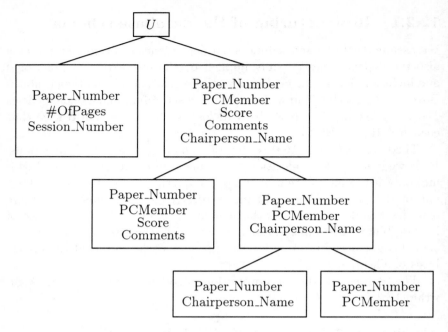

Figure 12.1   A decomposition tree.

Example 12.2 Suppose we are designing the conference database from scratch using the relational data model, without a preceding conceptual analysis phase. Suppose that we have found the dependencies

Paper_Number → #OfPages Session_Number,
Paper_Number PCMember → Score Comments, and
Session_Number → Chairperson_Name.

Let U = {Paper_Number, #OfPages, Session_Number, PCMember, Score, Comments, Chairperson_Name}. If we start to decompose U using the first dependency, continue by using the second dependency, and finally use the derived dependency Paper_Number → Chairperson_Name, we get the decomposition tree shown in Figure 12.1. Starting the decomposition with the last dependency, on the other hand, can yield the decomposition tree in Figure 12.2.

The decompositions do not differ much, especially after the schema {Paper_Number, PCMember} is eliminated from the first decomposition (see Exercise 12.7). Still, the decomposition in Figure 12.2 is clearly the better alternative. □

Example 12.2 illustrates a serious problem with Algorithm 12.2: the quality of the result depends a lot on the dependencies used in the decomposition, and on the order in which the dependencies are applied. A

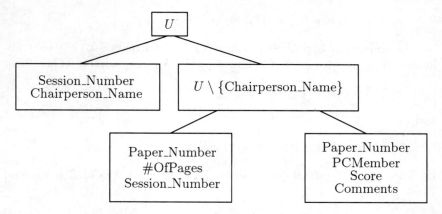

Figure 12.2   Another decomposition tree.

good heuristic seems to be that, instead of an arbitrary BCNF violating dependency $X \rightarrow Y$, one should use the derived dependency $X \rightarrow X_F^+$ as the basis of the decomposition (see Exercise 12.8). Another rule for choosing the dependencies is discussed in Exercise 12.9. There are still cases where only the designer knows which decompositions are natural. In general, the nondeterminism in the algorithm should be replaced by interaction with the designer.

Theorem 12.2 shows the correctness of Algorithm 12.2.

Theorem 12.2 Let U be a set of attributes and F a set of functional dependencies over U. Algorithm 12.2 produces a decomposition **R** of U such that **R** is lossless and each $R \in \mathbf{R}$ is in BCNF.

Proof. The BCNF property is immediate, since each schema in the decomposition is tested for the BCNF property just before it is output. Therefore it is sufficient to establish losslessness. For each node Z in the decomposition tree, define

$$\text{fringe}(Z) = \{X \mid X \text{ is a leaf in the subtree rooted at } Z\}.$$

By using induction on the height of the nodes in the decomposition tree, we shall show that $\text{fringe}(Z)$ is a lossless decomposition of Z for each node Z in the decomposition tree. Since the root node is U, the claim follows.

For any node Z of height 0, that is, for leaves of the decomposition tree, it is obvious that $\{Z\}$ is a lossless decomposition of Z, and we have the basis for the induction.

Suppose then that Z is a branch node of the decomposition tree, and that Z is decomposed into $\{XY, Z \setminus (Y \setminus X)\}$ using $X \rightarrow Y$. Let $\text{fringe}(XY) = \{R_1, \ldots, R_n\}$ and $\text{fringe}(Z \setminus (Y \setminus X)) = \{S_1, \ldots, S_m\}$; thus $\text{fringe}(Z) = \text{fringe}(XY) \cup \text{fringe}(Z \setminus (Y \setminus X)) = \{R_1, \ldots, R_n, S_1, \ldots, S_m\}$. We must show that for any relation r over Z,

$$r[R_1] \bowtie \cdots \bowtie r[R_n] \bowtie r[S_1] \bowtie \cdots \bowtie r[S_m] = r.$$

By the induction hypothesis, fringe(XY) and fringe($Z \setminus (Y \setminus X)$) are lossless decompositions of XY and $Z \setminus (Y \setminus X)$, respectively. Therefore

$$r[XY] = r[R_1] \bowtie \cdots \bowtie r[R_n]$$

and

$$r[Z \setminus (Y \setminus X)] = r[S_1] \bowtie \cdots \bowtie r[S_m].$$

By Theorem 10.8, the decomposition $\{XY, Z \setminus (Y \setminus X)\}$ of Z is lossless. Thus

$$r = r[XY] \bowtie r[Z \setminus (Y \setminus X)].$$

Combining these equations yields the result. $\qquad\qquad\qquad\qquad\square$

In addition to possibly producing unnatural decompositions, Algorithm 12.2 also suffers from efficiency problems. There are two potential sources of inefficiency:

(1) On lines 5 and 6 the projection of a dependency set is computed. This may take exponential time.

(2) The size of the decomposition tree may be exponential in $|U|$.

Note, though, that the BCNF test on line 1 can be carried out in polynomial time, since we have computed the projection of F. Alternatively, we could use F all the time instead of its projections, but then the Boyce-Codd normal form test would become expensive (by Theorem 10.7).

Both of the above inefficiencies can be eliminated. Exercises 12.10 and 12.11 show how to choose the dependency $X \rightarrow Y$ used in Algorithm 12.2 so that the XY schema is guaranteed to be in Boyce-Codd normal form. Then the BCNF test can be omitted: the $Z \setminus (Y \setminus X)$ schema is simply decomposed until it becomes sufficiently small that it is known to be in BCNF even without explicitly carrying out the test. Moreover, the size of the decomposition tree is linear in $|U|$.

Although it is thus possible to derive a decomposition algorithm that works in polynomial time, the use of this algorithm is not recommended. The special method for choosing $X \rightarrow Y$ favors short dependencies, and this increases the possibility of obtaining an unnatural decomposition. Moreover, the algorithm may needlessly decompose a schema that is already in Boyce-Codd normal form (see Exercise 12.12), again a feature that an algorithm intended for practical database design should not have.

A better approach is to maintain the structure of Algorithm 12.2, augment the algorithm with user interaction for choosing the dependency

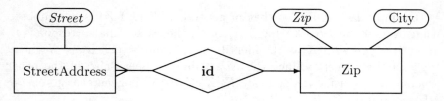

Figure 12.3   An entity-relationship diagram for street addresses and zip codes.

used for dividing the schema, and to develop more efficient methods for computing projections of dependencies or carrying out the BCNF test. Improved algorithms for computing projections were discussed in Section 10.4 (page 154). Chapter 13 describes an alternative representation for dependency sets. The representation makes possible an efficient implementation of many database design problems, as shown in Chapter 13.

Like Algorithm 12.1, Algorithm 12.2 assumes that the attribute set and the set of functional dependencies are known at the beginning of design. This assumption is unrealistic for larger designs, and hence the utility of Algorithm 12.2 is probably the same as that of Algorithm 12.1: it can be used for solving small subtasks that are otherwise hard.

12.2.2   Handling of inclusion dependencies

Inclusion dependencies pose two different problems for the decomposition algorithm. First, since the decomposition creates new relation schemas, should we perhaps add new inclusion dependencies to the database schema? And second, if the schema that is being replaced by its BCNF decomposition has entering or leaving inclusion dependencies, how should they be transformed?

We consider first the possibility of adding new inclusion dependencies. Example 12.3 should provide some intuition.

Example 12.3 Consider the attribute set {Zip, City, Street} discussed in Example 8.13 (page 128). A BCNF decomposition is ({Zip, City}, {Zip, Street}). This decomposition can be considered unwise, as it does not preserve the functional dependency City Street $\rightarrow$ Zip. Still, if one attempts to find an ER-interpretation for the database schema, the ER-diagram shown in Figure 12.3 appears fairly natural.

If we apply the *Rel* mapping to the ER-diagram in Figure 12.3, we get the relation schemas Zip(Zip, City) and StreetAddress(Zip, Street). One functional dependency, Zip $\rightarrow$ City, and one inclusion dependency, StreetAddress[Zip] $\subseteq$ Zip[Zip], would also be generated.   □

Example 12.3 indicates that in general, if R (XYZ) is decomposed using $X \rightarrow Y$ into $R_1(XY)$ and $R_2(XZ)$, the R_1 schema corresponds to an entity type with X as the identifying attributes (called an 'X entity type' in the sequel). Since the X attributes appear also in the other schema, an inclusion dependency $R_2[X] \subseteq R_1[X]$ is generated to ensure referential integrity.

Adding the inclusion dependency presumes that the schema $R_1(XY)$ really represents an X entity type. For this to make sense, there should not be two different X entity types; in other words, $R_1(XY)$ should not be further decomposed using a dependency with X as the left-hand side. Therefore Algorithm 12.2 should only be used with the modification discussed in Exercise 12.8, where instead of an arbitrary BCNF-violating dependency $X \rightarrow Y$ the basis of the decomposition is the derived dependency $X \rightarrow X_F^+$.

Consider then the second problem posed above: how are the inclusion dependencies entering or leaving R transformed when R is decomposed? Suppose $P[V] \subseteq R[W]$ is an inclusion dependency entering R. Four cases can occur.

- If $W \subseteq XY$, the dependency is replaced by $P[V] \subseteq R_1[W]$.

- Otherwise, if $W \subseteq XZ$, the dependency is replaced by $P[V] \subseteq R_2[W]$.

- Otherwise we must have $W \cap Y \neq \emptyset$ and $W \cap Z \neq \emptyset$. If $W \subset R$, a new schema $S(W)$ is created and the inclusion dependency is replaced by three inclusion dependencies: $P[V] \subseteq S[W]$, $S[W \cap XY] \subseteq R_1[W \cap XY]$, and $S[W \cap XZ] \subseteq R_2[W \cap XZ]$.

- If $W = R$, the inclusion dependency is simply replaced by its projections $P[V_1] \subseteq R[W \cap XY]$ and $P[V_2] \subseteq R[W \cap XZ]$. Here V_1 are those attributes of V that correspond to the attributes $W \cap XY$ of W in the inclusion dependency $P[V] \subseteq R[W]$; the sequence V_2 is defined analogously.

The motivation for this transformation is that since the W attributes appear together in an inclusion dependency, the connection among them is meaningful and should be preserved, if possible. If the connection disappears because of the decomposition, a new schema is created for maintaining the attributes W together. The inclusion dependencies are those that are implied by the original inclusion dependency. Fortunately, the situation where a new schema has to be added because of inclusion dependencies is rare: it requires among other conditions that the original inclusion dependency is not unary, and this is not true for most of the inclusion dependencies appearing in practice.

For an inclusion dependency $R[W] \subseteq S[V]$ leaving R, we have similar cases.

- If $W \subseteq XY$, the dependency is replaced by $R_1[W] \subseteq S[V]$.

- Otherwise, if $W \subseteq XZ$, the dependency is replaced by $R_2[W] \subseteq S[V]$.

- Otherwise, if $W \subset R$ we create a new schema $T(W)$ and replace the original inclusion dependency by the three dependencies $T[W] \subseteq S[V]$, $R_1[W \cap XY] \subseteq T[W \cap XY]$, and $R_2[W \cap XZ] \subseteq T[W \cap XZ]$.

- If $W = R$ the inclusion dependency is replaced by its projections as above.

The transformation may create new schemas that violate ERNF, or even BCNF. In such a case the decomposition algorithm is applied iteratively to the new schemas. Since they are smaller than the schema being decomposed, the process eventually terminates.

In this and many subsequent transformations a new schema may be generated for the purpose of keeping a set of attributes together, as for the set W above. The need for this arises because the connection between the attributes is lost by the splitting of some relation schema. However, it may well be the case that the attribute set is still contained in some other relation schema already present in the database schema. Then it is worthwhile to ask the designer whether the inclusion dependency could be redirected to that schema, instead of creating a new schema. We shall not mention this explicitly in the sequel, but it should be done before the introduction of a new schema.

12.3   A transformation for producing key-based inclusion dependencies

From now on we assume that each relation schema in the database schema is in BCNF. There are three other conditions that an entity-relationship normal form schema must satisfy. This section deals with key-basedness.

Suppose a schema S has an entering inclusion dependency $R[X] \subseteq S[Y]$ that is not key-based. If Y is a proper superset of some key K of S, then the inclusion dependency has the form $R[X_1X_2] \subseteq S[KY_2]$. As $K \rightarrow Y_2$, the pullback axiom FI1 (page 143) tells that also $X_1 \rightarrow X_2$. Since R is in BCNF, X_1 is a superkey. If no other dependencies reference the attributes in X_2 of R, these attributes are redundant in R, since for a given value of attributes X_1 the values of attributes X_2 can be retrieved by looking at the relation corresponding to S. Hence the attributes in

X_2 can be omitted from R, and the inclusion dependency is transformed to the key-based form $R[X_1] \subseteq S[Y_1]$. If, on the other hand, there is a dependency referring to the attributes X_2 of R, we leave X_2 in R, but shorten the inclusion dependency to the above key-based form.

Suppose then that in the dependency $R[X] \subseteq S[Y]$ the set Y is not a superkey of S. The existence of the inclusion dependency indicates that the attributes of Y describe some sort of an entity. If S has a leaving key-based inclusion dependency $S[Y] \subseteq T[Z]$, we remove $R[X] \subseteq S[Y]$ and replace it by $R[X] \subseteq T[Z]$. The intuition is that schema T represents the Y-entities better. If such a schema T does not exist, we create it. The attributes of T are exactly Y, and no functional dependencies hold. The inclusion dependency $R[X] \subseteq S[Y]$ is in this case replaced by the dependencies $R[X] \subseteq T[Y]$ and $S[Y] \subseteq T[Y]$.

Example 12.4 Consider the following relational database schema.

Site (*DeptName*, *Proj#*, Budget)
HighRiskProject (*Proj#*, MaxCost)

HighRiskProject[Proj#] $\subseteq$ Site[Proj#]

The inclusion dependency is not key-based. We therefore create a new relation schema Project(*Proj#*) and replace the inclusion dependency with two inclusion dependencies: HighRiskProject[Proj#] $\subseteq$ Project[Proj#] and Site[Proj#] $\subseteq$ Project[Proj#].

After the transformation, the Site schema is a weak entity schema according to the definition of ERNF. This is probably not what we want: the intuition guiding the transformation was that Site represents a relationship type. To turn Site into a relationship schema, we should add to the database schema the relation schema Department (DeptName) and the inclusion dependency Site[DeptName] $\subseteq$ Department[DeptName]. After these transformations the database schema is in entity-relationship normal form. The diagram shown in Figure 12.4 would be produced by *Ent*. □

In the above example, a weak entity schema was transformed to a relationship schema. Generally this can be done as follows. Assume T is a weak entity schema with (for simplicity) one leaving inclusion dependency $T[X] \subseteq R[Y]$. To make T really represent a relationship type, let Z be some key of T, and let $Z' = Z \setminus X$. We must cover Z' with the left-hand sides of leaving key-based inclusion dependencies. If necessary, a new relation schema and a new inclusion dependency are added to the database schema just as above.

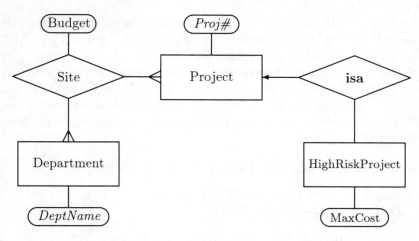

Figure 12.4   An entity-relationship diagram for departments, projects, and high risk projects.

Example 12.5 Consider the relation schemas $R(A)$, $S(AB)$, and $P(B)$, which can be thought to represent two entity types and a relationship type. Then the inclusion dependencies are $S[A] \subseteq R[A]$ and $S[B] \subseteq P[B]$. If the relationship type is not functional, the key of S is AB. Assume now the designer wants to state that the relationship type is mandatory for the R entities. This can be done by giving the inclusion dependency $R[A] \subseteq S[B]$. The addition makes the set of inclusion dependencies circular, and the new dependency is not key-based. Using the transformation for removing nonkey-based dependencies described above, we notice that there is an inclusion dependency leaving S, namely $S[A] \subseteq R[A]$. The transformation removes the dependency $R[A] \subseteq S[A]$ and inserts the (trivial) dependency $R[A] \subseteq R[A]$. Thus the transformation effectively removes the constraint that the relationship is mandatory.   □

12.4   A transformation for producing noncircular sets of inclusion dependencies

The next transformation step is to enforce noncircularity of the inclusion dependencies in the relational database schema.

If a circular subset of inclusion dependencies is found, the designer is asked to choose one schema in the cycle. Let S be the chosen schema, and let $R[X] \subseteq S[Y]$ and $S[Z] \subseteq T[V]$ be the inclusion dependencies involved in the cycle. Then the attribute set $Z \setminus Y$ is removed from S, a new schema $S'(YZ)$ is created, and the inclusion dependency leaving S is replaced by two inclusion dependencies: $S'[Z] \subseteq T[V]$ and $S'[Y] \subseteq S[Y]$. This is repeated until all cycles have been broken.

The idea is to leave S to represent the original entity type, to extract the portion of the entity type that participates in the cycle, and to revert one of the inclusions so that it is directed from the new schema (representing a relationship type) towards the original schema (representing an entity type).

Example 12.6 Consider the following database schema.

> Employee (*EmpName*, DeptName, Salary)
> Department (*DeptName*, Manager)
>
> Employee[DeptName] $\subseteq$ Department[DeptName]
> Department[Manager] $\subseteq$ Employee[EmpName]

Suppose Department is chosen as the breaking point for the cycle between Department and Employee. After the transformation, the new database schema has the following form:

> Employee (*EmpName*, DeptName, Salary)
> ManagedBy (*DeptName*, Manager)
> Department (*DeptName*)
>
> Employee[DeptName] $\subseteq$ Department[DeptName]
> ManagedBy[Manager] $\subseteq$ Employee[EmpName]
> ManagedBy[DeptName] $\subseteq$ Department[DeptName]

The effect is that ManagedBy now represents a relationship between department numbers and employees (the managers of the departments), and Department represents an entity, as it should.

If Employee had been chosen as the schema for breaking the cycle, the result would still be natural, though different (see Exercise 12.13).   □

12.5   Handling schemas that do not represent an object set

Suppose finally that the inclusion dependencies are noncircular and key-based, all relation schemas are in Boyce-Codd normal form, but the relational database schema still is not in entity-relationship normal form. Then it must have relation schemas that do not belong to any of the three classes in the definition of entity-relationship normal form.

There are three cases. The first and easiest is when the schema violates ERNF, but is in WERNF. Transforming such a schema is easy by introducing new relationship schemas. The second case occurs when the left-hand sides of inclusion dependencies leaving the schema are disjoint. Then the offending schema can be transformed to a relationship schema. The third and most complicated case occurs when a schema has several leaving inclusion dependencies whose left-hand sides intersect, but the conditions of weak entity schemas are not satisfied.

In the first case, when the schemas are in weak entity-relationship normal form, the situation is fairly easy. The difference between WERNF and ERNF is that WERNF allows foreign keys, that is, inclusion dependencies whose left-hand side does not intersect a key. If a schema R satisfies the conditions of WERNF, transforming it to ERNF is therefore easy. For each key-based inclusion dependency $R[X] \subseteq S[Y]$ such that X does not intersect any key of R, do the following. Let K be a key of R.

(1) Create a new schema $T(KY)$, with the key K.

(2) Remove the inclusion dependency $R[X] \subseteq S[Y]$.

(3) Remove the attributes of X from R.

(4) Add inclusion dependencies $T[K] \subseteq R[K]$ and $T[Y] \subseteq S[Y]$.

Suppose then the schema R does not satisfy even the conditions of WERNF. In such a case interaction with the designer is especially important, since R probably represents an odd connection between attributes.

Since R violates WERNF, there must be at least one inclusion dependency $R[X] \subseteq S[Y]$ such that X intersects a key of R, since otherwise R would be a strong entity schema with foreign keys.

The second case is as follows. Assume R has one or more leaving inclusion dependencies $R[X_i] \subseteq S_i[Y_i]$, for $i = 1, \ldots, k$, and assume their left-hand sides are disjoint. Denote $Z = \cup_{i=1}^{k} X_i$. If $k > 1$, then R looks like a relationship schema, so there either has to be an inclusion dependency entering R, or the conditions for the keys of relationship schemas are not satisfied. This means that Z is not a key of R, and $Z \setminus X_i$ is not a key of R for any $i = 1, \ldots, k$.

If Z is a subset of a key $Z' = ZW$, we can create a new schema $T(W)$ and add the inclusion dependency $R[W] \subseteq T[W]$. This transforms R to a relationship schema with participating entity schemas $S_1, \ldots, S_k$ and T.

If, on the other hand, the set Z is a superkey, and no $Z \setminus X_i$ is a key, schema R probably represents a k-ary relationship type with an atypical functionality constraint. For example, if $k = 3$ and X_1 is a key of R, then the idea can be that R represents a ternary relationship type where the value of X_1 determines the other values. Such a schema can be made to conform to the requirements of ERNF by dividing it into two schemas $R'(X_1X_2)$ and $R''(X_1X_3)$ representing binary relationships.

If the set Z is neither a superkey nor a subset of a key, the schema R is quite complicated. If K is a key of R, we can create a new schema $T(W)$ for the attribute set $W = K \setminus Z$ and add the inclusion dependency $R[W] \subseteq T[W]$ to reduce the case to the first one.

The third case occurs when the sets X_i intersect each other. Then the schema R might be a weak entity set where multiple inheritance is used. Finding a reasonable representation for such schemas requires considerable user interaction, and we omit even a short description of the possible transformations.

12.6   An example

As an example of the transformation algorithm, consider the following database schema.

    Country (*Country*, Capital, Currency)
    CurrencyValue (*Currency*, ValueIn$)
    CityPopulation (*City*, *Year*, Population)
    Membership (*Country*, *Organization*, EntryDate)
    Export (*Supplier*, *Consumer*, Amount)
    Company (*Company*, Country, Revenues)
    European (*Country*, *Year*, Population)

    Capital → Country
    Currency → Country

    Country[Currency] ⊆ CurrencyValue[Currency]
    Country[Capital] ⊆ CityPopulation[City]
    Membership[Country] ⊆ Country[Country]
    Export[Supplier] ⊆ Country[Country]
    Export[Consumer] ⊆ Country[Country]
    Company[Country] ⊆ Country[Country]
    European[Country] ⊆ Country[Country]

All the relation schemas are in BCNF.

The next thing to check is the key-basedness of the inclusion dependencies. There is one inclusion dependency that is not key-based: Country[Capital] ⊆ CityPopulation[City]. Following the transformation rules given in Section 12.3, we create a new schema: City(City), and replace the inclusion dependency by two new inclusion dependencies: Country[Capital] ⊆ City[City] and CityPopulation[City] ⊆ City[City].

The inclusion dependencies are noncircular, so the final step is the classification of the relation schemas. Most schemas can be uniquely classified as follows:

CurrencyValue	weak entity schema
CityPopulation	weak entity schema
Membership	weak entity schema
Export	relationship schema
European	weak entity schema
City	strong entity schema

Only two relation schemas, Country and Company, do not belong to any of the classes.

Consider first the Company schema. Since the left-hand side of the leaving inclusion dependency does not intersect a key of the schema, Company is a strong entity schema with foreign keys. Using the transformation given in Section 12.5, we remove the attribute Country from the Company schema and create a new schema CompanyCountry(Company, Country). The inclusion dependency Company[Country] $\subseteq$ Country[Country] is replaced by two inclusion dependencies, CompanyCountry[Company] $\subseteq$ Company[Company] and CompanyCountry[Country] $\subseteq$ Country[Country]. This transformation turns Company into a strong entity schema, and the new CompanyCountry schema is a relationship schema.

Finally, we have to deal with the Country schema. The left-hand side of the leaving inclusion dependency Country[Capital] $\subseteq$ CityPopulation[City] intersects a key of the schema, and hence Country is not even in weak entity-relationship normal form. However, as the schema has several keys, we can still use the transformation from WERNF to ERNF and produce the new schemas

CountryCapital (*Country*, Capital)
Country (*Country*, Currency)

Capital $\rightarrow$ Country
Currency $\rightarrow$ Country

CountryCapital[Country] $\subseteq$ Country[Country]
CountryCapital[Capital] $\subseteq$ City[City]
Country[Currency] $\subseteq$ CurrencyValue[Currency]

While the schema is now fairly natural, the two keys of Country can produce difficulties. We can remedy this by creating still new schemas:

Country (*Country*)
CountryCurrency (*Country*, Currency)

Currency → Country

CountryCurrency[Country] ⊆ Country[Country]
CountryCurrency[Currency] ⊆ CurrencyValue[Currency]

To summarize, the transformation to ERNF yields the following relational database schema.

Country (*Country*)
CountryCapital (*Country*, Capital)
CountryCurrency (*Country*, Currency)
CurrencyValue (*Currency*, ValueIn$)
CityPopulation (*City*, *Year*, Population)
Membership (*Country*, *Organization*, EntryDate)
Export (*Supplier*, *Consumer*, Amount)
Company (*Company*, Revenues)
CompanyCountry (*Company*, Country)
European (*Country*, *Year*, Population)
City (*City*)

Capital → Country
Currency → Country

CountryCapital[Country] ⊆ Country[Country]
CountryCapital[Capital] ⊆ City[City]
CountryCurrency[Country] ⊆ Country[Country]
CountryCurrency[Currency] ⊆ CurrencyValue[Currency]
CityPopulation[City] ⊆ City[City]
Membership[Country] ⊆ Country[Country]
Export[Supplier] ⊆ Country[Country]
Export[Consumer] ⊆ Country[Country]
CompanyCountry[Company] ⊆ Company[Company]
CompanyCountry[Country] ⊆ Country[Country]
European[Country] ⊆ Country[Country]

The *Ent* mapping described in Chapter 11 generates from this relational database schema the ER-diagram shown in Figure 12.5.

The result appears natural. Perhaps the most surprising point is that Membership is a *subclass* of Country, not a relationship type. This, however, becomes more understandable with a better choice of names. If Membership was called MemberCountry instead, its weak entity type nature would be clear. Membership cannot be a relationship type, since the relational schema does not allow recording information about organizations without information about their member countries. And since

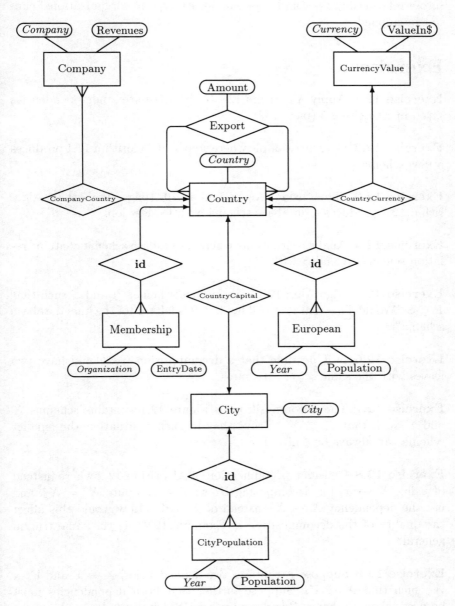

Figure 12.5   Result of the ER-mapping.

Membership can be represented in the ER-model in its original form, the normalizing transformation (that otherwise *would* transform Membership into a relationship type and create an entity type for organizations) cannot be applied.

Exercises

Exercise 12.1 Apply Algorithm 12.1 to the attributes and dependencies given in Exercise 8.5 (page 132).

Exercise 12.2 Give an example where step 4 of Algorithm 12.1 produces a new schema.

Exercise 12.3 Show using Algorithm 10.10 (page 165) that Algorithm 12.1 produces a database schema with lossless join.

Exercise 12.4 Analyze situations where a database schema contains relation schemas R and S with $R \subseteq S$.

Exercise 12.5 Algorithm 12.1 can produce schemas R and S such that $R \subseteq S$. Would Theorem 12.1 still hold, if R is left out of the final database schema?

Exercise 12.6 Is it possible that a decomposition tree could have two leaves with the same set of attributes?

Exercise 12.7 The decomposition in Figure 12.1 contains schemas X and Y such that $X \subset Y$. Prove that in such a situation the smaller schema can always be omitted.

Exercise 12.8 Consider a modification of Algorithm 12.2 where instead of using $X \to Y$ for decomposing U, we first compute $X' = X_F^+$ and use the dependency $X \to X'$ instead of $X \to Y$. How would this affect the quality of the decomposition in Example 12.2? Is the same true in general?

Exercise 12.9 Suppose F contains two dependencies, $X \to Y$ and $V \to W$, such that $X \subset V$. Suppose further that both dependencies must be used when a schema R is decomposed. Which dependency should be applied first? Why?

Exercise 12.10 Let F be a set of standard functional dependencies over U. Prove the following claims.

(a) Every set of attributes $X \subseteq U$ for which $|X| = 2$ is in Boyce-Codd normal form.

(b) If a set of attributes $X \subseteq U$ is not in Boyce-Codd normal form, there exist attributes $A, B \in X$ such that $(X \setminus AB) \to A$.

Exercise 12.11 Use the results of Exercise 12.10 to develop a decomposition algorithm that works in polynomial time with respect to $|F|$ and $|U|$. What is the complexity of your algorithm?

Hint. Use exhaustive search to find the attributes A and B in case (b) of Exercise 12.10.

Exercise 12.12 Give an example of a relation schema R and a set of functional dependencies F such that R is in BCNF with respect to F, but the algorithm suggested in Exercise 12.11 still decomposes R.

Exercise 12.13 Consider the relational database schema given in Example 12.6. Suppose Employee is chosen as the schema for breaking the cycle in the inclusion dependencies. What would be the result of the transformation given in Section 12.4? How does it compare with the schema obtained in Example 12.6 – which one is more natural?

Exercise 12.14 Transform the following relational database schema into ERNF and apply the *Ent* mapping to the result.

> Salesman(*EmpName*, Name, Salary, Manager)
> SoldPolicy(*Policy#*, Agent, Beneficiary, Amount)
>
> Salesman[Manager] $\subseteq$ Salesman[EmpName]
> SoldPolicy[Agent] $\subseteq$ Salesman[EmpName]

Bibliographic notes

Much of the literature on relational database design has concentrated on schema transformations, often using the term normalization. General studies of the equivalence of relational database schemas can be found in [BMSU81, MMSU80]; see [Ris78, AC78] for some early work. The algorithms in Sections 12.1 and 12.2 are the classical relational database design algorithms. The original synthesis algorithm was suggested by Bernstein [Ber76]. Variations have been proposed in [BDB79, BM87]. The decomposition algorithm of Section 12.2 has its origins in the work by Delobel and Casey [DC73], and the efficient decomposition method of Exercises 12.10 and 12.11 is by Tsou and Fischer [TF82b]. De Bra and

Paredaens [DP90] consider functional dependencies that almost hold and show how the exceptions can be removed by horizontal decompositions.

The method for transforming circular sets of inclusion dependencies comes from [MR86b], and the rest of the ERNF transformation algorithm is from [MR90].

Other proposals for entity-relationship transformation algorithms (usually combined with the ER-mapping) can be found in [Klu80, MZ80, JK89, RR88, RR89, SC89, NA88, DA83, DA88]. Many of the suggested methods do not use inclusion dependencies, and even when inclusion dependencies are used, they are often given only a secondary role, with the main emphasis being put on functional dependencies.

The example discussed in Section 12.6, as well as many of the smaller examples in this chapter, are from [JK89].

Chapter 13

Efficient Algorithms for Design Problems

Transformations of relation schemas occur in two-level database design in the cases where changes or additions on the relational level lead to schemas violating some normal form. The previous chapter showed what should be done to the violating schemas, but did not consider how these schemas are recognized and how the algorithmic problems are solved.

In Chapter 10 we saw that several of the computational problems encountered in database design tools are computationally intractable. Since these problems have to be solved in design tools, the basic solution has been to use trivial algorithms taking exponential time.

This situation is unsatisfactory in two respects. First, the problems do not appear to be that hard: hence it can be suspected that the intractability of these problems is due to some contrived cases not occurring in practice. Second, the exponential time algorithms are far too slow to be used in real situations: for example, an exponential search through all the subsets of a fifteen-attribute schema, where each subset has to be tested for some property, takes a long time.

In this chapter we introduce the concept of a *maximal set*, which remedies both these problems. A maximal set is an attribute set X which for some attribute A is a largest possible set *not* determining A, that is, any proper superset of X determines A.

The maximal sets for the attributes in a relation schema are in fact an alternative representation for the functional dependencies holding in that relation schema. The number of maximal sets for the attributes in a schema is closely connected to the difficulty of the computational problems for that schema. If a schema has few maximal sets, it is for example easy to decide whether a subschema is in some normal form. Schemas in normal form have few maximal sets, whereas highly unnormalized schemas have many maximal sets.

Maximal sets also give additional insight to the behavior of functional dependencies, and they will be crucial for the generation and analysis of example databases in Chapters 14 and 15.

We start in Section 13.1 by giving the basic definitions. In Section 13.2 we describe an alternative way of defining these sets; this way will be important in future chapters. Section 13.3 relates the maximal sets to the left-hand sides of dependencies. Section 13.4 considers the number of maximal sets, while Section 13.5 shows how maximal sets can be computed from a dependency set. The use of maximal sets in schema transformation methods is studied in Sections 13.6, 13.7, and 13.8.

13.1   Definitions

Recall that we assume that all functional dependencies are standard. Let F be a set of functional dependencies on a schema R, X a subset of R and $A \in X$. Then a set $Y \subseteq X$ is a *maximal set for A*, if $Y \not\rightarrow A$ and for any $Z \subseteq X$ such that $Y \subset Z$ we have $F \models Z \rightarrow A$. Hence a maximal set Y for an attribute A is a set that does not determine A, but the addition of any attribute to Y gives an attribute set that does determine A.

We denote by $\max(F, X, A)$ the collection of all maximal sets, that is

$$\max(F, X, A) =$$
$$\{Y \subseteq X \mid Y \text{ is a maximal set (with respect}$$
$$\text{to } \subseteq) \text{ such that } F \not\models Y \rightarrow A\}.$$

If F is clear from the context, we write just $\max(X, A)$. If $X = R$, we write $\max(F, A)$ or just $\max(A)$. The union of the sets $\max(X, A)$, where $A \in X$, is denoted by $\mathrm{MAX}(X)$.

Example 13.1 Let $R(AB)$ be a schema and let $F = \{A \rightarrow B\}$. Then $\max(F, R, A) = \{\{B\}\}$ (or, using the shorthand notation introduced earlier, $\max(F, R, A) = \{B\}$) and $\max(F, R, B) = \{\emptyset\}$.   □

Example 13.2 Let $R(ABCDE)$ be a relation schema and consider the dependency set $F = \{AB \rightarrow D, BC \rightarrow D, D \rightarrow E, E \rightarrow A\}$. Then

$$\max(F, R, A) = \{B, C\},$$
$$\max(F, R, B) = \{ACDE\},$$
$$\max(F, R, C) = \{ABDE\},$$

$$\max(F, R, D) = \{ACE, B\}, \text{ and}$$
$$\max(F, R, E) = \{AC, B\}. \qquad \qquad \qquad \square$$

The collection of maximal sets does not depend on the representation of the set of functional dependencies. If dependency set G is a cover of F, then $\max(F, X, A) = \max(G, X, A)$ for all X and A.

13.2   A characterization of maximal sets

In this section we give an alternative definition for the collection of maximal sets. The basic definition was in some sense local: it started from an attribute A, and went on to form the largest possible sets not determining A. The alternative definition is a global one: it considers the whole collection of subsets of a schema, and defines a subcollection, which turns out to contain exactly the maximal sets. This characterization gives us tools for developing algorithms based on maximal sets, and for developing methods for the use of example relations in Chapters 14 and 15.

Let X be a subset of a schema R with functional dependencies F, and let $Y \subseteq X$. We say that Y is F-*closed* in X, if $Y_F^+ \cap X = Y$. Thus an F-closed set Y in X does not determine (using F) any attributes of X outside Y. If F is clear from the context, we say that Y is closed in X; if X is the same set as the relation schema R, we say that Y is F-closed or just closed.

Denote

$$\mathrm{CL}(X) = \{Y \subseteq X \mid Y \text{ is closed in } X\}.$$

The collection of closed sets contains enough information about F for solving the implication problem. Let $\mathrm{CL}(R)$ be the collection of closed sets for F. Then $F \models X \rightarrow A$ if and only if for every $Y \in \mathrm{CL}(R)$ such that $X \subseteq Y$ we also have $A \in Y$.

Example 13.3 For the dependencies and attributes in Example 13.2 we have

$$\mathrm{CL}(R) \;=\; \{\emptyset, A, B, C, AC, AE,$$
$$ACE, ADE, ABDE, ACDE, ABCDE\}.$$

Looking at these sets we can for example determine that $F \not\models AD \rightarrow C$, since $ADE \in \mathrm{CL}(R)$, $AD \subseteq ADE$, and $C \notin ADE$. Similarly we see that $F \models D \rightarrow A$, since every set in $\mathrm{CL}(R)$ containing D contains A, too. $\square$

While the $\mathrm{CL}(X)$ family represents the same information as the original dependency set, it is often fairly large, as in Example 13.3. A possibility for representing this collection more succinctly is opened by noticing that the intersection of two closed sets is closed. This means that we can omit from $\mathrm{CL}(X)$ the sets that can be obtained as intersections of other sets in $\mathrm{CL}(X)$. Thus we define

$$\mathrm{GEN}(X) = \{Y \in \mathrm{CL}(X) \mid Y \subset \cap\{W \in \mathrm{CL}(X) \mid Y \subset W\}\}.$$

The intersection of an empty collection of subsets of X is taken to be X. Hence $\mathrm{GEN}(X)$ consists of those closed subsets of X that cannot be expressed as intersections of other closed sets.

Example 13.4 Continuing Example 13.3, we obtain

$$\mathrm{GEN}(R) = \{B, C, ABDE, AC, ACDE, ACE\}.$$

Note that this is exactly the collection of sets obtained in Example 13.2.
□

Lemma 13.1 Each set in $\mathrm{CL}(X)$ can be expressed as an intersection of the elements in $\mathrm{GEN}(X)$, and $\mathrm{GEN}(X)$ is the smallest subcollection of $\mathrm{CL}(X)$ with this property.
□

Using this lemma, we can define that $\mathrm{GEN}(X)$ is the *family of generators* for the collection $\mathrm{CL}(X)$.

We shall show that the MAX and GEN families are the same. For this, we need a preliminary lemma.

Lemma 13.2 If $Y \in \max(X, A)$, then Y is closed in X.

Proof. Let $Z = Y_F^+ \cap X$. Since Y does not determine A, we have $Z \not\rightarrow A$; since $Y \subseteq Z$ and Y is maximal, we have $Y = Z$. Thus Y is closed.
□

Theorem 13.1 $\mathrm{MAX}(X) = \mathrm{GEN}(X)$.

Proof. Let $Y \in \mathrm{MAX}(X)$ and let $A \in X$ be such that $Y \in \max(X, A)$. Then Y is closed in X, and can be expressed as an intersection of some members of $\mathrm{GEN}(X)$. Hence for each $B \in X \setminus Y$ the collection $\mathrm{GEN}(X)$ contains a set W_B satisfying $Y \subseteq W_B$ and $B \notin W_B$. Thus for A we have $Y \subseteq W_A$ and $A \notin W_A$. Because W_A is closed, it follows that $W_A \not\rightarrow A$. Since $Y \in \max(X, A)$, we have $Y = W_A$, and $Y \in \mathrm{GEN}(X)$.

Suppose then $Y \in \mathrm{GEN}(X)$. Since Y is closed in X, for each $B \in X \setminus Y$ there exists a set $Z_B \in \max(X, B)$ such that $Y \subseteq Z_B$. By Lemma 13.2 we know that $Z_B \in \mathrm{CL}(X)$ for all $B \in X \setminus Y$. Since

$$\cap\{Z_B \mid B \in X \setminus Y\} = Y,$$

the set Y can be expressed as an intersection of closed sets Z_B. But since $Y \in \mathrm{GEN}(X)$, this means that $Y = Z_A$ for some $A \in X \setminus Y$, and hence $Y \in \mathrm{MAX}(X)$.
□

13.3   Left-hand sides of dependencies

We saw that the two collections MAX and GEN are the same. In this section we relate this collection to the set of left-hand sides of dependencies. Given a relation schema R, a set F of standard functional dependencies, and an attribute $A \in R$, denote by lhs(A) the set of minimal attribute sets $X \subseteq R$ such that $X \rightarrow A$ follows from F. That is,

$$\mathrm{lhs}(A) = \{X \subseteq R \mid F \models X \rightarrow A \text{ and for all } Y \subset X : F \not\models Y \rightarrow A\}.$$

The families lhs(A) contain all the information about F, although F can be a much more succinct representation in some situations.

Example 13.5 For the dependency set of Example 13.2 the lhs-sets are as follows:

$$\mathrm{lhs}(A) = \{A, E, D, BC\},$$
$$\mathrm{lhs}(B) = \{B\},$$
$$\mathrm{lhs}(C) = \{C\},$$
$$\mathrm{lhs}(D) = \{D, AB, BC, BE\}, \text{ and}$$
$$\mathrm{lhs}(E) = \{E, D, AB, BC\}.$$

□

In this section we show that the families lhs(A) and max(A) are closely related. We assume throughout that R and F are fixed.

We need to borrow some material from the theory of hypergraphs. A collection $\mathcal{H}$ of subsets of R is a *(simple) hypergraph*, if no element of $\mathcal{H}$ is empty and if $X, Y \in \mathcal{H}$ and $X \subseteq Y$ imply $X = Y$.[1] The elements of $\mathcal{H}$ are called the *edges* of the hypergraph, and the elements of R are the *vertices* of the hypergraph.

We first note that lhs(A) is a hypergraph. The collection max(A) is not necessarily a hypergraph, since, as we saw in Example 13.1, the empty set can belong to max(A). However, the collection cmax(A) of complements of the maximal sets,

$$\mathrm{cmax}(A) = \{R \setminus W \mid W \in \mathrm{max}(A)\},$$

is a hypergraph.

Given a simple hypergraph $\mathcal{H}$ on R, a *transversal* T of $\mathcal{H}$ is a subset of R intersecting all the edges of $\mathcal{H}$, that is,

$$T \cap E \neq \emptyset \text{ for all } E \in \mathcal{H}.$$

Transversals are also called *hitting sets*. A *minimal transversal* of $\mathcal{H}$ is a transversal T such that no $T' \subset T$ is a transversal. The collection of minimal transversals of $\mathcal{H}$ is denoted be Tr($\mathcal{H}$). It is a hypergraph on R.

---

[1] Some authors require also that the union of the sets in $\mathcal{H}$ is R; we do not.

Example 13.6 Continuing Example 13.2, we compute the cmax families and the sets of their minimal transversals.

$$\mathrm{cmax}(F, R, A) = \{ACDE, ABDE\},$$
$$\mathrm{Tr}(\mathrm{cmax}(F, R, A)) = \{A, D, E, BC\};$$
$$\mathrm{cmax}(F, R, B) = \{B\},$$
$$\mathrm{Tr}(\mathrm{cmax}(F, R, B)) = \{B\};$$
$$\mathrm{cmax}(F, R, C) = \{C\},$$
$$\mathrm{Tr}(\mathrm{cmax}(F, R, C)) = \{C\};$$
$$\mathrm{cmax}(F, R, D) = \{BD, ACDE\},$$
$$\mathrm{Tr}(\mathrm{cmax}(F, R, D)) = \{D, AB, BC, BE\}; \text{ and}$$
$$\mathrm{cmax}(F, R, E) = \{BDE, ACDE\},$$
$$\mathrm{Tr}(\mathrm{cmax}(F, R, E)) = \{D, E, AB, BC\}.$$

Comparing with Example 13.5, we see that the minimal transversals of the cmax-sets are exactly the lhs-sets. □

The behavior in the example is no accident, as the following simple lemma shows.

Lemma 13.3 $\mathrm{Tr}(\mathrm{cmax}(A)) = \mathrm{lhs}(A)$.

Proof. We show that for any set $X \subseteq R$, the dependency $X \to A$ holds if and only if X is a transversal of the hypergraph $\mathrm{cmax}(A)$. Since the collections $\mathrm{lhs}(A)$ and $\mathrm{Tr}(\mathrm{cmax}(A))$ contain the minimal sets with these properties, the claim follows.

Assume $X \to A$ holds. If for some $W \in \max(A)$ we have $X \cap (R \backslash W) = \emptyset$, we have $X \subseteq W$ and thus $X \not\to A$, since W does not determine A as a maximal set. Thus $X \cap (R \backslash W) \neq \emptyset$ for all $W \in \max(A)$, and X is a transversal of $\mathrm{cmax}(A)$.

For the converse, let X be a transversal of $\mathrm{cmax}(A)$. Then for all $W \in \max(A)$ the intersection $X \cap (R \backslash W)$ is nonempty, and hence X is not included in any maximal set. But this means that $X \to A$ holds. □

Corollary 13.1 $\mathrm{cmax}(A) = \mathrm{Tr}(\mathrm{lhs}(A))$.

Proof. For any simple hypergraph $\mathcal{H}$ we have $\mathrm{Tr}(\mathrm{Tr}(\mathcal{H})) = \mathcal{H}$. □

The concept of a transversal of a hypergraph turns out to be useful for other applications, too. Next we give an algorithm for computing $\mathrm{Tr}(\mathcal{H})$ for a simple hypergraph $\mathcal{H}$.

Algorithm 13.1 Computing the set of minimal transversals for a simple hypergraph.
Input. A simple hypergraph $\mathcal{H}$ on a set R.
Output. The edges of the hypergraph $\mathrm{Tr}(\mathcal{H})$.
Method.

1.   Tr := $\{\emptyset\}$;
2.   **for** each $E \in \mathcal{H}$ **do**
3.   Tr := $\{X \cup \{e\} \mid X \in \text{Tr} \wedge e \in E\}$;
4.   Tr := $\{X \in \text{Tr} \mid$ there is no set $Y \in \text{Tr}$ with $Y \subset X\}$;
5.   **od**;

The output is Tr.   □

Algorithm 13.1 can sometimes generate the same set several times. Some optimizations are possible for special cases.

13.4   The number of maximal sets

The number of maximal sets in a relation schema has a twofold effect on database design. First, the number of maximal sets indicates the number of rows needed for an example relation (see Chapter 14). Second, the algorithms for several database design problems run in time which is proportional to the number of maximal sets, as we see later in this chapter.

This section contains a collection of results on the number of maximal sets. We first address the effect of the length of the left-hand side of the dependencies. After that, we address the question of modularity: if we have two parts in the relation schema, and they are (fairly) independent, what can be said about the number of maximal sets? After that we analyze the number of maximal sets in relation schemas that are in normal form, and give a very general result connecting the size of the max-family to the sizes of the left-hand sides of the dependencies.

We start by examining how the length of the left-hand sides of the dependencies affects the number of maximal sets. Suppose first that all dependencies of F are unary, that is, $|V| = 1$ for each $V \to Y \in F$.

Consider a set $W \in \max(F, X, A)$. Then $W = \{B \in X \mid B \not\to A\}$, by the definition of maximal sets and by the assumption that all dependencies are unary. Hence the family $\max(F, X, A)$ contains always exactly one set, and thus the schema R has at most $|R|$ maximal sets. Also, the collection of maximal sets is easy to compute.

Unfortunately, the step from unary dependencies to binary ones can cause an explosion in the number of maximal sets. Consider the following dependency set F_p.

$$
\begin{aligned}
A_1 A_2 &\to B \\
A_3 A_4 &\to B \\
&\vdots \\
A_{2p-1} A_{2p} &\to B
\end{aligned}
$$

This set of dependencies produces a MAX collection with (at least) 2^p members. Thus even sets of binary dependencies can have large MAX families.

Next we analyze how the structure of the dependency set influences the number of maximal sets. The first result states the intuitively obvious fact that only attributes that can be used in deriving A can have an effect on the number of maximal sets for A. The antecedents of an attribute set X, denoted by X_F^-, were defined in Exercise 10.18. Intuitively, X_F^- is the set of all attributes which can be used in deriving X using the dependencies in F. Formally, we defined this concept iteratively:

(1) $X_0 = X$;

(2) $X_{i+1} = X_i \cup \{B \mid B \in Y$ for some $Y \to Z \in F$
  such that $Z \cap X_i \neq \emptyset\}$.

The iteration stops after a finite number of iterations when $X_{i+1} = X_i$. The set X_i for which this holds was denoted by X_F^-.

We have the following simple result.

Theorem 13.2 (i) Let $k = |A_F^- \cap X|$. Then $|\max(F, X, A)| \leq 2^k$.
(ii) Let $k' = |(A_F^- \setminus \{B \in X \mid B \to A\}) \cap X|$. Then $|\max(F, X, A)| \leq 2^{k'}$.
  Proof. Exercise 13.6.   □

Theorem 13.2 is reassuring. If we add a new attribute B to the schema and B has nothing to do with A, then the number of maximal sets for A is not changed.

The key factor of a schema influencing the number of maximal sets is the number of essentially different starting sets for deriving an attribute. Thus the structure of the lhs-collection determines the number of maximal sets. The pathological example F_p has p independent dependencies with B on their right-hand side, and this results in a MAX collection of at least 2^p members.

Theorem 13.3 Let F be a set of functional dependencies over R, and let $X \subseteq R$. Then

$$|\max(X, A)| \leq \prod_{W \in \text{lhs}(A)} |W|.$$

  Proof. Exercise 13.7.   □

We continue by analyzing the effect of the structure of the dependency set on the number of maximal sets. The general result of Theorem 13.3 can be applied to BCNF and 3NF schemas: the size of the MAX family is bounded by (approximately) the product of the sizes of the keys. While a schema in normal form can have an exponential number of maximal sets, it at least requires a lot of keys.

Theorem 13.4 Let R be in BCNF with respect to F. Denote the keys of R by $X_1, \ldots, X_n$, and let Y be the set of nonprime attributes of R, that is, $Y = R \setminus (X_1 \cup \ldots \cup X_k)$. The size of MAX($R$) is at most

$$\left(\prod_{i=1}^{k} |X_i| \right) (|Y| + 1).$$

Proof. Exercise 13.8.   □

Theorem 13.5 Let R be in 3NF with respect to F, and let X_i and Y be as in Theorem 13.4. Denote by $Z_1, \ldots, Z_m$ the sets of attributes that are not keys but still imply some prime attribute. The size of MAX(R) is at most

$$\left(\prod_{i=1}^{k} |X_i| \right) \left(\prod_{j=1}^{m} (|Z_j| + 1) \right) (|Y| + 1).$$

Proof. Exercise 13.9.   □

13.5   Computing the collection of maximal sets

In this section we consider how the family of maximal sets can be computed for a given set of functional dependencies. Corollary 13.1 and Algorithm 13.1 give one way of computing the maximal sets from the collection of minimal left-hand sides, but this collection is seldom directly available.

Since there can be exponentially many sets in the MAX family, we cannot achieve a polynomial time algorithm. Our goal is rather to obtain a method which computes the maximal sets quickly with respect to their number. Even this seems difficult; however, we can formulate a simple incremental algorithm for the task which works fairly well in most situations.

We start with a preliminary lemma about recognizing maximal sets.

Lemma 13.4 Let F be a set of dependencies over R and $X \subseteq R$. Testing whether $Y \in \max(X, A)$ can be done in time $O(|X| \cdot \|F\|)$.

   Proof. Check first that $F \not\models Y \to A$, and then check that for each $B \in X \setminus Y$ we have $F \models YB \to A$. We have to compute the closure of at most $|X| + 1$ attribute sets, so the time needed is $O(|X| \cdot \|F\|)$ by Theorem 10.3 (page 152).   □

We denote the algorithm that performs the test of Lemma 13.4 by maximal(Y, A, F, X).

We aim at an algorithm for computing the family of maximal sets iteratively. That is, we start from the maximal sets for the empty dependency set, and then add dependencies one at a time and update the collection. The next theorem describes how the maximal sets with respect to a dependency set relate to the maximal sets with respect to a slightly smaller dependency set.

Theorem 13.6 Let $G = F \cup \{Y \to Y'\}$ and let $W \in \max(G, A)$. Either $W \in \max(F, A)$, or for some $B \in Y$, $Z \in \max(F, B)$, and $X \in \max(F, A)$ we have $W = X \cap Z$.

Proof. Assume $W \notin \max(F, A)$. Since $W \in \max(G, A)$, the set W does not determine A in G nor in F. Thus some proper superset X of W belongs to $\max(F, A)$. First, X must contain Y; otherwise X^+ would not change by going from F to G. Since X is F-closed, this would imply that X is a G-closed set that does not determine A. But this is impossible, since W is maximal among such sets, and X properly contains W.

On the other hand, Y cannot be contained in W. For if $Y \subseteq W$, then $YY' \subseteq W$, since W is G-closed as a member of $\max(G, A)$. Therefore $YY' \subseteq X$, and X is also G-closed. Again X would be a G-closed set extending W and not containing A, a contradiction.

Thus $Y \setminus W$ is nonempty; let $B \in Y \setminus W$ be arbitrary. Now W cannot determine B in F. This follows from the facts that W is F-closed and G-closed as a member of $\max(G, A)$, and that $B \notin W$. Therefore some member of $\max(F, B)$ must contain W. Let Z be an arbitrary set in $\max(F, B)$ with this property. We shall complete the proof by showing that $W = X \cap Z$.

The first part, $W \subseteq X \cap Z$, follows immediately from the facts that $W \subseteq X$ and $W \subseteq Z$. For the other direction it is sufficient to show that $X \cap Z$ does not determine A in G; the membership of W in $\max(G, A)$ then yields that $W = X \cap Z$.

We know that $X \cap Z$ is F-closed, since X and Z are. Also $Y \not\subseteq Z$, since $B \in Y$ and $B \notin Z$. Thus $Y \not\subseteq X \cap Z$ and $X \cap Z$ is G-closed. Since $X \in \max(F, A)$, we have $A \notin X$ and $A \notin X \cap Z$. Therefore $X \cap Z$ does not determine A in G. □

Using Theorem 13.6 we can now formulate an algorithm for computing the maximal sets for a set of functional dependencies.

Algorithm 13.2 Computation of maximal sets.
Input. A relation schema R and a functional dependency set F.
Output. Families $\max(F, R, A)$ for each $A \in R$.
Method.

```
1.     for all A ∈ R do
2.          max(A) := {R \ {A}};
3.     od;
4.     G := ∅;
5.     for all Y → Y' ∈ F do
6.          G := G ∪ {Y → Y'};
7.          for all A ∈ R do
8.               newmax(A) := max(A);
9.               for all W ∈ max(A) do
10.                   if not maximal(W, A, G, R) then
11.                        newmax(A) := newmax(A) \ {W};
12.                        for all B ∈ Y do
13.                             for all Z ∈ max(B) do
14.                                  if maximal(W ∩ Z, A, G, R) then
15.                                       newmax(A) := newmax(A)
16.                                            ∪ {W ∩ Z};
17.                                  fi;
18.                             od;
19.                        od;
20.                   fi;
21.               od;
22.          od;
23.          for all A ∈ R do
24.               max(A) := newmax(A);
25.          od;
26.     od;                                                 □
```

Algorithm 13.2 could be fine tuned further. For instance, it is not difficult to see that the test on line 10 could be replaced by the more efficient test

$$Y \subseteq W \land Y' \not\subseteq W.$$

However, since the algorithm works by computing the MAX sets for increasing subsets of F, the essential factor determining the complexity of the algorithm is the size of the collection of MAX sets.

13.6 Projecting maximal sets

A common feature of relational database design algorithms is that schemas are replaced by collections of smaller schemas. Assuming that the maximal sets are initially computed for a large schema, it would be useful if the maximal sets for the subschemas could then be computed fast. Suppose therefore that we are given a set of dependencies F over R, and the corresponding maximal sets $\max(F, R, A)$ for each $A \in R$. Let $X \subseteq R$. How do we efficiently find the sets $\max(F, X, A)$? The following lemma shows that this is easy.

Lemma 13.5 Let $W \in \max(X, A)$ for some $X \subseteq R$. Then $W = W' \cap X$ for some $W' \in \max(R, A)$.

Proof. By the definition of maximal sets, $W \subseteq X$ and $W \not\to A$. Thus $W \subseteq W'$ for some $W' \in \max(R, A)$, implying $W \subseteq W' \cap X$. If W is properly contained in $W' \cap X$, W is not a maximal subset of X not determining A (since $W' \cap X \not\to A$), a contradiction. $\square$

Thus we can compute $\max(X, A)$ by considering each set W' in $\max(R, A)$ and retaining those sets of the form $W' \cap X$ for which the call maximal$(W' \cap X, A, F, X)$ returns **true**.

Hence a subschema has no more maximal sets than the whole schema. For some dependency sets the size of any cover for a projection of the set is exponential in the size of the original set (see Exercise 10.17 (page 176)). Thus the representation of functional dependencies using maximal sets is more robust than the usual representation with respect to taking projections.

Lemma 13.5 can also be used to avoid the computation of projections of dependency sets needed in many design algorithms. Instead of an explicit representation of a cover for the projected dependencies, we are usually only interested in the implication problem: do the projected dependencies logically imply a given dependency? Exercise 13.3 shows how the maximal sets can be used to solve the implication problem. Thus to solve the implication problem for the projected dependencies, we can compute the projections of the maximal sets and use them as Exercise 13.3 indicates.

13.7   Testing the primality of attributes

We now move to showing how maximal sets can be used in design algorithms. The first problem is PRIMALITY, that is, deciding whether an attribute belongs to some key.

Lemma 13.6 If $(WA)^+ = R$ and $W^+ \neq R$, then A is a prime attribute.

Proof. If $(WA)^+ = R$, there must exist a key of R, say K, such that $K \subseteq WA$. Since $W^+ \neq R$, we have $K \not\subseteq W$; therefore, $A \in K$ and thus A is prime. $\square$

A straightforward primality test based on Lemma 13.6 would construct each subset W not containing A and test the conditions of the lemma. The time requirement is $O(2^{|R|-1} \cdot \|F\|)$. The following results show that instead of all possible subsets W, we can restrict ourselves to maximal sets and obtain a corresponding improvement in the time bound.

Theorem 13.7 Attribute A is prime if and only if $(WA)^+ = R$ for some $W \in \max(R, A)$.

  Proof. Suppose A is prime, and let K be a key that contains A; thus $K^+ = R$. Denote $Y = K \setminus \{A\}$. Thus Y is a proper subset of R not determining A (since K is a key). Therefore $Y \subseteq W$ for some $W \in \max(R, A)$. Since $K^+ = R$ and $K = YA \subseteq WA$, it follows that $(WA)^+ = R$.

  Conversely, let $W \in \max(R, A)$ such that $(WA)^+ = R$. Then $W^+ \neq R$, since W does not determine A. By Lemma 13.6, attribute A is prime. □

  We denote $|\max(X, A)|$ by m_A (the set X will be obvious from the context). We further denote

$$m = \sum_{A \in X} m_A;$$

thus $|\mathrm{MAX}(X)| \leq m$.

Corollary 13.2 Suppose that $A \in R$ and that the family $\max(R, A)$ is given. The time complexity of testing the primality of A is $O(m_A \cdot \|F\|)$.

  Proof. Follows from Theorem 13.7 and the linear time complexity of computing the closure of an attribute set. □

  In the worst case the quantity m_A is proportional to the number of subsets of R. Thus the algorithm for primality is exponential in the worst case. This is only to be expected, as PRIMALITY is an NP-complete problem. However, the primality test for attributes described above works fast, if the $\max(R, A)$ collection is available and small.

13.8   Testing the normal form properties

To characterize normal form properties using max sets, we introduce an additional concept. We say that a set W is *nonredundant*, if for no $V \subset W$ we have $V \to W$.

Theorem 13.8 Let F be a set of functional dependencies over R, and $X \subseteq R$. Then X is in BCNF if and only if each $W \in \mathrm{MAX}(X)$ is nonredundant.

  Proof. Suppose that X is not in BCNF: for some nontrivial dependency $Y \to A$ that follows from F we have $YA \subseteq X$ and $Y \not\to X$. Then

$Y \not\to B$ for some $B \in X$, and $\max(X, B)$ contains a set Y' extending Y. Since Y' is closed and $Y \subseteq Y'$, also $A \in Y'$. But then Y' is a redundant maximal set.

Assume $W \in \mathrm{MAX}(X)$ and W is redundant. Let $W \in \max(X, B)$ and suppose $W' \subset W$ and $F \models W' \to A$, where $A \in W \subseteq X$. Then W' is not a superkey of X and it determines an attribute of X, implying that X is not in BCNF. $\square$

Next we consider the two problems BCNFTEST for subschema and 3NFTEST. As for PRIMALITY, we are able to give algorithms for these problems that work in time proportional to the number of maximal sets.

Corollary 13.3 Let F be a set of functional dependencies over R, and $X \subseteq R$. Suppose $\max(R, B)$ is given for each $B \in R$. Then BCNFTEST for subschema can be solved for X in time $O(m \cdot |X| \cdot \|F\|)$.

Proof. First each $\max(X, B)$ set is computed using Lemmas 13.4 and 13.5, in time $O(m_B \cdot |X| \cdot \|F\|)$. By Theorem 13.8, it is then sufficient to check for each $A \in W \in \max(X, B)$ that $W \setminus \{A\} \not\to A$. Since $|\max(X, B)| \leq |\max(R, B)|$, this can be done in time $O(m_B \cdot |X| \cdot \|F\|)$, yielding the result. $\square$

Corollary 13.4 Let F be a set of functional dependencies over R. Suppose $\max(R, B)$ is given for each $B \in R$. Then 3NFTEST can be solved in time $O(m \cdot |R| \cdot \|F\|)$.

Proof. Each attribute $B \in R$ is first tested for primality. By Corollary 13.2, the total time required for this phase is $O(m \cdot \|F\|)$. The algorithm then proceeds as in the proof of Corollary 13.3 (using the $\max(R, B)$ sets), except that the test $W \setminus \{A\} \not\to A$ is only carried out if A is a non-prime attribute. $\square$

The above results show how the complexity of the normal form tests is strongly influenced by the number of maximal sets in the schema. Thus the number of maximal sets in a schema can be used as an indicator of the structural complexity of the schema: the existence of many maximal sets indicates that the functional dependencies have complicated interconnections in the schema.

For sets of inclusion dependencies, no such measure of complexity has been developed. A suitable candidate could be the number of different paths between relation schemas in the inclusion dependency graph (page 130). For circular sets of inclusion dependencies there are an infinite number of possible paths; for very simple sets of inclusion dependencies, the number of paths is small.

Exercises

Exercise 13.1 Let $R = ABCD$ and $F = \{A \rightarrow BC, B \rightarrow ACD, A \rightarrow D\}$ Compute the maximal sets for the attributes in R (i) using the definition, (ii) using Algorithm 13.2. Compare the number of sets with the bounds derived in Section 13.4.

Exercise 13.2 Prove that $F \models X \rightarrow A$ if and only if for each $Y \in \mathrm{CL}(X)$ the following holds: if $X \subseteq Y$, then $A \in Y$.

Exercise 13.3 Prove that $F \models X \rightarrow A$ if and only if for all $Y \in \max(A)$ we have $X \not\subseteq Y$. Thus, if the maximal sets for F are known, the implication problem for F can be solved without using an explicit representation of F.

Exercise 13.4 Give an example of dependency set F_n with $|F_n| = O(n)$ such that the collection lhs(A) has size $\Omega(2^n)$ for some attribute A.

Exercise 13.5 Improve Theorem 13.2 by considering the size of the largest family of incomparable subsets of a set of size n with respect to $\subseteq$.

Exercise 13.6 Prove Theorem 13.2.

Exercise 13.7 Prove Theorem 13.3.

Exercise 13.8 Prove Theorem 13.4.

Exercise 13.9 Prove Theorem 13.5.

Exercise 13.10 Let $(\mathbf{R}, F, \emptyset)$ be a database schema over U. Suppose $\mathbf{R} = (R_1, \ldots, R_k)$ is *not* dependency preserving. Let G be a set of functional dependencies over U. Consider the problem of deciding whether G is equivalent to

$$\bigcup_{i=1}^{k} F[R_i].$$

The problem is coNP-complete.

Suppose that in addition you are given the collections $\max(F, U, A)$ and $\max(G, U, A)$ for each $A \in U$. Show how the problem can be solved in polynomial time with respect to the size of this extended input.

Exercise 13.11 ** Let F and F' be sets of functional dependencies. Generalize Theorem 13.6 to relate the maximal sets of $F \cup F'$ to the maximal sets of F and of F'.

Exercise 13.12 ** The proof of Lemma 13.4 gives a way of deciding whether $Y \in \max(X, A)$ by computing the closures of the sets Y and YB, where $B \in X \setminus \{A\}$. Can one combine these closure computations so that the time requirement would be smaller?

Exercise 13.13 ** Show that for each collection W of subsets such that for each $X, Y \in W$ we have $X \not\subseteq Y$, there exists a closure operation such that W is the set of keys of this operation and there exists another closure operation such that W is the set of maximal sets of this operation.

Bibliographic notes

Theorem 13.1 is from [MR86a]; related characterizations are discussed in [DT88a, DT88b]. Lemma 13.4 is from [MR86a].

Thi [Thi86] considers the problem of computing the maximal sets in a relation schema when all the dependencies are produced by keys, that is, when the schema is in BCNF. His algorithm is fairly similar to Algorithm 13.2. He points out that the complexity of the algorithm is polynomial in the size of the schema, the number of keys, and the number of maximal sets. Exercise 13.13 is also from [Thi86]. For a thorough treatment of hypergraphs, see [Ber89].

The dependency set F_p on page 239 is given in [BDFS84]. The notion of the set A_F^- is from [Got87a]. For more material on incomparable subsets of a set needed in Exercise 13.5, see [Bol86]. Algorithm 13.2 is from [MR86a]. The coNP-completeness result in Exercise 13.10 is from [BH81].

Sections 13.6, 13.7, and 13.8 follow [MR89]. Lemma 13.6 is from [Kun85].

Chapter 14

Use of Example Databases in Design

We have described how database design proceeds using the ER-model and the relational model. The designer forms abstract concepts, entity types, relationship types, or relation schemas, that can be used to represent information about the target of the database.

Checking that the resulting design describes the target of the database correctly and adequately can be quite difficult. Of course, building the applications, loading the database with the actual data, and then checking how the system fulfills the needs of users is the ultimate test. But it is a costly way of detecting early mistakes.

As discussed in Chapter 2, providing feedback for the designer is important. The feedback can be formulated as *example databases* that the designer can use as tools for studying the properties of the suggested design.

In this chapter we discuss the properties of good examples and how one could generate such examples automatically. In Section 14.1 we investigate the desired properties of a good example database; these properties are enjoyed by so-called Armstrong databases. In Section 14.2 we define the concept of an Armstrong database formally and give results showing that Armstrong databases exist. Sections 14.3 and 14.4 show how such relations and databases can be generated automatically, given the database schema and the functional and inclusion dependencies holding in it.

14.1   Goals for example databases

When explaining a database schema to somebody, experienced designers tend to use examples. Some informal database design guidelines suggest the use of example values and relations during the design process. The advantages of examples are easy to see. An attribute name can easily mean different things to different people, but a concrete example of an allowed value for that attribute is more likely to be understood in the same way by everybody, and an example value also shows how the attribute name should be interpreted. Likewise, a relation schema expressing connections between attributes is an abstract concept and prone to misunderstandings. Concrete examples of a relation corresponding to the schema are easier to understand and evaluate.

Example databases can also be used as a tool for checking a more or less completed design: the examples help in finding missing or extraneous relationship types, shared subentities and so on. Also the queries and updates to be performed on the database can be tested using an example database: one can verify that there really is sufficient information in the database to fulfill the users' needs. Similarly, an application can be tested partly by using an example database.

Once we have decided to use examples of relations in the user interface of the design tool, the obvious question is what kind of example relations should be used.

An arbitrary example relation does not necessarily indicate all the important information about the relation schema or the database schema. An example row or two indicate what type of information can be stored using the schema. This is a valuable piece of knowledge, but such an example does not indicate the interrelationships of different rows and relations implied by the design. A suitable example relation can, however, clearly illustrate the problems in a suggested design.

Example 14.1 Recall Example 2.1 (page 14), where we obtained the relation schemas

Courses:	Name, Course number
Class times:	Course number, Room number, Time

No functional dependencies were imposed upon the latter table.

Suppose that we show the designer the following example relation filled with arbitrary tuples:

Course number	Room number	Time
CIS 510	DES 200	M 9:30
CIS 511	DES 200	W 13:30

Since no data dependencies were required to hold in the relation, this is an example of a legal relation. However, it should *not* be shown to the designer, since it gives the false impression that the suggested design is acceptable. Nothing prohibits many courses from meeting in the same room at the same time, or one course from meeting in two rooms at any given time. This cannot be seen from the relation above.

The example relation given in Example 2.1 was the following.

Course number	Room number	Time
CIS 551	PAC 30	M 9:30
CIS 510	PAC 30	M 9:30
CIS 510	DES 200	M 9:30
CIS 510	DES 200	W 13:30

In this example the problems discussed above are evident: Course CIS 510 meets in two rooms on Monday at 9:30, and Room PAC 30 is used by both CIS 510 and CIS 551 on Monday at 9:30. □

Thus a suitably chosen example can be very useful in pinpointing problems in a design. The following requirements seem to be necessary for good example databases. First, the example should satisfy all the constraints given by the designer. This also means that it will satisfy all the consequences of the given constraints. Second, the example should not satisfy any other constraints. These two conditions mean that the example is an *Armstrong database* for the given set of constraints. The technical definition of this concept follows in the next section. The relation given in Example 2.1 is an Armstrong relation for the empty set of constraints; this relation showed clearly the effects of the missing constraints.

The fact that a functional dependency is not required to hold is very easy to spot from an example relation that satisfies the Armstrong property: one only needs to compare two rows. Noticing that a constraint does hold is more difficult, since one has to inspect the whole table.

Examples can also make redundancy in a schema intuitively easy to comprehend. Suppose, for example, that in the schema

Employee (EmpName, Manager, Department)

the functional dependencies Department → Manager, Manager → Department, and EmpName → Department hold. This is represented by the following Armstrong relation.

EmpName	Manager	Department
Wilson	Hogger	Construction
Jones	Hogger	Construction
Wood	Drake	Sales

The first two lines of the example show how the information about the manager of the Construction department is represented twice. This can make it easier for the designer to understand why a design algorithm can suggest decomposing the schema into two smaller schemas, namely {EmpName, Department} and {Department, Manager}.

Although some things are easy to spot from the examples, also the explicit representation of the integrity constraints has its advantages. Therefore the designer can be shown both the list of constraints and the example table as representations of the constraint set. This double representation gives the designer two complementing views of the design.

For a given set of dependencies there exist several Armstrong databases. Which one of these is most useful for providing feedback to the designer? Clearly, the relation should be small if the designer is going to draw any conclusions from it.

The examples must also be realistic in the sense that the values occurring in the relations and the combinations of values in the tuples must correspond to some real world situation. This is a condition that can be hard to achieve when examples are automatically generated; however, allowing the user to edit the examples can remedy the problem.

The editing of the example database is useful also in remedying the problems spotted in the design. In Example 14.1 the designer probably notices that two courses meet at the same time in the same room. This can be changed directly in the example relation. Since an Armstrong database is a database satisfying exactly the consequences of a set of constraints, it can also serve as an alternative representation of the set of integrity constraints. A database represents those dependencies that hold in it. So after the user has edited the example database, one can automatically infer the dependencies that hold in the modified example, and use those dependencies to continue the design. The change in the dependency set can cause changes in the schemas of the database. The problem of inferring the dependencies holding in a database is considered in Chapter 15.

14.2   Armstrong databases

The discussion on the properties of good examples leads to the following definition. Given a class of dependencies $\mathcal{D}$ and a set $D \subseteq \mathcal{D}$ of dependencies over a set of relation schemas $\mathbf{R}$, a $\mathcal{D}$-*Armstrong database* for D is a database $\mathbf{r}$ over $\mathbf{R}$ such that for all dependencies $d \in \mathcal{D}$ we have $\mathbf{r} \models d$ if and only if $D \models d$. Hence an Armstrong database for a set $D \subseteq \mathcal{D}$ of dependencies satisfies exactly the logical consequences of D of the dependencies in $\mathcal{D}$. If the database schema contains only a single relation schema, we speak of *Armstrong relations*.

Example 14.2 The example relation given in Example 2.1 and reproduced above in Example 14.1 is an $\mathcal{F}'$-Armstrong relation for the empty set of dependencies, where $\mathcal{F}'$ consists of all functional dependencies. Hence in the relation no nontrivial functional dependencies hold.   □

Example 14.3 Consider the relation schema $R(AB)$, and the class of dependencies $\mathcal{F}'$ consisting of all standard or nonstandard functional dependencies over $R(AB)$. Then the following are examples of $\mathcal{F}'$-Armstrong relations for various dependency sets:

$$F = \emptyset \qquad\qquad F = \{A \to B\} \qquad\qquad F = \{A \to B, B \to A\}$$

A	B
0	0
1	0
0	2

A	B
0	0
1	0
2	3

A	B
0	0
1	1

In the Armstrong relation for $F = \{A \to B\}$ the first two lines show that B does not determine A; the third line is needed to show that the empty set does not determine B, that is, column B contains at least two different values. The relation

A	B
0	0
1	0

is an $\mathcal{F}$-Armstrong relation for the set $\{A \to B\}$, where $\mathcal{F}$ consists of all the standard functional dependencies. In fact, an empty relation is an $\mathcal{F}$-Armstrong relation for the set $\{A \to B, B \to A\}$; it is not a very intuitive one, however.   □

It should be noted that besides D, also the class $\mathcal{D}$ of all dependencies considered is an important parameter in the definition of Armstrong databases: it determines what dependencies have to be considered, in the positive or negative sense.

If the class $\mathcal{D}$ consists of all standard functional dependencies over **R**, we use the term $\mathcal{F}$-*Armstrong databases*; if $\mathcal{D}$ contains also all inclusion dependencies over **R**, the term is $\mathcal{FI}$-*Armstrong databases*. The prefix is often omitted, if it is clear from the context.

If Armstrong databases are to be useful, the first condition is that they have to exist. For arbitrary sets of constraints this does not necessarily hold. We start with a simple example.

Example 14.4 Let $\mathcal{D}$ consist of two dependencies:

σ_1 = 'relation r has at most one tuple',

and

$$\sigma_2 = \text{'relation } r \text{ has at least two tuples'.}$$

Let $\mathbf{R}$ consist of one relation schema R, and consider the empty set of dependencies, that is, $D = \emptyset$. We claim that there is no $\mathcal{D}$-Armstrong database for D. Let $\mathbf{r} = (r)$ be any database over $\mathbf{R}$. It satisfies exactly one of the dependencies in $\mathcal{D}$. But neither σ_1 nor σ_2 is a consequence of D. □

Luckily, for the cases encountered in database design Armstrong databases usually exist. Given the class of dependencies $\mathcal{D}$, we say that $\mathcal{D}$-Armstrong databases exist, if an Armstrong database exists for any set $D \subseteq \mathcal{D}$.

Theorem 14.1 $\mathcal{FI}$-Armstrong databases exist for (standard) functional dependencies and inclusion dependencies, that is, if I is a set of inclusion dependencies and F is a set of functional dependencies, there exists an $\mathcal{F}$-Armstrong database for the set $F \cup I$.

Proof. Let the database schema be $(\mathbf{R}, F, I)$. Denote by E the set of all functional and inclusion dependencies d over $\mathbf{R}$ such that $F \cup I \not\models d$. For any $d \in E$, let $\mathbf{r}_d$ be a database such that $\mathbf{r}_d \models F \cup I$, but $\mathbf{r}_d \not\models d$. Assume that for $d, e \in E$ with $d \neq e$ the values occurring in $\mathbf{r}_d$ and $\mathbf{r}_e$ are disjoint. Denote

$$\mathbf{r} = \bigcup_{d \in E} \mathbf{r}_d,$$

that is, relation r of $\mathbf{r}$ corresponding to relation schema R is the union of the corresponding relations in the databases $\mathbf{r}_d$. Since all functional dependencies are standard, and $\mathbf{r}_d \models F \cup I$ for all $d \in E$, we have $\mathbf{r} \models F \cup I$. Since the databases $\mathbf{r}_d$ are disjoint for different dependencies $d \in E$, we have that $\mathbf{r} \not\models d$ for all $d \in E$. □

We have required that all functional dependencies are standard. Theorem 14.1 is one place where this condition is necessary, as the following example shows.

Example 14.5 Consider relation schemas

$$R_1(A_1), R_2(A_2), R_3(A_3), R_4(A_4)$$

and the dependencies

$$F = \{\emptyset \rightarrow A_1\},$$
$$I = \{R_2[A_2] \subseteq R_1[A_1], R_2[A_2] \subseteq R_3[A_3]\}.$$

Let $d_1 = R_1[A_1] \subseteq R_3[A_3]$ and $d_2 = R_2[A_2] \subseteq R_4[A_4]$. One can show that any database satisfying $F \cup I$ satisfies d_1 or d_2, but $F \cup I$ does not imply d_1 nor d_2. Thus there is no $\mathcal{FI}$-Armstrong database for $F \cup I$. Note that I is a noncircular set. $\qquad\square$

Theorem 14.1 depends crucially on the assumption that the domains of attributes contain sufficiently many values. If only values from a small domain can be used, an Armstrong relation or database may not exist.

Example 14.6 Consider the schema $R(AB)$ and the dependency set $F = \{A \rightarrow B\}$. If $Dom(A) = \{0, 1\}$, any relation r over R can have at most two rows. If r has less than two rows, or if r contains two rows and these rows agree on B, then r satisfies $\emptyset \rightarrow B$. If r has two rows and these rows disagree on B, then r satisfies $B \rightarrow A$. Hence no Armstrong relation exists for F when the domain of A contains only two values. $\qquad\square$

Example 14.7 Consider the schemas $R(AC)$ and $S(BC)$, with keys A and B, and assume $Dom(C) = \{0, 1\}$. Assume (r, s) would be an $\mathcal{FI}$-Armstrong database for the set $\{A \rightarrow C, B \rightarrow C\}$. Then r would be an $\mathcal{F}$-Armstrong relation for $\{A \rightarrow C\}$, and hence $r[C] = \{0, 1\}$. Similarly, $s[C] = \{0, 1\}$. Therefore $(r, s) \models R[C] \subseteq S[C]$ and $(r, s) \models S[C] \subseteq R[C]$, a contradiction. $\qquad\square$

Examples 14.6 and 14.7 show in fact that the sizes of domains influence the interaction of functional and inclusion dependencies.

An Armstrong database for the set of functional and inclusion dependencies holding in the database provides good material also for testing the effects of insertions and other updates on the database. Since the relations violate every functional dependency that does not follow from the given set of dependencies, inserting the rows in the Armstrong relation one at a time gives a good indication of the allowed situations during the lifetime of the relation.

14.3   Generating Armstrong relations

In this section we address the problem of generating $\mathcal{F}$-Armstrong databases for single relation schemas. Given a set F of functional dependencies over a relation schema R, we want to produce a relation r satisfying a dependency $X \rightarrow Y$ if and only if $F \models X \rightarrow Y$.

Theorem 14.1 showed in particular that $\mathcal{F}$-Armstrong relations exist, and the proof gave a method for constructing such relations. But that method produces very large relations, and they are useless for database design. Our aim is to look for methods that can be used to produce small example relations.

We start with a definition. Given a relation r over a relation schema R, the *agree set of two rows* $u, v \in R$ is the set of attributes in R for which u and v have the same value. The *agree set* $\text{ag}(r)$ *of relation* r is the collection of all agree sets of pairs of tuples from r, that is,

$$\text{ag}(r) = \{\text{ag}(u, v) \mid u, v \in r\}.$$

Example 14.8 Consider again the relation in Example 2.1 (repeated in Example 14.1). Denoting the attributes by their first letters, the agree sets in this relation are RT, T, $\emptyset$, CT, C, CR, and CRT.   □

Recall also the definitions of $\text{CL}(R)$ and $\text{GEN}(R)$ from Chapter 13: given a set F of functional dependencies, $\text{CL}(R)$ is the set of all subsets of R that are closed with respect to F, and $\text{GEN}(R)$ is the subcollection of $\text{CL}(R)$ consisting of those closed sets that cannot be represented as an intersection of other closed sets. In Theorem 13.1 (page 236) we showed that the $\text{GEN}(R)$ family is exactly the family $\text{MAX}(R)$ of maximal sets not deriving some attribute.

The next result is an important characterization of Armstrong relations for functional dependencies.

Theorem 14.2 Let r be a relation over relation schema R and let F be a set of functional dependencies over R. Then r is an $\mathcal{F}$-Armstrong relation for F if and only if

$$\text{GEN}(R) \subseteq \text{ag}(r) \subseteq \text{CL}(R).$$

Proof. Assume $\text{ag}(r)$ satisfies the two inclusions in the statement of the theorem. We show that r is an Armstrong relation for F. Given $X \to Y \in F$, let t, t' be two rows from r. If $X \subseteq \text{ag}(t, t')$, then also $Y \subseteq \text{ag}(t, t')$, since $\text{ag}(t, t')$ is a closed set. Thus the dependency $X \to Y$ holds in r.

Assume then that the dependency $X \to A$ does not follow from F. Then $\max(F, R, A)$ contains a set W such that $X \subseteq W$. Since $W \in \text{MAX}(R) = \text{GEN}(R)$, and $\text{GEN}(R) \subseteq \text{ag}(r)$, relation r contains rows u, v such that $\text{ag}(u, v) = W$. But these two rows agree on X (since $X \subseteq W$) and disagree on A (since $A \notin W \in \max(F, R, A)$). Therefore $X \to A$ does not hold in r, and r is an Armstrong relation for F.

For the converse, assume r is an $\mathcal{F}$-Armstrong relation for F. Consider $X \in \text{ag}(r)$. Then $X = \text{ag}(u, v)$ for some $u, v \in r$. If X is not closed, some dependency of F would be violated by u and v. Hence $X \in \text{CL}(R)$.

Consider then a set $W \in \text{GEN}(R) = \text{MAX}(R)$. By the definition of $\text{GEN}(R)$ the set W is closed. Hence the dependency $W \to A$ does not follow from F for any $A \in R \setminus W$. Since r is an Armstrong relation for F, this means that r does not satisfy $W \to A$, and there exist rows $t_A, u_A \in r$ with $W \subseteq \text{ag}(t_A, u_A)$ and $A \notin \text{ag}(t_A, u_A)$. As above, $\text{ag}(t_A, u_A) \in \text{CL}(R)$ for all $A \in R \setminus W$. Now we have

$$W = \bigcap \{ \mathrm{ag}(t_A, u_A) \mid A \in R \setminus W \},$$

and since $W \in \mathrm{GEN}(R)$, we must have $W = \mathrm{ag}(t_B, u_B)$ for some $B \in R \setminus W$. Hence $W \in \mathrm{ag}(r)$. □

The proof shows also that a relation r satisfies the dependencies in F if and only if $\mathrm{ag}(r) \subseteq \mathrm{CL}(R)$.

Theorem 14.2 gives a method for constructing an Armstrong relation of a reasonably small size fairly quickly. The idea is to compute first for the given set F of functional dependencies the collection $\mathrm{MAX}(R)$. Then we form a relation r satisfying F so that the condition $\mathrm{MAX}(R) \subseteq \mathrm{ag}(r)$ holds. We start with the latter part, which we call *realization* of the collection $\mathrm{MAX}(R)$.

Algorithm 14.1 Realize a collection of closed sets.
Input. A relation schema R, a set F of functional dependencies over R, and a collection $\mathcal{C}$ of subsets of R with $\mathcal{C} \subseteq \mathrm{CL}(R)$.
Output. A relation r over R such that $\mathcal{C} \subseteq \mathrm{ag}(r) \subseteq \mathrm{CL}(R)$.
Method. For each attribute $A \in R$, let $c_{A,0}, c_{A,1}, \ldots$ be disjoint values from the domain of A. Apply the following steps.

1.   let r be the relation with a single tuple t_0
         such that $t_0[A] = c_{A,0}$ for all $A \in R$;
2. $i := 1$;
3.   **for** each $W \in \mathcal{C}$ **do**
4.   insert into r a tuple t_i such that
5. $t_i[A] = t_{i-1}[A]$ if $A \in W$, and $t_i[A] = c_{A,i}$ otherwise;
6. $i := i + 1$;
7.   **od**; □

Using Algorithm 14.1, construction of an Armstrong relation for a set of functional dependencies is easy.

Algorithm 14.2 Construction of an Armstrong relation.
Input. A relation schema R and a functional dependency set F.
Output. An Armstrong relation r over R for F.
Method.

1.   compute the collection $\mathrm{MAX}(R)$ with respect to F;
2.   use Algorithm 14.1 to form a
         relation r with $\mathrm{MAX}(R) \subseteq \mathrm{ag}(r) \subseteq \mathrm{CL}(R)$; □

Example 14.9 Consider the relation schemas

Employee (*EmpName*, DeptName),
WorksIn (*EmpName*, Proj#, Date), and
Project (*Proj#*, Site)

from Example 11.1 (page 182). Only one functional dependency is associated with the schema WorksIn, namely EmpName → Proj# Date. We apply Algorithm 14.2 to this schema. Abbreviating the attribute names by their first letters, we obtain the maximal sets PD, P, and D. If we use Algorithm 14.1 on these sets in this order, we obtain the following relation.

E	P	D
Wilson	A	Jan. 1991
Jones	A	Jan. 1991
Riordan	A	Feb. 1990
Wood	C	Feb. 1990

The agree set collection of this relation is $\{EPD, PD, P, \emptyset, D\}$. Note that there are more agree sets in the relation than maximal sets. □

Theorem 14.3 The result of Algorithm 14.1 on input C with $C \subseteq \mathrm{CL}(R)$ is a relation r satisfying $C \subseteq \mathrm{ag}(r) \subseteq \mathrm{CL}(R)$.

Proof. Consider the tuples t_i inserted into r. Since $\mathrm{ag}(t_{i-1}, t_i)$ is exactly the ith set from the collection C, we have $C \subseteq \mathrm{ag}(r)$ at the end.

We show that $\mathrm{ag}(r) \subseteq \mathrm{CL}(R)$ by induction on the number of tuples inserted into r. The base case is easy, since for a one-tuple relation the $\mathrm{ag}(r)$ collection contains only R, which is a closed set.

Let then the current relation be $s = \{t_0, \ldots, t_k\}$ and assume $\mathrm{ag}(s) \subseteq \mathrm{CL}(R)$. Consider the effect on the agree set of adding tuple t_{k+1} to the relation. We have that $\mathrm{ag}(t_{k+1}, t_j)$ is an intersection of sets from C for $0 \leq j \leq k$. Since $C \subseteq \mathrm{CL}(R)$, and $\mathrm{CL}(R)$ is closed under intersection, we have $\mathrm{ag}(t_{k+1}, t_j) \in \mathrm{CL}(R)$. □

Theorem 14.4 Given a set F of functional dependencies over a relation schema R, Algorithm 14.2 produces an Armstrong relation with $|\mathrm{MAX}(R)| + 1$ tuples.

Proof. Immediate. □

Theorem 14.4 can be combined with the results of Chapter 13 to show that for normalized schemas there exist reasonably small Armstrong relations.

Note that if in Algorithm 14.1 the example values from the domains of attributes are chosen to be disjoint, the columns of the example relations generated by the algorithm will be disjoint.

On some occasions it is useful to be able to modify an existing relation r so that we obtain an Armstrong relation for a given set F of functional dependencies. This can be done as follows.

Algorithm 14.3 Modification of an existing relation to yield an Armstrong relation.
Input. A relation schema R, a relation r over R, and a functional dependency set F.
Output. An Armstrong relation s over R for F. If r satisfies F, then $r \subseteq s$; otherwise s contains a copy of a chased version of r.
Method.

1. $r' := \text{chase}(r, F)$;
2. $\mathcal{C} := \text{MAX}(R) \setminus \text{ag}(r)$;
3.   use Algorithm 14.1 to form a relation r'' realizing the set $\mathcal{C}$;
4. $s := r' \cup r''$;   □

Example 14.10 Continuing Example 14.9, suppose we are given the following relation.

E	P	D
Wilson	A	Jan. 1991
Wilson	A	Feb. 1990
Riordan	B	Jan. 1991

This relation is not an Armstrong relation for the set $\{E \to PD\}$: it does not satisfy the dependency, and satisfies several other dependencies not implied by $E \to PD$. Using Algorithm 14.3, we first chase the relation. This gives the following relation r'.

E	P	D
Wilson	A	Jan. 1991
Riordan	B	Jan. 1991

Now $\text{ag}(r') = \{EPD, D\}$, and $\text{MAX}(R)$ is not included in $\text{ag}(r')$. Hence we have to realize the remaining maximal sets PD and P. We can use the last row of r' as the row t_0 in Algorithm 14.1. This yields the following relation.

E	P	D
Wilson	A	Jan. 1991
Riordan	B	Jan. 1991
Wood	B	Jan. 1991
Hogger	B	April 1988

The agree set collection for this relation is $\{EPD, D, \emptyset, PD, P\}$.   □

We conclude this section by considering the effect of the sizes of domains. Algorithm 14.1 assumes each domain has as many values as there are sets in the collection to be realized. What should one do if this is not the case? As Example 14.6 showed, there may not exist an Armstrong relation in this case. However, in many cases a relation exists, even though the domain has, say, two values. In this case one can obtain an example relation by using the values in the domain in a cyclic fashion: when the last one has been used, one starts again from the beginning. The result of this need not be an Armstrong relation, so one has to check in the end whether the resulting relation really satisfies the condition described in Theorem 14.2.

14.4   Generating Armstrong databases

In the previous section we considered the generation of example relations for single relation schemas. Now we turn to the problem of generating example databases.

There are two issues to be considered: global functional dependencies and inclusion dependencies. For global functional dependencies we take the easy way out by ignoring them in the construction of Armstrong databases. The relations of the example databases are constructed by considering only local functional dependencies. As long as the database schemas are independent, this causes no problems in the use of the examples.

Inclusion dependencies, on the other hand, require careful attention. A good example database must take them into account to show how the pieces of information present in different relation schemas interact.

The basic idea in producing $\mathcal{FI}$-Armstrong databases is to start with disjoint $\mathcal{F}$-Armstrong relations for the functional dependencies and to use the chase procedure to enforce the inclusion dependencies. As noted in Theorem 10.17 (page 170), this procedure does not introduce any additional inclusion dependencies.

To show how this result is applied, we give short and constructive proofs of two important special cases of Theorem 14.1.

Theorem 14.5 Let $(\mathbf{R}, \emptyset, I)$ be a database schema where I is noncircular. Then an $\mathcal{I}$-Armstrong database for I exists.

Proof.   We apply Theorem 10.17.   Starting from a database $\mathbf{r}$ over $\mathbf{R}$ with nonempty relations and disjoint columns, we compute $\mathbf{r}' = \text{chase}(\mathbf{r}, \emptyset, I)$. By Theorem 10.17, the result $\mathbf{r}'$ satisfies an inclusion dependency d if and only if $I \models d$. Thus $\mathbf{r}'$ is an Armstrong database for I.   □

Theorem 14.6 Let $(\mathbf{R}, F, I)$ be a dependency preserving database schema where each schema of $\mathbf{R}$ is in Boyce-Codd normal form and I consists of only key-based dependencies. Then an $\mathcal{FI}$-Armstrong database for $F \cup I$ exists.

Proof. Consider a database $\mathbf{r}$ consisting of disjoint Armstrong relations for the projections of F. Denote $\mathbf{s} = \text{chase}(\mathbf{r}, F, I)$. By Theorem 10.17 the database $\mathbf{s}$ satisfies an inclusion dependency if and only if the dependency follows from $F \cup I$. The database $\mathbf{s}$ satisfies exactly the functional dependencies following from F (or $F \cup I$), since we have $\mathbf{r} \subseteq \text{chase}(\mathbf{r}, F, I)$ by Theorem 10.19. □

We now describe the process presented in the above proof as an algorithm.

Algorithm 14.4 Armstrong database generation for Boyce-Codd normal form schemas with dependency preservation and key-based inclusion dependencies.
Input. A database schema $(\mathbf{R}, F, I)$. Assume that each schema of $\mathbf{R}$ is in Boyce-Codd normal form, that the database schema is dependency preserving, and that I consists of key-based dependencies.
Output. An $\mathcal{FI}$-Armstrong database $\mathbf{r}$ for $F \cup I$.
Method.

1.   generate disjoint Armstrong relations with disjoint columns
            for each relation schema in R;
2.   denote the result by $\mathbf{s}$;
3. $\mathbf{r} := \text{chase}(\mathbf{s}, F, I)$; □

Example 14.11 Continuing Example 14.9, we construct an example database for the database schema

> Employee (*EmpName*, DeptName),
> WorksIn (*EmpName*, Proj#, Date), and
> Project (*Proj#*, Site)

with the inclusion dependencies

> WorksIn[EmpName] $\subseteq$ Employee[EmpName] and
> WorksIn[Proj#] $\subseteq$ Project[Proj#].

We start with disjoint Armstrong relations for the relation schemas Employee and Project. (DeptName is abbreviated by N.)

E	N
Hogger	Computing
Drake	Computing
Budak	Manufacturing

P	S
E	Bonn
F	Bonn
G	Berlin

Using the chase procedure on these two relations and the WorksIn relation in Example 14.9, we obtain the following database.

E	N
Hogger	Computing
Drake	Computing
Budak	Manufacturing
Wilson	Mail-order
Jones	Administration
Riordan	Education
Wood	Transport

P	S
E	Bonn
F	Bonn
G	Berlin
A	New York
C	Stockholm

E	P	D
Wilson	A	Jan. 1991
Jones	A	Jan. 1991
Riordan	A	Feb. 1990
Wood	C	Feb. 1990

□

The problem with Algorithm 14.4 is that it produces unnecessarily large Armstrong databases, as we saw in Example 14.11. The reason for this is that no attempt is made to use the tuples produced by the chase for an inclusion dependency $R[X] \subseteq S[Y]$ for realizing the agree sets of S. We can improve Algorithm 14.4 by using the rows generated by the inclusion dependencies as a starting point for the relations for each relation schema.

Algorithm 14.5 Improved generation of Armstrong databases for Boyce-Codd normal form schemas with dependency preservation and key-based inclusion dependencies.
Input. A database schema $(\mathbf{R}, F, I)$. Assume that each schema of $\mathbf{R}$ is in Boyce-Codd normal form, that the database schema is dependency preserving, and that I consists of key-based dependencies.
Output. An $\mathcal{FI}$-Armstrong database $\mathbf{r}$ for $F \cup I$.
Method. Assume $\mathbf{R} = (R_1, \ldots, R_k)$, and assume that if I contains an inclusion dependency $R_i[X] \subseteq R_j[Y]$, then $i < j$.

1.   **for** $i := 1$ **to** k **do** $r_i := \emptyset$ **od**;
2.   let r_1 be an Armstrong relation for $F[R_1]$ with disjoint columns;
3.   **for** $i := 2$ **to** k **do**
4. $(r_1, \ldots, r_i) := \text{chase}((r_1, \ldots, r_i), F, I)$;
5.   **if** $\max(R_i) \not\subseteq \text{ag}(r_i)$ **then**
6.   use Algorithm 14.3 to add to s_i rows consisting of new values so that s_i is an Armstrong relation for $F[R_i]$;

7.   **fi**;

8.   add to r_i one row with values not occurring in any r_j
            with $j < i$, if such a row is not present;

9.   **od**;   □

Theorem 14.7 Algorithm 14.5 works correctly.

   Proof. By Theorem 10.21 (page 174), the functional dependencies
implied by $F \cup I$ are exactly those that follow from F. Each relation r_i
is made to be an Armstrong relation for $F[R_i]$ at some stage. After that,
the only operations applied to r_i are the chase and the addition of totally
new rows. By Theorem 10.19 (page 173), the chases do not modify the
original relations, and hence r_i remains an Armstrong relation for $F[R_i]$.

   For inclusion dependencies, denote by

$$\mathbf{r}^0 = (r_1^0, \ldots, r_k^0)$$

the relations consisting of those rows that are explicitly added to $\mathbf{r}$ in lines
2, 6, and 8 of the algorithm, that is, the rows not added by the chase.
Then

$$\mathbf{r} = \text{chase}((r_1^0, \ldots, r_k^0), F, I),$$

as the order of insertions of the rows is not significant. The database $\mathbf{r}^0$
has disjoint columns, and by Theorem 10.17 (page 170) $\mathbf{r}$ satisfies exactly
the inclusion dependencies implied by $F \cup I$.   □

Example 14.12 Continuing Example 14.9, we construct an example
database using Algorithm 14.5. Recall that the database schema is

   Employee (*EmpName*, DeptName),
   WorksIn (*EmpName*, Proj#, Date), and
   Project (*Proj#*, Site)

with the inclusion dependencies

   WorksIn[EmpName] $\subseteq$ Employee[EmpName] and
   WorksIn[Proj#] $\subseteq$ Project[Proj#].

   Starting from the relation

E	P	D
Wilson	A	Jan. 1991
Jones	A	Jan. 1991
Riordan	A	Feb. 1990
Wood	C	Feb. 1990

we first apply the chase, yielding the relations

E	N
Wilson	Computing
Jones	Accounting
Riordan	Manufacturing
Wood	Mail-order

P	S
A	Berlin
C	New York

The agree sets for the schema $\{E, N\}$ are EN and $\emptyset$; the collection of maximal sets is $\{\emptyset, N\}$. Thus we need to add one to realize the set N. For example, the row (Page, Mail-order) does this. Similarly, we have to add one row to the PS schema. These rows also ensure that no additional rows have to be added by line 8 of the algorithm. The resulting database is as follows.

E	N
Wilson	Computing
Jones	Accounting
Riordan	Manufacturing
Wood	Mail-order
Page	Mail-order

P	S
A	Berlin
C	New York
I	New York

E	P	D
Wilson	A	Jan. 1991
Jones	A	Jan. 1991
Riordan	A	Feb. 1990
Wood	C	Feb. 1990

□

Exercises

Exercise 14.1 Show that the following is a necessary condition for the existence of Armstrong structures for a class $\mathcal{D}$. For all $D \subseteq \mathcal{D}$ and $\phi_1, \phi_2 \in \mathcal{D}$: if $D \models \phi_1 \vee \phi_2$, then $D \models \phi_1$ or $D \models \phi_2$.

Exercise 14.2 Generate an Armstrong relation for the relation schema $R(ABCDE)$ and the dependency set $\{AB \rightarrow E, CD \rightarrow E\}$.

Exercise 14.3 A tempting way of trying to produce Armstrong relations for functional dependencies is to start from a relation satisfying no nontrivial functional dependencies, that is, an Armstrong relation for the empty set, and then apply the chase.

(a) Give a method to produce Armstrong relations for the empty set of functional dependencies.

(b) Show by an example how computing chase(r, F) for a relation r produced in part (a) is not necessarily an Armstrong relation for F.

Exercise 14.4 Use the proof of Theorem 14.1 to produce an Armstrong relation for the schema $R(AB)$ and the dependency set $\{A \to B\}$.

Exercise 14.5 The proof of Theorem 14.1, even when applied to single relation schemas, produces fairly large Armstrong relations. Estimate their size as a function of the number of attributes in the schema.

Exercise 14.6 Prove the claims of Example 14.5.

Exercise 14.7 Give an algorithm for minimizing an Armstrong relation. That is, design an algorithm that given a relation r produces a smaller relation $s \subseteq r$ such that s and r satisfy exactly the same functional dependencies.

Hint. An optimal solution is difficult, but consider the collection of agree sets of r to get at least in some cases a smaller relation.

Bibliographic notes

Armstrong relations for functional dependencies were introduced by Armstrong [Arm74]. A thorough survey of the concept, its counterparts in logic, and applications is given by Fagin [Fag82a]. Another paper by Fagin [Fag82b] proves the existence of Armstrong databases for a large class of dependencies. The concept is considered also in [GZ82] under the name of 'generators'. Armstrong relations are characterized using excluded functional dependencies by Gottlob and Libkin [GL90] (see also [Jan88, Jan89]).

The first proposal for using Armstrong relations in the design process was made by Silva and Melkanoff [SM81]. They suggest that the design tool should produce Armstrong relations for all the relation schemas, and then join the relations into a universal relation. Showing this relation to the designer should help in detecting potential anomalies in the database schema.

The structure of Armstrong relations for functional dependencies is addressed in [BDFS84]; see also [AD80]. Theorem 14.2 is from [BDFS84]. Algorithm 14.2 is from [MR86a]. Example 14.5 is from [FV83].

Chapter 15

Dependency Inference

Dependency inference is the task of deducing the integrity constraints that hold in an existing database or relation.

In the Design-By-Example design tool the designer can edit the example database generated by the tool. A new set of constraints is then inferred from the modified example. The example database and the set of functional and inclusion dependencies can be used as alternative representations of the same set of constraints.

Also an existing database can be analyzed by computing the functional and inclusion dependencies that hold in it. This information can for example be used to locate normal form violations in the schema. As discussed in Chapter 11, the set of functional and inclusion dependencies can also be used to form a first approximation of the conceptual schema for the database.

Care should be taken, however, to treat the results of dependency inference on an existing database only as tentative. Dependency inference tells only what dependencies hold in one instance of the database schema; the conceptual schema should be formed by looking at the dependencies which hold in every instance of the database schema.

Dependency inference can be compared to concept learning: it proceeds from a concrete example (the database) to an abstract concept (a set of dependencies). In dependency inference the situation is, however, fairly simple. For any database there is a finite set of functional and inclusion dependencies holding in it, and in principle we can compute this set by exhaustive search. Of course, more efficient algorithms computing only a small cover for the set of integrity constraints are preferable.

In this chapter we give three algorithms for inferring functional dependencies. The running times of the algorithms are exponential in the number of attributes, but polynomial in the number of rows. We also give lower bounds for this problem. Finally we consider the task of inferring the inclusion dependencies holding in a database. For unary dependencies this is fairly easy, for general dependencies quite difficult.

15.1   Algorithms for inferring functional dependencies

For functional dependencies, the dependency inference problem is the following: given a relation schema R and a relation r over R, find a cover for the set

$$\text{dep}(r) = \{X \to A \mid r \models X \to A\}.$$

Since $\text{dep}(r)$ contains many redundant dependencies, we are interested in finding small covers for it.

Example 15.1 Consider the following relation.

Employee	Department	Manager	Salary
Smith	Toys	Jones	200
Wilson	Administration	Brown	300
Barnes	Toys	Jones	300

In this relation, the following functional dependencies (and their consequences) hold:

> Employee $\to$ Department Manager Salary
> Department $\to$ Manager
> Manager $\to$ Department
> Department Salary $\to$ Employee

While the three first dependencies can be true for all instances of this schema, the fourth is probably only accidentally true in this small example.   □

If the relation r contains null values, there are two possibilities for defining the result of dependency inference. Either one can assume that all null values are distinct, or that they are all equal. Let B be an attribute for which null values occur. Assuming all null values are distinct means that fewer dependencies with B on the right-hand side hold than in the case where all null values are equal. Similarly, in the first case more dependencies with B on the left-hand side hold than in the second case.

A simple way of finding a cover of $\text{dep}(r)$ for a given relation r is to check all possible dependencies, as follows.

Algorithm 15.1 Naive computation of the functional dependencies holding in a relation.
Input. A relation r over R.
Output. A cover F for $\text{dep}(r)$.
Method.

1. $F := \emptyset$;
2.   **for** all subsets $X \subseteq R$ **do**
3.   **for** all attributes $A \in R \setminus X$ **do**
4.   **if** $r \models X \to A$ **then** $F := F \cup \{X \to A\}$ **fi**
5.   **od**;
6.   **od**;   □

Theorem 15.1 The set F computed by Algorithm 15.1 is a cover for the set $\text{dep}(r)$.

Proof. Clearly, F contains only dependencies that hold in r. Moreover, since the algorithm examines all possible nontrivial dependencies of the form $X \to A$, the set F will in the end contain all such dependencies that hold in r. Since all dependencies $X \to Y$ can be derived from dependencies with a single attribute on the right hand side, F is a cover of $\text{dep}(r)$.   □

Theorem 15.2 Algorithm 15.1 works in time $O(n^2 2^n p \log p)$, where n is the number of attributes in R and p is the number of tuples in r.

Proof. The dependency $X \to A$ can be chosen in $n2^{n-1}$ ways. Testing whether $r \models X \to A$ takes time $O(p^2|X|)$, if each pair of tuples is checked individually. Another possibility is to sort the tuples of r on X before making each test. Sorting takes time $O(|X|p \log p)$, and checking that the sorted relation satisfies $X \to A$ takes time $O(|X|p)$. Since $|X| \leq n$, the total complexity of this alternative is therefore

$$O(n2^{n-1}np \log p) = O(n^2 2^n p \log p).$$
                                                 □

Algorithm 15.1 is simple. Its drawback is that it uses exponential time for all inputs, no matter how regular the relation is. The next algorithm tries to be more adaptive to the input. It is based on the concept of a transversal of a hypergraph presented in Chapter 13.

Algorithm 15.2 Computation of the functional dependencies holding in a relation using transversals.
Input. A relation r over R.
Output. A cover F for $\text{dep}(r)$.
Method. First compute the complements of the maximal sets of $\text{dep}(r)$, and then form the cover F, as transversals (see Section 13.3) of these sets.

1.   **for** each attribute $A \in R$ **do**
2. $J_A := \{R \setminus ag(t, t') \mid t, t' \in r \text{ and } t[A] \neq t'[A]\}$;
3. $K_A := \{W \in J_A \mid \text{ there is no } V \in J_A \text{ such that } V \subset W\}$;
4. $\{$now $K_A = \text{cmax}(A)$, for each $A \in R.\}$
5. $L_A := \text{Tr}(K_A)$;
6.   **od**;
7. $F := \{X \rightarrow B \mid B \in R, X \in L_B\}$;   □

Example 15.2 Continuing Example 15.1, we use Algorithm 15.2 to compute the dependencies holding in the relation of that example. We abbreviate the attribute names by their first letters.

First we obtain the J and K sets:

$$J_E = \{EDMS, ES, EDM\}, \quad K_E = \{ES, EDM\}$$
$$J_D = \{DEMS, DEM\}, \quad\quad K_D = \{DEM\}$$
$$J_M = \{MEDS, MED\}, \quad\quad K_M = \{MED\}$$
$$J_S = \{SEDM, SE\}, \quad\quad\quad K_S = \{SE\}.$$

Now the L-families are transversals of the K sets:

$$\text{lhs}(E) = \{E, SD, SM\},$$
$$\text{lhs}(D) = \{D, E, M\},$$
$$\text{lhs}(M) = \{D, E, M\},$$
$$\text{lhs}(S) = \{S, E\}.$$

Thus the dependency set F is, with trivial dependencies removed,

$$SD \rightarrow E, SM \rightarrow E,$$
$$E \rightarrow D, M \rightarrow D,$$
$$E \rightarrow M, D \rightarrow M,$$
$$E \rightarrow S.$$

Forming a nonredundant and L-minimum cover, and combining dependencies with the same left-hand side we obtain the dependencies

$$SM \rightarrow E, M \rightarrow D, E \rightarrow MS, D \rightarrow M.$$

This is equivalent to the set obtained in Example 15.1.   □

Theorem 15.3 The dependency set F computed by Algorithm 15.2 for relation r is a cover for the set $\text{dep}(r)$.

Proof. By Lemma 13.3 (page 238) it would be enough to show that the collections K_A are the cmax(A) collections for dep(r). However, we prove the result without using Lemma 13.3.

Let $W \rightarrow A \in F$, that is, $W \in L_A$. We claim that $r \models W \rightarrow A$. Suppose not. Then there are rows $t, t' \in r$ such that $t[W] = t'[W]$ and $t[A] \neq t'[A]$. This means that $R \setminus ag(t, t')$ belongs to J_A and hence some subset V of $R\backslash W$ belongs to K_A. Thus each element of $\mathrm{Tr}(K_A)$ intersects V, and especially $W \cap V \neq \emptyset$. But this contradicts $V \subseteq R \setminus W$.

For the converse, suppose $W \to A \in \mathrm{dep}(r)$. We want to show that $F \models W \to A$. Suppose not; then there is no member $V \in L_A$ such that $V \subseteq W$. By the definition of transversals, this means that for some $X \in K_A$ we have $X \cap W = \emptyset$. Since $X \in K_A$, the relation r contains rows t and t' such that $X = R \setminus \mathrm{ag}(t,t')$ and $t[A] \neq t'[A]$. Since $X \cap W = \emptyset$, we have $W \subseteq \mathrm{ag}(t,t')$. But then t and t' violate the dependency $W \to A$, a contradiction. $\qquad\square$

Next we analyze the running time of Algorithm 15.2. The size of the J_A collection is $O(p^2)$, if the relation r has p rows. The family K_A is a subcollection of J_A. These families can be formed in time polynomial in p and n, the number of attributes in the schema.

Computing the sets in L_A can be done in polynomial time with respect to

$$\prod_{X \in K_A} |X|$$

by using Algorithm 13.1 (page 238). Hence the running time of Algorithm 15.2 is polynomial in p, n, and the product of the sizes of the cmax sets.

Algorithm 15.2 performs well on relations with simple dependencies. For example, if relation r has only one key X and no other nontrivial dependencies hold in r, then the K_A sets contain at most $|X|$ elements; namely, we have $K_A = \{AB \mid B \in X\}$ for $A \notin X$, and $K_B = \{B\}$ for $B \in X$. For these collections K_A Algorithm 15.2 works in polynomial time, provided the transversal algorithm can recognize the special case.

The drawback of the preceding methods is that they compute the collection of agree sets, a task which seems to require quadratic time in the number p of rows in the relation. Sorting a relation can, on the other hand, be done in time $O(p \log p)$, and several efficient methods for sorting are available. Thus we consider next an algorithm that is based on the idea of repeatedly sorting the rows of the relation with respect to different orderings of the attributes. The algorithm tries to minimize the number of sorts needed by collecting as much information from one sort as possible.

Algorithm 15.3 Computation of lhs(A) for dep(r) by consecutive sorts.
Input. A relation r over schema R, and an attribute $A \in R$.
Output. The collection lhs(A) for the dependency set dep(r).
Method. The algorithm maintains the following three collections of subsets of R:
    lhs: the left-hand sides already found;

nonlhs: sets X such that $X \to A$ does *not* hold in r; and
cand: sets still to be tested.

1.	lhs := $\emptyset$;
2.	nonlhs := $\emptyset$;
3.	cand := $\{\emptyset\}$;
4.	**while** cand $\neq \emptyset$ **do**
5.	let W be the first set of cand;
6.	remove W from cand;
7.	**if** some $L \in$ lhs is a subset of W **then**
8.	do nothing
9.	**else if** some $N \in$ nonlhs is a superset of W **then**
10.	cand := cand $\cup \{WD \mid D \in R \setminus (N \cup \{A\})\}$;
11.	**else**
12.	$Y := R \setminus WA$;
13.	sort r using attributes WYA as the sort key;
14.	let Y' be the longest prefix of WYA such that $Y' \to A$ does not hold;
15.	**if** Y' is not a subset of any set of nonlhs **then**
16.	remove subsets of Y' from nonlhs;
17.	nonlhs := nonlhs $\cup \{Y'\}$;
18.	**fi**;
19.	**if** $Y' \neq WY$ **then**
20.	let B be the attribute in WY following Y';
21.	**if** $Y'B$ is not a superset of any set of lhs **then**
22.	remove supersets of $Y'B$ from lhs;
23.	lhs := lhs $\cup \{Y'B\}$;
24.	**fi**;
25.	**fi**;
26.	cand := cand $\cup \{WD \mid D \in R \setminus WA\}$;
27.	**fi**;
28.	**od**;

$\square$

Example 15.3 Consider a relation r over schema $R(ABCD)$, and suppose lhs$(r, A) = \{CD\}$. Then Algorithm 15.3 would operate as follows on r.

First, cand is initialized to contain only the set $\emptyset$, and lhs and nonlhs are empty. Then the relation is sorted on attributes BCD (assuming that the attributes in Y are taken to be the attributes in R in cyclic order). The longest prefix of BCD not determining A is BC, and this set is added to nonlhs, and BCD is added to lhs. The cand collection is updated to contain sets B, C, and D.

Next we consider the first set in cand, namely B. Since B is a subset of $BC \in$ nonlhs, no sort is needed: B is removed from cand and the set

BD is added to cand. The next element from cand is C, and the same thing happens: C is removed and CD added.

The next set to be considered is D. The relation is sorted on attributes DBC, and DB is added to nonlhs. The set DBC is not added to lhs, since it is already there. No new sets are added to cand, since BD and CD are already in cand.

The next set from cand is BD. No sort is needed, since BD is a subset of an nonlhs set, namely BD itself. However, the set BCD is added to cand.

The next set from cand is CD. This leads to a sort on attributes CDB, and a new lhs set CD; it causes BCD to be removed from lhs. The collection nonlhs does not grow, since C is included in an existing nonlhs set, BC. The last set in cand is BCD. No action is needed, since BCD includes an lhs set. □

Theorem 15.4 Algorithm 15.3 works correctly.

Proof. Consider the following invariant.

(1) For each $N \in$ nonlhs we have $r \not\models N \to A$, and if $N, N' \in$ nonlhs, then $N \not\subseteq N'$.

(2) For each $L \in$ lhs we have $r \models L \to A$, and if $L, L' \in$ lhs, then $L \not\subseteq L'$.

(3) For each $X \subseteq R$ either

    (i) there exists $L \in$ lhs with $L \subseteq X$, or

    (ii) there exists $N \in$ nonlhs with $X \subseteq N$, or

    (iii) there exists $W \in$ cand with $W \subseteq X$.

Denote the disjunction of cases (i), (ii), and (iii) for set X by $\varphi(X)$.

Assume now that the invariant holds at the conclusion of the algorithm. Then the set lhs contains exactly the sets lhs(r, A).

The invariant holds trivially in the beginning of the algorithm. The algorithm stops, since the lengths of the sets in cand grow.

Next we show that the invariant continues to hold during the algorithm. First note that sets are added to lhs and nonlhs only if the sort and the subsequent check have shown that the corresponding dependency holds or does not hold. Also, the pruning of these collections does not cause violations of the last part of the invariant.

Thus it remains to show that when a set W is removed from cand, condition $\varphi(X)$ of part 15.4 continues to hold for each set $X \subseteq R$. We have to consider only subsets X such that $W \subseteq X$, since they are the only sets affected by the removal of W.

If $L \subseteq W$ for some $L \in$ lhs, nothing needs to be done to preserve the invariant: W can be removed directly.

If $W \subseteq N$ for some $N \in$ nonlhs, then part 15.4 requires that we take care of the condition $\varphi(X)$ for sets $X \subseteq R$ with $W \subseteq X$. This is done by adding the sets WD to cand, where $D \in R \setminus NA$. Namely, if $W \subseteq X$, then either $X \subseteq N$ (in which case $\varphi(X)$ holds by part (ii)), or $WD \subseteq X$ for some $D \in R \setminus NA$.

Assume then that neither of the previous cases hold. Then r is sorted using attributes WYA as the sort key.

To verify $\varphi(X)$ for all $X \subseteq R$ we note first that if $W \subseteq X$, either $WD \subseteq X$ for some $D \in R \setminus XA$ or $X = W$. The first case is handled by adding the sets WD to cand.

The remaining case is to check that $\varphi(W)$ holds after the loop has been completed. If Y' is a proper subset of W,[1] then a subset of W is added to lhs and hence $\varphi(W)$ holds after the loop. If $W \subseteq Y'$, then a superset of W is added to nonlhs and hence $\varphi(W)$ remains true.   □

To compute the whole dependency set, one can compute lhs(r, A) for each $A \in R$. In practice it is better to combine these computations, since the same sort can be used to check whether X is a suitable left-hand side for any attribute B.

Theorem 15.5 Algorithm 15.3 works in time $O(mnp \log p + n2^{2n})$, where m is the number of sorts done.

Proof.   Sorting the relation on attributes X takes time $O(|X|p \log p) = O(np \log p)$, assuming that values of single attributes can be compared in a single step. Finding the longest prefix Y' of WYA such that $Y' \to A$ does not hold can be done in time $O(np)$ using the sorted relation.

Maintaining the collections cand, lhs and nonlhs takes $O(nk)$ time per iteration, where k is the size of the collections. Then $k \leq 2^n$. The number of iterations is bounded by 2^n.   □

Algorithm 15.3 is easy to implement using the sort routines supplied by the database management system or the operating system.

15.2   Lower bounds for inferring functional dependencies

In this section we consider the computational complexity of dependency inference. The problem instances have two parameters: the number of

---

[1] In fact, this is not possible; it is, however, easier to prove the theorem by considering also this case.

attributes n and the number of rows p. If dependency inference is used to analyze modified example relations generated by a design tool, the quantity p is probably small. In the analysis of existing databases p can be quite large. We analyze the complexity of dependency inference with respect to both these parameters.

The naive algorithm showed that for fixed n the problem can be solved in time $O(p \log p)$, although the constant hidden by the O-notation is exponential in n. It is easy to show that $O(p \log p)$ is also a lower bound in a comparison-based model of computation, where the only way of obtaining information about equality and inequality of values is by pairwise comparisons.

Theorem 15.6 The dependency inference problem requires in the worst case $\Omega(p \log p)$ steps for two-attribute relations with p rows.

Proof. The *element uniqueness problem* is as follows. Given a sequence $a_1, \ldots, a_p$, determine whether $a_i \neq a_j$ for all $i \neq j$. This problem requires $\Omega(p \log p)$ steps in a comparison-based model.

The uniqueness problem can be solved using dependency inference by constructing a relation r over scheme $R(A, B)$ with tuples (a_i, i) for $i = 1, \ldots, p$. Then the elements of the sequence $a_1, \ldots, a_p$ are unique if and only if $A \to B \in \mathrm{dep}(r)$.   □

Thus the complexity of dependency inference as a function of the number of rows is $\Theta(p \log p)$. What about the complexity as a function of the number of attributes? We show next that for some relations over n attributes all the covers of their dependency sets are of exponential size.

Theorem 15.7 For each n there exists a relation r over R such that $|R| = n$, $|r| = O(n)$, and each cover of $\mathrm{dep}(r)$ has $\Omega(2^{n/2})$ dependencies.

Proof. Assume without loss of generality that $n = |R| = 2m + 1$. The following relation r with $3m + 2 = O(n)$ tuples is used to derive the size bound.

A_1	A_2	A_3	A_4	A_5	A_6	$\cdots$	A_{2m-1}	A_{2m}	A_{2m+1}
0	0	0	0	0	0	$\cdots$	0	0	0
1	1	0	0	0	0	$\cdots$	0	0	1
0	0	1	1	0	0	$\cdots$	0	0	2
		$\vdots$						$\vdots$	
0	0	0	0	0	0	$\cdots$	1	1	m
2	2	2	2	2	2	$\cdots$	2	2	0
3	2	2	2	2	2	$\cdots$	2	2	0
2	3	2	2	2	2	$\cdots$	2	2	0
2	2	3	2	2	2	$\cdots$	2	2	0
		$\vdots$						$\vdots$	
2	2	2	2	2	2	$\cdots$	2	3	0

Consider first a dependency $X \rightarrow A_{2m+1}$, where $X \subseteq \{A_1, A_2, \ldots, A_{2m}\}$. If for some i with $1 \leq i \leq m$ the set X contains neither A_{2i-1} nor A_{2i}, the relation does not satisfy $X \rightarrow A_{2m+1}$: tuples 1 and $i+1$ agree on X but disagree on A_{2m+1}. On the other hand, if X contains at least one attribute from each pair $(A_1, A_2), (A_3, A_4), \ldots, (A_{2m-1}, A_{2m})$, no two tuples agree on X, and the dependency $X \rightarrow A_{2m+1}$ holds vacuously.

The last $2m + 1$ tuples of the relation are included to ensure that if $X \rightarrow A_i$ holds for some A_i, where $1 \leq i \leq 2m$, then X must contain A_i. Therefore the minimum cover of $\text{dep}(r)$ (the cover having the smallest number of dependencies) is

$$F = \{X \rightarrow A_{2m+1} \mid \text{for each } i, \text{ where } 1 \leq i \leq 2m, X \text{ contains}$$
$$\text{exactly one of the attributes } A_{2i-1} \text{ and } A_{2i}\}.$$

The size of F is $2^m = \theta(2^{n/2})$.   □

Hence for some small relations the size of the output of dependency inference is exponential in the size of the input. Thus any algorithm for dependency inference must use exponential time, if it must output the result. In practice, relations r such that $\text{dep}(r)$ has only large covers are probably rare. Such a relation has many different keys, or the relation scheme is highly unnormalized (since lots of non-key dependencies hold). Both situations are unlikely.

Theorem 15.7 shows that the results of dependency inference can be large. This does not necessarily mean that identifying the dependency sets is hard. The following two theorems show, however, that this is the case, too.

We first show that there are a lot of nonequivalent dependency sets. By a standard information-theoretic argument, this implies that dependency inference is hard, at least for some relations.

Theorem 15.8 Denote by $K(n)$ the number of nonequivalent sets of functional dependencies over a fixed n-attribute set. Then

$$K(n) \geq 2^{S(n-1)},$$

where

$$S(n) = \binom{n}{\lfloor n/2 \rfloor}.$$

Proof. Let $|R| = n$, and let M be the collection of all subsets of size $\lfloor (n-1)/2 \rfloor$ of the first $n - 1$ elements of R. Then the size of M is $S(n-1)$.

Let A be the nth attribute of R. Given any subset $N \subseteq M$, let $F_N = \{X \rightarrow A \mid X \in N\}$. For $N \neq N'$, the dependency sets F_N and $F_{N'}$ are nonequivalent. There are $2^{S(n-1)}$ such sets F_N.   □

Theorem 15.9 Any algorithm for dependency inference uses in the worst case at least time $S(n-1)$ for an attribute set of n attributes.

Proof. A comparison-based algorithm for dependency inference chooses among $K(n)$ different sets. Any step in the algorithm can differentiate only between 2 (or some fixed number) of possibilities. Hence the result follows from the previous theorem.   □

The problem with the above result is that it is nonconstructive: we know that dependency inference is hard, but we have no idea of which sets are hard to find and which are not. Next we consider an alternative lower bound showing that the number of maximal sets of $\text{dep}(r)$ is connected to the complexity of dependency inference from r.

We consider a model of computation which is suitable for the application of finding the dependencies from a large existing database. We assume that we can only sort the relation with respect to the attributes in some sequence $X = A_1, \ldots, A_n$, and compare adjacent rows in the output of the sort; we do not have enough memory to study the whole relation.

Inspection of the sorted output gives us the closure of each set $\{A_1, \ldots, A_i\}$, where $i = 1, \ldots, n$.

This leads us to consider *closure queries*. They are defined as follows.

Given attribute set X, compute its closure with respect to $\text{dep}(r)$.

The following theorem gives a lower bound for the number of closure queries needed for dependency inference.

Theorem 15.10 Assume closure queries are the only way of obtaining information about the relation r. Then solving the dependency inference problem requires

$$|\text{max}(\text{dep}(r))|$$

closure queries for any relation r.

Corollary 15.1 Assume sorting the relation with respect to some attribute sequence is the only way of obtaining information about r. Then we need at least

$$|\text{max}(\text{dep}(r))|/|R|$$

sorts for dependency inference.   □

Proof of Theorem 15.10. Suppose an algorithm correctly finds a cover F for $\text{dep}(r)$ using queries that compute the closures of attribute sets $X_1, \ldots, X_k$, where $k < |\text{max}(\text{dep}(r))| = |\text{max}(F)|$. Then there exists $W \in \text{max}(F, A)$ such that $W \neq X_{iF}^+$ for all i.

Consider the dependency set

$G = \text{dep}(r) \cup \{W \to A\}$.

We show that the closures of the sets $X_1, \ldots, X_k$ are the same in G and in F. This, however, means that the algorithm cannot give correct results, since F and G are nonequivalent.

Consider the computation of the closure of X_i with respect to F. If $X_i \to W$ follows from F, then by the assumption $W \neq X_{iF}^+$ we have $W \subset X_{iF}^+$. Since $W \in \max(F, A)$, this means $A \in X_{iF}^+$. Therefore the new dependency in G does not increase the closure X_i, that is, $X_{iF}^+ = X_{iG}^+$.

If $X_i \to W$ does not follow from F, then $W \not\subseteq X_{iF}^+$, and again the closure of X_i is the same with respect to F as with respect to G.   □

15.3   Inference of inclusion dependencies

We now turn to the case of inclusion dependencies. Given a database schema **R** and a database **r** over **R**, we want to find the inclusion dependencies that hold in **r**.

Suppose we have a database schema consisting of two n-attribute relation schemas R and S. Then there are more than $n!$ possible nonequivalent inclusion dependencies of the form $R[X] \subseteq S[Y]$ between R and S. Checking them one by one is obviously impossible for any large value of n.

We can show that it is already NP-complete to decide whether an inclusion dependency of the form $R[X] \subseteq S[Y]$ holds, where Y contains all the attributes of S. Consider the following problem.

FULLINDEXISTENCE Let R and S be relation schemas, and denote by X the sequence consisting of the attributes of R in some order. Given relations r and s over R and S, respectively, decide whether there exists a sequence Y consisting of disjoint attributes of S in some order such that the dependency $R[X] \subseteq S[Y]$ holds in the database (r, s).

Theorem 15.11 FULLINDEXISTENCE is an NP-complete problem.

Proof. The problem is in NP, since we can nondeterministically guess a sequence Y and then in polynomial time verify that $R[X] \subseteq S[Y]$ holds.

To prove NP-hardness, we show that the following NP-complete problem is reducible to FULLINDEXISTENCE.

SUBGRAPH ISOMORPHISM Given undirected graphs $G = (V, E)$ and $H = (V', E')$, decide whether H contains a subgraph isomorphic to G, that is, whether there is an injective mapping $g : V \to V'$ such that for all $u, v \in V$ with $(u, v) \in E$ we have $(g(u), g(v)) \in E'$.

We reduce this problem to the FULLINDEXISTENCE problem as follows. The relation r corresponding to the graph $G = (V, E)$ has as schema R the set V, and it contains a row t_e for each $e = (u, v) \in E$. The values of t_e are defined by

$$t_e(u) = t_e(v) = 1,$$
$$t_e(w) = 0 \text{ for } w \in V \setminus \{u, v\}.$$

The relation s corresponding to graph H is formed in the same way: the schema S of s consists of the elements of V', and s has one row for each edge in E'. Denote by X the sequence of the attributes of R in some order.

We claim that there is an injective mapping g from V to V' preserving the incidence relation if and only if

$$(r, s) \models R[X] \subseteq S[Y]$$

for some sequence Y of disjoint attributes of S. The proof is left as Exercise 15.5. □

Thus it is in general not possible to check the existence of a long inclusion dependency fast. However, one should be cautious in interpreting a result like Theorem 15.11. The database used to prove NP-completeness is highly artificial. In real situations there are several ways to prune the set of possible inclusion dependencies. If an inclusion dependency $R[X] \subseteq S[Y]$ holds, then for all attributes A of X the corresponding attribute B of Y should be of the same type as A. That is, if A is a string-valued attribute, B should also be string-valued, and so on. Second, looking for inclusion dependencies of arbitrary length is typically not useful: the dependencies holding in a database are probably short. Furthermore, a necessary condition for an inclusion dependency $R[X] \subseteq S[Y]$ is that $R[A] \subseteq S[B]$ holds for each pair A and B of attributes of X and Y corresponding to each other. Hence one can start by looking at the unary inclusion dependencies holding in the database.

In a database schema with n attributes there are at most n^2 possible unary inclusion dependencies, so the collection

$$\{R[A] \subseteq S[B] \mid R, S \in \mathbf{R}, A \in R, B \in S, \text{ and } r[A] \subseteq s[B]\}$$

can be computed in time $O(n^2 p \log p)$, where p is the maximum number of rows in any one relation of the database $\mathbf{r}$. As mentioned earlier, the coefficient n^2 can further be lowered. There is no need to check inclusion between attributes with different domains. Hence instead of n^2 pairs of attributes one needs to investigate only $\sum_i n_i^2$ pairs, where i ranges over the different types of attributes (strings, numeric, and so on) and n_i is the number of attributes of type i.

Given that for most databases only relatively few inclusion dependencies hold, the checks for most dependencies should terminate rather quickly.

Exercises

Exercise 15.1 Show that Algorithm 15.2 can use exponential time for some inputs.

Exercise 15.2 Check the construction of Theorem 15.7 for $n = 5$.

Exercise 15.3 Enumerate all nonequivalent sets of functional dependencies over the relation schema $\{A, B\}$. Compare the result with the bound given by Theorem 15.8.

Exercise 15.4 A limited form of inference of functional dependencies is the inference of the keys of a relation. That is, given a relation schema R and a relation r over R, we want to find all keys of r. One can test whether a subset $X \subseteq R$ is a key by performing an SQL query that attempts to create a unique index for the attributes of X. If the index creation succeeds, then X contains a key; if it fails, X does not contain a key. Design an algorithm for key inference based on this operation.

Exercise 15.5 Complete the proof of Theorem 15.11.

Exercise 15.6 ** If the relation is large, say 100 000 tuples, then the inference of functional dependencies can be too time-consuming even for small sets of attributes. An alternative way of finding the dependencies is to select a small sample of the relation, compute the set of functional dependencies holding in the sample and then verify that they hold also in the original relation. Investigate the usefulness of this idea.

Exercise 15.7 Explain in detail the data structures and algorithms needed for the computation of the K_A sets in Algorithm 15.2. What is the worst case time requirement of your algorithm?

Exercise 15.8 ** In practical situations some dependencies 'almost' hold; that is, for most cases they are valid, except that there can be a small number of exceptions. Give a reasonable definition of the degree of validity of a functional dependency and develop an algorithm for finding the dependencies that almost hold.

Exercise 15.9 Investigate the problem of producing a short representation of the functional dependencies that do *not* hold in the given relation.

Exercise 15.10 ** Try to find a dependency inference algorithm that would work in polynomial time with respect to the number of MAX-sets of dep(r) and the size of the smallest cover of dep(r).

Exercise 15.11 (i) Give an SQL expression for checking whether the inclusion dependency $R[A] \subseteq S[B]$ holds. (ii) Write an embedded SQL program to infer all the unary inclusion dependencies holding in a database.

Exercise 15.12 ** Consider the problem of inferring some value-dependent constraints in a database.

Exercise 15.13 ** Develop an algorithm for finding all functional dependencies that hold in a given database in the sense of satisfaction by containing instance (Section 8.6).

Bibliographic notes

The dependency inference problem for functional dependencies was introduced in [MR86a]. Algorithms for the problem are presented in [MR87, BMT89, MR91]. Algorithm 15.3 is from [MR91].

The computation of transversals is studied in [EG91]. Section 15.2 follows [MR92]. Theorem 15.7 was stated in [MR87]; related results have been shown in [DG81, Thi86, GL90]. For the comparison-based model of computation and the element uniqueness problem the basic reference is [Rei72]. Theorem 15.6 uses a method similar to the classical example of information theoretic lower bounds, the $\Omega(p \log p)$ bound for sorting p keys using comparisons. The technique is also used in Theorem 15.9. Theorem 15.8 is from [BDK+91].

For an exposition of NP-completeness and the subgraph isomorphism problem, see the book by Garey and Johnson [GJ79].

The use of inference of inclusion dependencies in mapping relational schemas to conceptual schemas is considered in [CS91]. Papers dealing with inference of more complicated constraints are [Del87, TM89, PS89, Yas91, DRS91] and the collection [PS91]. Dependency inference can be considered as a special case of concept learning [MCM83, MCM86]. The lower bounds given in Section 15.2 generalize to more complex settings. Exercise 15.8 is from [KM92].

Bibliography

[AB86]   Abiteboul, S. and Bidoit, N. (1986). Non first normal form relations: An algebra allowing data restructuring. *Journal of Computer and System Sciences*, **33**(3), 361–393.

[ABD⁺90]   Atkinson, M., Bancilhon, F., DeWitt, D. J., Dittrich, K., Maier, D., and Zdonik, S. B. (1990). The object-oriented database system manifesto. In *Proceedings of the International Conference on Deductive and Object-Oriented Databases (DOOD'89)* (Kim, W., Nicolas, J.-M., and Nishio, S., eds.), pp. 223–240, Amsterdam: Elsevier Science Publishers B.V (North-Holland).

[ABLV83]   Atzeni, P., Batini, C., Lenzerini, M., and Villanelli, F. (1983). INCOD: A system for conceptual design of data and transactions in the entity-relationship model. In *Entity-Relationship Approach to Information Modeling and Analysis* (Chen, P. P.-S., ed.), pp. 375–410. Amsterdam: Elsevier Science Publishers B.V (North-Holland).

[ABU79]   Aho, A. V., Beeri, C., and Ullman, J. D. (1979). The theory of joins in relational databases. *ACM Transactions on Database Systems*, **4**(3), 297–314.

[AC78]   Arora, A. K. and Carlson, C. R. (1978). The information preserving properties of certain relational database transformations. In *Proceedings of the Fourth International Conference on Very Large Data Bases (VLDB'78)*, pp. 352–359.

[AC83]   Atzeni, P. and Carboni, E. (1983). INCOD (a system for interactive conceptual design) revisited after the implementation of a prototype. In *Entity-Relationship Approach to Software Engineering* (Davis, C. G., Jajodia, S., Ng, P. A., and Yeh, R. T., eds.), pp. 449–464. Amsterdam: Elsevier Science Publishers B.V (North-Holland).

[AC91]   Atzeni, P. and Chan, E. P. F. (1991). Independent database schemes under functional and inclusion dependencies. *Acta Informatica*, **28**(8), 777–799.

[AD80]   Armstrong, W. W. and Delobel, C. (1980). Decompositions and functional dependencies in relations. *ACM Transactions on Database Systems*, **5**(4), 404–430.

[AFS89]   Abiteboul, S., Fischer, P. C., and Schek, H.-J., eds. (1989). *Nested Relations and Complex Objects in Databases.* Berlin: Springer-Verlag. Lecture Notes in Computer Science 361.

[AHU74]   Aho, A. V., Hopcroft, J. E., and Ullman, J. D. (1974). *The Design and Analysis of Computer Algorithms.* Reading, MA: Addison-Wesley Publishing Company.

[AKW88]   Aho, A. V., Kernighan, B. W., and Weinberger, P. J. (1988). *The AWK Programming Language.* Reading, MA: Addison-Wesley Publishing Company.

[Arm74]   Armstrong, W. W. (1974). Dependency structures of data base relationships. In *Information Processing 74, Proceedings of IFIP Congress 1974* (Rosenfeld, J. L., ed.), pp. 580–583, IFIP, Amsterdam: North-Holland Publishing Company.

[ASU79]   Aho, A. V., Sagiv, Y., and Ullman, J. D. (1979). Equivalences among relational expressions. *SIAM Journal on Computing*, **8**(2), 218–246.

[AV88]   Abiteboul, S. and Vianu, V. (1988). Equivalence and optimization of relational transactions. *Journal of the ACM*, **35**(1), 70–120.

[AV89]   Abiteboul, S. and Vianu, V. (1989). Transaction-based approach to relational database specification. *Journal of the ACM*, **36**(4), 758–789.

[Bac69]   Bachman, C. W. (1969). Data structure diagrams. *Data Base*, **1**(2), 4–10.

[Ban92]   Bancilhon, F. (1992). Understanding object-oriented database systems. In *Advances in Database Technology –*

EDBT'92 (Pirotte, A., Delobel, C., and Gottlob, G., eds.), pp. 1–9, Berlin: Springer-Verlag. Lecture Notes in Computer Science 580.

[BB79]   Beeri, C. and Berstein, P. A. (1979). Computational problems related to the design of normal form relation schemes. *ACM Transactions on Database Systems*, **4**(1), 30–59.

[BC89]   Bagchi, T. P. and Chaudhri, V. K. (1989). *Interactive Relational Database Design – A Logic Programming Implementation*. Berlin: Springer-Verlag. Lecture Notes in Computer Science 402.

[BCN92]   Batini, C., Ceri, S., and Navathe, S. B. (1992). *Conceptual Database Design*. Redwood City, CA: The Benjamin/Cummings Publishing Company, Inc.

[BD83]   Bitton, D. and DeWitt, D. J. (1983). Duplicate record elimination in large data files. *ACM Transactions on Database Systems*, **8**(2), 255–265.

[BD91]   Biskup, J. and Dublish, P. (1991). Objects in relational database schemes with functional, inclusion and exclusion dependencies. In *3rd Symposium on Mathematical Fundamentals of Database and Knowledge Base Systems (MFDBS'91)* (Thalheim, B., Demetrovics, J., and Gerhardt, H.-D., eds.), pp. 276–290, Berlin: Springer-Verlag. Lecture Notes in Computer Science 495.

[BDB79]   Biskup, J., Dayal, U., and Bernstein, P. A. (1979). Synthesizing independent database schemas. In *Proceedings of ACM SIGMOD Conference on Management of Data (SIGMOD'79)*, pp. 143–152, New York, NY: ACM.

[BDD84]   Batini, C., De Antonellis, V., and Di Leva, A. (1984). Database design activities within the DATAID project. *Database Engineering*, **7**(4), 16–21.

[BDFS84]   Beeri, C., Dowd, M., Fagin, R., and Statman, R. (1984). On the structure of Armstrong relations for functional dependencies. *Journal of the ACM*, **31**(1), 30–46.

[BDK+91]   Burosch, G., Demetrovics, J., Katona, G. O. H., Kleitman, D. J., and Sapozhenko, A. A. (1991). On the number of databases and closure operations. *Theoretical Computer Science*, **78**(2), 377–381.

[BDK92]   Bancilhon, F., Delobel, C., and Kanellakis, P., eds. (1992).
          Building an Object-Oriented Database System – The Story of
          O_2. San Mateo, CA: Morgan Kaufmann.

[BDRZ84] Bragger, R. P., Dudler, A., Rebsamen, J., and Zehnder, C. A.
          (1984). Gambit: An interactive database design tool for
          data structures, integrity constraints and transactions. In
          *Proceedings of the International Conference on Data Engi-
          neering*, pp. 399–407, Silver Spring, MD: IEEE Computer
          Society Press.

[Bee90]   Beeri, C. (1990). A formal approach to object-oriented
          databases. *Data & Knowledge Engineering*, **5**(4), 353–382.

[Ber76]   Bernstein, P. A. (1976). Synthesizing third normal form re-
          lations from functional dependencies. *ACM Transactions on
          Database Systems*, **1**(4), 277–298.

[Ber89]   Berge, C. (1989). *Hypergraphs. Combinatorics of Finite Sets.*
          Amsterdam: North-Holland Publishing Company.

[BG80]   Bernstein, P. A. and Goodman, N. (1980). What does Boyce-
          Codd normal form do? In *Proceedings of the Sixth Interna-
          tional Conference on Very Large Data Bases (VLDB'80)*, pp.
          245–259.

[BGM85]   Bouzeghoub, M., Gardarin, G., and Métais, E. (1985).
          Database design tools: An expert system approach. In *Pro-
          ceedings of the Eleventh International Conference on Very
          Large Data Bases (VLDB'85)*, pp. 82–95.

[BH81]   Beeri, C. and Honeyman, P. (1981). Preserving functional
          dependencies. *SIAM Journal on Computing*, **10**(3), 647–656.

[BH84]   Bjornerstedt, A. and Hulten, C. (1984). RED1: A database
          design tool for the relational model of data. *Database Engi-
          neering*, **7**(4), 34–39.

[Bis89]   Biskup, J. (1989). Boyce-Codd normal form and object nor-
          mal form. *Information Processing Letters*, **32**(1), 29–33.

[BK86]   Beeri, C. and Kifer, M. (1986). An integrated approach to
          logical design of relational database schemes. *ACM Trans-
          actions on Database Systems*, **11**(2), 134–158.

[BM87]   Biskup, J. and Meyer, R. (1987). Design of relational database schemes by deleting attributes in the canonical decomposition. *Journal of Computer and System Sciences*, **35**(1), 1–22.

[BMS84]   Brodie, M. L., Mylopoulos, J., and Schmidt, J. W., eds. (1984). *On Conceptual Modelling: Perspectives from Artificial Intelligence, Databases, and Programming Languages*. New York: Springer-Verlag.

[BMSU81]   Beeri, C., Mendelzon, A. O., Sagiv, Y., and Ullman, J. D. (1981). Equivalence of relational database schemes. *SIAM Journal on Computing*, **10**(2), 352–370.

[BMT89]   Bitton, D., Millman, J. C., and Torgersen, S. (1989). A feasibility and performance study of dependency inference. In *Proceedings of the Fifth International Conference on Data Engineering*, IEEE Computer Society Press.

[Bol86]   Bollobás, B. (1986). *Combinatorics*. Cambridge: Cambridge University Press.

[BOS91]   Butterworth, P., Otis, A., and Stein, J. (1991). The Gem-Stone object database management system. *Communications of the ACM*, **34**(10), 64–77.

[BR86]   Bancilhon, F. and Ramakrishnan, R. (1986). An amateur's introduction to recursive query-processing strategies. In *Proceedings of ACM SIGMOD Conference on Management of Data (SIGMOD'86)*, pp. 16–52, New York, NY: ACM.

[BV84a]   Beeri, C. and Vardi, M. (1984a). Formal systems for tuple and equality generating dependencies. *SIAM Journal on Computing*, **13**(1), 76–98.

[BV84b]   Beeri, C. and Vardi, M. (1984b). A proof procedure for data dependencies. *Journal of the ACM*, **31**(4), 718–741.

[CAdS83]   Casanova, M. A. and Amaral de Sá, J. E. (1983). Designing entity-relationship schemes for conventional information systems. In *Entity-Relationship Approach to Software Engineering* (Davis, C. G., Jajodia, S., Ng, P. A., and Yeh, R. T., eds.), pp. 265–277. Amsterdam: Elsevier Science Publishers B.V (North-Holland).

[CAdS84]   Casanova, M. A. and Amaral de Sá, J. E. (1984). Mapping uninterpreted schemes into entity-relationship diagrams: Two applications to conceptual schema design. *IBM Journal of Research and Development*, **28**(1), 82–94.

[Cer83]   Ceri, S. (1983). Methodology and tools for data base design in the DATAID project. In *Methodology and Tools for Data Base Design* (Ceri, S., ed.), pp. 1–9. Amsterdam: North-Holland Publishing Company.

[CFP84]   Casanova, M. A., Fagin, R., and Papadimitriou, C. (1984). Inclusion dependencies and their interaction with functional dependencies. *Journal of Computer and System Sciences*, **28**, 29–59.

[CFT91]   Casanova, M. A., Furtado, A. L., and Tucherman, L. (1991). A software tool for modular database design. *ACM Transactions on Database Systems*, **16**(2), 209–234.

[CGT89]   Ceri, S., Gottlob, G., and Tanca, L. (1989). What you always wanted to know about Datalog (and never dared to ask). *IEEE Transactions on Knowledge and Data Engineering*, **1**(1), 146–166.

[CH88]   Chan, E. P. F. and Hernández, H. J. (1988). On generating database schemes bounded or constant-time-maintainable by extensibility. *Acta Informatica*, **25**(5), 475–496.

[CH91]   Chan, E. P. F. and Hernández, H. J. (1991). Independence-reducible database schemes. *Journal of the ACM*, **38**(4), 854–886.

[Cha89]   Chan, E. P. F. (1989). A design theory for solving the anomalies problem. *SIAM Journal on Computing*, **18**(3), 429–448.

[Che76]   Chen, P. P.-S. (1976). The entity-relationship model – toward a unified view of data. *ACM Transactions on Database Systems*, **1**(1), 9–36.

[CK85]   Cosmadakis, S. S. and Kanellakis, P. C. (1985). Equational theories and database constraints. In *Proceedings of the ACM Symposium on Theory of Computing (STOC'85)*, pp. 273–284, New York, NY: ACM.

[CK86]   Cosmadakis, S. S. and Kanellakis, P. C. (1986). Functional and inclusion dependencies: A graph theoretic approach.

In *Advances in Computing Research, Volume 3* (Kanellakis, P. C., ed.), pp. 163–184. Greenwich, CN: JAI Press, Inc.

[CKV90]   Cosmadakis, S. S., Kanellakis, P. C., and Vardi, M. Y. (1990). Polynomial-time implication problems for unary inclusion dependencies. *Journal of the ACM*, **37**(1), 15–46.

[CL80]   Chan, E. P. F. and Lochovsky, F. H. (1980). A graphical data base design aid using the entity-relationship model. In *Entity-Relationship Approach to Systems Analysis and Design* (Chen, P. P.-S., ed.), pp. 295–310. Amsterdam: Elsevier Science Publishers B.V (North-Holland).

[CM87]   Chan, E. P. F. and Mendelzon, A. O. (1987). Independent and separable database schemes. *SIAM Journal on Computing*, **16**(5), 841–851.

[CMNK88]   Choobineh, J., Mannino, M. V., Nunamaker, Jr., J. F., and Konsynski, B. R. (1988). An expert database design system based on analysis of Forms B. *IEEE Transactions on Software Engineering*, **SE-14**(2), 242–253.

[CMT92]   Choobineh, J., Mannino, M. V., and Tseng, V. P. (1992). A form-based approach for database analysis and design. *Communications of the ACM*, **35**(2), 108–120.

[CNC83]   Chung, I., Nakamura, F., and Chen, P. P.-S. (1983). A decomposition of relations using the entity-relationship approach. In *Entity-Relationship Approach to Information Modeling and Analysis* (Chen, P. P.-S., ed.), pp. 149–171. Amsterdam: Elsevier Science Publishers B.V (North-Holland).

[Cod70]   Codd, E. F. (1970). A relational model for large shared data banks. *Communications of the ACM*, **13**(6), 377–387.

[Cod72]   Codd, E. F. (1972). Further normalization of the data base relational model. In *Data Base Systems* (Rustin, R., ed.), pp. 33–64. Englewood Cliffs, NJ: Prentice Hall.

[Cod74]   Codd, E. F. (1974). Recent investigations in relational database systems. In *Information Processing 74, Proceedings of IFIP Congress 1974* (Rosenfeld, J. L., ed.), pp. 1017–1021, IFIP, Amsterdam: North-Holland Publishing Company.

[Cod79]   Codd, E. F. (1979). Extending the database relational model to capture more meaning. *ACM Transactions on Database Systems*, **4**(4), 397–434.

[Cod86]   Codd, E. F. (1986). An evaluation scheme for database management systems that are claimed to be relational. In *Proceedings of the Second International Conference on Data Engineering*, pp. 720–729, Washington, DC: IEEE Computer Society Press.

[Cod90]   Codd, E. F. (1990). *The Relational Model for Database Management, Version 2*. Reading, MA: Addison-Wesley Publishing Company.

[CS91]   Castellanos, M. and Saltor, F. (1991). Semantic enrichment of database schemas: an object-oriented approach. Manuscript.

[CTL91]   Casanova, M. A., Tucherman, L., and Laender, A. H. F. (1991). Algorithms for designing and maintaining optimized relational representations of entity-relationship schemas. In *Entity-Relationship Approach: The Core of Conceptual Modelling* (Kangassalo, H., ed.), pp. 349–362. Amsterdam: Elsevier Science Publishers B.V (North-Holland).

[CV83]   Casanova, M. A. and Vidal, V. M. P. (1983). Towards a sound view integration methodology. In *Proceedings of the Second ACM SIGACT-SIGMOD Symposium on Principles of Database Systems (PODS'83)*, pp. 36–47, New York, NY: ACM.

[CV85]   Chandra, A. K. and Vardi, M. Y. (1985). The implication problem for functional and inclusion dependencies is undecidable. *SIAM Journal on Computing*, **14**(3), 671–677.

[D+91]   Deux, O. et al. (1991). The O_2 system. *Communications of the ACM*, **34**(10), 34–48.

[DA83]   Dumpala, S. R. and Arora, S. K. (1983). Schema translation using the entity-relationship approach. In *Entity-Relationship Approach to Information Modeling and Analysis* (Chen, P. P.-S., ed.), pp. 337–356. Amsterdam: Elsevier Science Publishers B.V (North-Holland).

[DA88]   Davis, K. H. and Arora, A. K. (1988). Converting a relational
            database model to an entity-relationship model. In *Entity-
            Relationship Approach* (March, S. T., ed.), pp. 271–285. Am-
            sterdam: Elsevier Science Publishers B.V (North-Holland).

[Dat81]   Date, C. J. (1981). Referential integrity. In *Proceedings of the
            Seventh International Conference on Very Large Data Bases
            (VLDB'81)*, pp. 2–12, IEEE.

[Dat87]   Date, C. J. (1987). *A Guide to the SQL Standard*. Reading,
            MA: Addison-Wesley Publishing Company.

[Dat90a]   Date, C. J. (1990a). *An Introduction to Database Systems,
            Volume I, Fifth Edition.* Reading, MA: Addison-Wesley Pub-
            lishing Company.

[Dat90b]   Date, C. J. (1990b). *Relational Database. Writings 1985–
            1989.* Reading, MA: Addison-Wesley Publishing Company.

[DC73]   Delobel, C. and Casey, R. G. (1973). Decomposition of a
            data base and the theory of Boolean switching functions.
            IBM Journal of Research and Development, **17**(5), 374–386.

[DD85a]   De Antonellis, V. and Di Leva, A. (1985a). A case study of
            database design using the DATAID approach. *Information
            Systems*, **10**(3), 339–359.

[DD85b]   De Antonellis, V. and Di Leva, A. (1985b). DATAID-1: A
            database design methodology. *Information Systems*, **10**(2),
            181–195.

[DEF]   Deft™. 557 Dixon Road, Suite 111, Rexdale, Ontario,
            Canada.

[Del87]   Delgrande, J. P. (1987). Formal bounds on the automatic
            generation and maintenance of integrity constraints. In
            *Proceedings of the Sixth ACM SIGACT-SIGMOD-SIGART
            Symposium on Principles of Database Systems (PODS'87)*,
            pp. 190–196, New York, NY: ACM.

[Des]   Designaid. Nastec Corp. 24681 Northwestern Highway,
            Southfield, MI, USA.

[DF91]   Date, C. J. and Fagin, R. (1991). Simple conditions for guar-
            anteeing higher normal forms in relational databases. Re-
            search Report RJ8101, IBM, San Jose, CA. To appear in
            ACM Transactions on Database Systems.

[DG81]   Demetrovics, J. and Gyepesi, Gy. (1981). On the functional dependency and some generalizations of it. *Acta Cybernetica*, **5**(3), 295–305.

[DGS87]   Desai, B. C., Goyal, P., and Sadri, F. (1987). Fact structure and its application to updates in relational databases. *Information Systems*, **12**(2), 215–221.

[DP90]   De Bra, P. and Paredaens, J. (1990). Removing redundancy and updating databases. In *Third International Conference on Database Theory (ICDT'90)* (Abiteboul, S. and Kanellakis, P. C., eds.), pp. 245–256, Berlin: Springer-Verlag. Lecture Notes in Computer Science 470.

[DRS91]   Demetrovics, J., Rónyai, L., and Son, H. N. (1991). On the representation of dependencies by propositional logic. In *3rd Symposium on Mathematical Fundamentals of Database and Knowledge Base Systems (MFDBS'91)* (Thalheim, B., Demetrovics, J., and Gerhardt, H.-D., eds.), pp. 230–242, Berlin: Springer-Verlag. Lecture Notes in Computer Science 495.

[DST80]   Downey, P. J., Sethi, R., and Tarjan, R. E. (1980). Variations on the common subexpression problem. *Journal of the ACM*, **27**(4), 758–771.

[DT88a]   Demetrovics, J. and Thi, V. D. (1988a). Relations and minimal keys. *Acta Cybernetica*, **8**(3), 279–285.

[DT88b]   Demetrovics, J. and Thi, V. D. (1988b). Some results about functional dependencies. *Acta Cybernetica*, **8**(3), 273–278.

[EG91]   Eiter, T. and Gottlob, G. (1991). Identifying the minimal transversals of a hypergraph and related problems. Technical Report CD-TR 91/16, Technische Universität Wien.

[EN89]   Elmasri, R. and Navathe, S. B. (1989). *Fundamentals of Database Systems*. Redwood City, CA: The Benjamin/Cummings Publishing Company, Inc.

[ERD]   ER-Designer, SchemaGen, and Normalizer. Chen & Associates, Inc. Baton Rouge, LA, USA.

[ERV]   macScot ERVision. Andyne Computing Limited. Canada.

[Exc]   Excelerator. Index Technology Corp. One Main Street, Cambridge, MA, USA.

[Fag77]   Fagin, R. (1977). Multivalued dependencies and a new nor-
            mal form for relational databases. *ACM Transactions on
            Database Systems*, **2**(3), 262–278.

[Fag79]   Fagin, R. (1979). Normal forms and relational database op-
            erators. In *Proceedings of ACM SIGMOD Conference on
            Management of Data (SIGMOD'79)*, pp. 153–160, New York,
            NY: ACM.

[Fag81]   Fagin, R. (1981). A normal form for relational databases
            that is based on domains and keys. *ACM Transactions on
            Database Systems*, **6**(3), 387–415.

[Fag82a]   Fagin, R. (1982a). Armstrong databases. Research Report
            RJ3440, IBM, San Jose, CA.

[Fag82b]   Fagin, R. (1982b). Horn clauses and database dependencies.
            Journal of the ACM, **29**(4), 952–985.

[Fer85]   Ferrara, F. (1985). Easy ER: An integrated system for the
            design and documentation of data base applications. In
            *Proceedings of the 4th International Conference on Entity-
            Relationship Approach*.

[Fis88]   Fisher, A. (1988). *CASE: Using Software Development Tools*.
            John Wiley Inc.

[FJT83]   Fischer, P. C., Jou, J. H., and Tsou, D.-M. (1983). Succinct-
            ness in dependency systems. *Theoretical Computer Science*,
            24, 323–329.

[FMUY83]   Fagin, R., Maier, D., Ullman, J. D., and Yannakakis, M.
            (1983). Tools for template dependencies. *SIAM Journal on
            Computing*, **12**(1), 36–59.

[FV83]   Fagin, R. and Vardi, M. Y. (1983). Armstrong databases for
            functional and inclusion dependencies. *Information Process-
            ing Letters*, **16**(1), 13–19.

[FV86]   Fagin, R. and Vardi, M. Y. (1986). The theory of data depen-
            dencies – a survey. In *Mathematics of Information Process-
            ing* (Anshel, M. and Gewirtz, W., eds.), pp. 19–72. American
            Mathematical Society. Symposia in Applied Mathematics 34.

[FvH89]   Fleming, C. C. and von Halle, B. (1989). *Handbook of Rela-
            tional Database Design*. Reading, MA: Addison-Wesley Pub-
            lishing Company.

[GJ79]   Garey, M. R. and Johnson, D. S. (1979). *Computers and Intractability – A Guide to the Theory of NP-completeness.* New York: W. H. Freeman and Company.

[GL90]   Gottlob, G. and Libkin, L. O. (1990). Investigations of Armstrong relations, dependency inference, and excluded functional dependencies. *Acta Cybernetica,* **9**(4), 385–402.

[GMV86]   Graham, M. H., Mendelzon, A. O., and Vardi, M. Y. (1986). Notions of dependency satisfaction. *Journal of the ACM,* **33**(1), 105–129.

[Got87a]   Gottlob, G. (1987a). Computing covers for embedded functional dependencies. In *Proceedings of the Sixth ACM SIGACT-SIGMOD-SIGART Symposium on Principles of Database Systems (PODS'87),* pp. 58–69, New York, NY: ACM.

[Got87b]   Gottlob, G. (1987b). On the size of nonredundant FD-covers. *Information Processing Letters,* **24**(6), 355–360.

[GS89]   Goldstein, R. C. and Storey, V. C. (1989). Some findings on the intuitiveness of entity-relationship constructs. In *Proceedings of the 8th International Conference on Entity-Relationship Approach* (Lochovsky, F. H., ed.), pp. 6–20.

[GW86]   Graham, M. H. and Wang, K. (1986). Constant time maintenance or the triumph of the fd. In *Proceedings of the Fifth ACM SIGACT-SIGMOD Symposium on Principles of Database Systems (PODS'86),* pp. 202–216, New York, NY: ACM.

[GY84]   Graham, M. H. and Yannakakis, M. (1984). Independent database schemas. *Journal of Computer and System Sciences,* **28**(1), 121–141.

[GZ82]   Ginsburg, S. and Zaiddan, S. M. (1982). Properties of functional-dependency families. *Journal of the ACM,* **29**(3), 678–698.

[HC91]   Hernández, H. J. and Chan, E. P. F. (1991). Constant-time-maintainable BCNF database schemes. *ACM Transactions on Database Systems,* **16**(4), 571–599.

[HK87]   Hull, R. and King, R. (1987). Semantic database modeling: Survey, applications, and research issues. *Computing Surveys,* **19**(3), 201–260.

[HLY80]   Honeyman, P., Ladner, R. E., and Yannakakis, M. (1980). Testing the universal instance assumption. *Information Processing Letters*, **10**(1), 14–19.

[Hon82]   Honeyman, P. (1982). Testing satisfaction of functional dependencies. *Journal of the ACM*, **29**(3), 668–677.

[Hor91]   Horowitz, M. M. (1991). An introduction to object-oriented databases and database systems. Technical Report CMU-ITC-91-103, Carnegie Mellon University, Information Technology Center, Pittsburgh, PA.

[HPBC88]   Hsu, C., Perry, A., Bouziane, M., and Cheung, W. (1988). TSER: A data modeling system using the two-stage entity-relationship approach. In *Entity-Relationship Approach* (March, S. T., ed.), pp. 497–514. Amsterdam: Elsevier Science Publishers B.V (North-Holland).

[Hul86]   Hull, R. (1986). Relative information capacity of simple relational database schemata. *SIAM Journal on Computing*, **15**(3), 856–886.

[IEF]   IEF. Texas Instruments, Inc. P.O. Box 65562, MS 8474, Dallas, TX, USA.

[IEW]   IEW. KnowledgeWare Inc. 3340 Peachtree Road, Suite 1100, Atlanta, GA, USA.

[IL84]   Imieliński, T. and Lipski, Jr., W. (1984). Incomplete information in relational databases. *Journal of the ACM*, **31**(4), 761–791.

[Ioa92]   Ioannidis, Y. E., ed. (1992). Special issue on advanced user interfaces for database systems. *SIGMOD Record*, **21**(1), 4–64.

[Jan88]   Janas, J. M. (1988). On functional independencies. In *Foundations of Software Technology and Computer Science* (Nori, K. V. and Kumar, S., eds.), pp. 487–508, Berlin: Springer-Verlag. Lecture Notes in Computer Science 338.

[Jan89]   Janas, J. M. (1989). Covers for functional independencies. In *Proceedings of 2nd Symposium on Mathematical Fundamentals of Database Systems* (Demetrovics, J. and Thalheim, B., eds.), pp. 254–268, Berlin: Springer-Verlag. Lecture Notes in Computer Science 364.

[JF82]   Jou, J. H. and Fischer, P. C. (1982). The complexity of recognizing 3NF relation schemes. *Information Processing Letters*, **14**(4), 187–190.

[JK84]   Johnson, D. S. and Klug, A. (1984). Testing containment of conjunctive queries under functional and inclusion dependencies. *Journal of Computer and System Sciences*, **28**(1), 167–189.

[JK89]   Johannesson, P. and Kalman, K. (1989). A method for translating relational schemas into conceptual schemas. In *Proceedings of the 8th International Conference on Entity-Relationship Approach* (Lochovsky, F. H., ed.), pp. 279–293.

[JNS83a]   Jajodia, S., Ng, P. A., and Springsteel, F. N. (1983a). Entity-relationship diagrams which are in BCNF. *International Journal of Computer and Information Sciences*, **12**(4), 269–283.

[JNS83b]   Jajodia, S., Ng, P. A., and Springsteel, F. N. (1983b). The problem of equivalence for entity-relationship diagrams. *IEEE Transactions on Software Engineering*, **SE-9**(5), 617–630.

[Kal91]   Kalman, K. (1991). Implementation and critique of an algorithm which maps a relational database to a conceptual schema. In *Advanced Information Systems Engineering. Proceedings of the Third International Conference CAiSE'91* (Andersen, R., Bubenko jr., J. A., and Sølvberg, A., eds.), pp. 393–415. Berlin: Springer-Verlag. Lecture Notes in Computer Science 498.

[Kan88]   Kangassalo, H. (1988). CONCEPT D: A graphical language for conceptual modelling and data base use. In *Proceedings of the 1988 IEEE Workshop on Visual Languages*, pp. 2–11, Washington, DC: IEEE Computer Society Press.

[Kan90]   Kanellakis, P. C. (1990). Elements of relational database theory. In *Handbook of Theoretical Computer Science, Volume B* (van Leeuwen, J., ed.), pp. 1073–1156. Amsterdam: Elsevier Science Publishers B.V (North-Holland).

[Ken78]   Kent, W. (1978). *Data and Reality*. Amsterdam: North-Holland Publishing Company.

[Ken79]   Kent, W. (1979). Limitations of record-based information models. *ACM Transactions on Database Systems*, **4**(1), 107–131.

[Ken81]   Kent, W. (1981). Consequences of assuming a universal relation. *ACM Transactions on Database Systems*, **6**(4), 539–556.

[Ken82]   Kent, W. (1982). Choices in practical data design. In *Proceedings of the Eighth International Conference on Very Large Data Bases (VLDB'82)*, pp. 165–180, Saratoga, CA: VLDB Endowment.

[Ken83a]   Kent, W. (1983a). A simple guide to five normal forms in relational database theory. *Communications of the ACM*, **26**(2), 120–125.

[Ken83b]   Kent, W. (1983b). The universal relation revisited. *ACM Transactions on Database Systems*, **8**(4), 644–648.

[KL89]   Kim, W. and Lochovsky, F. H., eds. (1989). *Object-Oriented Concepts, Databases, and Applications*. Addison-Wesley Publishing Company.

[Klu80]   Klug, A. (1980). Entity-relationship views over uninterpreted enterprise schemas. In *Entity-Relationship Approach to Systems Analysis and Design* (Chen, P. P.-S., ed.), pp. 39–59. Amsterdam: Elsevier Science Publishers B.V (North-Holland).

[KM92]   Kivinen, J. and Mannila, H. (1992). Approximate dependency inference from relations. In *Proceedings of the International Conference on Database Theory (ICDT'92)*, Berlin: Springer-Verlag. To appear.

[KMR+91]   Kantola, M., Mannila, H., Räihä, K.-J., Siirtola, H., and Tuomi, J. (1991). Design-By-Example: A tool for database design; user guide for version 3.0. Manuscript.

[KS86]   Korth, H. F. and Silberschatz, A. (1986). *Database System Concepts*. New York, NY: McGraw-Hill.

[Kun85]   Kundu, S. (1985). An improved algorithm for finding a key of a relation. In *Proceedings of the Fourth ACM SIGACT-SIGMOD Symposium on Principles of Database Systems (PODS'85)*, pp. 189–192, New York, NY: ACM.

[LD80]   Liu, L. and Demers, A. (1980). An algorithm for testing lossless join property in relational databases. *Information Processing Letters*, **11**(2), 73–76.

[Lie82]   Lien, Y. E. (1982). On the equivalence of database models. *Journal of the ACM*, **29**(2), 333–362.

[Lip79]   Lipski, Jr., W. (1979). On semantic issues connected with incomplete information databases. *ACM Transactions on Database Systems*, **4**(3), 262–296.

[LLOW91]   Lamb, C., Landis, G., Orenstein, J., and Weinreb, D. (1991). The ObjectStore database system. *Communications of the ACM*, **34**(10), 50–63.

[LLPS91]   Lohman, G. M., Lindsay, B., Pirahesh, H., and Schiefer, K. B. (1991). Extensions to Starburst: Objects, types, functions, and rules. *Communications of the ACM*, **34**(10), 94–109.

[LO78]   Lucchesi, C. L. and Osborn, S. L. (1978). Candidate keys for relations. *Journal of Computer and System Sciences*, **17**(2), 270–279.

[LP82]   LeDoux, C. H. and Parker, Jr., D. S. (1982). Reflections on Boyce-Codd normal form. In *Proceedings of the Eighth International Conference on Very Large Data Bases (VLDB'82)*, pp. 131–141, Saratoga, CA: VLDB Endowment.

[LT83]   Loizou, G. and Thanisch, P. (1983). Testing a dependency-preserving decomposition for losslessness. *Information Systems*, **8**(1), 25–27.

[Mai80]   Maier, D. (1980). Minimum covers in the relational database model. *Journal of the ACM*, **27**(4), 664–674.

[Mai83]   Maier, D. (1983). *The Theory of Relational Databases*. Potomac, MD: Computer Science Press.

[Mai91]   Maier, D. (1991). Comments on the "Third-generation data base system manifesto". Technical Report 91-012, Oregon Graduate Institute, Beaverton, OR.

[Man84]   Mannila, H. (1984). On the complexity of the inference problem for subclasses of inclusion dependencies. In *Proceedings of the Winter School on Theoretical Computer Science* (Back, R., Mannila, H., Räihä, K.-J., and Ukkonen, E., eds.), pp. 182–193, Finnish Society for Computer Science.

[Man87]   Mannila, H. (1987). Generating example databases from ER-
            schemes. Report C-1987-48, University of Helsinki, Depart-
            ment of Computer Science, Helsinki, Finland.

[Mar87]   Martin, J. (1987). *Recommended Diagramming Standards
            for Analysts and Programmers – A Basis for Automation.*
            Englewood Cliffs, NJ: Prentice Hall.

[Mar90]   Markowitz, V. M. (1990). Referential integrity revisited:
            an object-oriented perspective. In *Proceedings of the Six-
            teenth International Conference on Very Large Data Bases
            (VLDB'90)* (McLeod, D., Sacks-Davis, R., and Schek, H.,
            eds.), pp. 578–589, Palo Alto, CA: Morgan Kaufmann.

[Mar91]   Markowitz, V. M. (1991). Safe referential integrity struc-
            tures in relational databases. In *Proceedings of the Seven-
            teenth International Conference on Very Large Data Bases
            (VLDB'91)* (Lohman, G. M., Sernadas, A., and Camps, R.,
            eds.), pp. 123–132, San Mateo, CA: Morgan Kaufmann.

[Mas]   MastER Plus: The information architect. Gestione Sistemi
            per l'Informatica S.r.l. (GESI). 32 Via Rodi, Rome, Italy.

[MB89]   Mylopoulos, J. and Brodie, M. L., eds. (1989). *Readings in
            Artificial Intelligence and Databases.* Morgan Kaufmann.

[MBGW84]   Mylopoulos, J., Borgida, A., Greenspan, S., and Wong, H.
            K. T. (1984). Information system design at the conceptual
            level – the Taxis project. *Database Engineering*, **7**(4), 4–9.

[McC89]   McClure, C. (1989). *CASE Is Software Automation.* Engle-
            wood Cliffs, NJ: Prentice Hall.

[MCM83]   Michalski, R. S., Carbonell, J. G., and Mitchell, T. M., eds.
            (1983). *Machine Learning: an Artificial Intelligence Ap-
            proach.* Palo Alto, CA: Tioga.

[MCM86]   Michalski, R. S., Carbonell, J. G., and Mitchell, T. M., eds.
            (1986). *Machine Learning: an Artificial Intelligence Ap-
            proach*, volume II. Los Altos, CA: Morgan Kaufmann.

[Meh84]   Mehlhorn, K. (1984). *Data Structures and Algorithms, Vol-
            umes 1–3.* Berlin: Springer-Verlag.

[MH89]   McCune, W. W. and Henschen, L. J. (1989). Maintaining
            state constraints in relational databases: A proof theoretic
            basis. *Journal of the ACM*, **36**(1), 46–68.

[Mit83a]   Mitchell, J. C. (1983a). The implication problem for functional and inclusion dependencies. *Information and Control*, **56**(3), 154–173.

[Mit83b]   Mitchell, J. C. (1983b). Inference rules for functional and inclusion dependencies. In *Proceedings of the Second ACM SIGACT-SIGMOD Symposium on Principles of Database Systems (PODS'83)*, pp. 58–69, New York, NY: ACM.

[MM86]   Markowitz, V. M. and Makowsky, J. A. (1986). Unifying entity-relationship and universal relation approaches to user interfaces. Technical Report 412, TECHNION – Israel Institute of Technology, Computer Science Department, Haifa, Israel.

[MM87]   Markowitz, V. M. and Makowsky, J. A. (1987). Incremental reorganization of relational databases. In *Proceedings of the Thirteenth International Conference on Very Large Data Bases (VLDB'87)*, pp. 127–135, Los Altos, CA: Morgan Kaufmann.

[MM88]   Markowitz, V. M. and Makowsky, J. A. (1988). Incremental restructuring of relational schemas. In *Proceedings of the Fourth International Conference on Data Engineering*, pp. 276–284, IEEE Computer Society Press.

[MMR86]   Makowsky, J. A., Markowitz, V. M., and Rotics, N. (1986). Entity-relationship consistency for relational schemas. In *Proceedings of the International Conference on Database Theory (ICDT'86)* (Ausiello, G. and Atzeni, P., eds.), pp. 306–322, Berlin: Springer-Verlag. Lecture Notes in Computer Science 243.

[MMS79]   Maier, D., Mendelzon, A. O., and Sagiv, Y. (1979). Testing implications of data dependencies. *ACM Transactions on Database Systems*, **4**(4), 455–469.

[MMSU80]   Maier, D., Mendelzon, A. O., Sadri, F., and Ullman, J. D. (1980). Adequacy of decompositions in relational databases. *Journal of Computer and System Sciences*, **21**(3), 368–379.

[MR83]   Mannila, H. and Räihä, K.-J. (1983). On the relationship of minimum and optimum covers for a set of functional dependencies. *Acta Informatica*, **20**, 143–158.

[MR86a]   Mannila, H. and Räihä, K.-J. (1986a). Design by example:
            An application of Armstrong relations. *Journal of Computer
            and System Sciences*, **33**(2), 126–141.

[MR86b]   Mannila, H. and Räihä, K.-J. (1986b). Inclusion dependen-
            cies in database design. In *Proceedings of the Second In-
            ternational Conference on Data Engineering*, pp. 713–718,
            Washington, DC: IEEE Computer Society Press.

[MR87]   Mannila, H. and Räihä, K.-J. (1987). Dependency inference.
            In *Proceedings of the Thirteenth International Conference on
            Very Large Data Bases (VLDB'87)*, pp. 155–158, Los Altos,
            CA: Morgan Kaufmann.

[MR88]   Mannila, H. and Räihä, K.-J. (1988). Generating Arm-
            strong databases for sets of functional and inclusion depen-
            dencies. Report A-1988-7, University of Tampere, Depart-
            ment of Computer Science, Tampere, Finland.

[MR89]   Mannila, H. and Räihä, K.-J. (1989). Practical algorithms
            for finding prime attributes and testing normal forms. In
            *Proceedings of the Eighth ACM SIGACT-SIGMOD-SIGART
            Symposium on Principles of Database Systems (PODS'89)*,
            pp. 128–133, New York, NY: ACM.

[MR90]   Mannila, H. and Räihä, K.-J. (1990). A mapping from re-
            lational database schemas to ER-diagrams using inclusion
            dependencies. Manuscript.

[MR91]   Mannila, H. and Räihä, K.-J. (1991). Algorithms for infer-
            ring functional dependencies. Report C-1991-41, University
            of Helsinki, Department of Computer Science, Helsinki, Fin-
            land. To appear in *Data & Knowledge Engineering*.

[MR92]   Mannila, H. and Räihä, K.-J. (1992). On the complexity
            of inferring functional dependencies. To appear in *Discrete
            Applied Mathematics*.

[MRS85]   Maier, D., Rozenshtein, D., and Stein, J. (1985). Represent-
            ing roles in universal scheme interfaces. *IEEE Transactions
            on Software Engineering*, **SE-11**(7), 644–652.

[MRW86]   Maier, D., Rozenshtein, D., and Warren, D. S. (1986). Win-
            dow functions. In *Advances in Computing Research, Volume
            3* (Kanellakis, P. C., ed.), pp. 213–246. Greenwich, CN: JAI
            Press, Inc.

[MS89a]   Markowitz, V. M. and Shoshani, A. (1989a). Name assign-
            ment techniques for relational schemas representing extended
            entity-relationship schemas. In *Proceedings of the 8th Inter-
            national Conference on Entity-Relationship Approach* (Lo-
            chovsky, F. H., ed.), pp. 21–39.

[MS89b]   Markowitz, V. M. and Shoshani, A. (1989b). On the correct-
            ness of representing extended entity-relationship structures
            in the relational model. In *Proceedings of ACM SIGMOD
            Conference on Management of Data (SIGMOD'89)* (Clifford,
            J., Lindsay, B., and Maier, D., eds.), pp. 430–439, New York,
            NY: ACM.

[MUV84]   Maier, D., Ullman, J. D., and Vardi, M. Y. (1984). On the
            foundations of the universal relation model. *ACM Transac-
            tions on Database Systems*, **9**(2), 283–308.

[MZ80]   Melkanoff, M. A. and Zaniolo, C. (1980). Decomposition of
            relations and synthesis of entity-relationship diagrams. In
            *Entity-Relationship Approach to Systems Analysis and De-
            sign* (Chen, P. P.-S., ed.), pp. 277–294. Amsterdam: Elsevier
            Science Publishers B.V (North-Holland).

[NA88]   Navathe, S. B. and Awong, A. M. (1988). Abstracting rela-
            tional and hierarchical data with a semantic data model. In
            Entity-Relationship Approach (March, S. T., ed.), pp. 305–
            333. Amsterdam: Elsevier Science Publishers B.V (North-
            Holland).

[Nic82]   Nicolas, J.-M. (1982). Logic for improving integrity checking
            in relational databases. *Acta Informatica*, **18**(3), 227–253.

[NN90]   Nummenmaa, J. and Numminen, O. (1990). Graphic editors
            for knowledge acquisition and conceptual schema design. In
            Information Modelling and Knowledge Bases (Kangassalo,
            H., Ohsuga, S., and Jaakkola, H., eds.), pp. 318–328. Ams-
            terdam: IOS Press.

[NO89]   Nishiyama, S. and Obana, S. (1989). The E-R editor: an
            editor for database conceptual schema design based on E-R
            model. In *Proceedings of the 8th International Conference
            on Entity-Relationship Approach* (Lochovsky, F. H., ed.), pp.
            361–375.

[NP89]   Navathe, S. B. and Pillalamarri, M. K. (1989). OOER: To-
            ward making the E-R approach object-oriented. In *Entity-
            Relationship Approach: A Bridge to the User* (Batini, C.,

ed.), pp. 185–206. Amsterdam: Elsevier Science Publishers B.V (North-Holland).

[OY87]   Ozsoyoğlu, Z. M. and Yuan, L.-Y. (1987). A new normal form for nested relations. *ACM Transactions on Database Systems*, **12**(1), 111–136.

[PDGV89]   Paredaens, J., De Bra, P., Gyssens, M., and Van Gucht, D. (1989). *The Structure of the Relational Database Model*. Berlin: Springer-Verlag. EATCS Monographs on Theoretical Computer Science 17.

[PS89]   Piatetsky-Shapiro, G. (1989). Discovery and analysis of strong rules in databases. In *ADSS'89*, pp. 135–142.

[PS91]   (Piatetsky-Shapiro, G., ed.) (1991). *Proceedings of 1991 AAAI Workshop on Knowledge Discovery in Databases*. American Association for Artificial Intelligence.

[Put91]   Put, F. (1991). Schema translation during design and integration of databases. In *Entity-Relationship Approach: The Core of Conceptual Modelling* (Kangassalo, H., ed.), pp. 399–421, Amsterdam: Elsevier Science Publishers B.V (North-Holland).

[RBB+84]   Reiner, D., Brodie, M. L., Brown, G., Friedell, M., Kramlich, D., Lehman, J., and Rosenthal, A. (1984). The database design and evaluation workbench (DDEW) project at CCA. *Database Engineering*, **7**(4), 10–15.

[RBF+86]   Reiner, D., Brown, G., Friedell, M., Lehman, J., McKee, R., Rheingans, P., and Rosenthal, A. (1986). A database designer's workbench. In *Proceedings of the 5th International Conference on Entity-Relationship Approach* (Spaccapietra, S., ed.), pp. 127–140.

[RC88]   Rogers, T. R. and Cattell, R. G. G. (1988). Entity-relationship database user interfaces. In *Entity-Relationship Approach* (March, S. T., ed.), pp. 353–365. Amsterdam: Elsevier Science Publishers B.V (North-Holland).

[Rei72]   Reingold, E. M. (1972). On the optimality of some set algorithms. *Journal of the ACM*, **19**(4), 649–659.

[Rei84]   Reiter, R. (1984). Towards a logical reconstruction of relational database theory. In *On Conceptual Modelling: Perspectives from Artificial Intelligence, Databases, and Programming Languages* (Brodie, M. L., Mylopoulos, J., and

Schmidt, J. W., eds.), pp. 191–233. New York: Springer-Verlag.

[Ris77]   Rissanen, J. (1977). Independent components of relations. *ACM Transactions on Database Systems*, **2**(4), 317–325.

[Ris78]   Rissanen, J. (1978). Theory of relations for databases – a tutorial survey. In *Proceedings of the Seventh Symposium on Mathematical Foundations of Computer Science (MFCS'78)*, pp. 536–551, Berlin: Springer-Verlag. Lecture Notes in Computer Science 64.

[RK87]   Roth, M. A. and Korth, H. F. (1987). The design of NFNF relational databases into nested normal form. In *Proceedings of ACM SIGMOD Conference on Management of Data (SIGMOD'87)*, pp. 143–159, New York, NY: ACM.

[RKS88]   Roth, M. A., Korth, H. F., and Silberschatz, A. (1988). Extended algebra and calculus for nested relational databases. *ACM Transactions on Database Systems*, **13**(4), 389–417.

[RR88]   Rosenthal, A. and Reiner, D. (1988). Theoretically sound transformations for practical database design. In *Entity-Relationship Approach* (March, S. T., ed.), pp. 115–131. Amsterdam: Elsevier Science Publishers B.V (North-Holland).

[RR89]   Rosenthal, A. and Reiner, D. (1989). Database design tools: Combining theory, guesswork, and user interaction. In *Proceedings of the 8th International Conference on Entity-Relationship Approach* (Lochovsky, F. H., ed.), pp. 391–405.

[Sag83]   Sagiv, Y. (1983). A characterization of globally consistent databases and their correct access paths. *ACM Transactions on Database Systems*, **8**(2), 266–286.

[SC89]   Springsteel, F. N. and Chuang, P.-J. (1989). ERDDS: The intelligent E-R-based database design system. In *Entity-Relationship Approach: A Bridge to the User* (Batini, C., ed.), pp. 349–368. Amsterdam: Elsevier Science Publishers B.V (North-Holland).

[Sci86]   Sciore, E. (1986). Comparing the universal instance and relational data models. In *Advances in Computing Research, Volume 3* (Kanellakis, P. C., ed.), pp. 139–162. Greenwich, CN: JAI Press, Inc.

[Sci91]   Sciore, E. (1991).   An extended universal instance data model. *Information Systems*, **16**(1), 21–34.

[SDPF81]   Sagiv, Y., Delobel, C., Parker, Jr., D. S., and Fagin, R. (1981). An equivalence between relational database dependencies and a fragment of propositional logic. *Journal of the ACM*, **28**(3), 435–453.

[SK91]   Stonebraker, M. and Kemnitz, G. (1991). The POSTGRES next-generation database management system. *Communications of the ACM*, **34**(10), 78–92.

[SKK83]   Sakai, H., Kondo, H., and Kawasaki, Z. (1983). A development of a conceptual schema design aid in the entity-relationship model.   In *Entity-Relationship Approach to Information Modeling and Analysis* (Chen, P. P.-S., ed.), pp. 411–428. Amsterdam: Elsevier Science Publishers B.V (North-Holland).

[SM81]   Silva, A. M. and Melkanoff, M. A. (1981). A method for helping discover the dependencies of a relation. In *Advances in Data Base Theory* (Gallaire, H., Minker, J., and Nicolas, J.-M., eds.), pp. 115–133. New York: Plenum.

[SQL86]   SQL (1986).   Database language SQL.   Technical Report ANSI X3.135-1986 and ISO/TC97/SC21/WG3 N117, ANSI and ISO/TC97/SC21/WG3.

[SQL92]   SQL2 (1992).   Information technology – database language SQL. Technical Report ISO/IEC/JTC1/SC21 N6789, ISO/IEC/JTC1/SC21.

[SS77a]   Smith, J. M. and Smith, D. C. P. (1977a). Database abstractions: Aggregation. *Communications of the ACM*, **20**(6), 405–413.

[SS77b]   Smith, J. M. and Smith, D. C. P. (1977b). Database abstractions: Aggregation and generalization. *ACM Transactions on Database Systems*, **2**(2), 105–133.

[SS90]   Scholl, M. H. and Schek, H.-J. (1990). A relational object model. In *Third International Conference on Database Theory (ICDT'90)* (Abiteboul, S. and Kanellakis, P. C., eds.), pp. 89–105, Berlin: Springer-Verlag. Lecture Notes in Computer Science 470.

[STH91]   Spencer, R., Teorey, T. J., and Hevia, E. (1991). ER standards proposal. In *Entity-Relationship Approach: The Core of Conceptual Modelling* (Kangassalo, H., ed.), pp. 425–432. Amsterdam: Elsevier Science Publishers B.V (North-Holland).

[SU82]   Sadri, F. and Ullman, J. D. (1982). Template dependencies: A large class of dependencies in relational databases and its complete axiomatization. *Journal of the ACM*, **29**(2), 363–372.

[Teo90]   Teorey, T. J. (1990). *Database Modelling and Design: The Entity-Relationship Approach.* San Mateo, CA: Morgan Kaufmann.

[TF82a]   Teorey, T. J. and Fry, J. P. (1982a). *Design of Database Structures.* Englewood Cliffs, NJ: Prentice Hall.

[TF82b]   Tsou, D.-M. and Fischer, P. C. (1982b). Decomposition of a relation scheme into Boyce-Codd normal form. *SIGACT News*, **14**(3), 23–29.

[The89]   The Laguna Beach Participants (1989). Future directions in DBMS research. *SIGMOD Record*, **18**(1), 17–26.

[The90]   The Committee for Advanced DBMS Function (1990). Third-generation database system manifesto. *SIGMOD Record*, **19**(3), 31–44.

[Thi86]   Thi, V. D. (1986). Minimal keys and antikeys. *Acta Cybernetica*, **7**(4), 361–371.

[TL82]   Tsichritzis, D. C. and Lochovsky, F. H. (1982). *Data Models.* Englewood Cliffs, NJ: Prentice Hall.

[TM89]   Tseng, V. P. and Mannino, M. V. (1989). Inferring database requirements from examples in forms. In *Entity-Relationship Approach: A Bridge to the User* (Batini, C., ed.), pp. 391–405. Amsterdam: Elsevier Science Publishers B.V (North-Holland).

[TYF86]   Teorey, T. J., Yang, D., and Fry, J. P. (1986). A logical design methodology for relational databases using the extended entity-relationship model. *Computing Surveys*, **18**(2), 197–222.

[Ull83]   Ullman, J. D. (1983). On Kent's "Consequences of assuming a universal relation". *ACM Transactions on Database Systems*, **8**(4), 637–643.

[Ull88]   Ullman, J. D. (1988). *Principles of Database and Knowledge-Base Systems*, volume I. Rockville, MD: Computer Science Press.

[Ull89]   Ullman, J. D. (1989). *Principles of Database and Knowledge-Base Systems*, volume II. Rockville, MD: Computer Science Press.

[Var84]   Vardi, M. Y. (1984). A note on lossless database decompositions. *Information Processing Letters*, **18**(5), 257–260.

[Var88]   Vardi, M. Y. (1988). Fundamentals of dependency theory. In *Trends in Theoretical Computer Science* (Börger, E., ed.), pp. 171–224. Computer Science Press.

[Vos88]   Vossen, G. (1988). A new characterization of FD implication with an application to update anomalies. *Information Processing Letters*, **29**(3), 131–135.

[Vos90]   Vossen, G. (1990). *Data Models, Database Languages and Database Management Systems*. Wokingham, England: Addison-Wesley Publishing Company.

[Vos91]   Vossen, G. (1991). Bibliography on object-oriented database management. *SIGMOD Record*, **20**(1), 24–46.

[Wan89]   Wang, K. (1989). Can constant-time-maintainability be more practical? In *Proceedings of the Eighth ACM SIGACT-SIGMOD-SIGART Symposium on Principles of Database Systems (PODS'89)*, pp. 120–127, New York, NY: ACM.

[Wan90]   Wang, K. (1990). Polynomial time designs toward both BCNF and efficient data manipulation. In *Proceedings of ACM SIGMOD Conference on Management of Data (SIGMOD'90)* (Garcia-Molina, H. and Jagadish, H. V., eds.), pp. 74–83, New York, NY: ACM.

[Wed84]   Wedekind, H. (1984). Supporting the design of conceptual schemata by database systems. In *Proceedings of the International Conference on Data Engineering*, pp. 434–438, Silver Spring, MD: IEEE Computer Society Press.

[WG92]   Wang, K. and Graham, M. H. (1992). Constant-time main-
          tainability: A generalization of independence. *ACM Trans-
          actions on Database Systems*, **17**(2), 201–246.

[Wie87]   Wiederhold, G. (1987). *File Organization for Database De-
          sign*. New York, NY: McGraw-Hill.

[WP87]   Wassermann, A. S. and Pircher, P. A. (1987). A graphical,
          extensible integrated environment for software development.
          In *Proceedings of the ACM SIGSOFT/SIGPLAN Software
          Engineering Symposium on Practical Software Development
          Environments* (Henderson, P., ed.), pp. 131–142, New York,
          NY: ACM.

[Yas91]   Yasdi, R. (1991). Learning classification rules from database
          in the context of knowledge acquisition and representation.
          IEEE Transactions on Knowledge and Data Engineering,
          3(3), 293–306.

[YP82]   Yannakakis, M. and Papadimitriou, C. H. (1982). Algebraic
          dependencies. *Journal of Computer and System Sciences*,
          25(1), 2–41.

[ZM83]   Zhang, Z.-Q. and Mendelzon, A. O. (1983). A graphical
          query language for entity-relationship databases. In *Entity-
          Relationship Approach to Software Engineering* (Davis,
          C. G., Jajodia, S., Ng, P. A., and Yeh, R. T., eds.), pp. 441–
          448. Amsterdam: Elsevier Science Publishers B.V (North-
          Holland).

[ZM90]   Zdonik, S. B. and Maier, D., eds. (1990). *Readings in Object-
          Oriented Database Systems*. San Mateo, CA: Morgan Kauf-
          mann.

Index

Notes

Notes

Notes

Notes

Notes